THE CONSERVATIVE PARTY

D0488657

PRAISE FOR THE CONSERVATIVE PARTY

'There haven't been a lot of good books published about the Conservative Party in recent years, but Tim Bale has written one that fills the gap . . . he tells the story well, combining breezy prose with academic rigour and anecdotes from the key participants.'

Andrew Sparrow, *Guardian.co.uk*

'A wonderful insightful account of the Conservative Party from the denouement of Margaret Thatcher's leadership in 1989/90 through to the ascent of David Cameron.'

Party Politics

'A hugely impressive achievement – and required reading for anyone who wants to understand the party most likely to run Britain in the new decade.'

Sunday Business Post

'Excellent . . . a very useful first account of how the oldest and most successful political party in the western world lost its electoral advantage and then, finally, took years to find its way again.'

Total Politics

'An intelligent and informative account of the Party's decline from 1990 to its recovery from 2005 onwards. This is a refreshing and hugely enjoyable study which brings the subject matter and dramatis personae to life, written by a highly-respected political scientist who has interviewed many of the people involved, and who also has a wry sense of humour which makes his writing sparkle.'

Politics & Policy

'A highly insightful, and often very funny, commentary on the party's dysfunctionality in the post-Thatcher era.'

Irish Times

'A detailed yet splendidly readable study.'

British Politics

'In his new, rather good book, the academic Tim Bale provides a history of the Tories in the 15 years that preceded Mr Cameron's ascent. Read it and it isn't hard to work out the party's problem.'

Daniel Finkelstein, *The Times*

'For a contemporary history of British politics, deliciously free of the jargon which usually masks the failure of academics to understand their subject, you will read nothing better than this.'

Tribune

'A mountain of insights about the tiny amount of space in which political leaders make their moves.'

Independent Arts and Books Supplement

'[An] exhaustive and authoritative account.'

London Review of Books

'A solid, meticulous account.'

Financial Times

'It's hard to think of anyone with an interest in British politics who will not enjoy, and profit from, Tim Bale's outstanding book. His chapters on the Hague and Duncan Smith years in particular – the latter a man for whom the word "hapless" could almost have been invented – form a kind of "how not to do it" manual for any political party in opposition. I suspect Messrs Miliband and Balls have already ordered theirs.'

Waterstones.com Bookseller's Review

'Contains the best account so far of the "decontamination" strategy pursued by Cameron after his surprise win in the leadership contest of 2005.'

Progress

'Bale provides a well-researched and very readable account of [his] thesis.'

Times Higher Education

'Bale's book is a useful reminder of the chronology of the main political events, often stormy, which have taken place over the past 20 years.'

House Magazine

'Tim Bale's book firmly avoids "big picture" explanantions focused on single issues like "sleaze" or Europe, and instead offers a detailed analytical narrative of the party leadership from the fall of Thatcher to the rise of Cameron. Bale in essence updates the old approach of High Politics, epitomized by the late Maurice Cowling, in which political history is the actions of a narrow band of senior politicians, and fuses this with a modern social scientist's understanding of the interrelationship between ideas, interests, and insitutions.'

Planet Magazine

'Tim Bale's study of the death and re-birth of the post-Thatcher Conservative Party is a delight to read. It is perky, cheeky, irreverent, packed with revealing quotes and in places deliciously funny. But Bale is not just an entertaining guide to the tribulations of the accident-prone Conservative leaders of the recent past. Only half-concealed by his jaunty prose and witty asides is a thorough scholar and insightful analyst. His anatomy of the modern Conservative Party will hold the field for a long time to come.'

David Marquand, Oxford University

'How did David Cameron find the key to success which the Tory Party has lost since 1997? Tim Bale's book, while thoroughly readable, covers this subject more convincingly and in greater depth than most political journalists. He has done an excellent job.'

Douglas Hurd

'Much the best book that has been written on the contemporary Conservative Party. Bale's analysis is extremely impressive. It will make this book the leading book in the field, and very unlikely to be quickly surpassed.'

Andrew Gamble, Cambridge University

'Tim Bale's well-researched volume is essential reading for anyone who wants to understand the Conservative Party's recent history. It is extremely accessible to the lay reader and chronicles not only some of the party's darkest days, but also its rediscovery of the will to win under David Cameron.'

Jonathan Isaby, Co-Editor, *ConservativeHome.com*

'Tim Bale has produced the best guide to the changing nature of the Conservative Party yet published. He appears to have read everything and spoken to everyone that matters to produce an eminently readable and interesting book. It should be required reading for all students of politics, as well as anyone wanting to know more about the contemporary Conservative Party.'

Philip Cowley, Nottingham University

'This is an excellent book immaculately researched. Tim Bale traces the downfall of the Conservative Party leading to the catastrophic defeat of 1997. He sheds new light on the party's continuing slide, which was only conclusively ended when David Cameron became leader and moved back onto the centre ground of politics. He reveals the "villains" of the story – not least the ideologically driven commentators – but his central question goes wider. He asks how it was that a party which had consistently sought power through the years lost the will to win? It is a book which Conservative politicians would be well advised to read now that, at long last, they have the opportunity of returning to government.'

Norman Fowler

'This is the first comprehensive treatment of the Conservative Party since Margaret Thatcher. The period has seen extraordinary changes in the Party's fortunes and now we have a well-researched and balanced account of what happened.'

David Willetts

'Now poised for national success again, Conservatives should treat Tim Bale's timely account of their recent history as essential reading. Detailing the Party's highs and lows, this book reminds us of the scale of the challenge that faced David Cameron's new leadership, and illuminates his strategy for recovery.'

Jo-Anne Nadler, author of *Too Nice to be a Tory*

THE CONSERVATIVE PARTY

FROM THATCHER TO CAMERON

TIM BALE

polity

Copyright © Tim Bale 2010
Afterword © Tim Bale 2011

The right of Tim Bale to be identified as Author of this Work has been asserted in
accordance with the UK Copyright, Designs and Patents Act 1988.

First published in 2010 by Polity Press
This edition published in 2011 by Polity Press
Reprinted 2011

Polity Press
65 Bridge Street
Cambridge CB2 1UR, UK

Polity Press
350 Main Street
Malden, MA 02148, USA

All rights reserved. Except for the quotation of short passages for the purpose of
criticism and review, no part of this publication may be reproduced, stored in a
retrieval system, or transmitted, in any form or by any means, electronic, mechanical,
photocopying, recording or otherwise, without the prior permission of the publisher.

ISBN-13: 978-0-7456-4857-6
ISBN-13: 978-0-7456-4858-3 (pb)

A catalogue record for this book is available from the British Library.

Typeset in 10.75 on 14 pt Adobe Janson
by Servis Filmsetting Ltd, Stockport, Cheshire
Printed and bound by MPG Books Group, UK

The publisher has used its best endeavours to ensure that the URLs for external
websites referred to in this book are correct and active at the time of going to press.
However, the publisher has no responsibility for the websites and can make no
guarantee that a site will remain live or that the content is or will remain appropriate.

Every effort has been made to trace all copyright holders, but if any have been
inadvertently overlooked the publisher will be pleased to include any necessary credits
in any subsequent reprint or edition.

For further information on Polity, visit our website: www.politybooks.com

BLACKBURN COLLEGE
LIBRARY
Acc. No. BB49977
Class No. UCL 324.241 BAL
Date 7.2.2012

CONTENTS

ACKNOWLEDGEMENTS

I am grateful, firstly, to the Leverhulme Trust for providing me with the time and funding to work on this book and, secondly, to all those who gave up some of their time to be interviewed for it, whether on or off the record. I would also like to acknowledge those whose help was less consciously given but was nonetheless vital, namely the journalists, many of whom are name-checked in the notes. Similarly, I owe a great debt to those who run and contribute to *http://conservativehome.blogs. com/* and *http://www.iaindale.blogspot.com/*, especially Jonathan Isaby.

I would like to thank my Sussex University colleagues (particularly Dan Hough, Sally Marthaler, Paul Taggart, and Paul Webb) for their understanding and advice, and some of my students (Amy Busby, Dan Keith, Ed Maxfield, and Rebecca Partos) for editorial assistance. Academics at other universities have also helped: they are too numerous to mention but most of them belong to the Conservatives and Conservatism specialist group of the Political Studies Association, information on which can be found at *http://www.sussex.ac.uk/polces/ ConservativesandConservatism*. I would also like to thank the editorial and production staff at Polity.

Finally, of course, I would like to thank my family and friends. Many are mystified by my love affair with the Tories, but have always shown (or convincingly feigned) interest – and in Wendy's and Simon's case helped, once again, with proof-reading. The biggest debt of all, as always, goes to Jackie and to Javier, Belén and Jack.

A Note on Sources

When interviewees chose to speak off the record, their words or the information they imparted are not accorded a note, since to cite an anonymous and confidential interview would pointlessly take up space. For the same reason, once a book or article is cited in a chapter, it can be assumed to inform the account thereafter and is not cited again unless the text makes reference to a specific quote, fact, or idea. References to speeches are not routinely cited since their approximate date is given, thus allowing the reader to find them easily on *http://www.conservatives. com/*.

Autobiography in Five Short Chapters

Chapter *One*

I walk down the street.
  There is a deep hole in the sidewalk.
  I fall in.
  I am lost. . . .. I am helpless.
    It isn't my fault.
It takes forever to find a way out.

Chapter *Two*

I walk down the same street.
  There is a deep hole in the sidewalk.
  I pretend I don't see it.
  I fall in again.
I can't believe I am in this same place.
      But, it isn't my fault.
It still takes a long time to get out.

Chapter *Three*

I walk down the same street.
  There is a deep hole in the sidewalk.
  I *see* it is there.
  I still fall in. . . it's a habit. . . but,
    my eyes are open.
    I know where I am.
It is *my* fault.
I get out immediately.

Chapter *Four*

I walk down the same street.
  There is a deep hole in the sidewalk.
  I walk around it.

Chapter *Five*

I walk down another street.

Copyright © 1993, by Portia Nelson, from the book *There's a Hole in My Sidewalk*, reprinted with permission from Beyond Words Publishing, Hillsboro, Oregon; copyright © 2004, by Portia Nelson, from the book *Me in You and You in Me: How Love Works*, reprinted with permission from Souvenir Press, London

1

SOLVING THE PUZZLE

AN INTRODUCTION

Politicians, most people think, will say anything to get elected. Parties, if they are in opposition, will do whatever it takes to get into power and, if they are in government, whatever it takes to stay there. This book challenges that common wisdom and tries to explain why it's wrong. It does this by focusing on a party that for decades had a reputation for its ruthless pursuit of power but which, until very recently, seemed to have forgotten how to win. If at the heart of every story there has to be a question, then it is this: how and why did the Conservative Party, of all parties, not do what it had to do in order, firstly, to stay in Downing Street after 1992 and, secondly, to get back there as soon as possible after 1997? Just as importantly: why and how was it able, after 2005, to apparently put things right so quickly?

This book's task, then, is not so much to explain why the Conservative Party lost elections – there are, after all any number of reasons why that can happen, many beyond the control of politicians, especially when they are in opposition and not government. Rather it tries to explain why those politicians were unwilling and unable to act in a way that might have given them more hope of winning or at least losing less badly. In so doing, it argues that, while there is no point trying to find and then flog a simple, superficially attractive answer to such a difficult problem, we can nevertheless provide an explanation that is both realistic and intelligible – and one that not only works in this case but might get us thinking about others, too.

The key to such an explanation lies in realizing, firstly, that party politics, indeed all politics, is essentially the interaction of ideas, interests, institutions, and, of course, individuals – people who, however intelligent and well intentioned, are, like the rest of us, hardwired to make what, objectively speaking, are sometimes irrational decisions; people who are both the product and the producers of the organizations they work in and the ideas they work with. Secondly, we need to bear in mind that politics is 'path-dependent': things said or done early on can constitute 'critical junctures' which then make certain courses of action (even if they are misguided) almost inevitable and others (even where they would seem to make more sense) almost impossible.

Thirdly, it is worth paying attention both to the people who actually do politics (which is why this book makes use of extensive interviews with politicians at all levels of the Conservative Party) and to the people who make their living reporting on it. This is not simply because they can give us a crucial insight into what, significantly, is a very small world. It is also because the line between players and recorders in politics is a very blurred one. Indeed, one of the main contentions of this book is that one cannot understand the Conservative Party, its recent travails and its future triumphs, without acknowledging the existence of what I call 'the party in the media' – the editors, commentators, and journalists who have a huge impact on Tory strategy, or whatever passes for it.

Finally, it is worth taking notice of another group of people who are paid to observe politics – the academics – just to see if they have anything to say which might give us a few clues. As an academic myself, I am well aware of and sympathize with the standard criticisms made against them – that they live in ivory towers working up abstract theories which have little or no purchase on the real world, that they phrase their findings in language that obscures rather than illuminates, and that they seem to know more and more about less and less. But I also know that academics do have something to contribute if only they can communicate it in a way that most of us who simply take an intelligent (and possibly an active) interest in politics can understand and even enjoy. Judging from high-street bookshops, historians have managed to do this. There is no real reason why political scientists – especially if they can weave together narrative and analysis – cannot join them.

Academics are lucky people. They can get behind the headlines and beyond the collective memories and conventional narratives about parties that often disguise and distort what actually went on inside them. Academics can get at what people were thinking, saying, and doing at the time rather than what we (or those same people) hazily recollect. And, by treating politics as a science as much as an art, academics collect data about parties and elections all over the world, thereby discovering patterns and regularities which suggest that some of the stuff we might think of as strange – the failure of politicians and parties to do whatever it takes to snatch and cling onto power, for example – can actually make perfect sense, at least to those directly involved. Knowing all this means that we stand a much better chance of producing a satisfying rather than a simplistic, silver-bullet-style explanation – an explanation which fits with how things work in the messy, nuanced, accident-prone, and incident-packed real world in which politicians (and even academics!) try their best to live.

And that, when it comes down to it, is the purpose of this book. One of the biggest compliments paid to me by a Tory politician as I was trying out my ideas on this topic was that I had 'really got under the skin of the Conservative Party'. I don't know if he was right. But what I do know is that only by doing that can we see where and why it went so wrong under and after Margaret Thatcher and how its current leader, David Cameron, appears to have put things right.

The puzzle

Once upon a time, every book written about the Conservatives contained an obligatory reference to what one expert calls 'the party's quite remarkable facility for adaptation and, closely allied to this, its appetite for power, often indeed its readiness to subordinate all other considerations to that one objective'.[1] The Tories, after all, could claim to be not just the world's oldest political party but also one of its most successful. First emerging in the eighteenth century, they governed Britain for much of the nineteenth and most of the twentieth. Naturally, they suffered the occasional reverse. But part of the key to their success in the twentieth century was their uncanny ability, following the loss of an election or two, to pick themselves up, dust themselves off, and start all over again. In short, the Tories could claim to be the country's 'natural party of government' because, whenever they found themselves in opposition, they rapidly managed to do whatever it took to get back into office.

Precisely what that was is no mystery. Without forgetting the wisdom of the old saw that 'governments lose elections, oppositions don't win them', the party out of office essentially has to present itself as a convincing alternative. In the words of one investigation into how the Tories traditionally managed to recover power, this normally means the opposition is able to demonstrate that 'it has a credible leader, is united, . . . and has policies which are not unwelcome to the electorate and which have enough coherence and content to be sustainable against attack'. Consequently, the same study concluded, there are five ways in which the Party normally places itself in a position to win next time around.

> The first of these is 'fresh faces': a new leader or leadership team, and especially the sense of a change of generations. The second is 'cohesion': the maintenance of unity and discipline within the party, which is essential to convey a sense of purpose and effectiveness. The third is 'visibility': a new agenda or a distinctive position, and a distancing from past unpopular policies and their legacy. Here it is important to have an impact upon the political elite and opinion formers, in order to give credibility to revival and reorientation, and for this to be communicated to a wider audience. The fourth element links to this, and is 'efficiency': not just an improved or revived party organization, but the sense that the party is at least master in its own house and can respond with speed and authority when the need arises. The final element is 'adaptability': a hunger for office, and a pragmatic or unideological approach which gives room to manoeuvre and seize the openings that appear.[2]

When the Tories ran into trouble at the end of a decade of success during which Margaret Thatcher won three elections on the trot, they failed to do these five things – or certainly failed to do them all simultaneously – until at least 2005, when David Cameron was elected leader.

Some of Cameron's predecessors over the previous fifteen years (John Major, William Hague, Iain Duncan Smith, and Michael Howard) could claim, more or less convincingly, to be a fresh face. But all of them, bar one, led a fractious party and none of them managed to convey a sense that the Conservatives were really moving on and coming together organizationally. As for elevating pragmatism over ideology, forget it. Inasmuch as they did so at all, they were left looking not realistic but opportunistic. For the most part, however, they did nothing of the kind, focusing instead on policies which made them look, at best, out of touch and old-fashioned and, at worst, mean-spirited and obsessive.

This might not have mattered so much had the Tories been facing the same Labour Party they had managed to beat so easily in 1979, 1983, and 1987. But they were not. Labour had been making progress, at first halting and then headlong, towards what it continually and persuasively claimed was the centre ground of British politics.[3] As a result, first in opposition under Neil Kinnock and John Smith and then in government under Tony Blair, Labour managed to tap into the widespread belief among the British that there need not be – indeed should not be – a trade-off between social justice and economic growth, between fairness and efficiency, between quality public provision and higher net disposable incomes. At the same time, it also managed to persuade people that a trade-off does exist between lower taxes and investment in the NHS and state education, which, along with economic wellbeing and the control of crime (and immigration), remain at the top of voters' lists of things governments are supposed to deliver. In so doing, Blair effectively neutralized – at least until 2007 – the classic Conservative argument that Labour's heart might have been in the right place but that it couldn't run the economy. 'New Labour' also made any claim by the Tories that they could simultaneously deliver lower taxes and maintain public services look like a pathetically transparent attempt to have their cake and eat it too. That Conservative politicians – when they weren't too busy talking up threats to national identity and law and order – continued to make that claim suggests that they, to some extent at least, were the authors of their own misfortune.

Doing things differently would probably not have won the Tories the elections of 1997 and 2001. It might not even have seen them win in 2005, when Labour was much more vulnerable. But it would almost certainly have seen them perform significantly better than they did. Moreover, what they needed to do was not rocket (let alone political) science. Following on from the list of the five things a Tory opposition traditionally did to get back in the game, the Conservative Party needed a leader who would cause it consistently, cohesively, and therefore convincingly to project some kind of progress back to the moderate mainstream or centre ground on which British elections are (unless the other main party deserts that territory) generally won or lost.[4] None of those in charge between the Tories' landslide election victory in 1987 and the election of David Cameron in 2005 came even close to meeting that need. Instead, especially after 1997, they 'banged on' about issues which people may have cared about (tax, crime, immigration, and Europe) but which were never going to help the Conservatives endanger Labour's overall majority. Meanwhile, they ceded ownership of the issues that did really count (health, education, and the economy) to a Labour Party determined to portray its Tory opponent as divided, extreme, and stuck in the past. Accordingly, most voters (notwithstanding attempts by the odd academic to insist otherwise) believed that the Conservative Party was stranded on the right, while Labour continued its relentless progress to what they saw as the centre ground.[5]

This book, then, is not so much about what the Conservative Party needed to do after 1989 as it is about why and how the Party proved unable (or unwilling) to do it. It also looks at how and why it suddenly decided to do things so differently from 2005 onwards. This is a puzzle worth solving not only because it tells us something about the Tories, but because solving it may add to our understanding of political parties more generally. After all, even if we forget about the Conservative Party's supposedly characteristic 'appetite for power', its behaviour after 1989 and especially after 1997 is, at first glance, hard to explain – especially if we believe that politicians, and therefore the parties they lead, are, at root, self-interested 'rational actors'. On the face of it, after all, the prospect and certainly the experience of a bad defeat should encourage the party that looks like losing, or that has in fact lost, to move towards the position of the winner, potential or actual. As one study which looked at parties across a range of different countries puts it, 'Past election results serve the same function as a very good opinion poll': they show the losing party – especially if it is beaten badly – that its prior beliefs about the voters were wrong; they also point to where it has to move in order to do better next time around.[6]

Why parties don't always do what we expect

Theory, however, is one thing. Practice is another – and not just when it comes to Britain's Conservative Party. Large-scale cross-national comparisons often show, of course, that parties can and do change – most commonly in response to defeat and a change of leader, and often in the direction of their more successful rivals.[7] But they also show that parties are prone to inertia and that they often adopt more intense or even extreme policies than one would expect if the default option really was to close down the space between themselves, the electorate, and their sometimes more successful competitors.[8] Studies in the same field also suggest some clues as to why. Stripped of the specialized jargon that accompanies them, some of them would seem to make a lot of sense and are therefore worth taking seriously when observing the Conservative Party's behaviour since 1989.

Of the reasons put forward by political scientists to explain why a badly beaten party might not make a more sensible and attractive offer to the electorate next time round, there are several which, as we will see, seem particularly relevant in the case of the Tories. These include the following:[9] the threat posed by smaller, newer parties; the influence of party activists and campaign donors, neither of whom see their party's stances as quite as 'extreme' as ordinary voters might do; the fact that less moderate stances are at least distinctive and therefore reduce confusion among potential supporters and may even persuade them; the possibility that politicians cannot be certain (at least initially) that their preferred policies will actually lose them an election and the fact that (contrary to common wisdom) politicians do genuinely believe in the policies they prefer. Associated with this tendency to take ideas seriously is a tendency among politicians to believe that they can draw voters towards them instead of accepting the worrying possibility that little they say and do makes much difference. We might expect parties to 'accommodate' (i.e. move towards) the preferences of the electorate – preferences which are 'exogenous' in the sense of being determined outside politics by a combination of voters' personal backgrounds and their reactions to economic, social, and cultural developments. However, the politicians who run those parties are often convinced that those preferences are in fact 'endogenous' (determined by political argument and events) and can therefore be 'shaped'.

Indeed, political scientists can provide us with even more, potentially useful explanations of why parties might not necessarily act as 'rationally' as we might expect. For instance, the fact that a party is seen as (or complacently assumes it is) more competent or credible than its opponent can lead it to think it can get away with policies that most voters would consider 'ideological' or radical. And a party can still expect a large number of voters to remain loyal to it whether it moves to the centre or not. Furthermore, a party expecting a low-turnout election may believe an ideological appeal to those loyal partisans will ensure they show up at the polling station whereas the more centrist, but alienated majority is less likely to vote. Again, as we shall see, all these have a role to play in helping us to explain how and why the Tories did what they did after 1989.

But even with these additional explanations, the list of reasons put forward by political scientists for why a party might head for the hills rather than the centre ground is incomplete. And those that complete the list also make a lot of sense when we look at the Tories after 1989. We would do well to assume, for example, that, given how little even the experts really know about what voters think and what motivates them to choose one alternative over another, parties are likely to stick to, rather than compromise, their ideology. The latter, after all, performs so many functions: it not only 'provides politicians with a broad conceptual map of politics into which political events, current problems, electors' preferences and other parties' policies can all be fitted', it also has a vital 'role in maintaining the separate identity of the party and promoting activist involvement in the first place'.[10] Inertia may also be the default option for parties because change is, quite frankly, a bloody difficult, lengthy, and risky business. Because it involves convincing suspicious voters who are familiar with the party's existing brand, its electoral payoff might not come quickly enough for leaders either to attempt change in the first place or to stick with it even if they do, especially in the face of severe internal and public criticism.[11] Recent research covering the entire postwar period and 25 countries shows there are almost inevitably time lags between any shift in position and the electoral benefits to which that shift might contribute – not least because it takes time for a change in a party's policies to help bring about a change in its public image.[12]

This focus on what might put a party off doing things differently, of course, assumes that its leaders even realize they are doing something wrong. As hinted at by some of the reasons already mooted for their failure to adjust in the expected direction, however, this may not be the case. Political parties might actually find it harder to get the message than we might expect, not least because they share certain characteristics with other large organizations where communication (as well as acting on what is communicated) is inherently problematic. Without lapsing into too much jargon, the way parties are put together and run means that, even when they are faced with 'exit' (of members or voters), they are systematically likely to value and reward 'loyalty' (to an ideology as well as to an individual leader or to the institution) rather than 'voice' (insisting that something is going badly wrong and has to change).[13] In an ideal world, of course, a political party – indeed any organization – should seek to institutionalize feedback so as to maximize the chances that it will notice things aren't right. At the same time, it needs to promote loyalty so that people (a) don't give up on it without giving it a chance or (b) don't kick up so much fuss that they end up damaging its reputation or capacity to respond. In the real world, unfortunately, it is difficult to strike this balance.

This trade-off between exit, voice, and loyalty is hard to get right, for three main reasons. Firstly, while the long-run interest of those at the top is not to cut themselves off, maintain their autonomy and continually prove their authority, their short-run interest lies in doing precisely that: exit then becomes treason and voice mutiny. Secondly, those in charge will be able, for the most part, to rely on the majority of people under them wanting to carry on without too much complaint, either because those people feel their time will come or because they fear their going will leave things in even worse shape than they already are. Thirdly, both the leader and those around (or just under) him or her are prone to believing that things aren't fundamentally as bad as they seem, to making excuses which blame unlucky contingencies or unfair competition. Interestingly, though, it is sometimes those (including those at the very top) who are most heavily invested in the organization – and therefore most likely to deceive themselves that things are OK – who, once they wise up, begin to advocate, facilitate, or even drive change. This, as we shall see, is relevant if one is interested not just in how a party took so long to sort itself out but also why, when it decided to do so, it happened relatively quickly.

One can of course push the analogies between parties and commercial firms too far. Indeed, in the words of a young Tory MP with a private-sector background interviewed for this book, 'You get from business to politics by taking your organization structure, removing it so there's no direct reporting . . . , have every employee think that they could be the chief executive within quite a short period of time, and then have them not all quite agreed on what the product range is, or the customers.'[14] Yet, as we go on to look in detail at what went on inside the Conservative Party after 1989, it becomes obvious that many of these apparently generic explanations have some traction.

Appropriately, though, for a party which has traditionally looked askance at abstract schemas and solutions (especially when they originate overseas), most writing on the Tories makes little or no reference to these generic explanations, preferring instead those that are essentially historical and home-grown.[15] The (very considerable) upside of this is that its authors – many of whom know the Conservative Party inside out – seek, quite rightly, to situate the Party firmly in a particular context and to pin responsibility on real people in real time.[16] The downside of such an approach is that it misses out on the suggestive insights that come from treating the Tories not as unique but as a party like any other. Worse, it can in some cases lead us into making arguments which sound striking but have little real substance. To assert, as does one author of a recent book on the Party, that one 'great truth of the age is that the right has won politically while the left has won culturally' assumes, rather bizarrely, that a Labour government that has spent unprecedented amounts on the welfare state has self-evidently capitulated to Thatcherism while the socially liberal attitudes held by the educated middle class are all-pervasive. Meanwhile, the same author's claim that the Party's collective guilt at the matricide of Margaret Thatcher saw it take 'refuge in the form of group therapy that Tories have always understood, based on nostalgia, mythology and selective memory' is great fun but just too pat.[17]

There are, however, a couple of recent exceptions to the rule just outlined. One of these argues, for example, that the Tories in 2001 were out of sync with the prevailing 'policy mood' and stranded way outside the so-called 'zone of acquiescence' in which any party hoping to win must be located. [18] In so doing, it touches on (though it doesn't have the time or space to investigate) a number of explanations that are clearly informed by those we have already referred to, adding one – a candidate recruitment process that results in MPs who are 'one-of-us' rather than in tune with the times or the electorate – that is clearly worth bearing in mind. Thinking about why Tory candidates and MPs surveyed tended to think Tory voters were more right-wing and Eurosceptic than in fact they were also leads the study into some suggestive speculation on the role of what social psychologists call 'selective perception' – the tendency to interpret evidence according to one's existing convictions, even to the extent that discordant information actually reinforces those convictions. Evidence to support such a proposition, of course, would require the approach taken in the study (a 'quantitative' one, based on survey research) to be complemented by a 'qualitative' approach (involving things like interviews and the analysis of written sources) – in other words by the approach used in this book.

The potential of such an approach is amply demonstrated by the other stand-out study of the Party which brings to bear generic explanations in an attempt to overturn what has become something of a consensus among journalists, academics, and even some politicians. This is that the Tories' focus on, say, Europe and immigration at the elections of 2001 and 2005 represented an attempt simply to mobilize what Americans would call 'the base' – the so-called 'core vote' strategy. In fact, the study points out, even in theory the Tory leadership had far less need than is popularly assumed to pander to its 'core support' in the electorate: such voters were more likely than not to follow their party than to put pressure on it, not least because they had nowhere else to go. After talking to some of those involved in the campaigns, the study makes what this book also suggests is a convincing case that the Party's decision to focus on such issues during the elections in question was about more than simply enthusing its own supporters. In fact, it also believed – not unreasonably by that stage – that it had little alternative but to stress the issues it 'owned' (and on which it had opinion poll leads amongst all voters) rather than fight on those, like the economy, health, and education, which had become Labour territory.[19]

Ideas, interests and institutions – and individuals: high politics and the Conservative Party

This book, of course, touches on general elections, including those of 2001 and 2005, as well as those of 1992 and 1997. But they are by no means its main focus. Instead, it is much more interested in how and why, by the time those elections came round, the Conservative Party ended up feeling it had no choice but to fight them in the way it did. And while this book, too, holds that generic explanations can help solve that puzzle, it also believes that any solution will involve not one but several explanations and inevitably involve the particular as well as the general.

Any solution, certainly, has to reject from the outset the notion – commonplace, believe it or not, among academics but probably crazy to everyone else – that anyone seeking to explain something political should have to choose between a focus on ideas (the ideology that drives those involved and the policies they favour), a focus on interests (the material considerations that motivate them or at least those that fund and support them), or a focus on institutions (organizations, rules, and customary ways of doing things). Instead we have to appreciate that politics, including party politics, can only be understood not just by melding contextual and generic explanations but by focusing on the intersection, the interrelationship, and the reciprocal influence of ideas, interests, and institutions.[20] Just as importantly, we have to remember that, because we are trying to understand the real world (a place more akin to a movie than to a snapshot), we are dealing with a situation in which actions and decisions taken early in the piece influence, constrain, and even determine what happens later on – a commonsense idea that academics call 'path dependence'.[21]

Because of all this, finding a solution to our puzzle will involve delving deep into the sequence of events that began with the ousting of Margaret Thatcher in 1990 and saw the Party go through four more leaders until finding one who finally looked remotely capable of saving it from what, getting on for 250 years ago, the greatest of all Tory thinkers referred to as 'the unpitied calamity of being repeatedly caught in the same snare'.[22] To do this is to enter the realm of what is sometimes called 'high politics'. As characterized by the Conservative historian who made that phrase his own, this is an environment in which only 'fifty or sixty politicians in conscious tension with one another' really count – a world where politics is 'primarily a matter of rhetoric and manoeuvre' driven not by genuinely held ideas but by '[a]ntipathy, self-interest and mutual contempt', a place where arguments over policy, strategy, and tactics are 'inseparable from disputes about persons'.[23]

Clearly, of course, there is rather more to it than this essentially pessimistic, even cynical, caricature implies: we have already stressed, after all, that politics boils down not to interests, or for that matter institutions or ideas, but to the interaction between them. To pursue to the letter an approach to understanding the political world which has so little time for ideology and so little appreciation of institutions, as well as one which focuses only on parliamentary elites and not on the relationships they have with other actors and groups, would be blinkered indeed.[24] That said, the idea of 'high politics' contains more than a grain of truth – as anyone who has read the best insider accounts of New Labour will realize.[25] When it comes to the Conservative Party from Thatcher to Cameron, for example, the cast of characters can seem surprisingly small. Indeed, it is striking the extent to which people who play a part early on (perhaps behind the scenes, perhaps in parliament or maybe in the press) pop up again a few years later.

For the moment, a few illustrations will have to suffice, but they are important ones. David Cameron himself, and indeed many of his inner circle like George Osborne, Ed Llewellyn, George Bridges, and Steve Hilton, are obvious examples, joining the Conservative Research Department just after university, going on to work as special advisers when the Tories were in government, perhaps dropping out of politics for a while before coming back to play a significant role in the counsels of the leaders who took the Party through a period of opposition in which it couldn't (or wouldn't) do a thing right, only to emerge, apparently, as its saviours. But there are others. Andrew Lansley advised Norman Tebbit under Thatcher, headed up the Conservative Research Department under Major, was closely involved in the catastrophically bad election of 2001, then ducked out of frontbench politics to emerge as a modernizer and a shoo-in for an important Cabinet position in the next Conservative government. The same can be said of Michael Gove, who started out on the *Times* as a media cheerleader for Michael Portillo when he was still a Thatcherite, travelled with him towards modernization, led the press pack against Iain Duncan Smith, and, having become an MP, became a key part of 'project Cameron's' apparent move to the centre ground – a location which, as we shall see, he had earlier professed to despise. Also part of that project is Michael Ashcroft. He helped bankroll the Party, attracted huge media criticism (not least from Gove) as Treasurer under Hague, became a big critic himself of the way the Party went about trying to win elections under Iain Duncan Smith and Howard, and was then brought into the heart of the Party's effort to help David Cameron win next time round. A small world indeed.

More generally, the 'high politics' approach is a useful reminder that institutions do not think, nor do ideas act. Only individuals do, even if they are more or less constrained and to some extent formed by those same institutions and ideas. To privilege measures (or anything else) over men is, as Britain's shortest-lived Prime Minister once insisted, to suppose 'that it is the harness and not the horses that draw the chariot along'.[26] It may be going too far to say, as does one hugely enjoyable account of life on the inside, that 'the story of the decline of the Tory Party' in recent years 'is largely one of human frailties and misjudgements'.[27] But it is undoubtedly true, as one of our most prominent political journalists once put it, that politics, whether or not one regards it as an art or a science, 'tests the frail personalities and skills of real people under pressure'.[28] If we take human agency seriously, and if we accept, too, the notion that to be human is to possess quirks and qualities as well to indulge in the pursuit of self-advancement, we have to add individuals to ideas, interests, and institutions in order properly to understand and explain any political puzzle.

For all that, it would be a big mistake to follow the 'high politics' focus on a few individuals so rigorously that 'Back-benchers and party opinion . . . appear off-stage as malignant or beneficent forces with unknown natures and unpredictable wills.'[29] Nevertheless, one has to avoid the opposite error: it is too easy – especially with the advent of internal democracy – to give a party's grassroots membership and dyed-in-the-wool supporters in the electorate much more weight than they actually have. Blaming, for instance, the anticipated reaction of ideologically purist activists and dyed-in-the-wool Tory voters for the Conservative Party's failure to do what it should have done after 1989, and especially after 1997, is problematic – for two reasons.

The first is that the bulk of in-depth research, both by academics and by journalists, on the attitudes of ordinary members and activists, both in parties in general and in the Conservative Party in particular, suggests that they are no more likely to be uniformly ideological zealots than those who run and represent the party at the national level.[30] The stereotype of what a political scientist would call 'the party in the country' or 'on the ground' suggests, as one long-suffering Tory member memorably puts it, that 'by default we are all racist, misogynist, uncaring, dim-witted, nationalistic, homophobic, selfish, materialistic, militaristic, jingoistic, meat-eating, double-barrelled, unsophisticated, fox-hunting, anti-intellectual, brutish, elitist, high-church, no church, reactionary, iconoclastic, country dwelling, two-house owning, bulldog walking, white, English men'.[31] To many of the Tory MPs they select and help elect, this is a travesty of the truth: the people they like to think about as 'my members' are the salt of the earth, are by no means unrepresentative of the public at large, and (for MPs, this is the best bit) are largely happy (barring scandals involving sex or money) for the man or woman they like to think of as 'their Member' to get on with things.

To other MPs, of course, Tory activists do live up to the familiar stereotype and, as such, are assumed to operate as a considerable constraint on the leadership's freedom of manoeuvre. As one put it in an interview for this book, 'They're all obsessed with law and order and hanging people, and obsessed with foreigners and immigration and Europe, basically. So a lot of concessions have to be made to these people – a lot of bones have to be thrown out of the sledge to appease these wolves.' Sentiments like these, however, tend to come from the small minority on the centre-left of the Party who are understandably keen to clutch at a simple explanation for the otherwise unfathomable failure of their leaders – men whom they assume are for the most part as urbane and intelligent as they are – to drive the Party in their direction.

The reality is clearly far more complex than this. Some activists do fit the caricature, yes. But, taken as a whole, the Conservative Party in the country is not a baying mob capable of reducing the leadership to a quivering wreck at the mere thought of going against its supposedly settled will. Whether, in practice, the leadership realizes quite how biddable even these 'core' supporters are is more of a moot point, of course, especially when it is up against it and worrying about its position – a position which ultimately relies on MPs who will hear and pass on any grumbling going on at the grassroots. Even so, we should not go so far the other way that the party in the country becomes, like the proverbial 'core vote', a phantom we can call up every time a Tory leader is accused, in that well-worn phrase, of 'lurching to the right'.

The second reason why we have to be careful not to overdo the influence of ordinary members is that in many parties – particularly centre-right parties like the Conservative Party – leadership autonomy is not only a recognized right but a reality. Labour leaders, like their counterparts in other social democratic parties all around the world, are often obliged, out of office anyway, to put up with people and policies foisted on them by their parties. When it comes to the Tories, however, not even the parliamentary party and the Shadow Cabinet, let alone the grassroots, have any appreciable say on strategy, or what passes for strategy. This is especially the case in opposition. In government, a Prime Minister's relationships with his or her ministers are inevitably marked by interdependence.[32] When the Conservative Party is out of office, that interdependence – a mutual reliance which in government is institutionally reinforced by the civil service and the doctrine of Cabinet collective responsibility – is, if not wholly absent, then highly attenuated.

Not one Tory politician or staffer interviewed for this book dissented from the suggestion that the Conservative Party in opposition is an essentially top-down organization. In marked contrast with its main political opponent, its leader (and those he recruits to his Leader's Office and admits into his 'inner circle', 'kitchen cabinet', 'personal entourage', call it what you will) has, both in theory and in practice, the main and final say on the strategic direction of the Party. It is this (as well as the fact that Neil Kinnock, John Smith, Tony Blair, and Gordon Brown all began to work to change their party after its first, rather than its third, landslide defeat) which means we cannot explain what happened to the Tories simply by pointing out that Labour, too, was out of office for well over a decade. Turning around the Labour Party was bound to be like turning round an oil tanker. No-one would ever compare the Tory

Party to a speedboat, but turning it around could and should have been much easier.

A change of leadership in the Conservative Party is, in effect, regime-change: a new leader, like a new American President, brings in 'his people' and for the most part gets rid of many of those who worked for or alongside his predecessor. This essentially presidential set-up is why this book is divided into chapters that deal with each leader in turn. But it is also why Shadow Cabinet has, at best, a consultative role. Although its individual members are sometimes given considerable autonomy to develop policy, and although they meet together so as to achieve buy-in for the leader's plans and to ensure that each spokesman knows approximately what the others are up to, it is by no means like a firm's board of directors. And even its most prominent members, some of who may be involved in so-called 'strategy groups' with the leader and his inner circle, are under no illusions that they are on an equal footing with their boss – something they are constantly reminded of, as one of the supposedly 'big beasts' who served under William Hague recalls: 'The leader is everything in the Conservative Party. It's perfectly true. You find that in all sorts of ways, even little things. Like if you went with him to make a speech somewhere, he'd be whisked away by a car and flown away in a helicopter and you'd be left to walk to the station.' Of course, this concentration of power has a flipside. It is highly contingent on results, actual and potential. A Tory leader who is seen as a winner can (within reason) do pretty much what he or she likes. Someone who looks like a loser, however, will still be 'everything' – but not, perhaps, for very long. In the words of one of the handful of political scientists to have managed to bridge the gap between popular and academic understandings of party politics, 'when appointed, the Leader leads and the party follows, except when the party decides not to follow; then the Leader ceases to be Leader'. [33] This stark reality also makes a difference to the way the Party reacts to defeat: as one of the contenders for the Tory leadership in 2005 puts it, 'Defeat is seen not as a corporate act but something for which someone has to be personably culpable.' [34] This may be good for accountability but, as we shall see, normally ends up preventing the Party from thinking seriously about where, collectively, it went wrong. And the fact that the Conservative Party is essentially an 'autocracy tempered by assassination'[35] means that the anticipation or expectation of

defeat encourages, well in advance of any election, destabilizing speculation about whether a Conservative leader can or should remain in post
or instead make way for someone who might do better.

'The party in the media'

Leadership speculation occurs not just in private but in public, too;
normally via the media. Indeed, the latter's role as a conduit is one
reason why any account has to take it very seriously indeed. But its role
in providing a public sphere or forum for internal debate, even an arena
for gladiatorial combat, is not the only one the media plays in party
politics – and maybe not even the most important one. Most analysis
of the media's political impact focuses on its much-debated (and on the
balance of evidence much-exaggerated) capacity to influence voters,
whether by telling them what to think (very unlikely) or at least by
telling them what to think about (possible but by no means categori-
cally proven).[36] In fact, however, the media may well have more power
to influence the mood and behaviour of those who claim to serve the
voters rather than the mood and behaviour of the voters themselves –
something, which, as we shall see, many politicians will admit to, albeit
indirectly.[37]

Certainly, there is every reason to suppose that leader-writers, columnists, and even reporters exert more influence on the Conservative
Party's leadership (especially if they write for the *Mail*, the *Telegraph*,
the *Sun*, and to a lesser extent the *Times*) than any fabled 'core vote'
or fanatical bunch of grassroots activists – or even those MPs who are
(sometimes laughably) labelled 'Senior Tories' or members of a supposedly 'important backbench group' by journalists desperately seeking
to stand up or string out a story on a quiet news day. Of course, there
are Tories who have been in parliament longer than their colleagues.
And, of course, they and their more junior colleagues still belong to
groups and dining clubs, some of which ('No Turning Back', the ''92
Group', and 'Fresh Start', for instance) may have played a part in the
disintegration of the party at Westminster under John Major. But many
of those groups are as much about social and generational bonds as
they are about ideology. As such, as journalists will admit in private,
these individuals and groups have nowhere near the cohesion and clout

imputed to them, especially when the Conservative Party is in opposition and therefore has little need of their votes in parliament. The 1922 Committee – a forum for Tory backbenchers – is a slightly different beast, but, again, is only very rarely a force to be reckoned with: except when some misstep means MPs are particularly unhappy with their leader or a certain Shadow minister, its weekly meeting is a routine gallop through Commons business for the next seven days.[38]

Politicians nowadays spend an awful lot of time worrying about and talking to the media. For its part, the media spends considerable resources on covering politics, be it on sending reporters to report it, or employing columnists to comment on it, or paying a polling company to gauge the public mood, giving it an additional angle and another excuse to up the ante. Indeed, as one of Britain's most acute journalistic observers of politics notes, 'The views of politicians, journalists, party members and the general public, as reflected in opinion polls, bounce off and reinforce one another in a constant and occasionally volatile feedback loop.'[39] Inasmuch as there is a line between the media and politicians, it is a blurred rather than a fine one – a membrane rather than a barrier. Indeed, the existence of what in Britain is now routinely referred to as the 'Westminster village' has important implications for how we understand parties and account for their actions.

Parties, we have to realize, are not impermeable institutions – and, when it comes to the media, osmosis has been occurring for decades. Even in the 1930s, according to one historian, 'The Lobby was merely an important and sophisticated part of contemporary Conservatism.'[40] And even the 'high politics' approach, first developed to deal with the politics of Britain as it became a democracy, included 'a handful of publicists' – proprietors and journalists – in the 'network of plebiscitary demagogues' it deemed worthy of study.[41] Whether it should or not, then, press comment matters deeply to politicians. Those who make it are listened to. They are buttered up. Bones are thrown to them, but brickbats almost never – at least in public. As a result, a party cannot really be said to begin and end with its grassroots, its paid professionals, and its elected representatives. To what political scientists call 'the party on the ground' or 'in the country' (the activists), 'the party in central office' (the office-holders and staffers) and 'the party in public office' (the elected politicians), we have to add 'the party in the media'.

And we have to acknowledge that the latter may well be as (if not more) influential in determining a party's overall direction and its composition as those who are formally its members and its employees.

A route map

This book begins at the beginning, with the ousting of Margaret Thatcher, and ends at the point at which it became clear that David Cameron had not only put the Conservative Party back in contention but stood a very good chance indeed of becoming Britain's next Prime Minister. Between those two points it looks at the leadership provided by four men under whom the Tories clearly lost what Enoch Powell – no mean vote-getter himself – called their 'grand sense for where the votes are'.[42] It does this by re-creating what actually happened rather than relying on what many of us recall happening.

So, for instance, it shows there is little or no truth in the idea that William Hague suddenly switched from a 'modernizing' to a 'core vote' strategy: he showed little real understanding of or enthusiasm for the former, while the latter is a misnomer; indeed, it could be argued that Hague had never really had a strategy worth the name. Likewise, attempts at modernization by Iain Duncan Smith and Michael Howard either were similarly unconvincing or never really occurred. On the other hand, to suggest that, for example, Michael Portillo, could have done in 1999 or 2000 what David Cameron did in 2005 is to overstate the extent to which Portillo's views on the economy or the size of the state were – at that stage anyway – as 'progressive' as his views on 'social' or 'moral' issues. More contemporaneously, it becomes obvious that once Cameron entered the leadership contest he was always likely to triumph, not least because the favourite, David Davis, was simply never going to win. It also becomes evident that Cameron's move to the centre ground is as much rhetorical as real – facilitated not just by opinion poll leads (and by the fact that he understands strategy and how to implement it) but by his combining counter-intuitive initiatives with more caution and reassurance to the right than he is often credited with. Cameron, in short, has done as little as he can get away with and as much as he can afford. He may be 'the heir to Blair' in the sense of realizing that, when both main parties are evenly matched, elections can only be won by moving towards voters rather than hoping they will move towards you. But rather than re-engineering his party, as Blair (and to a lesser extent Kinnock and Smith) did, the Tory leader has only re-styled it.

These and other points, as well as the overall explanation, emerge as a result of immersing the reader in the surprisingly small but heavily mediatized world inhabited by those leaders and the people around them. This 'high politics' approach proceeds chronologically on the grounds that earlier events have a marked impact on what the actors involved are able (or choose) to do later on. Politics is a path-dependent activity, and so time – and timing – matters. So, too, do ideas, interests, institutions, and individuals. The aim is always to highlight the interplay between them in order to explain not only why the Conservative Party failed to display its supposedly customary pragmatism but also why it seemed to recover it so quickly after 2005. This explanation is pulled together in a conclusion which also, firstly, suggests why we might need to mitigate our criticisms of the Tory leaders we discuss and, secondly, extends the study to the present day.

2

LOSING THE PLOT

THATCHER TO MAJOR, 1989–1997

Two decades after the event, many Tories still believe that getting rid
of Margaret Thatcher and replacing her with John Major was one of
their party's biggest mistakes. How, they wonder, could her colleagues
in Cabinet and parliament have been so stupid? Sure, the Party had run
into trouble in the late 1980s. But here was a proven election-winner
with an unassailable overall majority who had transformed Britain from
a union-dominated basket case into a low-tax, property- and share-
owning democracy that once again counted for something in the world.
Major, in contrast, is caricatured as a grey and uninspiring loser of no
fixed principles – a likeable but weak and needy character who would
always cut a deal rather than come out fighting, a Prime Minister whose
economic policy ended up around his ankles, who raised rather than
reduced taxes, who caved into Europe, and who presided over a sleazy,
divided government that probably deserved to lose in 1997.

In reality, the decision of the Party to get rid of its leader in November
1990 was a rational act that reflected 'the wisdom of crowds' rather than
a lemming-like leap over the cliff exploited by a tightly knit cabal of
irreconcilable, pro-European opponents. To believe that, had they stuck
with Mrs Thatcher, the Tories would – just as they had done in 1982 and
1986 – have climbed out of the hole they had dug themselves into and
won the next election is to ignore the sheer size of the hole compared to

the other mid-term dips the Party had experienced during the decade. True, the Conservatives managed (even if only just) to climb out of it under Mr Major. But under Mrs Thatcher there was no sign that they had even stopped digging.

Means, motive, and opportunity: setting Thatcher's fall in context

Thatcherism was an iconoclastic instinct more than it was a clearly thought-out or consistently executed ideological project. It is often afforded, notes one expert, 'a coherence and a consistency which is hard to reconcile with the improvisation, muddle, opportunism and changes of direction which characterised the Thatcher government in so many areas of policy'.[1] It may have had a winning formula – no-nonsense policies on crime and immigration, spending as little on welfare and health as voters will allow you to get away with, maintaining the military, boosting the private sector, encouraging entrepreneurship, ending subsidies, undermining union power, keeping inflation low, and delivering a rolling programme of tax cuts. But it was contingent rather than hegemonic. Thatcher didn't win elections because she converted a majority of citizens to her cause (she didn't) or because she was personally popular (she wasn't). She won them because her governments delivered just enough tangible benefits to just enough voters at just the right times in order to defeat an opposition whose record in office was woeful and whose attempt to put things right – hampered, first, by the Social Democratic Party and, second, by the National Union of Mineworkers – was proving protracted and not entirely convincing.[2]

After the Tories' victory in 1987, however – and this is the third point – their luck seemed to run out. Tax cuts designed to mitigate the stock market crash that followed the election combined with financial deregulation and property inflation to create an inflationary boom necessitating higher interest rates and the start of a long economic slowdown. The misery that many in the North, and in Scotland and Wales had experienced earlier in the decade now started to spread to Southern voters who hitherto had done very nicely. A local government finance reform (the infamous 'Poll Tax') that looked set to cause household bills to rocket made things even worse. Before long, the Party's opinion poll ratings began to plummet.

For a leader thoroughly in tune with the ideological instincts of her parliamentary party, this might have been survivable – just. But research suggested that Thatcher's support among her colleagues was far less ideological, and therefore far more contingent, than many imagined: with diehard Thatcherites making up no more than 25 per cent of Tory MPs, any failure on the Prime Minister's part to deliver the electoral goods would mean she was in serious trouble.[3] The Party's poor performance in elections to the European Parliament in June 1989 – a contest that took place in the wake of public splits within the government over European and economic policy – worried many MPs. And backbencher Anthony Meyer's decision to lay down a symbolic challenge to Thatcher by triggering a leadership contest in the autumn of 1989 effectively broke down 'the moral barrier that stopped members of the Parliamentary Party from competing for the leadership while the Leader was still Prime Minister'.[4] The ensuing ballot of MPs revealed that nearly 60 of them were not prepared to support her, suggesting that she was far from invulnerable. Even more worrying, up to 60 MPs who did support her sent her campaign manager a warning that their support could not be guaranteed next time around.

Deputy Chief Whip Tristan Garel-Jones felt duty-bound to tell Thatcher that unless something was done to smooth the introduction of the Poll Tax and to tone down her hostility to Europe, then 'the daylight assassination of the Prime Minister' might not be far off.[5] But although this apparently prompted her to make a little more room in her diary to meet with backbenchers, her enemies, if not her friends, could see that 'the clear message' sent by the 1989 leadership challenge was not sinking in.[6] At Cabinet level, hopes of a move towards more 'collective government' came to nothing and 'the bunker mentality', as well as the wilfully abrasive treatment of colleagues who worried about her increasingly undiplomatic language on Europe, continued.[7] Meanwhile, Tory MPs were really beginning to panic about losing their seats as 'it was becoming clear that the Poll Tax was not so much an albatross as a ticking time-bomb, ready to explode'.[8] Anxiety in the Whips' Office grew, but the Prime Minister – distracted by Cabinet arguments and media criticism – did not seem to take its warnings as seriously as she might.[9]

By-elections are a pretty poor guide to the outcome of the next general election. But they can seriously impact on party morale – especially when things go badly. And in Eastbourne on 18 October 1990 they went very badly indeed. The sitting MP, Ian Gow, who had been one of Mrs Thatcher's closest confidants and had been assassinated by the IRA in July, bequeathed his successor a majority of almost 17,000 on a vote share twice that of his nearest challenger. But this was turned by the Liberal Democrats into a majority of just over 4,500 on a swing of 20 per cent, thereby matching the swing to Labour the Tories had suffered at the Mid Staffs by-election in March, which was itself the largest in half a century. Exit polls from the earlier contest suggested that 90 per cent of switchers felt that Thatcher had 'gone too far in her policies and lost touch with ordinary people', while 77 per cent said she should 'not remain as leader at the next election'; meanwhile her plummeting satisfaction rating as Prime Minister continued to set new records.[10] If an apparently rock-solid seat like Eastbourne was vulnerable, reasoned many Conservative MPs, then no-one was safe. If the price of safety – which for many meant the end of the Poll Tax, with which the Prime Minister was so personally associated – was the removal of Margaret Thatcher, then enough of them were now prepared to pay it. Many in their constituency associations, of course, felt differently, but by no means all of them. As one MP who took the trouble to canvass opinion later observed,

> The idea that [Thatcher] was toppled by a parliamentary cabal against the general sentiment in the party is a fantasy of the Right. . . . They threw her out because the constituency parties were losing faith in her too. On the surface all the talk was of loyalty to the leader, yet I was not the only MP who knew that the reality [at the grassroots] was different.[11]

Contest and resignation

In November 1990 Geoffrey Howe resigned as Deputy Prime Minister in protest at being continually undermined by a woman to whom he had given sterling service since the late 1970s. His unexpectedly electrifying speech to the Commons explaining his reasoning triggered the contest that was to lead to Thatcher's downfall by prompting a challenge by Michael Heseltine. The charismatic ex-minister had used his time out of government to establish his credentials as a policy thinker and to strengthen his support in the media. Just as importantly, he built up his reputation in the party in the country by doing the rounds on 'the rubber chicken circuit' – fund-raising dinners in the constituencies of fellow MPs, who, even if they might have preferred to see more of him in the Commons and resented what they saw as his aloof manner, nonetheless owed him a debt of gratitude for helping them to meet the cost of an agent or other hired help. His loyal lieutenants had also been privately collecting names of Tory MPs who would support him should Thatcher be forced out.[12] Now, however, he was forced to break cover – not only by Howe's implicit call on him to stand but also by the needlessly provocative 'put up or shut up' briefing by some of Thatcher's inner circle, who initially believed that he did not have the numbers to beat her so may as well be taken on sooner rather than later.

Heseltine stood as the man who could get Conservative MPs re-elected, not least by going back to the drawing board on the Poll Tax. And no fewer than six opinion polls in as many Sunday newspapers just before the ballot appeared to confirm that, with him as leader, the Party stood a much better chance against Labour: indeed, the average of all six suggested that, under Thatcher, the Tories would be 11 per cent behind Labour but, under Heseltine, they would enjoy a 5 per cent lead.[13] Given the fact that, between Howe resigning and making his resignation speech, Labour had won another by-election (Bradford North), with the Tory vote falling by nearly 23 percentage points, MPs could hardly be blamed for wavering. And if this was true even of those who felt they owed the Prime Minister something, it was even more the case for the 68 Conservative MPs who had lost their places on the frontbench and the 97 who had never even been asked to serve during her 11 years in Downing Street.[14]

Faced with Heseltine's challenge, Margaret Thatcher, however, made no promises to change anything and gave no guide to how she planned to turn things around. She thought instead that she could see off Heseltine, who she believed was as flaky as he was flashy, by standing on a record that she considered self-evidently superior – so self-evidently that it would have been pointless to be seen to be actively soliciting the support of backbenchers who, after all, knew all they needed to know about her.[15] Convinced that Tory MPs would prefer to see her getting on with the business of government by going to a summit in Paris instead of trawling the Commons to drum up support, she put her faith in a combination of the payroll vote (the third of Conservative MPs with government jobs, however lowly) and what she assumed was a reasonably efficient mopping-up operation by her Parliamentary Private Secretary (PPS), Peter Morrison. In reality, however, that operation was shambolic.[16] Not all MPs were canvassed, let alone properly followed-up or cross-checked, meaning that Thatcher's numbers were hopelessly overestimated.[17] Heseltine's lieutenants, in contrast, were not great persuaders, but at least they could do the maths.

Some belated activity on the part of Thatcher's self-appointed praetorian guard of MPs in the 20- to 30-strong 'No Turning Back' group may have garnered a few extra votes but, in the absence of her failure to campaign personally, it was not enough to achieve the total she needed to win on the first ballot, namely an absolute majority of Conservative MPs and a lead of 15 per cent of the total number of Conservative MPs over her challenger. Even if she had won over the handful of extra votes she needed, however, there must be some doubt about whether she could have carried on – or at the very least carried on regardless. She commanded the support of only half (and perhaps less than half) of the parliamentary party. It was precisely to try to prevent a leader with such limited support carrying on, of course, that the Tory Party's rules for such contests stipulated that he or she win more than just a majority of those voting. And even if Thatcher had responded to a first-round defeat by winning a second ballot and staying on as Prime Minister at the head of a 'cabinet of all the talents' that included Heseltine and abandoned the Poll Tax, exercising due authority over her colleagues, the House, and the country would have been next to impossible.

In short, after the result of the first ballot was announced, Thatcher was effectively dead in the water. Support, the Chief Whip reported, was slipping away at all levels, not least among ministerial colleagues, whose thoughts were already turning not to how she might win but, firstly, to who might be better placed to 'stop Heseltine' and, secondly, to how she must be protected from 'humiliation'. Unable even to muster a convincing campaign team, realizing that she could not win, and anxious to ensure she had at least some say in the succession (many were already suggesting to her that John Major was the man), the Prime Minister cut her losses and announced her resignation.[18]

Why she couldn't hold on: ideas, interests, institutions – and individuals

Margaret Thatcher had become incapable not simply of responding to a threat to her leadership but even of recognizing how serious that threat was and realizing it demanded a convincing and possibly accommodating response. How did it come to this? During her own successful strike against Ted Heath in 1975, after all, she had shown herself willing to grub up votes by cajoling and hinting, flattering and entreating, promising and persuading, well aware that Heath was throwing away support by refusing to play the game. As Leader of the Opposition, she was cautious, making it clear to the public and to her party that changes were needed but not revealing quite how extensive those changes might be. And, when in government, she did not, contrary to common wisdom, generally pursue her objectives, however 'ideological', without a care for public opinion or party unity: she calculated, bided her time, went with the grain whenever she could.[19] That such a consummate politician should have the rug whipped from under her feet not by the electorate but by her own party illustrates the importance of the interplay between interests, institutions, ideas, and also individuals. It also shows how vital it is for a political party – or at least those who want to continue leading it – to maintain mechanisms that ensure that they get the message that all is not well and act upon it too.

The problem for Thatcher was that, from the end of 1987 onwards, these mechanisms either were unavailable or were not working as they should have done. Cabinet was dysfunctional: in the words of one former civil servant and future Tory minister, who saw at first hand 'the intimidation [Thatcher] had come to exercise over her ministers', 'When people say that in her last few years in office she had stopped listening to anyone, they are right. But one reason she had stopped listening was that a lot of the people around her had stopped talking.'[20] Those who did not tended to be her ideological soulmates and, as such, did nothing to prevent her losing touch with reality.

Other institutionalized lines into the parliamentary party also proved inadequate – at least in terms of saving its leader. When the Conservative Party is in power, the main focus of the Whips' Office is on getting the government's business through the Commons and advising on the ups and downs of reshuffles. It may report on the mood among MPs as gleaned both from its own efforts and from reports from the Chairman of the 1922 Committee, formed by backbenchers to represent their interests and whose meetings potentially provide a forum for two-way communication. But it is not necessarily dedicated to watching the leader's back – unless of course there is an especially close individual or ideological tie that binds the leader and the Chief Whip. In 1990, however, when the latter post was occupied by Geoffrey Howe's old friend, Tim Renton, this was far from the case. Not only was Renton unable to prevent a challenge, he was determined, once it came, to defend what he saw was the traditional impartiality of the Whips' Office during leadership elections – a stance he had already adopted during Meyer's symbolic stalking-horse challenge the year before.[21] Perversely, the one institution that did attempt to help the Prime Minister was the one expressly charged with neutrality or at least representing backbenchers, namely the 1922 Committee, and in particular its Chairman, Cranley Onslow. Felt by Thatcher's supporters 'to be both reliable and on her side', Onslow tried to help Thatcher by agreeing to shorten the period during which she could be challenged that year – a decision which may, ironically, have helped precipitate Heseltine's move against her.[22]

But it wasn't just individuals in charge of institutions who mattered. For one thing, Thatcher's final PPS 'was an unmitigated disaster. Peter Morrison . . . was a toff's toff, and made it very clear from the outset that he did not intend to spend time talking to the plebs' on the backbenches, virtually guaranteeing he could do nothing to counter Thatcher's 'growing isolation from her colleagues'.[23] Just as seriously, he did not enjoy a relationship of trust or confidence with the Chief Whip. This meant feedback to the Prime Minister was even further reduced. As a consequence, one of Thatcher's greatest fans confided to his diary, she simply didn't realize how bad things were: 'It's the Bunker syndrome. Everyone round you is clicking their heels. The saluting sentries have highly polished boots and beautifully creased uniforms. But out there at the Front it's all disintegrating. The soldiers are starving in tatters and makeshift bandages. Whole units are mutinous and in flight.'[24] Even those who were loyal to her thought the Prime Minister was too prone to listen to her Press Secretary, Bernard Ingham, and her Foreign Affairs Adviser, Charles Powell, neither of whom apparently 'understood how the Party worked or how to spot the signs of discontent amongst members of the Party, nor for that matter how to set about diffusing the anger that was being stored up'.[25] She refused entreaties to get rid of them from some of those who organized her leadership campaign in 1989.[26] Moreover, she continued to take calls from unwavering admirers like the News International columnist Woodrow Wyatt, who thought it more important to buck her up than tell the truth.[27]

The effect of all this may have been offset in previous years by the presence of two individuals who, unfortunately for her, were now no longer around. Adviser-cum-troubleshooter Willie Whitelaw had been forced into retirement after a stroke at the end of 1987. But perhaps an even greater loss was that of Ian Gow, who had remained close to Thatcher, even though he had stopped being her PPS in 1983. He was also a great friend of Geoffrey Howe and as such was able to effect running repairs to the relationship between the two after the latter was moved from the Foreign Office to become Deputy PM. Moreover, Gow had continued to operate as a vital link between Thatcher and the parliamentary party and had been very involved in the team that saw off Meyer's challenge in 1989. His assassination by the IRA not only caused the Eastbourne by-election that so spooked Tory MPs in October 1990, but deprived their leader of the man who, as Howe himself acknowledges, might have prevented the fatal breach between Thatcher and himself and who could conceivably have helped her scrape through the leadership contest that it helped precipitate.[28]

Finally, when emphasizing the role of individuals, one cannot forget the leader herself. Whether it was due to the euphoria or fatigue that followed three election victories in a row, Thatcher's personality underwent something of a change. Even before she became Prime Minister, the Tory leader 'had a well-developed ability to draw down the blinds': 'her face would blank over whenever anybody started to tell her something unhelpful'.[29] After over a decade at Number Ten, however, this trait was not only more pronounced but accompanied by a tendency to speak without pausing for thought: 'She was less inclined to listen to anything but applause. In her the brake which in all of us imposes a pause between what we think and what we say was wearing dangerously thin.'[30] This was exactly what happened when she allowed the cheers of Eurosceptic backbenchers to send her off-message in the parliamentary performance that led directly to Howe's resignation. Certainly, then, John Major was not alone in feeling that Thatcher's 'increasingly autocratic approach' meant that too many reasonable arguments were running into 'the slammed door of a closed mind' and that she had 'lost her political agility'.[31]

'The best we had': John Major becomes Prime Minister

Thatcher was, however, sufficiently clear-thinking, before going public with her resignation, to secure from her colleagues an agreement that they should come out collectively against Heseltine. They were easily persuaded: not only did they have little sympathy with Heseltine's Europhile interventionism but they also had doubts about his temperament and judgement. And, like many backbenchers, they found it hard to believe that the man who had toppled Thatcher would be able to win over the grassroots members they were going to need to campaign for them at the next election – a suspicion shortly reinforced by a newspaper survey of constituency associations which revealed support for the Chancellor, John Major (whose team had admittedly put a lot of effort into winning them over), was outstripping support for Heseltine seven to one. This exceeded even the very generous estimate that the Chairman of the National Union, Sir Peter Lane, had given the 1922 Committee in private. MPs were also influenced by opinion polling which, by the time they came to vote, showed Major was likely to give the Tories a bigger boost than Heseltine.

But if electoral self-interest mattered, so too did ideas. The notion that support for Major – or for that matter Heseltine – had less to do with policy and philosophy than it did with personality and background is patently false: ideology mattered as much in this contest as it did in any of the contests that followed it.[32] True, the third candidate, Foreign Secretary Douglas Hurd, stood more as a 'safe pair of hands' (and as a useful repository of votes that might otherwise have gone to Heseltine) than as a representative of a particular wing of the party.[33] But Thatcher and her ilk regarded him as irredeemably centrist. Major might not have been a Thatcherite zealot, but he was located towards (if not actually on) the right of the Party. As one of his colleagues from that side of the spectrum later put it, 'We knew he wasn't a hard-core Thatcherite, but he was the best we had.'[34] As such, he could bank on the right's support, especially when Thatcher herself made it clear to her most loyal MPs that she expected them to vote for him. This allowed his team, in turn, to concentrate on projecting a unifying 'One Nation' image in order to pull in the 'floating votes' of more moderate MPs.

Institutional strength also mattered. Major's campaign team was also better run than Heseltine's. Relying on the silky skills of Richard Ryder and Francis Maude, as well as Norman Lamont, it had begun tentative preparations even before the contest which triggered Thatcher's resignation and it was staffed by MPs able to tap support from different (if sometimes overlapping) groups and networks within the parliamentary party.[35] Major and his team also encouraged the media to draw a contrast between his rise from humble beginnings and the privileged backgrounds of his two opponents. Research shows that his supporters were less likely than theirs to have been to the best schools and universities, and that parliamentary inexperience was also a factor: Major's supporters had served slightly less time in the House. But ideology counted too. Heseltine won most support among those thought of as 'left-wingers' and 'wets', whereas Major won bigger in the larger group who made up the 'drier' right of the party – those keenest on keeping the state out of the economy. The most significant divide, however, was between those who shared Heseltine's pragmatic enthusiasm for European integration and those who shared Mrs Thatcher's increasing hostility to it. Major might not be quite as 'anti' as the woman who had made him Foreign Secretary and Chancellor, but he was a long way from being a Europhile in the Heseltine mould. In this way, as in so many other ways, then, Major picked up support not so much because of who he was but because of who he wasn't, although to suggest that his was therefore a 'default victory' rather than a genuine one is too harsh.[36] For many Conservatives, a vote for Major and against Heseltine looked like it would simultaneously provide the change and the stability they craved in equal measure.

That said, Major did not in fact win outright. He may have won hands-down in terms of newspaper endorsements – of the dailies only the *Telegraph* (Hurd) and the anti-Tory *Guardian* and *Independent* (Heseltine) declined to support him. But in the ballot, he failed – just – to make it over the official hurdle which required that he get more votes than the other two men put together: Major got 185 to Heseltine's 131 and Hurd's 56. But if this hinted at trouble for the future, it was all but forgotten at the time as Heseltine and Hurd immediately withdrew from the contest. Their doing so, it was unilaterally decided by the Chairman of the 1922 and the Chief Whip, rendered a third ballot unnecessary. John Major became Tory leader and, as a result, Prime Minister. Yet, even to some of those who had elected him, he would never be much more than 'a club Hon. Sec. pushed forward on the sudden death of the chairman' – a man who owed everything to Thatcher and whose election as leader could be seen as 'a farewell and rather guilty gift to her from her party'.[37]

Clearing up and cleaning out

Before he had entered the race, the Conservatives' new leader was not exactly a household name. Indeed, this, along with his seemingly straightforward, rather likeable personality, may have won him public favour in the opinion polls that suggested to his fellow MPs that not only would he stand a much better chance of pulling the party together than Heseltine, but he would be just as capable of reversing Labour's lead. At Westminster, of course, Major was a much more familiar figure. A former Whip who had been careful not to lose touch with the tea room as he rose through the ranks, he was (unlike both Thatcher and Heseltine) a clubbable type with the happy knack of getting on with a wide variety of people, whatever their ideological persuasion. Though privately he was far from blind to her faults, Major was regarded by most as something of a Thatcher loyalist, but one with whom even her critics could do business.

Major was in an odd and delicate position. The endorsement he had been given by Margaret Thatcher during the leadership contest was undoubtedly a key – if not the key – to his victory. And he and Lamont were clearly desperate to avoid any criticism from her in its aftermath.[38] But he had also been charged, implicitly if not explicitly, with breaking with both her presentational style and at least some of her policies. The first task was relatively easy: Major was so obviously more of a listener and less of a lecturer than his predecessor, and he, along with many of those closest to him, always had a much less black-and-white view of the world in general and politics in particular.[39] Major's style of leadership, then, was bound to look and sound very different to that of his predecessor.

Changing policy was more difficult. Major may not have been quite the acolyte that Thatcher and her supporters hoped for, but he nevertheless believed in a lot of what his predecessor believed, particularly when it came to a low-inflation, low-tax economy and a state that was both as small as possible and open to private-sector management methods. Norman Lamont, who had worked under Major at the Treasury before he became his first Chancellor, realized that the new Prime Minister would not turn out to be as right-wing as many imagined, but saw no signs of a radical departure from his predecessor's policies. The difference would be tactical rather than strategic: Major combined orthodoxy with emollience and was therefore 'an ideal person to consolidate the achievements of the last decade into a "kinder, gentler Thatcherism"'.[40] But while Major was more than prepared, as he put it, to lead 'the Thatcherite march onwards with conviction', he knew he had 'to talk up my inheritance, while moving with the minimum of fuss to correct my own party's mistakes', and to avoid, on the one hand, being labelled 'son of Thatcher' by her enemies and, on the other, being accused of 'wrecking her legacy' by her friends.[41] Doing this would of course revolve not just around policy but around the individuals appointed to make and implement it.

Matching Heseltine's promise to do something about the Poll Tax had been a necessary condition of contesting the leadership. But, as the closely fought administrative war of attrition conducted largely behind closed doors in Whitehall was to show, coming up with a suitable replacement in time for a general election was something else entirely. It may have been clever politics to appoint Heseltine as Secretary of State for the Environment with a clear remit to do just that, but he could not of course be given *carte blanche*. After all, the newly appointed Chancellor, Norman Lamont, was understandably keen to demonstrate to the Treasury, the public, and the markets that he owed his appointment to something more than his role as manager of Major's leadership campaign. It was also important, given Lamont's identification with the Thatcherite right, that Heseltine not be seen to walk all over him, and it was hoped (by all concerned, including Heseltine) that the retention of Michael Portillo as local government minister would ensure that the eventual replacement for the Poll Tax – the Council Tax – was acceptable to the right. The appointments of Thatcher-trusties Kenneth Baker as Home Secretary and Richard Ryder as Chief Whip, along with the fact that 13 of her 22-strong Cabinet remained in post, were likewise a sign that, notwithstanding the promotion of Chris Patten to the Party Chairmanship, the Iron Lady's departure hardly presaged a lurch to the (pro-European) left.

Ideological considerations proved slightly less important when it came to making party political appointments to the Number Ten Policy Unit. Out went dyed-in-the-wool, dry-as-a-bone Thatcherites and in came an ideologically rather more flexible and eclectic team headed up by the (mildly pro-European) Tory journalist Sarah Hogg, who was charged mainly with encouraging the flow of ideas between the Prime Minister and his ministers (not one of whom, incidentally, was a woman like herself).

The real link between government and Party, however, was supposed to be provided by the Political Office, headed by the Political Secretary, whose 'overall role is to ensure that while the Prime Minister is busy being Prime Minister he does not forget that he is also the leader of a political party in whose name he stands for office'.[42] Again, a card-carrying Thatcherite gave way to a rather less dogmatic appointee, one of John Major's special advisers from the Treasury, Judith Chaplin. Although she retained Major's confidence, Chaplin proved a problematic appointment because an increasing proportion of her time was devoted to winning a parliamentary seat. As a result, a young Central Office staffer who had already gained a reputation for emotional intelligence and political judgement beyond his years, David Cameron, was drafted in to help Major with Prime Minister's Questions. Meanwhile, Jonathan Hill (formerly a special adviser to Ken Clarke and now of the Policy Unit) had to cover much of Chaplin's work liaising with Central Office and other party organs. Ideology, and appeasing the right, also played no part in Major's decision to retain Graham Bright, who had worked assiduously on his leadership campaign, as his PPS. Bright was to be his eyes and ears in the House of Commons, a place in which the new Prime Minister, previously so assiduous in such matters, henceforth spent barely more time than his two immediate (and famously detached) predecessors as Tory leader.

Away from Westminster, the party in the country was shell-shocked and sore rather than vengeful, although a few well-known Heseltine supporters were hauled in front of their constituency associations to explain themselves and even, in a handful of cases, made to face reselection. But things were not plain sailing for the leadership. In March 1991 Major and many of his Cabinet addressed the Conservative Central Council meeting in Southport against a background of opinion polls which suggested that, despite Lamont's first and supposedly vote-winning Budget, Labour were back in the lead. Although they laid into the opposition and in particular its leader, Neil Kinnock, none of the leading figures who spoke fared very well in front of an audience of 3–400 activists and councillors still reeling from, and resentful about, the events of the autumn.

Major's first few months, however, were made much easier by the overnight transformation in the Party's opinion poll rating achieved by dumping Thatcher. At the time of Howe's resignation, a Gallup poll put the party on 34 per cent and the Labour Party on 46 per cent – precisely the average for both parties in the 15 months prior to Thatcher's departure; after the latter, in December 1990, the same poll put the Conservatives on 45 per cent and Labour on 39 – a lead which, although it diminished in size (the average was 40–38), was maintained over 10 of the next 15 months.[43] The question as to whether this stunning reversal of fortune really had more to do with Thatcher going than Major replacing her is an interesting one. But it was not one that most Tory MPs really cared about at the time: many of them were basically back from the dead – and at a time when the economy seemed if anything to be deteriorating. For most of them, it stood to reason that John Major must be at least partly responsible for the miracle.

Gratitude appeared to give Major leeway to soften the Tories' tone on matters European. March 1991 saw him alarm Thatcher's die-hard supporters by declaring that Britain belonged '[a]t the very heart of Europe, working with our partners in building the future'. Meanwhile concerted, albeit indirect, action was taken to ensure the arch-Eurosceptic Bill Cash was unseated as Chairman of the parliamentary party's European Affairs Committee.[44] Rather more publicly, in the autumn at Maastricht, Major and his negotiating team pulled off the seemingly impossible trick of creating a European Union Treaty that avoided mention of federalism, that did not oblige the UK to sign the so-called Social Chapter, that maintained the possibility of national vetoes on foreign and security and justice and home affairs matters, and that enshrined the British opt-out on the single currency. The substance of this achievement, together with the highly effective PR operation undertaken in the media and the Commons, ensured that most sceptics gave the leadership the benefit of the doubt, at least for the time being and with an election looming. One who did not, however, was Margaret Thatcher, who, while she did not go so far as the hardline Eurosceptics who voted against the government in the post-Maastricht debate, did join the handful who abstained. It is a moot point whether she was driven by purely ideological motives or was in fact disguising her rage at losing the leadership – using what appeared to be an issue of principle the more effectively 'to get her own back', as some have suggested.[45] So too is the suggestion that one of her successor's biggest mistakes was his decision not to press straight on with parliamentary ratification of the Treaty but instead delay it until after the election.[46]

Away from Europe, Major pressed ahead with a couple of minor but symbolic departures from his predecessor's policies. Child benefit – which Thatcher had frozen and hoped to see wither on the vine – was up-rated, and proper compensation arranged for haemophiliacs given HIV-infected blood. This 'effort to nudge Conservatism towards its compassionate roots' was, according to Major, 'far more than a calculated remarketing of a brand whose image had become tarnished'. But, along with a later high-profile meeting with the gay actor Ian McKellen at Downing Street in September 1991, it alarmed some on the right, including Thatcher herself, who, having lost an empire, was clearly finding it difficult to find a role, her frustration fed by acolytes (Alistair McAlpine, Nick Ridley, Tim Bell, and Robin Harris) and Tory journalists (Charles Moore and Simon Heffer) for whom Major had 'committed the ultimate crime of not being Margaret Thatcher'.[47] The target for their vitriol was understandably resentful. The right – Major reasoned – had little to complain about when it came to his early focus on, say, education, which was all about reducing local authority control, more testing, less coursework, traditional methods, tougher inspections, and raised expectations. Likewise, the attempt to improve public services more generally via the so-called Citizen's Charter had been delegated to a supposedly Thatcherite junior minister, Francis Maude, and was, after all, about those services mimicking the consumer focus of the private sector. On the other hand, Major's belief that the Party mustn't be seen to regard public services simply as 'historical relics' or 'an embarrassing problem, ever demanding money' was bound to create tensions with those Conservatives who saw them in exactly that light.[48]

Many of those who were now accusing Major of straying from the path naturally blamed those around him, with Chris Patten, his pick as Party Chairman, frequently fingered as the most malign, 'left-wing' influence. In fact, Patten was probably far too busy trying to whip Central Office into shape to play much of a role as an *eminence grise*. He 'was appalled to find the Party's HQ split into little empires, sometimes more concerned with internal turf battles than with the Labour Party' – a place that contained 'unsung heroes and heroines with a great deal of experience' but also 'its fair share of time-servers and political novices'.[49] Even the Party's Treasurer, and Thatcher devotee, Alistair McAlpine, who had left his post that summer, thought 'the place was out of control' with senior officials 'in the pay of businessmen and promoting their interests', while Patten's predecessor, Kenneth Baker, supposedly 'sat resplendent in his magnificent office'.[50] Neither Baker nor Thatcher, it seemed, had thought a great deal about the next election, and the new Chairman reported to Major in January 1991 that '"the cupboard was bare" on planning, money and policy'.[51]

However, despite an accumulated deficit of £12 million – made worse by the decision by business backer and Thatcher fan Michael Ashcroft to demand repayment of his £3 million loan, Patten was able to replace some staff and commission polling.[52] The latter suggested the Party could still win an election, particularly if it focused on exploiting Labour's vulnerability on taxation. This finding chimed with the advice coming from Saatchi and Saatchi, which Patten had reappointed as the Conservatives' advertising agency, ignoring the qualms of some Central Office staffers who thought it had let the Party down in 1987. Of course, the agency counselled, the PM 'should be asking for his own term not for Margaret Thatcher's fourth', but the campaign 'should focus on a negative approach, denigrating Labour and their suitability for office, rather than . . . on the virtues of Major and the Tories'.[53]

'Keep a-hold of Nurse for fear of finding something worse': beating Labour in 1992

In the long run-up to the 1992 election, John Major held more 'Political Cabinets' – occasions where the civil service secretariat withdrew and ministers reverted to first names and talked about Tory performance, prospects, and strategy – than his predecessor. But, as the election got nearer, he set up an 'A-team' to run the election campaign. Individual qualities counted for far more than ideological fervour: the presence of Heseltine, Hurd, Clarke, and Patten meant that Lamont was the only fully paid-up Thatcherite on board. That said, there was little sense in which the Party's pitch at the 1992 election was more 'centrist' than it had been in the 1980s. Thatcher may have slain some dragons but there was still plenty to do. A Conservative government would, the manifesto promised, privatize the railways and the coal industry. Resisting the temptation to admit Labour had changed but to focus on its opportunism – a strategy that some were suggesting even before Thatcher left office – the opposition and its leader were tagged, very traditionally, as unreliable and incompetent, stuck in the socialist past and as addicted to taxing and spending as ever. Some, particularly those who analysed opinion research in Central Office, believed that the Party had to risk straying on to Labour's home turf, particularly on health, and Major's speech to the Tory Conference in Blackpool in 1991, while stressing 'the power to choose – and the right to own', was also an obvious attempt to emphasize his own use of the NHS as a guarantee of his Party's commitment to it.

As the election loomed, however, the view that the Party would be obliged to confront Labour on its own territory lost out to the argument pushed on Chris Patten and those around John Major by Maurice Saatchi. Effectively trashing the brief given to his agency by its supposed political masters, Saatchi laid out the following at a meeting in the early autumn of 1991:

In retrospect, at least, 1979, 1983 and 1987 appeared very simple elections to win. The choice was clear: 'efficient but cruel' Tories versus
'caring but incompetent' Labour. The difficulty for the Conservatives
in 1991 was that the recession had killed the 'efficient' tag – leaving
only 'cruel'. While the Tory party had successfully blunted the 'cruel'
image by replacing Margaret Thatcher with someone seen as more
'caring', . . . John Major should [not] fight the election on soft 'caring
issues'. Instead it should be fought on the old economic battleground –
although the Tories would have to rely on claiming relative rather than
absolute 'efficiency'. They would therefore have to demonstrate that
under Labour, conditions would be even worse.[54]

Despite misgivings that the electorate was now more willing to pay a
little more to improve public services, Saatchi's advice was taken. It was
heavily backed by Lamont, who was positively evangelical in his conviction that tax was the Tories' trump card.[55] And it was supplemented,
though only at the eleventh hour, by the Party playing another of its
strongest suits – immigration. Major and Patten had initially been
rather more reluctant to bring up the subject but had eventually lent
their support to Kenneth Baker, who, with the help of the *Express*, made
a last-minute splash with a speech touching (not very obliquely) on the
issue.[56]

Allied to the decision to sell Major over and above his party (the
name of which was not even mentioned in its prime-time Party Election
Broadcast, for instance) the negative strategy paid off, even if implementing it did exacerbate the perennial campaign tensions between
the two institutions (Number Ten and Central Office) jointly charged
with getting the manifesto together and running things.[57] Certainly,
the Party's victory owed more to the overall thrust of a campaign that
capitalized on the electorate's continuing uncertainty about Labour
than it did to Tory organization. Campaigning in marginal constituencies and the fortune the Party spent on polling in them proved relatively
ineffective: the Conservatives did less well in those seats than in their
strongholds; what is more, they failed to strangle at birth the anti-Tory
tactical voting that would, at general elections to come, serve to amplify
Labour's margin of victory.[58] That few if any paid much attention to such
details is understandable. The Party had, after all, not only won a fourth

successive general election but, many Tories believed, done something even more crucial: Margaret Thatcher may have killed socialism in Britain but, as someone who had served under her put it, 'by winning in 1992 John Major put it in a grave and stuck a damn great slab of marble on top of it so it was never going to come out again'.[59]

'Ashes in our mouths'

Whichever party had emerged victorious in 1992 would have been faced with an economy in recession. It would also have had to try to maintain an unsustainable exchange rate, necessitating a politically catastrophic devaluation and the consequent need to raise taxes, hold down spending, and maintain relatively high interest rates in order to ensure that the export-led benefits of that devaluation were not squandered by public or private consumption. Meanwhile, it would have needed to ratify a controversial treaty with an organization, the European Union, whose ambitions for a single currency many people – not least in the media – blamed for worsening or even creating those difficult economic circumstances. All this would have been a lot to ask of a government with a majority that might have allowed it to ride out internal dissent. But the electoral system that for much of the twentieth century had worked in the Conservatives' favour denied John Major's administration even that. As he plaintively noted,

> We won half a million more votes than Labour would in their landslide of 1997, and a third of a million more than Margaret Thatcher had managed in 1987. On an even national swing, our lead in terms of seats would have been over seventy. And when the parties' respective shares of the vote were calculated, the Conservatives received 42.8 per cent across Britain, against Labour's 35.2 per cent: a lead of over 7 per cent. It was one of the biggest leads in votes since 1945, but it yielded only a miserly majority of [21] seats.[60]

Perhaps in a normal parliament this might have been enough. But this was no normal parliament. Major barely had time to put together a Cabinet before his government was hit broadside by Black Wednesday – named after the day on which the UK was forced to suspend sterling's membership of the Exchange Rate Mechanism (ERM), the currency system into which the Tory leader had, Eurosceptics insisted, dragged the country in the first place. Then his pick as Minister of Trade and Industry, Michael Heseltine, made things even worse by announcing a month later the virtual winding-up of Britain's coal industry in a closure programme that would affect over 30 pits and over 30,000 jobs. The programme – even to grassroots Tory members in constituencies completely unaffected by it and notwithstanding a plan to soften the blow that was cobbled together over a weekend – came over as a callous kick in the teeth for those miners who, during the 1984–5 strike, had defied and helped defeat the National Union of Mineworkers. For all his reputation as a centre-left Tory, Heseltine had, not for the first or the last time (his abortive Post Office privatization was still to come), ironically succumbed to the temptation to assume, like many Thatcherites, that the worse the medicine tasted, the better it would ultimately be for the patient.[61] And he had utterly (but characteristically) failed to anticipate backbench reaction. As a result, the Major government came over as not only incompetent but just as harsh as that run by his predecessor.

The effect on public opinion of all this was nothing short of catastrophic. Overnight, the Party's opinion poll ratings dropped below those it had experienced during even the most difficult periods under Thatcher. Moreover it also lost its previously impregnable lead over Labour as the party best equipped to handle the economy. The county council elections of May 1993 were disastrous, allowing the Liberal Democrats to consolidate their strength in the South West of England – a position that gave them a great platform for future general elections. More immediately, the Lib Dems won two famous by-election victories in Newbury and then Christchurch on swings (28.4 per cent and 35.4 per cent) that put into the shade even those contests that had so alarmed Tory MPs in the dying days of the Thatcher regime. Even more worrying, because it went to Labour (by then under the leadership of Tony Blair) on a swing of 29.1 per cent, was the by-election in Dudley West in December 1994. The consequences of such defeats were not only bad for morale, as they had been under Thatcher, but also led to '[t]he haemorrhaging away' of the Party's majority in Parliament – the institutional factor that is all too easy to forget when set against the more colourful story of the clash of ideas and individuals that otherwise may not have mattered so much.[62]

Against this backdrop, the government was committed to securing the parliamentary ratification of the Maastricht Treaty. Prior to the general election, Major had been able to present the document (not unreasonably perhaps) as a victory for Conservative caution and his own negotiating skills. However, the contest had seen a number of loyalists – most notably Chris Patten – lose their seats and also brought in just over 50 new Tory MPs. Whether this represented an exchange of 'Major's Friends' for 'Thatcher's Children' is arguable.[63] It is too simplistic to suggest that out went the 'older county and aldermanic guard, steady under fire and largely without ministerial ambitions' and in came 'a breed of professional politicians who, as ideologues', failed to appreciate the need for 'institutional self-discipline'.[64] Similarly, it is overstating the case to say that 'although the right held most of the Parliamentary party, the Government was run from the centre left'.[65] On the other hand, there was indeed an increasing mismatch between the Cabinet, where by the 1990s only a handful of ministers could be described as thoroughgoing Thatcherites, and the parliamentary party, where their ranks were swelled at each passing election.[66] Certainly, the balance of the parliamentary party with regard to Europe tilted more towards the overtly sceptical than did the Cabinet.[67] Veterans of the cause on the backbenches were joined by new recruits like Iain Duncan Smith and Bernard Jenkin, who seemed to think that making a name for themselves as skilful troublemakers would do more for their long-term prospects than a few years of loyal anonymity – a calculation that may militate against party cohesion but may not be far off the mark.

Even for Tory MPs outside the ranks of the hardline sceptics, the ERM 'turned a quarter of a century of unease into a flat rejection of any wider involvement in Europe'.[68] Worse than that, many of them began to see the Treaty not just as a clear and present danger to national sovereignty but as a symbol of everything that had gone wrong since Mrs Thatcher's departure – an event which some still felt guilty or angry about and which the most determined sceptics had always interpreted as some kind of Europhile coup.[69] In this they were only encouraged by the increasingly frequent and strident interventions on the issue, in public as well as private, by the former Prime Minister and her fans, some of whom had even taken to calling her 'the lady across the water'. And while the leadership, always skilled at rigging Conference, might still be able to write and plant friendly resolutions on Europe at Blackpool in 1993, it could not prevent big beasts like Norman Tebbit making inflammatory public speeches on them.[70]

Even more serious, perhaps, were the nods and winks given by current ministers like Michael Portillo, Peter Lilley, and John Redwood. Cabinet sceptics were, it must be admitted, in a difficult position: resignation from the Cabinet on what for them had become a point of principle was tempting; but it risked precipitating further resignations and perhaps the fall of the government, which would in turn have handed the resulting election to a Labour Party committed to the single currency.[71] Hoping to avoid this, and perhaps to nudge fellow Cabinet members in their direction, they therefore stayed in but found it difficult to keep completely quiet. The consequent erosion of collective responsibility not only emboldened rebels, it undermined support even amongst those loyal to a Prime Minister whose authority was clearly in question. So serious, indeed, did the leaks from and in-fighting in Cabinet become that in February 1995 the Executive of the 1922 Committee – the representatives of the backbenchers – actually warned their leader that he had to warn his colleagues to stop.

The party in the media turns on Major

Major had previously been able to count on the broad support of most of what we have chosen to call 'the party in the media'. But not any more. The editor of the best-selling *Sun* famously told Major on the night of Black Wednesday, 'I've got a bucket of shit lying on my desk and tomorrow morning I'm going to pour it all over your head.' He rarely stopped pouring (and stirring) it from then on. The *Times* (also owned by Rupert Murdoch's News International) was slightly more measured but gave no quarter to anyone in its Euroscepticism. And the *Telegraph* and *Mail* titles made little effort to disguise their contempt for Major, and especially his European policy. Their antagonism was based both on personal and ideological animosity and on the commercial imperative to reflect the preferences of readers who were clearly disappointed with the government their newspapers had urged them to vote for. And it went way beyond the single currency. As one journalist who joined the lobby while working for an ostensibly Conservative-supporting newspaper during the Major years recalls, 'It was quite clear that my task was to get the Tories. Quite simple. "Go and cause trouble", that's what I was told.'

This media hostility played a significant role in the disintegration of the Tories after 1992, especially at Westminster. Clearly both print and broadcast outlets became both a conduit and a weapon used by politicians to fight each other. But commentary also mattered, especially at the elite level, and in a way that means Conservative colomnists have to be seen as an integral part of, not simply an outside influence on, the Party. Not even the most sympathetic Tory MP, for instance, could avoid the 'acid rain' of highbrow (but below-the-belt) invective that rained down on Major from the likes of William Rees-Mogg and Simon Heffer, supported if not spurred on by their editors, who, in their turn, were backed by their proprietors. In the words of a former Tory minister – himself 'with one foot in Parliament and another in the press' – both the parliamentary party and the Tory newspapers, particularly the *Telegraph*, 'were gravitating towards the fogeyish, ultra-patriotic Right' and its view that 'Major was a booby and the party had made a mammoth mistake in ditching Mrs Thatcher'. The only means of escape, apparently, 'was to turn the Conservatives to the Right and lead the country in revolt against Europe, up to and if necessary including withdrawal'.[72]

An understandably resentful John Major later railed against a Tory press that 'enmeshed itself closely with the more active elements of the Euro-sceptic cause', thereby creating 'a group in Parliament and the media whose superficial gossip, intellectual posturing and flock mentality endlessly swung rebellion this way and that, behind one right-wing hustler for the leadership and then another, between flashes of patronising loyalty . . . and then outright defiance'.[73] This was not paranoia. But it was perhaps a little hypocritical given that the Tory leadership was inevitably no less willing than its enemies to form and exploit relationships with journalists in its conflict against troublemakers inside the parliamentary party.[74] Nor did it always behave sportingly when it came to dealing with higher-profile dissidents, most obviously Norman Lamont and John Redwood. And of course Major frequently did himself no favours: it was not just that he chose rather mild-mannered civil servants rather than a more savvy media professional to run his press operation; he allowed his guard to slip too many times, calling right-wingers in Cabinet 'bastards', claiming to hear 'the flapping of white coats' whenever the hardcore parliamentary rebels were around, and even allegedly suggesting he was going to '"fucking crucify the right" for what they have done'.[75]

Unfortunately for Major, the personal peccadilloes of individual Tory MPs allowed opponents in the media to open up yet another front in their war against the leadership – to go for the crotch as well as the jugular.[76] His suggestion at the 1993 Conference that it was 'time to get back to basics' was intended to reassure the right that, after Maastricht, the Party would be returning to its Thatcherite roots – more Conservatism and less State – and was initially successful as such. But, with the unwitting aid of Central Office media managers (notably Tim Collins), it was immediately spun by journalists as some kind of moral crusade on the part of the government, thereby rendering any departure from those basics a matter of supposedly legitimate public interest. Soon 'sleaze' was everywhere, whether it be sexual – Piers Merchant, David Mellor, Stephen Milligan – or financial, as in the case of MPs accepting cash for questions or Jonathan Aitken's stay at the Ritz. The apparent failure of the leadership to take firm and decisive action was also an easy target – never mind that the latter was often impossible given considerations of natural justice and the limited powers that parties (especially those with small majorities) actually possess to dismiss MPs. Moreover, it could be slotted into the prevailing narrative of dithering and weakness. The need to respond to this, and to public outrage, resulted in Major, in October 1994, tasking the well-respected Law Lord, Michael Nolan, with heading a committee to examine standards in public life – an inquiry that, instead of kicking the whole issue into touch, would end up providing the Prime Minister with even more problems.

Central Office and the constituencies

The Conservatives' problems were not confined to parliament and the media. Money was also a worry. Donations were drying up and the Party's deficit stood at nearly £20 million; nor, contrary to popular wisdom, do such deficits automatically improve between elections since routine (and research) spending is higher than many assume.[77] After the election, Major made the veteran minister Norman Fowler Party Chairman. Fowler's rationalization of Central Office meant cuts in London and led to the ten Area Offices in England being slimmed to just six Regional Offices which would no longer dovetail with the provincial organizations of the voluntary party under the National Union.[78] This achieved its main goal, namely to cut current costs and establish better financial control under the watchful eye of a new Board of Management. But it could do nothing to prevent the Tories' European election campaign in 1994 being the first in history at which they found themselves outspent by Labour or from getting less out of the Boundary Commission's review of parliamentary constituencies than they had hoped for. The reforms also impacted negatively on staff and morale without necessarily meeting their other aim – improving relationships with, and financial contributions from, constituency associations.

The latter, whose size could vary between fewer than 50 members in the safest Labour seats to up to 5,000 in rock-solid Tory seats, have often chafed at handing over their full 'quota' payment to Central Office and, according to some, have always 'nurse[d] an ancient hatred of the party machine in London'.[79] That Fowler's reforms increased their represen- tation on the Executive of the National Union (the body representing the party in the country) did not make up for the creation of the Board, which many saw simply as a way of allowing the bureaucracy to get its hands on association funds.[80] Associations were also finding it increas- ingly difficult to hold on to members, let alone recruit new ones or get those who did stay to campaign actively – problems that were only emphasized when the press got wind of academic work on the party that famously showed the average age of the party's members was 62.[81] The same work also suggested, in fact, that the so-called 'blue-rinse brigade' were not simply the Thatcherite zealots and purists of popular imagina- tion. True, they were almost as keen on lower taxes and privatization as they were on capital punishment and the repatriation of immigrants. True, also, that over 80 per cent of them agreed the Party 'should always stick to its principles even if this should lose it an election'. But many expressed attitudes to European integration, to the welfare state, public services, trade unions, market regulation, and the need to position the

Party in the centre ground that were (to use the terms employed by the study) surprisingly 'progressive' rather than 'individualistic'. This more nuanced picture, however, failed to attract much attention.

Fowler stepped down in the summer of 1994 and was replaced by Jeremy Hanley, who, while he brought with him accountancy skills and an ebullient personality (potentially useful for a raiser of both funds and morale), was relatively inexperienced. To make up for this Major appointed two new Deputy Chairmen, John Maples and Michael Dobbs, both with political marketing skills. Day-to-day liaison between Central Office and Number Ten was also improved by the move of George Bridges from the former to the latter, although the Downing Street machine definitely suffered as a result of the departures of Jonathan Hill and Sarah Hogg. Nor could anyone do much to prevent differences in the spin put out by Major's new Press Secretary, Christopher Meyer, recruited from the diplomatic service, and the considerably more Eurosceptic Communications Director, Tim Collins. Nor was Major's attempt to use the Number Ten Policy Unit to kick-start more radical policy initiatives that would feed into the manifesto for the next election coordinated with Central Office, which at the time (March 1995) was developing what was known as the 'reassure the middle-classes strategy'.[82] Both locations were, in fact, receiving letters from the constituencies to the effect that they had little idea of what was going on in the country, leading Norman Blackwell, who took over as Head of the Policy Unit in 1995, to liken the government to 'the board of a major corporation that was out of touch with its shareholders and its customers'. They also led Hanley to put forward a consultation exercise ('Operation Disraeli') with ministers meeting the party in the country with a view to involving them in shaping a 'people's policy' – an idea attacked from the right as symbolic of the lack of initiative and leadership at the very top of the party.[83]

The leadership in question

Thatcher's removal not only destroyed the assumption that Conservative leaders could not be challenged while they held the premiership but showed that a government in trouble could be rescued from the abyss by a swift change at the top. The need to find an alternative to Major was already the subject of gossip at Westminster as early as the spring of 1993, especially after the Party's appalling performance at the local elections in May, where it lost some councils that had been Conservative since their creation in 1888. The talk intensified after Major subsequently removed Norman Lamont from the Chancellorship following a whispering campaign against him emanating from Central Office – a move that also meant the departure of his special adviser, David Cameron, much to the disappointment of one Tory backbencher, who noted in his diary that he 'may come from the Right, but he has astute political antennae and a fabulous turn of phrase'.[84] The new Chancellor, Ken Clarke, had proved his worth since Black Wednesday as a stout defender of a government down on its luck – so much so, indeed, that some were touting him as a replacement for Major.[85] Also promoted was John Redwood, apparently in the belief that Clarke's appointment – controversial since he was anything but a Eurosceptic or a single-minded tax-cutter – needed to be balanced by bringing in some right-wing ballast.

For Major, though, this and other clear-outs made no difference. The tea-room talk of who would replace him rumbled on throughout 1994. And it was fuelled in the early part of the year by suspicions among the Prime Minister's closest allies that Heseltine's fan club was once again actively gauging the level of support for its hero, especially after a *Sunday Times* poll in April suggested many Tory MPs were warming to the idea of Heseltine taking over. In contrast to Clarke and other Cabinet ministers, Heseltine had emerged from the Scott Inquiry into arms sales to Iraq with his reputation enhanced. Moreover, his enthusiasm for the doomed plan to privatize the Post Office seemed designed to court the right. Despite a public denial by Heseltine's PPS, these suspicions only subsided (and even then only temporarily) with the death of the Labour leader, John Smith, from a heart attack – a reminder of the cardiac problems Heseltine had himself suffered and which, for some of his colleagues, now ruled him out of the leadership.

When the results came in from the European Parliament elections in mid-June 1994, they left the Tories with their lowest share of the vote since the advent of universal suffrage; moreover, many of the seats they held onto were won by the smallest of margins.[86] By-elections held on the same day were no less disastrous: under Thatcher, the party had got used to sacrificing around a third of its vote at such contests; now it was losing between two-thirds and three-quarters.[87] Right-wing Eurosceptics in parliament had already begun talking publicly about Major as finished after what they saw as the government's capitulation over EU Qualified Majority Voting at the end of March 1994 – a 'betrayal' that had led Tory backbencher Tony Marlow to ask the PM on the floor of the House why, given he had 'no authority, credibility or identifiable policy', did he not 'stand aside and make way for somebody else who can provide the Party and the country with direction and leadership?' The results of the European Parliament elections ensured that the question was no longer confined to hard-core sceptics. In Hugo Young's words, Major had become 'a permanently contingent leader. Whether he could actually be removed was another matter.'[88]

With Heseltine seemingly out of the race, speculation began to centre on the man who had been touted as his right-wing running mate, Michael Portillo. Fortunately for Major, however, many Tory MPs were not yet convinced that the young pretender was sufficiently experienced, while his willingness to bend if not break collective Cabinet responsibility on the single currency did not go down well with everybody. Major, although not his government, was also helped by the fact that another potential challenger from the right, Michael Howard, was by that stage considered by many to have made a hash of the two big law-and-order measures the Tories tried to push through parliament in the face of an impressive opposition campaign spearheaded by the man who, in the summer of 1994 was chosen as Labour leader.

Blair's election as leader, as one of Major's advisers puts it, 'tipped the Conservatives from having a mild attack of the nerves into a full-scale nervous breakdown. Our compass went haywire.' Combined with the Tories' self-inflicted wounds caused by rebellions over the EU budget and the raising of VAT on fuel in the autumn, it boosted Labour's lead to a stratospheric 39.5 percentage points. More detail on their plight was provided in a memo leaked to the media written by John Maples, one of the Party's two Deputy Chairmen, on the findings from focus groups of former Tory voters. The latter, clearly, had a very low opinion of the Party, with many of them accusing it of being dishonest, uncaring, and unable to understand their concerns and problems. There was 'a feeling of powerlessness and insecurity about jobs, housing, health service, business, family values, crime etc. and no vision of where we are heading', with many voters seeing the Major government as 'ineffectual and unable to deliver its promises'. People thought little of Major's aspiration for a 'classless society' when 'the reality is now that the rich are getting richer on the backs of the rest, who are getting poorer'.

Equally telling, because they reflected underlying political realities and attitudes, were Maples' recommendations: a worryingly impressive Blair needed knocking about a bit by some Tory 'yobbos' in the Commons; tax cuts were needed if voters were to be persuaded that the economy was improving; the government should think about bringing forward law-and-order and trade-union legislation to embarrass the opposition; the Tories' NHS reforms had gone down like a lead balloon and '[t]he best result for the next 12 months would be zero media coverage of the National Health Service' on the grounds that 'we can never win on this issue'. Conservative arguments were not getting through because they were too complex for most people, and because 'What we are saying is completely at odds with their experience.' The Tories had to remember, said Maples, that 'While ABC1s can conceptualise, C2s and Ds cannot. They can relate only to things they can see and feel. They absorb their information and often views from television and tabloids.' Not surprisingly, Labour, and its supporters in the media, loved it: 'The destructive power of the Maples Memorandum', gloated the *Guardian*, 'is that it rings so true and talks so dirty at the same time', thereby confirming voters' worst suspicions about a cynical and patronizing government desperate to do anything it could to arrest its decline.[89]

Not surprisingly, speculation about replacing Major continued apace into 1995 and was now by no means confined to his sworn enemies. Even in advance of that year's local election disaster, despairing Tory MPs were drawing up 'dream teams': Ken Clarke's enthusiasm for Europe apparently disqualified him yet there was renewed talk of Michael Heseltine, with Michael Portillo as his running mate. Aware of this, Heseltine's fan club urged him to tone down his pro-Europeanism in anticipation of a contest to come – a contest in which apparently both the *Mail* titles and even the Murdoch press would support him.

In May 1995, the Nolan Committee's first report recommended MPs stop working for multi-client lobbying organizations and disclose extra-parliamentary earnings. Major promised to accept the 'spirit' and 'broad thrust' of the report, at which point, in the words of one minister, 'the parliamentary party erupted'.[90] Whips reported that forcing through Nolan would result in a rebellion bigger than those on Europe. Major was unable to persuade the Tory majority on the Commons Committee in question to recommend implementing Nolan in full. However, on the vote on the Committee's more limited recommendations in November 1995 (specifically on an opposition amendment obliging MPs to disclose any income they earned for parliamentary work in addition to their Commons salary), over 20 Tory MPs deserted their outraged colleagues and either abstained or joined Labour and the Liberal Democrats in the aye lobby.[91]

It was hard, however, to insist that Tory MPs knuckle down on Nolan when so many were already being asked to set aside their misgivings on Europe, the issue that threatened to balkanize the backbenches. After Black Wednesday and as the Maastricht ratification process began in earnest, 'Divisions in the party were prised open; fissures became chasms; factions became entrenched.'[92] In February 1994, an MP responsible for organizing the Maastricht rebels, in conversation with Chief Whip Richard Ryder, estimated that, based on that experience, there were 50 Tory MPs 'staunchly opposed to the European Union with a further 80 undeclared fellow travellers' ranged against 'fewer than 90 committed Integrationists', with 'the balance of 130' who would 'go whichever the wind is blowing'.[93] The language is telling, confirming not just academic research but also the contemporary impression of one disillusioned ex-minister that 'the civility and camaraderie' between Tory MPs that had struck him when he had first entered the Commons in 1983 had been blown apart by Europe, with the Party 'falling into fragments, literally, physically, before your eyes'.[94]

The zealotry of Eurosceptic 'true believers' meant that they were able to resist either the threats or the blandishments offered by Whips once it became clear that reasoned persuasion had failed.[95] The inability to sanction or reward them in the customary way eventually led, in November 1994, to Major withdrawing the whip from eight MPs following their rebellion (in the wake of the Maples memorandum) over a European Finance Bill. This highly unusual step, by effectively removing nine of Major's critics from the parliamentary party,[96] had

the immediate advantage of making it more difficult for those hoping
to gather the 34 signatures needed to precipitate a leadership contest.
But in the longer term it was counterproductive: the decision was taken
without much idea of what would happen after they were deprived of
the whip and their being allowed back into the parliamentary party in
April 1995, against the wishes of the Chief Whip and clearly without
conditions or an apology on their part, in effect 'awarded them a campaign medal rather than . . . a dressing down'.[97] And it only made it more
difficult to maintain a grip on those Tory MPs who had remained loyal,
often with teeth gritted and nose held. It also renewed tea-room talk
about the possibility of replacing Major.

   To the party in the country such factionalism at Westminster could
seem self-indulgent. Many ordinary members, whatever their views on
Europe, were also aware that their friends and neighbours just didn't
care that much about it in comparison to much more pressing domestic
concerns. The idea, then, that the parliamentary Eurosceptics were
invariably reflecting the views of a bunch of rabid activists is highly misleading, as even some of the 'Whipless Eight' realized.[98] Seen from the
leadership's perspective, however, many constituency associations did
nowhere near enough to bring their rebellious representatives into line,
in spite of the fact that they were encouraged to do so. During the passage
of the Maastricht Treaty, for example, Basil Feldman, the Chairman of
the National Union, sent associations a letter explaining that the fate of
the government was at stake and that they should communicate accordingly with their MP. However, the tradition of local autonomy often
trumped that of party hierarchy: if there was ideological agreement on
Europe between an individual member and his or her association, then
the leadership had no institutional leverage whatsoever.

   This kind of loyalty to the local member removed one of the few
remaining weapons available to the Whips' Office, which was already
having to come to terms with the fact that Maastricht and other aspects
of European policy had given some backbenchers a taste for rebellion.[99]
But, once again, the problem was as much individual as it was ideological or institutional. The Chief Whip, Richard Ryder, not only had
health problems but, in the words of his predecessor, 'lacked an ability
to command that would have weighed more on the scales than his good
brain and pleasant personality'.[100] His authority was further diminished

once it became known he wished to retire, probably sometime in the summer of 1995. The suggestion of 'a cooling of relations' with Major, particularly after the readmission of the 'Whipless Eight', did not help matters.[101] Nor did the fact that his relatively inexperienced lieutenants seemed incapable of inspiring the fear or respect that had been the almost automatic due of their more 'old school' colleagues in the past.

Moreover, there was no other institution at Westminster that could help the leadership crack down on Eurosceptic MPs. Certainly, the 1922 Committee's Executive, primarily elected by all Tory MPs to represent backbenchers, could do little to help. In the summer of 1993, when criticism of Major first began to mount dangerously, its Chairman, Marcus Fox, urged MPs to get behind their leader and briefed the press that they were doing so. But, by supporting, in November 1994, the leadership's decision to make a vote on the EC Finance Bill a matter of confidence, he precipitated a challenge for his post – beaten off, but only just – by the more right-wing Nicholas Bonsor. On the other hand, Fox had little truck with those who called for Euro-rebels on the Executive to resign and it was he who had recommended Major bring Redwood into the Cabinet.[102] Nor was he averse to communicating the feeling of backbenchers to Number Ten if he thought it might stiffen Prime Ministerial resolve on EU matters.

Other backbench groups and committees predictably proved even less useful to the leadership. Most of the subject committees that provide a forum for Tory MPs who wish to gain a useful reputation as a subject expert and that theoretically facilitate two-way communication between back- and frontbenchers fell into desuetude over the course of the parliament. Indeed, by 1995 most were attended 'by the chairman, secretary and a couple of loners with nowhere else to go'.[103] More informal groups – sometimes as much social as ideological – also had little sway over those who joined them and in any case were often tiny. The exception to the rule was the 100-strong '92 group, not least because it was sufficiently large and cohesive to set up and back slates of 'Thatcherite' candidates for other bodies within the parliamentary party. Unfortunately, however, it proved impossible to unseat its troublemaking Chairman, George Gardiner (who had apparently promised Portillo the group's support 'when the time came').[104] However eccentric, Gardiner's instincts reflected those of many of his fellow members:

so convinced were they, for example, that the leadership had it in for anyone on the right that they were prepared to defend the indefensible, censuring Major in October 1994 for obliging Neil Hamilton to step down while he conducted his doomed libel action against the *Guardian* over 'cash for questions'.

'Put up or shut up': the 1995 leadership contest

By the spring of 1995 John Major was well aware that he would probably face a leadership challenge in November. He also had to endure yet another round of criticism in the media from Thatcher, who was launching the second volume of her memoirs. And at a meeting with 50 or so MPs belonging to the Eurosceptic Fresh Start group on 13 June, during which he tried to defend his 'wait and see' policy on the single currency (later changed to the supposedly more decisive-sounding 'negotiate and decide'), the Tory leader was ambushed, barracked, and heckled by backbenchers who seemed to believe not only in ruling out the single currency in principle but that doing so would sweep the Party back to power at the next election. Deciding it could not go on like this, Major shocked everyone by announcing that he would be triggering a leadership contest that he himself intended to enter and win. It was time, he said, for his critics 'to put up or shut up'.

After a frantic few days it became clear that, much to the relief of his campaign team, the Prime Minister's only opponent in the first ballot would be John Redwood, the right-wing Secretary of State for Wales.[105] Michael Portillo decided not to challenge Major directly in the hope that, unlike Michael Heseltine in 1990, he could avoid being seen as the assassin and come through in the second ballot. In any case, Major had cleverly made it very difficult for Portillo to enter in the first round by telling him in private that he was calling the contest, effectively giving him just seconds to decide whether to resign and fight or (as he decided to do) to wish the Prime Minister good luck.[106]

Although he had been toying with the idea of a challenge for some time, Redwood's campaign was a disorganized one. Nor could he count on the support of all Eurosceptics, partly because of ambivalence about him as an individual but also because there were many ideological varieties of Euroscepticism. That said, Redwood, as the challenger, did have the advantage of a simple – indeed sledgehammer – message, set out by his supporters in a flier to all Conservative MPs, whose order of priorities it tellingly took for granted: 'No Change Equals No Chance. The choice is stark. To Save Your Seat, Your Party, and Your Country, vote for John Redwood.' But the fact that it was felt necessary to distribute such a flier points to one of Redwood's key disadvantages – one he shared with Michael Heseltine – namely that he 'found the task of hanging around in the House of Commons for hours on end a very great bore', ensuring that the enthusiasm of his tiny fan club was not accompanied by more general goodwill.[107] Major, on the other hand, was careful not to make Thatcher's mistake and took time during the contest to work the tea room, and was encouraged to do so by his campaign team, who also ensured any wavering MPs were given a 'Cabinet Cuddle'.

Like his predecessor, however, Major was unable to take advantage of the institution that would have been best equipped to provide his campaign with ready-made intelligence and organizing ability, namely the Whips' Office. Other institutions, though, proved more malleable – as they had in previous contests. A month or so earlier, after the May 1995 local elections, the 1922 Committee had rejected calls for an immediate leadership election on the grounds that the rules stipulating such a contest had to be held at the start of the parliamentary session.[108] Now, having been briefed beforehand, the '22's Chairman, Marcus Fox, followed up Major's shock announcement by letting it be known that potential opponents only had a week to declare their candidacy and then only four full days to fight the PM for the crown. Once Redwood entered the fray, Fox then refused his team's request that the ballot be genuinely secret, meaning that the Executive, who were due to oversee voting, would have a very good idea who had failed to vote for the incumbent – something that was bound to put off those who hoped for preferment.[109] Much to the chagrin of Redwood's team, Central Office, in marked contrast to its studied neutrality during the previous leadership election, also appeared to side clearly with one candidate. Director of Communications, Tim Collins, they claimed, 'directed a vitriolic character assassination of Redwood and his parliamentary colleagues'.[110] Major's campaign was also assisted by young Central Office staffers whom many judged to have a bright future, like George Bridges, Rachel Whetstone (Michael Howard's special adviser), and

George Osborne. Only one of the bunch, Steve Hilton, elected to help John Redwood.

Redwood's real problem, however, was not organization but the fact that few thought he could actually win, either in the leadership ballot or in the country. Early polls suggested, indeed, that less than a third of voters put Europe among the most important issues facing the country and that a Redwood-led party would lose over 60 additional seats to Labour. As a result, media attention turned early to the possible contenders should he do enough to force a second ballot. Fortunately for Major – and in marked contrast to the contest which toppled Thatcher – newspaper polls did not suggest that the two frontrunners identified, Michaels Heseltine and Portillo, would give the Party a significantly greater chance of winning the next election.[111] If anything, Major, whose personal ratings, while terrible, were – in contrast to Thatcher's – still above those of the Party, appeared to be getting something of a poll boost in the light of his 'brave' decision. Meanwhile, the negative editorials in the *Times*, *Telegraph*, *Mail*, and *Sun* (which famously characterized the choice as 'Redwood vs Deadwood') were so familiar that they were to some extent discounted and, in any case, most were assumed to be backing Redwood simply as a stalking horse. Whether the survey of constituency chairmen by the *Sunday Express* (which, like its daily stablemate, did stay loyal) had much of an impact is difficult to tell. It certainly indicated overwhelming support for Major: well over 90 per cent were recommending their MP to stick with him. Whether by accident or design, Major had conveniently timed the leadership contest to coincide with a meeting with over 150 of them at Central Office – a meeting which, he ensured, only he had a chance to address.

But the decision made by most Tories at Westminster to support Major probably had a lot more to do with, firstly, a calculation that he would win (ensuring that he, unlike Redwood, could make credible offers of patronage to potential waverers) and, secondly, the lack of anyone else who could win round voters and hold the Party together. Of the two Michaels, Portillo was widely seen by his colleagues to have 'bottled it', willing to wound (and install telephone lines) but afraid to strike by mounting a first-round challenge. Many of his putative supporters in the parliamentary party were also afraid that voting for Redwood in order to force a second round might backfire by giving the latter momentum – exactly what had helped Thatcher in 1975. Heseltine was anathema to many Eurosceptics and Thatcherites and in any case he believed on this occasion that discretion – and the Deputy Prime Ministership he was offered – was the better part of valour. The only other serious possibility, Chancellor Ken Clarke, was likewise happy to bide his time, had attracted the ire of the right by putting up taxes instead of cutting spending, and, worst of all, was as unapologetically Europhile as Heseltine.

Major, it turned out, was indeed, as former minister Steve Norris rather injudiciously put it when talking to the television cameras on the day of the contest, 'the least worst option'. Over a third of the parliamentary party did not vote for the Prime Minister, who garnered 218 votes against Redwood's 89, all but two of whom, research reveals, were hardline Eurosceptics.[112] There were 22 abstentions, and later research suggests that nearly half of Tory MPs not holding government office had failed to endorse Major's leadership.[113] But if Major won fewer votes than he had hoped for, he had won more than he had feared – and enough to prevent a second ballot. Moreover, Major's team spun brilliantly what otherwise might have been seen as a 'default victory' rather than a genuine vote of confidence.[114] And, once again, Marcus Fox, Chairman of the 1922, also helped out, persuading the Executive unilaterally to declare that this would be the last contest until after the next election.

Meet the new boss, same as the old boss

Major's win did allow him to make some personnel changes, the most important of which was to replace gaffe-prone Party Chairman, Jeremy Hanley, with Brian Mawhinney, renowned for being both a fixer and a bruiser. Mawhinney's main task was to try to get the party in a fit shape to fight the election, not just logistically but also in terms of presentation, big ideas, and a 'narrative' – something to which the new Director of the Research Department, think-tanker Danny Finkelstein, was expected to contribute significantly. At the other key department, Communications, however, Hugh Colver resigned as Head a few months into Mawhinney's term after the new Chairman brought the former head, Tim Collins (now a parliamentary candidate), back as a consultant. He also managed to secure the services of the reliably partisan Charles Lewington of the *Sunday Express* as Director of Communications and switch the Party's polling and advertising to ICM and M&C Saatchi, respectively. What Major did not do, however, was widen his circle of trusted advisers, continuing to rely heavily on his one-time PPS, Graham Bright, and on his old parliamentary friends Robert Atkins and Tristan Garel-Jones (loathed by Eurosceptics as 'the Member for Madrid Central' and therefore a useful lightning conductor). They were capable men but, by failing to bring Cabinet colleagues into his inner circle, the PM isolated himself and perhaps helped to bring about more disloyalty than he would otherwise have had to put up with.

Any boost that the 1995 leadership contest provided to Major's authority within the parliamentary party was pitifully temporary, partly because the Party's poll ratings did not pick up but also because Major, hoping he had seen off the right, saw no need to conciliate it.[115] The subsequent reshuffle, which saw Michael Howard stay at the Home Office rather than move to the Foreign Office, did not see the shift to the right that some MPs thought they had been promised by Major's campaign team. And any advantage accruing to the PM from his having finally persuaded his Cabinet in April 1996 to concede that an attempt to join the single currency would require a referendum was neutralized by Blair. Labour announced that it too would consider a vote before joining, ensuring that only a pledge to rule out the single currency for the next parliament would put 'clear blue water' between the two parties – and that was further than Major (and in particular Clarke and Heseltine) were prepared to go. Indeed, they had already done too much for some Europhiles: Tory MP Alan Howarth defected to Labour on the eve of the 1995 conference in Blackpool and his former colleague Emma Nicholson crossed the floor to the Lib Dems at the end of December.

By the New Year of 1996 the Tory leader was once again 'openly derided', and by the spring MPs were 'back to the old tea room talk: the leadership is decent but weak, roll on defeat and let's get a new leader'.[116] Major was looked upon with pity or contempt by both sides of the divide on Europe, who knew they were being played by a man hoping (against hope) that he could 'offer different messages to different audiences and get away with it'.[117] Just as Thatcher's strengths were reinterpreted as flaws once she ran into trouble (determination and certainty, for instance, became stubbornness and arrogance), what had been an asset when Major had stood for the leadership in 1990 – his uncanny ability to convince whomever he was talking to that he sympathized with them – became, once he won the leadership and had to make tough choices, a liability. The conciliator became a confidence trickster.

Looking back, Major claimed that by this stage his abiding priority was to ensure his Party stayed in one piece until either something turned up to help it win the next election or it was put out of its misery by a Labour victory. Yet on the modalities and the extent of the split he supposedly so feared, he is, tellingly, rather vague. True, any move to rule out the single currency might have seen the defection of more than just two or three pro-European MPs and this would have inflicted serious short-term damage, particularly if the Chancellor Ken Clarke had been one of them. But whether this would really have constituted the kind of rupture occasioned by, say, Peel's repeal of the Corn Laws in the 1840s is highly unlikely. Any defectors would have been deselected as Conservative candidates at the next election – a move which may have prompted some resignations from their constituency associations but hardly a mass exodus from the party in the country. The alternative (much less probable) scenario – the government suddenly signing up to the single currency, precipitating a loss of confidence in the Prime Minister among the majority of his backbenchers and a walkout by a large minority of his Cabinet – would have led either to Major's immediate replacement or a general election, the loss of which would have had pretty much the same effect, namely the selection of a Tory leader more in tune with majority feeling in the parliamentary party on Europe.

Given, then, that the existence of the Conservative Party was not really at issue, what really drove Major was not so much an institutional imperative as an idea, namely that the national interest was best served by a Conservative government remaining in office as long as humanly possible and by keeping the UK's options open on Europe.[118] In this he was hardly unique among Tory Prime Ministers, but he was uniquely unfortunate in having a predecessor who not only believed the opposite but was more than happy to share her thoughts with the party in the media, most of whom had little sympathy or respect left for the current Prime Minister.[119] This powerful combination led Major to become ever more sensitive to what the papers were saying about him but also to try to limit the damage he and others felt Thatcher was doing by holding talks with her and elaborately choreographing her appearances at conference. But it was never enough. After a brief lull following Major's victory over Redwood, Thatcher launched into her first set-piece speech on domestic politics since her resignation: speaking in January 1996, she claimed 'policies and performance' had not lived up to Conservative 'analysis and principles'; the middle class and aspiring voters had been let down; the Party had to resist the siren call of the middle ground; as far as she was concerned, 'One Nation Conservatism' was 'No Nation Conservatism'; the avoidance of 'honest principled debate' on 'important issues' would do more harm than 'splits and disagreements' and risked 'directionless failure'.

This was particularly galling for Major because his government had by no means abandoned the path first cut by his predecessor. It was a path, he had always insisted in private (where he referred to 'Thatcherism with a human face'), that he wanted to follow in substance if not in style, even at a time when, research suggested, voters were moving to the left – a shift that might have prompted an electorally more 'rational' party to have made for the much-maligned middle ground.[120] That Major and his colleagues 'could think of little more than continuing what Mrs Thatcher had begun' was partly inertia: it was as if 'the ideological engine could not stop itself going forward'.[121] But it was also an intellectual and institutional difficulty to which all long-serving governments are prone, namely the failure to renew whatever project animated and sustained them in their early years, with the result that they fall instead into the trap of simply serving up more of the same. Theoretically, this could have been offset by, say, think-tanks, backbenchers, former ministers, and media commentators. But in reality nearly all of them were calling for privatization to go further and faster, for the welfare state to be rolled back, and for a final stand against corporatist-socialist Europe. These calls may have been a factor in preventing the leadership from moving more visibly towards more centrist positions on policy, not simply because it felt it would incur internal opposition if it did so, but because, as a famously 'wet' ex-minister later put it, operating in this ideologically and institutionally confined space meant 'Major and other Ministers did not seem to realise how right-wing they were'.[122]

Going, going, gone: the long campaign for the 1997 general election

On 11 April 1996 the Conservative Party lost the South East Staffordshire by-election on a swing of 22 per cent to Labour and a *Sunday Times* survey published the following weekend suggested that only around a quarter of Tory MPs believed they could win the next election. The *Telegraph* once again weighed in – the Party had to replace Major.[123] This was followed by the official launch of the Referendum Party, whose founder, James Goldsmith, was apparently willing to spend £20 million to field 600 candidates nationwide. Local election results in May were predictably dire. Europe was still a problem. And time was running out. Major would have to call an election in a year's time.

The strategy for that election was supposed to be hammered out by a group meeting at Central Office, comprising the Chairman and Deputy (Mawhinney and Michael Trend), the Directors of Research, Campaigns, and Communications (Danny Finkelstein, Tony Garrett, and Charles Lewington), the Director of the Number Ten Policy Unit (Norman Blackwell), and Major's Political Secretary (Howell James), along with veterans like Tim Bell, Peter Gummer, and Maurice Saatchi, responsible for advertising. But from the summer of 1996 there was a tension between the latter, who believed that the electorate had to be sold the positive side of the story before being warned not to 'let Labour ruin it', and those (like Mawhinney and Garrett) who believed they had to go on the offensive straight away. This view won out and the summer saw the launch in earnest of the 'New Labour, New Danger' campaign that in August saw the controversial Tony Blair 'Demon Eyes' poster dreamed up by Saatchi protégé and former Central Office staffer Steve Hilton. However, this was not the only tension within the group. The other, almost inevitably perhaps, was Europe. Saatchi in particular was convinced that a more aggressively sceptical stance – ideally, indeed, ruling out joining the single currency in the next parliament – would unite the party and allow it to focus on one of the few areas where Labour appeared to be out of touch with the electorate. Others, including Mawhinney, Finkelstein, Bridges, Blackwell, and in the end Major, plumped for a more positive, optimistic, and less jingoistic appeal – 'Opportunity for all' rather than Saatchi's 'True to Britain'.

This was partly out of conviction, but partly because they figured that the alternative risked provoking big beasts like Heseltine and especially Clarke. They were right: when in the autumn of 1996 attempts were made by both the party in the media and, it seems, Central Office and even perhaps Number Ten to bounce the government into ruling out joining the single currency in the next parliament, both reacted sharply, obliging Major to support them and dash the hopes of his Eurosceptics. Clarke in particular left Mawhinney in no doubt about where power had to lie when the Party was in government: 'Tell your kids', he apparently warned the Chairman, referring to both junior and senior staff at Central Office, 'to get their scooters off my lawn'. Clarke's fellow parliamentarians, however, were less chastened. At a meeting of the 1922 Committee that followed the media-fuelled spat, many could not seem to accept that the Chancellor of the Exchequer had any right to determine government policy on such a vital economic issue whether they agreed with him or not. Any sense of what it meant to govern, let alone due deference, had long gone.

The Conservative leadership was also unable to exert any more control over the Party's candidates than its current MPs. Despite strong behind-the-scenes and even public pressure, it failed to prevent the re-adoption of 'sleazy' incumbents like Piers Merchant or Neil Hamilton. Nor was the leadership able – notwithstanding an explicit appeal by Michael Heseltine to a packed meeting of the '92 group – to persuade some of its members to drop personal commitments not to sign up to a single currency in the next parliament that were in clear breach of the official 'negotiate and decide' position. There were certainly powerful incentives for Tory candidates not to toe the leadership line. Firstly, those who went against party policy in their personal address – a group which included, incidentally, David Cameron – hoped (often in vain, it turned out) to avoid a challenge by a candidate of the Referendum Party. Secondly, they were offered up to £3,000 additional campaign funding by another Eurosceptic multi-millionaire, Paul Sykes – something only government members and about 25 pro-Europeans turned down. Perhaps some were even so desperate as to believe that they might be saved by the *Times*, which declared it would recommend voters to choose candidates not on the basis of their party but according to whether they rejected the single currency. Once again, local autonomy – this time combined with 'external' patronage and press power – trumped party hierarchy, leaving the leadership institutionally and ideologically compromised.

In the event, candidates' stands made no difference to how they fared at the election: voters did not distinguish between self-proclaimed Eurosceptics and alleged Europhiles; they just wanted the Tories out. But even if, in retrospect, the Conservatives' efforts to prevent that happening were doomed to failure, it is still possible to criticize their 1997 election campaign for doing less than it might have done. Clearly, internal arguments about Europe prevented them focusing on what could, had it been argued consistently, been one of their plus points, namely the strong and sustainable economic recovery achieved by Norman Lamont and Ken Clarke. But the problem wasn't just one of ideas, or rather one idea blotting out another. It was also institutional. Firstly, there were tensions between, on the one hand, elected politicians (and their professional staff) and, on the other, the advertising and PR people they had hired: the latter felt they were forced to fight with one hand tied behind their backs by an essentially amateur leadership that would not let them get on with their job and go for the jugular, while the former felt Saatchi and Bell in particular were exceeding their brief, trying to alter the product rather than do the best they could to sell it. Secondly, and especially once the campaign proper began, there was the very same struggle for control between the Central Office machine and the leader's staff that had also plagued the Party in 1992.

The institutional and intellectual confusion which characterized the Conservative effort in the long- and near-term campaign in 1997 may also have been down to individuals. As well as ensuring they themselves were in safe seats – Cabinet members like Brian Mawhinney, Peter Lilley, and Stephen Dorrell all joined the so-called 'chicken run' from the marginals – ministers found their minds turning not so much to how the election might be fought and won, but to how they might best position themselves for the seemingly inevitable post-defeat leadership contest. Even those who in retrospect had no chance whatsoever of becoming Tory leader began publicly to harden their positions on Europe without much thought as to any embarrassment thus caused to the government. And in private, the jockeying and preparation continued apace: according to one Whip, writing in mid-March 1997, there were 'at least four campaign teams in an advanced state of readiness', ready to swing into action as soon as the election was over.[124] Michael Howard's strong sense that politics was a team game meant he was always scrupulously loyal to Major, even off the record. But he had, thought some, been positioning himself since 1996, keeping up with old friends in the tea room and making new ones by inviting them in for a chat about policy, as well as visiting constituency associations. Even Michael Heseltine, who performed heroically during the election campaign itself, admits to using 'what little time there was to spare . . . to consider the likely turn of events', fortified as usual by his fan club's assurances 'of a wave of new converts' to his cause.[125]

By that stage, in fact, any Conservative managing to attract fresh recruits deserved a medal. Certainly, the Party as a whole had long since stopped doing so. One expert analysis just before the general election suggested that membership, which had stood at around 1.2 million in 1979 and had declined to 600,000 by 1992, now stood at around 400,000 – a post-war low that meant the Tories were, for the first time ever, fighting a Labour Party that could claim to be at least its equal in terms of bodies on the ground. And although they could still claim to have more agents, the total had fallen to 264 from 299 in 1992 and 359 in 1979. Many of those, however, were employed in the wrong places, reinforcing the seemingly perennial mismatch between the voluntary manpower that their safe and marginal constituencies could call on: the former averaged 1,200 members; the latter just 750.[126] In 1994 the same analyst suggested that membership in vital marginal seats had averaged 1,000 but could be much lower. In Slough, where the Tories' 1992 majority of just over 500 was converted in 1997 to a Labour majority of just over 13,000, the Party reportedly had only 83 members in 1994 and was without an agent. In Stratford-upon-Avon, by contrast, where John Maples won the seat with a majority of 14,000 in 1997, the party had 5,000 members – more than enough to employ an agent whether they needed one or not. In the Party as a whole, only around 5 per cent of members were under 35 and only 1 per cent under 25, while the Young Conservatives were 'virtually defunct'.[127] Not all the remaining stalwarts were elderly, but far too many of them were.

A week or so into the campaign proper, once it became clear that there was nothing likely to blow Labour off course, no-one at the top of the Conservative Party believed it could win. Even its leader thought the best he could do was to restrict a Labour majority to 20 or 30 seats. Nevertheless, there was arguably a duty of care on its representatives to do everything in their power to avoid making the impending defeat worse than it had to be. As Major put it, 'the scale of the defeat . . . mattered desperately' not just to candidates but 'to the sort of opposition the Conservative Party would be able to provide after the election'.[128] Many individual MPs seemed to forget this, hoping against all the evidence that they could buck the trend and survive the wave that was about to break. This may have been in part because few came close to guessing quite how big that wave would be. Many believed that the improving economy and a residual fear of Labour would see a large (if not necessarily sufficient) number of voters return to the Party at the last minute. And even in the final week the best guess by Tony Garrett in Central Office – the man who had accurately forecast the 1992 result when so many others had written the Tories off – was a Labour majority of 40 to 60 seats, possibly rising to 90 depending on tactical voting. That even the most hard-headed estimate got it so wrong suggests just how far from reality, and from the mood of the country, the Conservative Party had travelled – and how much work and time it would take it to get back on track.

3

TACTICS OVER STRATEGY

WILLIAM HAGUE, 1997–2001

The scale of the Conservative Party's defeat in 1997 is hard to over-state. With less than 31 per cent of the vote, compared to 42 per cent in 1992, it lost more seats – over 170 – than it held on to, leaving just 165 Conservative MPs at Westminster, 41 of whom were new to the place and only 36 of whom had any experience of life in opposition.[1] Not a single one represented a Scottish or Welsh constituency. They faced a Labour Party with 418 MPs and an overall majority of 179. However, while the extent of the defeat may have been unprecedented, the reasons behind it were not. A fascinating historical analysis of the fall of Tory administrations since 1783 identifies the following common factors: 'failure of leadership, and in particular a negative image of the party leader'; 'confusion over policy direction'; 'manifest internal disunity'; 'a revived and credible opposition'; 'a hostile intellectual or media environment'; '[c]oncern over the party's management of the economy'; 'depleted party finance'; 'organizational sclerosis'; and 'strength of feeling of "time for a change"'.[2] John Major's government ticked all these boxes.

But there was something else. The Conservative Party lost the 1997 general election in no small part because it could not adjust to the fact that voters had banked the gains made from the rescue and liberaliza-tion of the British economy under Thatcher and were now concerned to ensure sufficient investment in public services like health and education. That this sentiment had not resulted in a Labour victory in 1992 was down mainly to the fact that Neil Kinnock had been unable to persuade voters that he and his party could be trusted to look after the welfare state without jeopardizing economic efficiency. Blair's (and Brown's) genius was to convince people that this was the *raison d être* of New Labour. Whether many Conservatives saw it that way, however, was extremely doubtful. To them the proximate causes (the ERM débâcle and the tax rises that followed it, the disunity over Europe, the sleazy behaviour of a few bad apples) loomed much larger than the apparent exhaustion of the Thatcherite project. Indeed, to many of them, Labour had won not because it had come to its senses and worked out where the country wanted to go after Thatcher, but because it had shamelessly embraced everything she stood for and had simply stolen their clothes.[3] This, combined with Major's immediate resignation, plus the widespread illusion that their defeat had been so bad that things could only get better, meant that, instead of embarking on what might have been a useful post-mortem, the Tories went straight into a leadership contest.

Hague wins the leadership

The 1997 election simplified the choices for Conservative MPs. Portillo was out of parliament and therefore out of the running. The strain of the campaign almost certainly contributed to the recurrence of the cardiac problems that meant Michael Heseltine, though still an MP, would not figure in any leadership contest. Ken Clarke was still around, but his views on Europe (and to a lesser extent the economy) were as unacceptable as ever. Indeed, they were more so given that the parliamentary party that returned to Westminster after the election was more uniformly Thatcherite than the one that had left it for the hustings – a change confirmed not just by academic research but by the victory of Archie Hamilton, Thatcher's former PPS, over the ultimate 'safe pair of hands', John MacGregor, in the contest for the chairmanship of the 1922 Committee.[4] Redwood and Howard (and Peter Lilley, who also stood) might have had sounder views on Europe, but there was no reason to think that they were any more likely to appeal to the electorate now than before. William Hague, on the other hand, was

Major's youngest Cabinet minister and had enjoyed what was generally recognized as a good campaign.

To Redwood's followers, the young pretender was simply a soulless careerist – 'train-spotting vacuity overlaid by the gloss of management theory' or simply 'John Major with A-levels'.[5] To them, his campaign emphasis on the modernization of party structures was a distraction from the European issue, which had to be settled once and for all. They also tried to paint Hague as 'the establishment candidate' since his promise of organizational reform and greater party democracy chimed with like-minded calls coming from the Executive Committee of the National Union and in particular its Chairman, Robin Hodgson. This taunt had the potential to hit home: many MPs, after all, took umbrage at the idea that the Tory defeat could in part be pinned on the bad behaviour of a parliamentary wing that needed to share some of its rights, privileges, and power, starting with the forthcoming leadership contest. Others, however, believed that the resentment of ordinary members had to be assuaged rather than ignored, which made the position adopted by Hague the smarter move. Still, with Howard and Redwood handing out plenty of red meat to Eurosceptics, Hague had to convey some sense of a departure that was ideological rather than simply institutional lest he come over as some kind of consensus-seeking centrist in the Major mould. In late May, he duly attacked the 'constantly shifting fudge' of the past few years and had his 'friends' hint that Clarke would not make it into his Shadow Cabinet. He also sought Margaret Thatcher's blessing, even though in the first round, at least, she was known to favour Michael Howard, whose invitation to stand as his junior running mate Hague had first accepted and then spurned.

Howard was supported by former ministers like Francis Maude, now re-elected to parliament, and David Davis, who had never been away but who had failed to prosper as much as he might have hoped under Major. Howard also recruited Tim Collins, the Party's former Director of Communications and now an MP, to handle the media, but it was the latter that, in the end, effectively did for his campaign. The suggestion by Ann Widdecombe that there was 'something of the night' about her former boss at the Home Office was damaging, but Howard might just have overcome it had not someone on his team responded with off-the-record insinuations about Widdecombe that, to many

MPs, simply went too far. This, along with a notoriously difficult inter-view on BBC's *Newsnight* programme, effectively scuppered Howard's chances.[6] Similarly crass – and possibly just as counterproductive – was the innuendo apparently emanating from the Redwood camp about the 'bachelor boys' running Hague's operation.

Clarke's campaign was clean but reportedly disorganized, relying more than perhaps it should have done on the former Chancellor's posi-tion as the public's preferred choice and his hope that his colleagues at Westminster could be made to see that (as he put it in an open letter to them) 'if the Conservative Party is perceived to swing further to the ideo-logical right and also to become hard-line nationalist and anti-European, it will make itself unelectable'. This was a message that predictably went down like the proverbial lead balloon with the party in the media. Clarke's campaign was not the only one to suffer organizational prob-lems, however. Redwood's putative campaign manager, Iain Duncan Smith, failed to declare for him until he had consulted his constituency association – a move which many interpreted as an effort to buy time so he could consider a possible bid of his own. Once on board, Duncan Smith apparently proved competent enough but was suspected of using the consequent publicity for his own ends rather than his candidate's.[7]

Hague's victory always looked likely from the moment the results of the first ballot were announced. Clarke, whose support came mainly from pro-Europeans but also from those who thought he would at least be able to hit Blair where it hurt, had garnered just 49 votes to Hague's 41. And this in spite of the apparent pressure to vote for him put on some reluctant Eurosceptics by their constituency associations. The former Chancellor seemed less likely than Hague to pick up votes from the three also-rans who had fatally split the rest of the right-wing vote – Redwood, who, on 27, stayed in the race, and Lilley and Howard, who, on 24 and 23 apiece, dropped out and endorsed the less zealously right-wing Hague. The latter's first-round votes had come largely from the centre of the Party but he now moved to reinforce his Eurosceptic credentials by declaring that he was 'opposed to a Single Currency in principle' and even implying that those who were not would be barred from the Shadow Cabinet.[8] Even so, not all those who had voted for Howard and Lilley went with them. A few went to Redwood anyway, but a surprising number seem to have gone to Clarke, firstly on the basis that if they couldn't get the policy they wanted they would at least get personality, and, secondly, because they simply couldn't stomach the idea of being led by 'a shifty little bureaucrat' like Hague.[9] Some claimed simply to be following the wishes of their constituency association: the 'advisory' ballots held by the National Union showed chairmen supporting Clarke in both the first and second rounds, although there was clearly a move towards Hague between the two ballots: Clarke beat Hague hands-down first time around, but in round two he lost momentum, slipping back while Hague moved up.

The contest proper entered a third round. Clarke, who had bested Hague on the second ballot by only two votes (64 to 62), had little choice but to gamble – 'shit or bust' were his words – on an unlikely deal with the arch-sceptic John Redwood, who finished third. The latter would accept a free vote on the single currency and the Shadow Chancellorship in return for recommending his 38 voters from the second ballot to vote for Clarke, who, having parked Europe, would call on the Party to focus on electorally more important issues like the economy, health, and education.[10] Clarke himself had little faith in the idea; indeed, he would have stood down had Heseltine been able to overcome the opposition of his family (and his own considerable doubts) and enter the contest on the third ballot. In any case, the so-called 'Molotov–Ribbentrop pact' met with an almost uniformly negative reaction in the press and the parliamentary party, and it prompted Thatcher publicly to back Hague. Most Redwood supporters saw which way the wind was blowing: even his campaign manager, Iain Duncan Smith (who made it clear to journalists he would be running on his own account next time round), accepted a pre-emptive offer of a place in Hague's Shadow Cabinet. Hague was duly elected with 93 votes to Clarke's 70.

In fact, there was less than met the eye to Hague's winning margin. As numerous analysts have pointed out, he was chosen mainly because – in a largely Eurosceptic, economically liberal but socially conservative parliamentary party – there was no one better placed to beat Clarke and because he had by far the fewest enemies. He was also helped by a large number of older Tory MPs retiring or being defeated at the general election, ensuring that many of those eligible to vote identified with Hague as a relative newcomer.[11] Because there were so many apparently deep-seated differences over ideas and the individuals that were associated with them, the institutional rules ensured that inoffensiveness and novelty triumphed, producing a winner whose support was broad but not deep. Even the confirmatory ballot held prior to Hague's first Party Conference as leader suggested only limited enthusiasm for him: true, nearly 81 per cent voted for him, but only 44 per cent of ballot papers were even returned. Not even his worst enemy, however, would have predicted that, by the next Conference, in October 1998, Hague's ratings with the public would stand, along with his party's, at just 25 per cent – a figure that inspired the *Sun* to run a front-page picture of him as Monty Python's proverbial parrot hanging lifelessly (and upside down) from his perch, the headline proclaiming 'This party is no more . . . it has ceased to be . . . this is an Ex-party.' How did things begin so badly?

Initial complacency

Perhaps the most striking thing about the 1997 leadership contest is how much discussion seemed to turn on Europe and the single currency, and how little it was concerned with either why the Party lost and what on earth it was going to do about New Labour. The lack of a proper post-mortem allowed a number of all-too-comforting myths to grow up, particularly on the right of the Party. The first of these was that 'natural' Conservative voters had stayed at home and that the solution to the Party's problem was to reconnect with them. In fact, research suggested there was no reservoir of hidden Conservative support just waiting to be tapped by a more robustly right-wing, Eurosceptic stance: Tory abstention was probably no more than three quarters of a million, whereas defections to Labour and the Lib Dems ran at something like 3.5 million. But such findings simply could not penetrate such deeply held instincts, even when published by people who could claim to have the Party's best interests at heart.[12]

The second myth was even more pervasive, attaining the status of common wisdom in the Party to this day. This holds that the intellectual and moral victory was won by the Tories and that New Labour beat them simply by stealing their clothes and stressing sleaze and division rather than by convincing voters that it stood a better chance of delivering both growth and improved public services than a right-wing opponent all-too-easily portrayed as wedded to narrow-minded individualism.[13] On this reading, Tony Blair was a lightweight who had won on false pretences: sooner or later (and very probably sooner) he and his supposedly socialist colleagues would be found out, fall flat on their faces, and fail to rise to the task of running the country, at which point the electorate would come back home. As neatly expressed by the think-tanker who would soon become the Director of the Conservative Research Department under Hague, the Party effectively 'behaved like a disappointed middle-aged wife whose husband's just run off with his PA and thinks, "Well, give it three or four months and when he needs his socks darned and a home-cooked meal, he'll come crawling back, begging for forgiveness."' [14] In short, the country would return to the Tories as the 'natural party of government', especially if, without taking things too far, they expressed contrition for putting up taxes and washing so much dirty linen in public during the Major years.

   To some of those who had not survived the Labour landslide of 1997 and were now perforce living outside the Westminster bubble, deprived of the creature comforts of office but mixing in wider circles, this seemed ridiculously complacent. But those who survived – many of whom after all moved up in the pecking order as a result – could carry on relatively regardless, even feeling, perhaps, that, since they had held on to their seats, they must know better than their defeated ex-colleagues.[15] This, in the words of one MP later associated with calls for the Party not just to modernize but also to moderate, was deeply damaging because 'Our tendency to underestimate Labour affected our own strategy. We didn't really believe that we needed to change very much. . . . If you look back there's no indication really that the Party leadership accepted that the public had rather tired of quite significant parts of our overall outlook.' [16] This complacency was evident in Hague's first big speech as leader in July 1997. Since voters apparently 'still embraced our ideas', he told his audience, the 'fresh start' that would provide the platform for a Tory comeback would be institutional not ideological: organizational rationalization – and to a lesser extent democratization – would be the order of the day.

Institutional fixes and individual missteps

This focus on institutions rather than ideas was consistent with Hague's leadership campaign and reflected his individual predilections

– structural reform being the first resort of the management consultant. But there was also a political rationale. Hague and his colleagues
were painfully aware that in the first year of the new Labour government, the media and the electorate would pay no attention to what the
Conservatives had to say on policy.[17] It might be possible, however, to
convey at least a vague impression of change by pursuing structural
reform that many felt anyway was long overdue and in any case was
exactly what the Party had done as a response to losing office from
the nineteenth century onwards.[18] Rewarding the voluntary party for
agreeing to rationalization by giving ordinary members a say in electing
the leader also responded to a widespread feeling in the constituencies
that the Party had been let down by wayward Tory MPs – a mood much
in evidence at the 1997 Conference when Archie Hamilton, Chairman
of the '22, was sensationally booed from the floor as he tried to defend
the primacy of the parliamentary party.

At root, however, Hague's plans involved centralization when the
demands from the party in the country were really about democratization. This potential tension was finessed by conceding a little of the
latter in return for being allowed to get on with the former, as well as
by the appointment of Cecil Parkinson, now in the Lords, to what was
his second stint as Party Chairman. A popular choice, Parkinson would
hopefully help smooth the feathers that reform was bound to ruffle, not
least because it was to be driven by the Asda supermarket boss, Archie
Norman, who, though recently elected as an MP, was unfamiliar with
the culture of the Conservative Party and indeed politics in general.
Hague also made much of his decision to move his private office from
the Commons to Central Office in Smith Square.

The so-called 'Fresh Future' reforms – far-reaching reorganization
of the Party that saw it bring together its voluntary, professional, and
parliamentary components into a unified structure for the first time –
were ultimately approved by a membership ballot in March 1998, with
96 per cent supporting the reforms (a figure slightly undermined by
the fact that only 33 per cent bothered to return their ballot papers).
Theoretically at least, the new system would make it slightly harder to
depose an incumbent leader by requiring 15 rather than 10 per cent of
MPs to call in writing for a vote of confidence; this would be decided
by a simple majority, with a leader who lost being obliged to resign,

triggering an initial contest, possibly over a number of rounds, among MPs, with two going forward into a final contest in which all grassroots members would be able to participate on a one-member-one-vote basis. MPs, in other words, would lose their exclusive right to select the Party's leader but they would remain crucial gatekeepers by ensuring that the party in the country could only choose between the two candidates that emerged from their ballots at Westminster.[19]

This was not the electoral college sought by some grassroots reformers (such as the tiny Conservative Charter Movement). Nor did the new Policy Forum engendered by 'Fresh Future' have anything more than an advisory role. The reforms also granted unprecedented rights to the centre (via newly created Area Executives) to intervene in the affairs of associations deemed to be failing to meet specified 'minimum criteria' on membership, fund-raising, and campaigning – rights which would in years to come be exercised on a number of sometimes quite controversial occasions. In addition, 'Fresh Future' established, for the first time, a consolidated and centrally held and administered membership list which might allow the leadership to communicate directly with grassroots Conservatives without first going through associations, theoretically allowing it to appeal to the membership over the heads of activists for financial or policy support. The upside was that the associations managed to secure a majority on the new Party Board for elected representatives of the National Convention (the body that would supersede the National Union in the newly unified party structure). Henceforth the voluntary party would in theory be able to control the expenditure of the professionals in Central Office. However, progress on another front – the right of associations, on a majority vote, to deselect a sitting MP who wasn't performing or was past his or her sell-by date – was stymied by an eleventh-hour veto by the Executive of the 1922 Committee.

Hague's enthusiasm for fashionable management techniques also went so far as to see the introduction of 'away-days' for Tory MPs, focusing on team-building, motivation, and presentations – some from overseas speakers (invariably American or Australian right-wingers) who had helped turn around their own parties. These occasions were also used as a chance to project a less buttoned-up, more casual style, though it was a moot point whether holding them in places like

Eastbourne, firmly established in the public imagination as part of South East England's *costa geriatica*, was really the best way of appearing in-tune-with-the-times. And the fact that, to some in the Party, going without a jacket and tie was the height of cool is indicative of quite how far they had to go to catch up with contemporary Britain. Just possibly, fewer crimes against fashion might have been committed had more Tory MPs been women, but any progress on significantly increasing their numbers looked an awfully long way off. Anything which smacked of positive discrimination was an absolute non-starter and Peta Buscombe, appointed the Party's Vice-Chairman with responsibility for women in 1997, soon encountered resistance, not least from the Conservative Women's National Committee, to her attempt to mainstream rather than hive off women's representation in the Party.[20]

Progress on the reforms to the Party's paid professional operation was put off until the overarching structure was agreed, but it quickly became a bruising battle. Already widely mistrusted as someone who didn't really understand the difference between politics and business, Archie Norman, now Chief Executive of the Party, did himself no favours by appointing a Lib Dem as his assistant. He was soon on a collision course with Tony Garrett, veteran Campaign Director at Central Office, over his plans to close the Regional Offices set up under Norman Fowler and switch resources to a more direct relationship between London and smaller operations organized on county lines – plans which Parkinson was persuaded to back, leading to Garrett's departure. Whether the loss of past expertise was worth the future savings was a moot point, but it was clear that something had to be done. The Party had spent well over £25 million on the election, £15 million on advertising from M&C Saatchi alone; it was now overdrawn to the tune of nearly £4 million, and its income of £6 million would leave it hard pressed to meet annual running costs of over twice that amount.[21] The shortfall could be covered temporarily with the help of loans and donations made and drummed up by Michael Ashcroft, who took over as the Party's Treasurer in the summer of 1998. But cost-cutting measures begun by Norman and his lower-profile but equally determined successor, David Prior, would not bring things back into balance – and allow the Party, for example, to begin long-overdue investment in IT – until the spring of 2000.[22] Prior to that, Hague had been rebuffed or simply ignored by constituency associations (many of which were already failing to meet their fund-raising quotas) when he asked their permission to approach their members directly for much-needed cash – an embarrassing rejection which illustrated, firstly, how little authority Hague had personally and, secondly, how a fierce commitment to local autonomy had survived his 'Fresh Future' reforms.[23]

Hague's lack of authority had been a concern to his advisers right from the start. That he had long been depicted as a 'Hansard-reading teenage conformist and tweed-jacketed Young Conservative' was bad enough.[24] But things got even worse almost as soon as he assumed the leadership when, overcompensating, he ran into ridicule for wearing an irretrievably naff baseball-cap and cagoule combo for a photo-opportunity and then, not long afterwards, having himself snapped with his fiancée sipping rum punch from a coconut at the UK's biggest Afro-Caribbean festival, presumably in order to display his multicultural street-cred. When, soon after that, the pseudo-events gave way to real drama as the Princess of Wales died in a high-speed car crash in Paris, Hague's restrained tribute compared poorly with Blair's pitch-perfect performance – an embarrassment compounded, firstly, by Hague and other Tories wondering out loud whether the PM might not be making political capital out of the tragedy and, secondly, by Hague's going too far the other way by backing cringe-worthy calls to rename Heathrow airport after Diana. The Tory media machine's evident desire a few weeks later to have journalists note that he and his fiancée were (gasp!) sharing a bedroom at their Blackpool conference hotel only served to make their desperation to market their man as an ordinary guy even more painfully obvious. Certainly nothing he (or indeed Blair) did that summer and autumn suggested to the electorate that they had been wrong to boot out Hague's party: the second by-election of the parliament was fought in November after the Conservative candidate defeated at the general election in Winchester had successfully argued that the result in the constituency had been too close to call; it saw the Lib Dems increase their majority over the Tories from 2 to 21,556.

These early missteps were crucial because they put Hague on the back foot almost from the start, denying him the sort of early success and legitimacy that might have made him more confident about formulating and pursuing the wider change agenda that was being urged on him by people like Archie Norman.[25] They were in part down to the Tories' press operation being overstretched throughout Hague's first year-and-a-half as leader. Hague's friend Alan Duncan, who had done sterling media work for him during the leadership contest, soon began to attract flak from resentful (and more senior) colleagues, one of whom stooped so low as to observe to a journalist that 'Margaret Thatcher said "every Tory leader should have a Willie"; our leader has a prick.'[26] Moved out of his media-handling role to the supposedly more strategic role of 'Parliamentary Political Secretary' to the leader, he was replaced by the twentysomething Gregor Mackay, who became Hague's press officer. But – incredibly – Central Office was without a Director of Communications until March 1999.

Not everything remained in limbo, of course. Some of the earliest changes made were literally structural: the internal walls built during the expensive refit that Smith Square had undergone under Thatcher's last Chairman were torn down in order to promote more 'joined-up thinking'. This physical reconfiguration was accompanied by other organizational and personnel changes. The Research Department and the Press Office were merged, with the Head of the former, Danny Finkelstein, moving into the Leader's Office as head of Hague's own Policy Unit, while the new 'Political Operations' department was headed up by two more thirtysomethings – Rick Nye and, as Director, Andrew Cooper – both of whom, like Finkelstein, had begun life in the Social Democratic Party (SDP) before moving on to head the right-of-centre think-tank the Social Market Foundation. Norman, perhaps underestimating the mistrust that the former Social Democrats were bound to encounter from more tribal Tories, was determined to bring in new people who were not 'steeped in Central Office tradition', thereby making it easier to 'reshape the central office machinery into a modern political communications outfit' – something that was badly needed since the existing set-up was 'still very much stuck back in the glory days of the late 1980s'.[27]

Instincts not ideas

If the Party was beginning to re-tool itself institutionally, progress on the ideas front was more limited. Indeed, the only significant development was to push the Party further towards Euroscepticism. This seemed to make sense. Firstly, opposition freed it from needing to worry about preserving Britain's national interest in keeping its options open on a single currency. Secondly, around 140 out of a total of 165 Tory MPs could now fairly be described as Eurosceptic.[28] Thirdly, it was widely (and possibly correctly) assumed that there might have been more Tories returned to Westminster in 1997 had it not been for the intervention of the Referendum Party (and its then smaller competitor, the UK Independence Party or UKIP) at the general election.[29] Finally, research confirmed that Euroscepticism had the potential to become, on balance, an electoral asset if the Party could convince the public that Europe was no longer the cause for the kind of division that had rendered it a liability in 1997.[30] Accordingly, Hague wasted little time. His appointment of confirmed Eurosceptics Peter Lilley and Michael Howard as Shadow Chancellor and Shadow Foreign Secretary set the tone, as did his bringing in both John Redwood and Iain Duncan Smith to a Shadow Cabinet which soon endorsed his promise not to join any single currency by the next election and for the lifetime of the following parliament – the so-called 'two parliaments' line. The consequent resignations of the Party's Northern Ireland spokesman, Ian Taylor, and then Shadow Cabinet member David Curry were clearly seen as a price worth paying. So too, apparently, was Ken Clarke and Michael Heseltine's contemptuous dismissal of the new line.

Within months, Hague (possibly concerned not to be outdone by Michael Portillo, out of parliament but still talking tough on Europe) was upping the ante with a hard-hitting anti-euro speech at INSEAD, the business school near Paris that he had attended in the 1980s. This much-hyped intervention provoked predictably withering and worldly-wise criticism from the Party's pro-European grandees. This in turn prompted Hague to seize what looked like an opportunity to demonstrate his authority and curry favour with the party in the media in the face of the whispers about his leadership that had begun within less than a year of his taking over.[31] Despite the considerable logistical difficulties in sending out ballot papers caused by the fact that the Party still didn't have a central list of what it guessed were around 350,000 members, it would hold a vote on his 'two parliaments' line. The result, announced on the eve of the 1998 Party Conference, did little, however, to impress either the public or the press in the short term. In the long term, the fact that 84 per cent of the 59 per cent of members who voted in the ballot supported the leader's line lent it a good deal of legitimacy and persuaded most pro-Europeans that there was no point in carrying on the argument, at least within the Party.[32] The flipside of the leadership's victory, though, was that it was going to be much more tempting for it to play the European card if it found itself up against it in the future.

Hague's first speech as leader to the 1997 Conservative Party Conference, which delighted Eurosceptics by declaring that the ERM had been 'a great mistake', was spun as an attempt to distance the Tories from their reputation as not only disunited but sleazy, incompetent, and intolerant of lifestyles that departed from 'the traditional family', for which Hague nonetheless declared his undying affection. What the speech lacked, however, was any sign that the leadership realized that the Tories might not have lost in 1997 purely because they were seen as venal, cack-handed, and small-minded or because they had departed from the true path of (Thatcherite) righteousness. No-one seemed to be putting forward, even as devil's advocate, an alternative thesis – namely that, after eighteen years, the widespread unpopularity of the policies the Party had pursued since the 1980s could not be compensated for indefinitely by patching together a series of evanescent electoral coalitions capable, every four years or so, of beating a divided, distrusted, and disorganized Labour opposition.

To some extent this failure to think the unthinkable was individual. Those who had served in government anytime between 1979 and 1997, Hague included, were understandably reluctant to see them as anything but years of real, positive, and lasting achievement. Partly as a result, Hague, his biographer concluded, 'remained at heart an unreconstructed Thatcherite at a time when reconstruction was vital'.[33] Hague's precocious ambition may have led him to avoid joining backbench groups that would have labelled him as on one particular side of the party, but this did not mean he had no fixed opinions. Far from it, in fact. He was 'an instinctive Eurosceptic'. His economic thinking was in line with that of his first boss, Norman Lamont, whose PPS he became soon after entering parliament. Hague had tolerant views on homosexuality, but he also believed in promoting the traditional family (he opposed divorce law reform, and one of his first promises as leader was to reverse the Major government's decision to phase out tax allowances for married couples). And he was big on law and order, voting, for example, for the return of capital punishment in February 1994 and even admitting, while Secretary of State for Wales, that he favoured bringing back the birch. However much Hague's intellect may have nudged him towards a less traditional outlook, the Tory leader's instincts (his 'gut politics [were] traditionally populist and nationalist right-wing . . . overlaid with Thatcherite economic libertarianism') chimed with those of many grassroots members.[34] This cannot be ignored when trying to understand why his leadership was marked by what one of his Shadow Cabinet colleagues called 'the politics of the nineteenth tee' (a reference to the politically incorrect ideas that presumably get bandied around in the golf club bars of Middle England). As the same colleague put it, 'William was a right winger. Let's not pretend he was a prisoner of the right. He was a man of the right.'

But the failure of the Party's senior figures to think the unthinkable was also ideological. Holding down public spending in the face of mass unemployment, increasing inequality, and an ageing population; selling basic utilities and transport infrastructure to the private sector; pouring the money not into the NHS and schools but into tax cuts which disproportionately benefited those on higher incomes; standing up to Europe, whatever the cost: these were policies to be proud of. Senior Conservatives might – just – be able to countenance some kind of muffled apology for looking sleazy and divided, for losing control of the currency, and having to raise, rather than lower, taxes, and for being perhaps a little hard-hearted and moralistic when it came to people who didn't qualify as members of a nuclear family. But they didn't seem even to consider the possibility – suggested by survey after survey which showed the average voter moving leftward at every election after 1983 – that a significant proportion of the electorate might object as much to what they were proud of as what they were (ever so) slightly ashamed of.[35]

The failure to challenge this mindset was also institutional: there seemed to be no mechanism inside the Party which would ensure that alternative explanations and solutions were seriously canvassed or contemplated. Consequently, while Hague may have made vague references, as he did in his address to the spring 1998 Central Council, to the 'One Nation' tradition, rejecting the notion that the Tories were 'a bunch of Blue Trotskyites trotting into the wilderness', they had little substance. They were in any case contradicted by the content of many of the contributions to the full conference in the autumn – an event so poorly attended that rumour had it that the organizers had moved the stage forward so that the hall would look less empty.[36] Hague himself, for example, contrasted Labour's 'third way' with the Tory commitment to what he called the 'British way', which apparently meant economic and personal liberty, less taxation and regulation, 'smaller government and bigger citizens'. Shadow Health spokesman Ann Widdecombe, striding without notes around the Ikea-furnished platform, emphasized the Party's commitment to private healthcare. Peter Lilley, Hague's deputy, admittedly hinted at the fact that the Party may have to accept some of New Labour's changes and work hard to overturn the carica-ture of the Tories as 'the selfish party'. But how he hoped to reconcile all this with his evident enthusiasm for lower public spending was far from obvious. Away from the podium, Michael Portillo, setting out his stall in advance of an eagerly awaited return to the Commons, did nothing to suggest that his much-vaunted foray into social liberalism also meant a pitch for the centre ground: the government's signing up to the Social Chapter would see Britain, like the rest of the EU, experi-ence 'a continuing haemorrhage of low-skill jobs . . . , and so high levels of unemployment'; extra resources for the NHS and education would result in no improvements; indeed, insisted Portillo, 'we must allow the enterprise economy to flourish by holding down public spending and reducing taxes to the levels in the USA and Japan. That will require substantial reform of the public sector.'[37]

Search for a strategy

Just prior to the 1998 Conference, the Conservative Party had launched 'Listening to Britain' (LtB), which, inspired by a US Republican initiative, involved a series of meetings held between Shadow Cabinet members and representatives of interest groups and 'ordinary people'. Now that the Party's finances were a little less pre-carious, it also began its first serious polling since the general election a year and a half previously. Public surveys by its pollster ICM, like the one published by the *Guardian* as the Conference opened, suggested not only that Labour enjoyed a massive 51- to 29-point lead, but that the Conservatives were stranded well to the right of the average voter. True, some 35 per cent thought of Labour as to the left of where they stood, but 33 per cent thought it was where they were, with the same percentage thinking it stood to the right of them. But when it came to the Tories, only 21 per cent thought the Party was where they were, while 63 per cent thought it was to their right. ICM's private research likewise suggested that the Tories had made little progress in changing public perceptions since losing the election, and that, to quote from internal documents, LtB had 'made absolutely no impact whatsoever' and was 'rapidly running out of steam', failing in its 'overriding purpose', which was not so much to generate policy as 'to *show* that we are listening'.

ICM's research also informed a paper for Hague, Chief Executive Archie Norman, and Michael Ancram, who took over as Chairman at the 1998 Conference, by Central Office staffers Andrew Cooper and Danny Finkelstein, who had grown increasingly concerned that the Party was simply treading water. 'Kitchen Table Conservatives' – so named because it stressed the need for the Party to concern itself with issues that ordinary people talked about – began with some very basic questions: 'Where are we now? Where do we want to be? How are we going to get there?' It then suggested ways forward. In the short term, the Party had to 'understand that a lot of the things that people said about us before the election were true. . . . We *were* out of touch. We *had* stopped listening. We *were* undisciplined and divided. We *didn't* have any clear idea of the direction in which we wanted to take Britain.'[38] The Party also had to do something about the dire impression that voters had formed about its leader – a man routinely dismissed as 'aloof, out of touch, remote from ordinary people and weak'. Just as importantly, it had to spend every waking hour doing what it should have done in the first 18 months after the election in 1997, namely to communicate that 'the Conservative Party is changing' and was 'a different kind of party' from the one that had lost that election – a party that could credibly claim that it 'knows what people really care about, says what people really think and has policies to deal with the things that really matter'. This would involve, above all, four things:

First we must understand that, the more Conservatives talk like (and, as a party, look more like) the rest of Britain – in both language and content – the more credible our political messages will be and sound. . . .

Second we must ensure that we are once again trusted more than Labour on the economy. . . .

Third we must neutralise our vulnerabilities on key policy issues – principally the perception that our instincts are to undermine and under-fund our public services, especially schools and hospitals. Other things being equal we will not win re-election while people suspect our motives on those issues.

Fourth out of the issues we identify and the new ideas we develop – we must define our purpose for the years ahead, fashioning a new narrative, which embraces the exciting opportunities as well as the new threats and challenges facing Britain in a new century.[39]

All this, it noted, 'is only possible with thorough and frequent opinion research and with the discipline to apply it – including the concentration to keep on and on repeating the same messages'. The paper also stressed that survey and focus group research was 'only of value if politicians are prepared to believe it, and where necessary act on it, even when it runs contrary to their own gut instinct', and that the Party had to stop being 'overly pre-occupied with what the papers say, and with the Today programme, at the expense of TV'.

'Kitchen Table Conservatives', then, betrayed a degree of frustration with the attitudes and the custom and practice of Tory politicians, up to and including a leader who, in the words of one of his colleagues, 'didn't have a strategic sense, . . . wasn't actually interested in policy', but rather in 'reacting to newspaper headlines'. What the paper failed to do, however, was to work through or spell out the logical implications – ideological and institutional – of its findings. This was partly because its authors were barely beginning to come to terms with them themselves. After all, it was Cooper himself who, just a few months earlier when challenged by a visiting journalist on the lack of new ideas emanating from the Party, had simply fallen back on phrases like 'free markets, freedom, opportunity and choice' at the same time as talking about 'changing our body language'; there was apparently 'no policy reason why we lost. It was the Conservatives who were thrown out of office not Conservatism' – all of which left his visitor feeling that the logic was 'if it ain't broke, don't mend it, just put it in a new box'.[40] Consequently 'Kitchen Table''s suggestions for the kind of '10,000-volt' shocks required to communicate to the public that the Conservative Party was changing were laughably inadequate. Rather than, say, setting a target for the number of female candidates chosen for winnable seats or taking on those who wanted to promote private provision in education and healthcare, Hague was urged to challenge traditionalists in the Carlton – the gentlemen's club to which all Tory leaders were invited to become honorary members – to drop their opposition to full membership for ladies, or to use the Party's Ethics and Integrity Committee to expel someone for sleaze.

The same mismatch between ends and means was evident in Cooper's follow-up paper in February 1999, entitled 'Conceding and Moving On'. Like his earlier paper, it drew inspiration from New Labour's guru, Philip Gould, but again it failed fully to appreciate that, to Gould, 'conceding' meant admitting that his party lost the election not only because it was out of touch, incompetent, incredible, and untrustworthy, but also because its main opponent had got it right on some key policy issues. Just as Labour had to admit that the Tories had made the correct call on, for example, council house sales, trade-union reform, privatization, or tough sentencing, the Tories might have to admit that Labour were on the money by, for instance, concentrating on trying to improve the NHS rather than keeping it on short rations and worrying about how to help more people go private. In fact, Cooper was indeed coming to this conclusion but it was not yet fully formed, nor one that he thought he could sell to Hague in any case. As he later admitted, 'Conceding' was written partly out of frustration that the Tory leader, despite his being well aware he needed something he could call a strategy, wasn't actually implementing 'Kitchen Table' – because he either didn't really understand it or didn't in fact agree with it.[41]

In public, however, Hague remained on message – at least for a while – even if, given 'Kitchen Table''s limited recommendations, what he came up with inevitably went nowhere near far enough. The strategy (if it can be called that) was deliberately leaked to the media in early March 1999 and laid the ground for Hague's speech to the Conservative Spring Forum held a few days later. The Party apparently needed to break '[f]ree of old structures, free of old habits, free of old thinking' – which would mean being prepared to change language and policies that gave the misleading impression that Conservatives were 'harsh and uncaring', as well as 'obsessive' about Europe, even if this meant admitting that 'for all our successes, we made some mistakes'. Conservative governments *had* sometimes been preoccupied with containing the costs of the NHS to the detriment of improving its services; they *had* alienated teachers with excessive regulations; and they *had* centralized too much power in Whitehall. Unfortunately, however, even that limited list of errors was not accompanied by any eye-catching and concrete promises to put things right. Indeed all that was offered was a vague promise to produce new policies that would 'respond to people's concerns and values about security and family breakdown, about over-powerful government and failing public services' (all of which sounded rather like *Conservative* people's concerns), as well as a pledge to cut red tape on business and to restore 'explicit and special recognition of marriage' in the tax and benefits system. Anyone expecting a '10,000-volt shock', let alone a 'Clause IV moment' – a sure-fire opportunity for Hague to show voters that he would follow Blair by taking on his own party in order to do what was right – would have been sorely disappointed.

Up to the job?

Hague's failure to take even the modest recommendations of 'Kitchen Table' and 'Conceding' beyond the merely rhetorical was not just because he and his closest colleagues were ideologically incapable of taking them sufficiently seriously. It was also because his attention was distracted by events that challenged his own authority and sapped the morale of those serving under him. One such occurred in December 1998 when the leader of the Party in the Upper House, John Major's old friend Robert Cranborne, went behind Hague's back to negotiate a deal whereby the Blair government, in return for Conservative peers supporting the first round of Lords reform, would allow just over 90 hereditary peers (of which Cranborne was one) to retain their seats after the other 659 were removed from the Upper House. Cranborne's concession of support for the bulk of Blair's reforms was further than Hague was prepared to go and, as news of the deal leaked out, he tried to persuade Tory peers in a tense two-hour meeting to back down. Having failed (they were apparently against him by a margin of about four to one), he then sacked Cranborne and only prevented the departure of the entire frontbench team in the Lords by persuading Cranborne's right-hand man, Tom Strathclyde, to take his place. To do this he even had to ignore the fact that Strathclyde had himself been party to the deal with Blair and continued to insist on the right of Tory peers to carry on supporting it. Hopes that this compromise might prove a face-saver were then cruelly dashed when the Tory leader decided to appear on the BBC's flagship late-night current affairs show, *Newsnight*, and its famously waspish anchor, Jeremy Paxman, began by observing, 'You can't even control a toff in the House of Lords' and ended by enquiring, 'Do you ever wonder if you are up to the job?'

The Cranborne episode, then, played into nagging (and, to be frank, slightly snobbish) doubts that Hague, a mere provincial, was not as quick-witted as his gift of the gab suggested. The man who claimed to be modernizing the Tory Party somehow ended up looking like even more of a throwback than the hereditary peers themselves, having forgotten the cultural premium placed on consensus and compromise in the Upper House and being forced into a show of authority that its members resented and which ultimately backfired. The episode also confirmed what one leader writer called 'one of British politics' most enduring themes', namely 'the lucklessness of William Hague'.[42] But there was more to it than that. Hague's need to act so swiftly also had roots in his desire to be seen to be, in the words of one observer, 'de-Majorising his party by showing he has core beliefs he will not trim for short-term gain'.[43] Just as Hague's predecessor, then, had been deter-mined to distance himself from the leader who went before him – in style if not always in substance – so was Hague. And so too were his closest advisers (Seb Coe, David Lidington, George Osborne, Danny Finkelstein, Gregor Mackay, and Alan Duncan) – a group already mis-chievously labelled as 'the nursery' because of their relative youth and supposed lack of nous. Both he and they forgot one of the first rules of political leadership, namely that any attempt to demonstrate 'the smack' of firm leadership always risks accentuating its absence.

Hague's reception at the 1922 Committee held after Cranborne's sacking saw him noisily supported by his backbenchers, but many made it privately clear to journalists that they considered the whole thing an embarrassing mess. The fact that the Conservatives' poll ratings appeared not to have suffered in the immediate aftermath of the event, and that those who had said they would vote Tory backed Hague three-to-one over the sacking, was cold comfort given the Party remained under 30 per cent while the Labour government was some 20 points ahead on just under 50 per cent. Even more alarmingly, rumours were now rife that the 25 names needed to trigger a leadership contest were being collected in order to mount a challenge should things fail to improve. Shadow Health Secretary Ann Widdecombe, beginning to be touted as a possible successor, warned in a radio interview that 'the party has got to get out of the habit of thinking that as soon as anything goes wrong the answer is a change of leadership' – which, of course, merely served to confirm that this was still the case.

Running back to mummy

The row over Lords reform did nothing to ease the concerns of Central Office staffers like Cooper and Nye about the internal arguments that the approach laid out in 'Kitchen Table Conservatives' might provoke unless properly sold, understood, and implemented. Even some members of Hague's inner circle and his Shadow Cabinet thought they were being asked to apologize for the Party's years in government. There were also those who were highly sceptical about the use of focus groups and opinion polling, not simply because they were methods associated with New Labour, but because they represented a cowardly abdication of leadership and an abandonment of ideology.[44] Hadn't Margaret Thatcher shown that both leadership and ideas were crucial to Conservative success? Indeed, one only had to look to John Major, they reasoned, to show where such a wimpish strategy led. In any case, they did their own research by meeting voters on their doorsteps or down at the *Dog and Duck*, and, surprise, surprise, they apparently thought very differently.

It was against this background that, in mid-April 1999, Peter Lilley, Hague's deputy, was due to give the annual R.A. Butler Lecture. Lilley was widely thought of as a thorough-going Thatcherite and as one of the Eurosceptic 'bastards' in Major's Cabinet. However, he was now overseeing 'Listening to Britain' and had been closely following both the quantitative and qualitative research carried out by the Party's pollster, ICM. This had convinced him, he admitted to the BBC in March 1999, that the Party could only win back power by pitching its policies in the centre ground rather than picking them solely because they put 'clear blue water' between the Tories and Labour. Conservatives didn't need to apologize, but they did need to stop 'glorying in past successes' and 're-fighting battles we've already won'. They also needed to 'break free of the perceptions' of the Party that were established during the 1980s, particularly the idea that it was only interested in the economy. Now that the latter was sound and Labour were not attempting to depart from the policies that had made it so, the Tories needed to move on and show, for instance, that they were equally interested in 'quality of life' issues. They also needed to avoid Labour's mistake after 1979 when 'they thought they could win without changing'.[45] In particular, Lilley (whose plans for pensions had been torn apart by Labour accusations of privatization during the election) had become convinced that the Party had to reassure the public that any plans to reform the public services – particularly health and education – arose out of a genuine commitment to improve them, not out of what many voters clearly still saw as the Tories' essential antipathy to a publicly funded welfare state.

Lilley of course knew that any speech by him to that effect would have to be squared with colleagues, particularly those with responsibility for health and social security, all of whom were (rather awkwardly) keen on the private sector playing a bigger role. Somehow, however, they were never shown the final draft – and Hague's office did not pay it sufficient attention – before advance briefings of its apparently hard-hitting message were given to journalists, who billed the speech as a conscious repudiation of Thatcherism by one of its chief acolytes.[46] Worse still, they then revealed that many of Lilley's Shadow Cabinet colleagues were upset and angry about the speech – hardly surprising since he was not simply saying that bringing the free market into health and welfare was politically unwise but telling the Party that anyone who thought it could and should play a bigger role was theoretically mistaken and going against all sorts of real-world evidence that it wouldn't work.

The reaction inside the Party to what really was a '10,000-volt shock' – albeit an unlicensed one – was overwhelmingly negative, from top to bottom. The Shadow Cabinet met the day after the speech, and achieved the notable feat of uniting Michael Howard and Ann Widdecombe, who spoke for most of its members when they objected to what was seen as an attempt to bounce it into a line that restricted frontbenchers' room for manoeuvre in their own policy areas. To them, this blurred the Party's identity, disavowed what they regarded as the impressive record of achievement between 1979 and 1997, and was bound to provide ammunition for Labour.[47] Lilley came in for harsh criticism at the 1922 Committee, led by Eric Forth and Edward Leigh of the Thatcherite 'No Turning Back Group'. Thatcher, it was reported, had 'gone ballistic', especially as Lilley had made his remarks on the same night as a big celebration, attended by Hague, of the twentieth anniversary of her move into Number Ten. Constituency associations, meanwhile, complained to their MPs, who in turn passed on their concerns to the Whips' Office.[48]

Significantly, attempts to defend Lilley, let alone argue that what he was saying was only the logical extension of what Cooper and Finkelstein had been groping towards, were few and far between. Some of this reluctance may have had something to do with the individual involved. Those Thatcherites – and there were many – who never forgave those who supposedly stabbed their heroine in the back in 1990 saw the speech as confirmation of Lilley's treachery and were never going to believe his protests that it was not intended as some kind of repudiation of her.[49] Meanwhile, the shrunken group of more centrist Conservative MPs, whether high profile or less well known, could hardly be blamed for failing to leap to the defence of one of Thatcher's own. But it was more than about Lilley as an individual: no-one at Westminster stood up for him because, in an overwhelmingly Thatcherite parliamentary party, there was no-one *to* stand up for him. If it looked as if he had gone out on a limb, that was because he had.

Unfortunately for Lilley, the reaction in the traditional Tory press – the party in the media – was equally if not more negative. Indeed, the withering criticism of what one columnist called 'the madness of disowning Maggie' simply confirmed the strength of the delusions that anyone seeking fundamental change was up against.[50] Even those who would eventually calm down and come around were, at the time, similarly convinced – and no less hyperbolic. Michael Gove was later to make the switch not just from journalism into politics but from Thatcherite to modernizer. At this stage, however, he spoke for many Conservative commentators when he suggested 'no location is as undignified as being "in the centre"', somewhere 'where the lowest common denominator and the highest possible public spending meet' – 'an arid region where no principles can take root, no institution can be sure of its foundation, no banner can be firmly placed. For that reason, it is a particularly shameless place for politicians to be.' Indeed, 'The natural inhabitants of the centre are those politicians of easy virtue, happy to massage public opinion but never to challenge it.' 'The Tories did not lose in 1997 because they failed to emphasise their commitment to the public sector, they lost because they debauched the public finances in pursuit of the "centre ground".' The government could never spend as wisely or as effectively 'as freer citizens liberated by a smaller state'.[51]

More ominously still, perhaps, was that the man whose biography Gove had penned a few years before, Michael Portillo, evidently agreed with him. According to one newspaper report, he had 'scathingly accused Mr Hague of seeking to copy Tony Blair's repositioning of New Labour while he was Opposition leader' and 'advised the Tory leader not to "follow fashion"'. 'You cannot,' Portillo warned, 'ditch policies that succeeded so convincingly that they were adopted by our opponents, and much of the free world'.[52] Coming from the man regarded by some of his most ardent fans as the rightful leader of the Conservatives, this was dangerous stuff. Had Portillo not been out of parliament, things might have been even more difficult for Hague: his Chief Whip, James Arbuthnot, was reporting that he had 'massively underestimated the scale of dissent on the backbenches' occasioned by Lilley's speech. Central Office, too, was in crisis. The Party's Director of Marketing and Membership, widely seen as a *Portillista*, had to be dismissed for leaking an earlier, even more incendiary version of Lilley's speech to the press at the height of the row – a decision that added to an already unhappy, even slightly hysterical, atmosphere among staffers, some of whom were prepared to confess to the press that morale was now 'subterranean, not low'.[53]

Others took the opportunity to use the episode to air long-running grievances. To the *Mail's* leader, it was 'all too plain . . . that Conservative thinking is now dominated not by belief or commitment but by focus groups and a jejune cabal of courtiers who are long on intelligence but short on common sense'.[54] And not for the first or the last time, two of the inner circle were singled out for particular criticism from both the Party's professionals and its parliamentarians: as one newspaper put it, 'The guilty men are held to be Sebastian Coe, Mr Hague's chief of staff and, most of all, "Gorgeous" George Osborne, Hague's 28-year-old Political Secretary, whose political acumen has long been the subject of criticism within Conservative circles.'[55] This was more than a little disingenuous and opportunistic: if any of the backroom boys had backed Lilley it would have been Cooper and Finkelstein rather than Coe and Osborne. The resentment they provoked was therefore easily (perhaps too easily) dismissed as mere jealousy, typical of an age-old tendency for those without the king's ear to blame not the king himself but his closest courtiers.

To the public, inasmuch as they were paying any attention to the affair, this backlash would simply serve to reinforce suspicions that the Tories were both divided and deep down still wedded to their 'private good/public bad' ideas – unless, of course, the leadership decided to seize the day and face down rather than head off knee-jerk criticism of Lilley's approach. At first this looked possible. Hague, feeling initially that he had little choice but to back his deputy or else look a complete idiot, stitched together a piece for the *Times* which asserted there was no contradiction between support for Thatcherite ideals and, for instance, the NHS.[56] Then, despite the painfully obvious (and headline-grabbing) refusal of Michael Howard during a television interview to back the Lilley line, Francis Maude, the Shadow Chancellor, went ahead with a speech in which he, too, insisted the Tories (who in the past, he said, had 'sometimes sounded as if we were only interested in markets and accountancy') had to show people they were committed to public provision. Even more significantly, he promised to do so by saying a Conservative government would stick to Labour's increases in health and education spending – increases he had previously called reckless.

However, it quickly became clear that, for all Hague's bravado about 'the odd bit of lively discussion' in the Shadow Cabinet and his claim that he was 'not afraid of controversy', this was as far as the Tory leader felt comfortable with going.[57] Indeed, steps were instantaneously taken to dilute Maude's commitment in order to render it palatable. It was balanced the very same day by sources close to Hague telling journalists that the next manifesto would include tax cuts funded by savings on social security. This, in turn, allowed Shadow Social Security spokesman Iain Duncan Smith, who had earlier made his unhappiness with the Lilley line very clear, to declare his relief that it 'left him "free" to pursue plans to reduce the "dependency culture" in the welfare state through reform which "involves and embraces the voluntary and private sector"'.[58] And just in case anyone was still worried, a few days later, Hague, having apparently telephoned Thatcher, spoke to backbenchers at the 1922 Committee, focusing on what he admitted had been the poor media handling of the episode. He also tried to reassure party activists that 'We will always be proud of Margaret Thatcher and we will always be champions of the free market' – words that were slightly undermined a few days later when a confidant of Hague's described Thatcher as 'a mad old bag' and told a newspaper that his boss, who had apparently disliked being photographed next to his former pin-up at the 1998 Party Conference, was hatching plans to keep her off the platform when the Tories met again in 1999.[59]

The firestorm of internal and media protest at Lilley's speech put off anyone trying anything like that again for the foreseeable future – even the handful of Tory MPs who thought he was saying what needed to be said.[60] This group did not include Hague, but his relationship with the party in the country undoubtedly took a hit as the result of the episode, even if it had ended in him 'running back to mummy'.[61] This was not merely because many activists balked at what they, too, saw as an unnecessary and/or inept attempt to distance the Party from its past, but also because it was so badly timed. While MPs were in meltdown at Westminster, members of their constituency associations, the Chairman of the National Convention reminded Hague, were trudging up and down the streets canvassing for local elections taking place in the first week of May – elections which would inevitably be used by MPs and the media as a test of Hague's leadership.

A question of survival: 'Project Hague'

In the wake of the Lilley crisis, that leadership began for the first time to be seriously questioned. One newspaper reported 'the desperation in Tory ranks' had grown so serious that a member of the Executive of the 1922 was suggesting Hague would have to go; it also claimed that Whips were 'telephoning Tory MPs in an attempt to prevent them deserting him', and quoted an unnamed frontbencher to the effect that self-preservation could lead some to 'press the panic button'.[62] Word was that Hague would need the Party to gain at least 1,000 seats at the local elections before he could breathe easy – at least until the European Parliament elections in June. The polls, however, were appalling both for the Party and, even more so, for its leader, although whether the Lilley speech made things worse simply because of the internal arguments it generated or because those arguments reminded the public of quite what an 'ideological party' the Tories had become is a moot point.[63] MORI gave Labour, on 56 per cent, a 31 point lead over the Tories on just 25 per cent – a lead four points higher than the previous month. Meanwhile, Hague's personal approval rating stood at minus 31 per cent, five points down on the previous month. Indeed, Hague seemed to be doing not only worse than Neil Kinnock at the same point in his leadership but worse even than Michael Foot. Against Labour's current leader, Hague was beaten out of sight by Blair on every measure of leadership used.

Fortunately for Hague, who was much closer to resigning in the wake of the row over Lilley's lecture than many at the time realized, the Conservative Party did indeed do better in the 1999 local elections than national polls predicted.[64] Labour, despite moving into mid-term territory, finished first but polled just 36 per cent and suffered in some of its urban strongholds at the hands of the Lib Dems. The Tories, on 34 per cent, could boast a two-point improvement in their vote share compared to 1997, as well as 1,400 seats regained. Hague was also helped by the distraction provided by the government's surprisingly poor performance in elections to the new Scottish and Welsh legislatures. The underlying picture, however, was still worrying. The Conservative vote share was still below what Labour had managed in its darkest days under Foot and its gains were for the most part in traditional Southern strongholds where by rights they should never have lost seats in the first place. Moreover, rather more challenging prospects in the South-East did not turn from red to blue. The Party failed to make an impact in the North, even less in the cities, and actually dropped back in Scotland and Wales. And it was still a long way short of the traditional dominance it had enjoyed prior to taking office at a national level in 1979: then the Party had about 12,000 seats; now it had just 4,000.[65]

The better-than-feared results provided a breathing space for Hague, although they were marred by his having to issue a dressing down to, of all people, his old friend, junior Health spokesman Alan Duncan, for confessing in an interview that the Party had 'got to go back to the drawing-board and no longer just scrabble around in the hope of winning short-term engagements and battles'.[66] Duncan's loose lips made Hague all the more determined to try to get a grip on his Party's press operation. The appointment of Amanda Platell as Head of Media in the spring of 1999 was intended to do precisely this and out went Gregor Mackay, whose role went to *Times* veteran Nick Wood – an intensely political figure with right-wing views but who knew his way around the lobby. Platell had lost her job as editor of the *Sunday Express* in response to falling circulation and, her critics claimed, knew next to nothing about politics. She was, though, thought to have her finger on the pulse of 'Middle England' and good relations with other Fleet Street editors, both of which would help get Hague better coverage in the media. Wood and Platell's brief was both to re-sell 'the real William Hague' to an unconvinced electorate and to establish better contacts with senior journalists so that briefings from the Leader's Office, Central Office, and the Shadow Cabinet did not cut across each other.

Unfortunately Wood and Platell's attempts to convince the electorate that it was wrong about a man who was widely perceived as having 'something of the nerd about him' soon ran into trouble. Things looked up briefly during the European Parliament elections, although a wheeze to have Hague's wife Ffion sport a £2,000 pound-sign pendant that he had given her ended up backfiring when it was revealed that Platell had organized the whole thing and the jeweller was still waiting to be paid. Platell's task was made all the more difficult, however, when the strategy to improve the Tory leader's image, apparently nicknamed 'Project Hague', leaked. The *Telegraph* quoted liberally (cruelly even) from a memo supposedly drawn up at a meeting in the early summer just before the Tory leader and his wife left for a break in the USA:

Among the proposed ideas for capitalising on the trip are photographs. . . . The memo describes these as: 'Holiday shot with Ffion - evening

walk on beach? Relaxing; quality time with wife; Sailing in USA, informal shot on board? Teaching Ffion (or godson) to sail on holiday.'
    Others include an aborted plan to attend the *Star Wars* premiere,
and 'pre-conference walk in the Dales, country pub, colourful locals'.
To toughen his image the party plans to stress his hopes of securing a
blue belt in judo and his interest in abseiling. 'Late August: judo with
Army, no shots of actual fight, shot with Army fighters in kit? blue belt
to be attempted before conference.'[67]

This concern with getting the papers onside was reinforced by Hague's
desperate need to claw back some of the political capital he had lost
within the Party, including the party in the media, after the Lilley
speech. Since he could hardly conjure an opinion poll lead out of thin
air, and since his own instincts were in any case in tune with those of the
Tory press, the way ahead seemed obvious. As an official who worked
closely with Hague later observed,

> If he was to remain leader he had to shore up his base, or create a base
> where he hadn't had one. . . . And that meant giving inordinate weight
> to the opinion of Conservative commentators, columnists, editors, on
> the first level. And, on the second level, it meant giving Conservative
> Party activists something to rally around and that meant very much
> concentrating on those issues that mattered to those people rather than
> issues that actually mattered to voters. Some of that was out of necessity.
> Some of it, temperamentally, William quite enjoyed.[68]

The inordinate attention paid to what the papers said was in part a
function of the belief Hague shared with most politicians that what
those papers have to say really matters – an assumption based not so
much on the idea that the press swings votes during election campaigns
(although many continue to think it does, especially when it comes to
the *Sun*), but that it contributes to a climate of opinion. This 'mood
music' can potentially harm or help politicians, be it electorally or
simply in terms of how they are thought of by their parliamentary colleagues, who (in admittedly circular fashion) are assumed to be deeply
influenced by what they read, especially (in order of importance in Tory
circles) if it appears in the *Mail*, the *Telegraph*, and (some way behind

the other two) the *Times*.[69] But this obsession with the papers was also a function of Hague allowing two people who were essentially media tacticians – Wood and Platell – to drive (or rather drive out) strategy. That their primary loyalty, like Seb Coe's, was to the leader rather than to the Party as a whole was important. Even more important, however, was their belief (not wholly misplaced perhaps) that his survival as leader was in danger and that the Party would get nowhere unless it could persuade the electorate that its leader was a man who should be taken seriously. They were not impressed, ideologically speaking, with 'Kitchen Table Conservatives'. But even if they had been, they concluded, it was not a strategy which the leader the Party had picked could sell. The Tories, they argued, had no choice but to 'let William be William', and William simply wasn't a modernizing, kitchen-table kind of guy; trying to pretend otherwise would mean him coming over as inauthentic – a cardinal sin in PR terms.[70] As Nick Wood put it,

> Our job was to work out what was the most effective political strategy for Hague and then go and deliver it. And we thought that a right-wing strategy – for want of a better word – was the right strategy for him. It stood the greatest chance for shoring up support, which was what we were really focused on through that period when we were in grave political trouble in all sorts of ways. It was a bit of a lifeline strategy in the sense that I could see the danger of our seriously imploding in that period. My judgement was we had to hang on to our base vote. . . . There were some terrible, terrible opinion polls where we dropped to 23, 24. We were being hit by the Liberals and we were certainly being hit very hard by Labour. And I knew at various points in that period that if William had not performed well in local elections or European elections he'd have been out.[71]

Going hard on Europe

Given this, the obvious course of action, at least in the short term, was to play the Eurosceptic card: as one 'senior source' told journalists, 'We managed to upset 95 per cent of the party by appearing to break with Thatcherism. If we go hard on Europe, we will have 95 per cent of the party with us.'[72] Alienating the remaining 5 per cent might even be helpful since any fuss on their part would serve as a useful warning to Tory MPs swayed by opinion polls and op-eds suggesting they would be doing better under Ken Clarke, even if his decision to join Blair in the Britain in Europe all-party campaign for the euro in fact made it less likely than ever that the Party would turn to him.[73] A determinedly sceptical campaign in the run-up to the European Parliament elections might also take some of the wind out of the sales of Michael Portillo, still considered the biggest threat, notwithstanding the fact that 'friends' of Ann Widdecombe let it be known that the Shadow Health Secretary (who was apparently wooing the grassroots on the proverbial 'rubber chicken circuit') was interested in the leadership. Just as importantly, a strongly sceptical stance would, it was hoped, bring erstwhile and still loyal supporters in the press back onside – apparently 'said by some party insiders secretly to have been the most important objective of the whole electoral campaign'.[74]

This was not a stance that the leadership had any difficulty in selling to the bulk of Conservatives. Surveys of both MPs and candidates revealed that a degree of Euroscepticism was becoming pretty much the taken-for-granted, default position for all but a shrinking minority of confirmed pro-Europeans, only a handful of whom failed to vote as instructed against ratification of the Amsterdam Treaty in 2000.[75] The pro-European cause inside the Party, already weakened by losses at the general election, was further damaged by the decision of some of its advocates (none of whom were MPs) to form the breakaway Pro-Euro Conservative Party, which went on to win only 1 per cent of the votes at the European elections. This contrasted poorly with the 7 per cent won by UKIP – a performance which suggested that, unless the Tories were careful, the party could cause them problems at the next general election. Meanwhile, the fact that the sceptical rhetoric which so enthused the party in the media risked alienating many sectors of British business did not appear to worry the Conservative leadership – further confirmation, if it were needed, that the Party is no more a front for serving the interests of finance (or any other kind of) capitalism than its main opponent is simply a mouthpiece of the trade unions. A firm stance on Europe did help, however, in attracting one particular capitalist, namely the spread-betting tycoon Stuart Wheeler, who eventually donated £5 million to the Tories in the run-up to the general election.

A more sceptical stance also made sense when it came to voters, who were in the main unenthusiastic about Europe, because the Party could more or less convincingly claim that its internal arguments on the subject were behind it. Hague had in effect purged the Europhiles from his Shadow Cabinet and won his internal referendum on the single currency. Clarke and Heseltine promised not to rock the boat during the campaign as long as they were free to campaign for a single currency after it. Likewise, many Conservative MEPs, who were far less Eurosceptic than their counterparts in Westminster, agreed to toe the line in return for a selection system that ensured that most who wanted to stay in Brussels and Strasbourg would be ranked high enough on the lists used for the new PR electoral system to ensure their safe return. The Tory leader had also adopted a slogan that tested well with focus groups – one which, like Labour's 'Tough on crime, tough on the causes of crime', signalled the Party was hard-headed but not completely narrow-minded. Anyone voting for the Conservatives was voting to be 'In Europe, not run by Europe' and, (unusually given the fact that most European elections are not really fought on European issues) may well have cast their ballot with that slogan, and their opposition to the euro, in mind.[76] In the event, the 36 per cent share of the vote that the Tories received was not particularly impressive, especially given Labour's poor campaign, apathy in its heartlands, and a turnout of just 24 per cent. Nevertheless, it put them ahead of Labour in a nationwide contest for the first time since 1992. It also appeared to represent an advance on their general election performance in 1997, even if polls taken soon after the elections continued to show Labour on around 50 per cent and the Tories still stuck at around 30 per cent. The European contest was a real election, and one in which the Conservatives had done better than many had expected them to do. As such, it was a big morale-booster.

Locking in the new line

Had a boost to morale been the only impact of the European elections then it might have been fairly benign, although even then it is possible to argue counterfactually that the Party might have done better by doing worse. A poor result might have meant that Tory MPs paid more attention to another 'real' contest. The result of the by-election at Eddisbury on 22 July was not quite as bad as the opinion polls. But it still suggested that the Party would win just seven seats from Labour at a general election – a long way short of the 80-plus it needed to deny Blair a majority. All this might have led to Hague being obliged to stand down and a more effective leader being installed in his place; it might also have led whoever had replaced him to question the idea that making a hard line on Europe central to the Tory offer could help deliver electoral success. Instead, Hague looked likely to keep his job, and, at a press conference called to hail the Tory 'triumph', was already making it clear that he intended to turn the next general election into a battle over the single currency.

Just as importantly, the apparently successful European campaign set in train a series of promotions and demotions that was to have important consequences for the Tories' wider ideological positioning and electoral approach in the short and medium term. The reshuffle carried out after the results were announced was packaged as Hague finally being able to create a Shadow Cabinet in his own image and one that distanced him from the Major years. The most obvious victim was Peter Lilley, but there was also the voluntary departure of Michael Howard, whose relations with Hague's youthful inner circle had sometimes been difficult, as well as Norman Fowler and Gillian Shephard. Rather surprisingly, Howard was replaced as Shadow Foreign Secretary by John Maples, not known as particularly Eurosceptic, with his job as Defence spokesman going to Thatcher-favourite and former soldier Iain Duncan Smith. Possibly following the same logic, former GP Liam Fox, also a right-winger, was promoted to Health – a vacancy arising as the result of another right-winger, Ann Widdecombe, being rewarded with the post of Shadow Home Secretary. Perhaps the most significant promotions, however, involved two less senior politicians, Andrew Lansley and Tim Collins, who would join the leader's inner circle and complement rather than contradict the advice of Wood and Platell.

Lansley had served as Private Secretary to Norman Tebbit at the Department of Trade and Industry before going on to head up the Conservative Research Department in 1990 – a job that gave him a key role in the production of the 1992 manifesto. Entering parliament in 1997, he had quickly been appointed a Vice-Chairman and played a big part in coordinating and disciplining the Party's European campaign, not least by obliging senior colleagues to fit into an Alastair Campbell-style timetable which later earned the nickname 'Stalingrid'. His reward was promotion into the Shadow Cabinet to cover the Cabinet Office and Policy Renewal, with a brief to accelerate and pull together the policy process, which, under Lilley (and Finkelstein), seemed to have lost momentum. Lansley at least gave the impression that he knew what the Party had to do, and also looked and sounded good on the television, even when propounding ideas which put him on what one unfriendly journalistic profile reckoned was 'the carnivorous old Right' of the Party.[77] Looking back, however, many who worked with him under Hague suggest that he was simply very good at giving his boss what he thought he wanted and convinced it was better to follow some kind of strategy (or whatever passed for one) than none at all. Interestingly, Lansley later contended, this did not extend as far as agreeing with Hague's belief that the 1999 European campaign was a blueprint on which the national contest in 2001 could be based: 'The whole point about the EP elections', he noted, 'was that we had created a campaign that was geared to exploiting some very particular areas of Labour weakness and Conservative strength which were quite clearly not salient at a general election.'[78] At that stage in his career, however, even if he didn't really share his leader's faith in the electoral power of Europe and the other two components of what later got labelled the 'Tebbit trinity', namely tax and immigration, he would (rather like the even more junior George Osborne) try to make things work.

If Lansley was simply adapting to his environment, however, Collins was a true-believer – 'Redwood with knobs on', as one fellow MP put it. He, too, had been heavily involved in the 1992 election as Major's Press Secretary before becoming the Party's Director of Communications. The fact that he was responsible for the fateful briefing at the 1993 Conference which appeared to confirm that 'Back to Basics' covered matters of personal morality did not, however, prevent him from being elected to the Commons in 1997, where he straight away began work on the leadership campaign of Michael Howard (for whom he had acted as an adviser). He was now promoted from the Whips' Office to the post of senior Vice-Chairman. His task was to link senior ministers (and Hague) with the Party's expanded 'War Room', which combined media and research. As a 'dyed-in-the-wool right-winger', 'more-Thatcherite-than-Thatcher',

Collins was convinced from the outset that any moves to the centre would be wrong in principle and doomed to failure in practice.[79] In the 1980s and early 1990s an increasingly radical Conservative Party had, after all, been able to win elections in spite of the fact that the average voter was moving, ideologically speaking, in the opposite direction. Why should it not pull off the same trick in the new millennium?

Common sense: populism emergent

The approach pursued by Hague and his closest advisers after June 1999 was built on the belief that the Party should, within reason, fight the government to a draw on traditional Labour issues but should spend most of its time and effort trying to focus voters' attention on those iconic issues that had served the Tories well in the past and on issues where they could claim to be in tune with majority opinion. In the eighties, voters' love of tax cuts, the argument ran, was what kept Conservative governments in power, despite people telling pollsters time and again that they cared more about fighting unemployment and saving the welfare state – something supposedly 'proved' by the fact that the Party had been kicked out of office once it stopped delivering what, in their heart of hearts, people 'really' wanted. Similarly, saying no to Europe was something they respected Margaret Thatcher for even if they didn't like her; it also mainlined into the nationalism that still resonated with so many voters. And bringing up asylum was, claimed critics, the politically correct way of playing the so-called 'race card', a means to bring up immigration – an issue which, as Lansley had noted in a newspaper article a few years before, 'played particularly well in the tabloids and has more potential to hurt'.[80] All that was needed was a narrative frame that could encompass and weave together all these themes into a coherent whole. This was provided by populism – a way of appealing to voters which typically 'pits a virtuous and homogeneous people against a set of elites and dangerous "others" who are together depicted as depriving (or attempting to deprive) the sovereign people of their rights, values, prosperity, identity and voice'.[81]

The showcase for this populist approach was to be the 1999 Conference, which would also give the leadership the chance to respond to criticism that the Party had produced little in the way of concrete policies. Lansley was charged with kick-starting a process that had stalled after Lilley's Butler speech – a task likely to be made easier by the announcement that, on the recommendation of the Neill Committee on Standards in Public Life, the Tories would receive a threefold increase in public funding for their parliamentary activities. Although the largest single sum went to the Leader of the Opposition, the rest was channelled through Central Office, which then provided each minister with a researcher from the Research Department, as well as some media assistance. With many desk officers thus devolved, the Research Department itself would concentrate on supporting the Party's central campaigning and media effort in the so-called 'War Room', run by Rick Nye. The problem was that, although the extra funding allowed the Party to double the War Room's staff between July and October, the extra bodies took a little time to train up and bed in.[82] This meant that the document produced for the 1999 Conference – *The Common Sense Revolution* – was a rush-job prepared by only a handful of people (including Hague, Finkelstein, Lansley, and Osborne) by no means all of whom were, in their heart of hearts, really convinced that it was the best approach. On the other hand, it was at least an approach that the leader the Party was stuck with might convincingly be able to sell: as one of its authors later put it, 'You've got to fit the message to the messenger.'[83]

The policy document, then, dovetailed with Hague's speech, which sought to counterpose the 'instincts' and good sense of the people against 'the patronising elite who think it's small minded to believe in our country and the chattering classes who think it's intolerant to be tough on law and order and the progressive intellectuals who think that caring is spending other people's money'. *Common Sense* listed over 50 policy proposals intended to support and symbolize the outlines of the Conservative offer at the next general election. The family would be promoted and marriage would once again be recognized and rewarded by the tax and benefit systems. State interference would be stopped. Car-drivers would not be 'despised or penalised'. Taxes and red tape would be cut. Schools would be freed from local authority control. Welfare would be made harder to get. Prison sentences would get longer. A cooler reception would be given to asylum-seekers. The number of ministers and MPs would be reduced. There would be 'English votes on English laws'. The UK's relationship would be 'renegotiated' so that it could refuse to implement laws it didn't like. And the pound would be saved. 'Come with me,' cried Hague, 'and I will give you back your country.'

To the relief of Hague's inner circle, who were understandably concerned he would be overshadowed by Mrs Thatcher's return to the Conference scene, this tub-thumping drew an enthusiastic response from delegates. It certainly went down better than a fringe speech by Heseltine, who warned an audience pelted by peanuts and cocktail sausages thrown by rowdy Eurosceptics that the Party had to appeal not just to its natural supporters but to the millions of voters in the 'disengaged centre'. The party in the media also seemed pleased with the 'common sense' that Hague managed to mention 39 times in tones rendered, according to one press report, 'less nasal and northern' by a female voice trainer.[84] The approach as a whole seemed to reassure it that, in the words of the *Telegraph*'s headline on 5 October, 'Hague takes party back to Thatcher' – and about time too, some commentators claimed.[85] An admiring Michael Gove spoke for the majority when, writing in the *Times* the next day, he declared Hague had 'the guts' to stay true to Thatcherite principles – in marked contrast, apparently, to John Major, whose memoirs (predictably critical of his predecessor as Prime Minister) had just been published.[86]

As Gove himself hinted, however, there were some both inside and outside the Party who wondered whether it might be storing up problems for itself by trying, some way out before a general election, to ape Labour's 1997 pledges by offering five so-called 'guarantees'. A 'parents' guarantee' gave the public the power to get rid of the management of inadequate schools. A 'patients' guarantee' gave people a fixed, needs-based waiting time for NHS treatment which, if not met, would allow them to seek private treatment paid for by the state. Then there was a 'Can work, must work' guarantee that those claiming benefits would lose them if they refused job offers, and the 'sterling guarantee' that the Tories would make opposition to adopting the euro a manifesto commitment. Most controversial, however, was a 'tax guarantee' which declared that taxes would fall as a share of the nation's income over the term of the next parliament – a pledge which was immediately labelled economic nonsense since it would oblige a government operating in a recession to make massive reductions in public expenditure as tax and social security receipts fell. If this were a Tory administration – especially one simultaneously pledged to match its Labour predecessor's spending plans for health and education – it would soon discover the difference between being populist and remaining popular.

Judgement calls

The potential problem posed by the tax guarantee, however, was temporarily eclipsed by a couple of unwelcome (though hardly unforeseeable) developments. A few days after the Tory Conference both Ken Clarke and Michael Heseltine shared a platform with Tony Blair at the launch of the Britain in Europe group, at the time widely regarded as the beginning of a campaign to persuade the public that the UK should sign up to the single currency. Hague immediately demanded his media team come up with something that would upstage them. Its instant response, which was immediately briefed to the media with little or no consultation of Shadow Cabinet colleagues (some of whom were expected to participate in the farce), was that Hague would be taking the fight to the people by addressing a series of open-air meetings around the country, standing (and this was the gimmick) on the back of a flatbed truck festooned with Union flags and red, white, and blue balloons.[87] Some of his colleagues were left, in the words of one, 'slack-jawed and horrified' at the plan, but those closest to him (including Amanda Platell, whose attempt to effect a reconciliation with the *Sun* in particular seemed at least temporarily to be paying off) were convinced that it would be a chance for Hague to prove that he really was a man of the people.[88]

But while the no doubt eager public had to wait four months until the truck was hired and decorated – its first appearance was in mid-February 2000 – Hague (not for the first time, especially after he appointed Platell) had to cope with yet more whispers about his judgement. In late November 1999, the Conservative Party was left reeling by accusations in the *Times* newspaper about the business dealings and political influence of its Treasurer, Michael Ashcroft, and the news that its candidate for the London mayoralty, Jeffrey Archer, had fabricated the alibi that had secured his famous libel victory against the *Daily Star* in 1987 – a crime which eventually led to his conviction and jailing for perjury in

2001. The Ashcroft row was complicated – and eventually resulted in legal action on his part. It did not, in the end, prevent him being awarded a peerage in the spring of 2000 – a move that cynics saw as a reward for the fact that Ashcroft, as he casually (but, given his hard work and generosity, not inaccurately) reminded one journalist, had 'helped the Conservative Party and, some people would say, . . . stopped it from really going out of existence.'[89]

The Ashcroft saga, however, paled in comparison with the Archer story. There were longstanding doubts about Archer within the Party. But despite such misgivings, Hague joined his two predecessors in endorsing the novelist's candidacy for London mayor and had praised him at the 1999 Conference as a man of 'probity and integrity'. Now, just a few weeks later, he was having to pretend the disgraced peer didn't exist and to begin a process that eventually saw him kicked out of the Party. It was an embarrassing blow to Conservative credibility and something that Hague could and should have acted to prevent happening in the first place, most obviously by making Archer's candidacy conditional upon his voluntarily subjecting himself to clearance by the Party's newly minted Ethics and Integrity Committee. The failure to do so was down to Hague as an individual, and to some extent down to his senior colleagues, all of whom allowed hope (and Archer's obvious popularity with grassroots Tories) to triumph over experience.

Even worse, the indecision continued. Instead of immediately passing the mayoral candidacy onto the man who had come second to the lying Lord, former minister Steve 'shagger' Norris, the leadership permitted the selection process to be re-opened, allowing those who objected to being asked to campaign for a well-known womanizer to mount a media campaign against him. Then, having been left off the shortlist as a result, Norris won the nomination after he was reinstated via a last minute rule-change passed by the Party Board with the apparent support of the leadership – only to lose the election in May to an independent candidate, the former Labour MP Ken Livingstone. By that time, however, the Conservatives' leader had rather more important matters on his mind.

Dismissing talk of any threat to Hague in the summer of 1999, Michael Heseltine had noted almost in jest that 'it's only when Michael Portillo comes back in the House of Commons that William will have to watch his back'.[90] In November of the same year, Portillo duly won a by-election in the safe seat of Kensington and Chelsea occasioned by the death of Alan Clark. From then on some of Hague's closest advisers, particularly his Head of Media, Amanda Platell, spent an inordinate amount of time and effort trying to protect him from a threat to his leadership that their paranoia probably made even more serious than it already was.[91] Institutionally, Portillo's entry into parliament demanded a reorganization of the Shadow Cabinet: he was too highly regarded, even by his opponents, to be left on the backbenches, and anyway might have been even more dangerous there, untainted by the mistakes of the leadership and therefore a rallying point for internal discontent. Individually, Portillo had the star quality that Hague so obviously lacked: indeed, the media career he had carved out for himself after losing his seat in 1997 had made him not only more famous but also better-liked than he had been as a minister in Major's government. Ideologically, Portillo represented a serious alternative for those Tories worried about the principles and the electoral impact of Hague's populist turn – an alternative that, especially as Portillo seemed to be revising the purist position he had adopted in the wake of Lilley's heresy, even looked as if it might extend beyond a more liberal attitude on social and moral issues to encompass more centrist positions on bread-and-butter issues like the economy and public services.

Portillo walked straight into the Shadow Chancellor's job at the beginning of February 2000, replacing Francis Maude, who was saved from the sack himself by Hague's last-minute decision to move him sideways into the foreign affairs portfolio, which he freed by the sacking, after just a few months as Shadow Foreign Secretary, of John Maples. Understandably upset, Maples, who after his famous memo in 1994 had something of a reputation for speaking truth to power, published an open letter to Hague in which he echoed what were to become familiar criticisms from those opposed to populism. Promising to 'save the pound' was all very well, but if Blair went on to grant a referendum on the decision to adopt the euro, then 'we will have a dead fox at our feet'. Moreover, voters might not want a European superstate but they did want to stay in the EU; they would be scared off, and the Party split again, if Tory policy were 'allowed to move from "flexibility" to "renegotiation"'. He went on to warn, 'You have surrounded yourself with a private office operation which is almost completely cut off from the Shadow Cabinet and the parliamentary party.' Even though 'most of the major departments [were] now shadowed by rightwingers', Hague should use his elected colleagues more and listen to those inside 'the bunker' less: 'You have got some very bright people with real experience of government and of policy. . . . Kids do not know everything and grey hairs have their part to play.' Just as important, 'don't set too much store by being able to command media adulation; all they want is a row' – something briefing against colleagues was also helping to generate. And most important of all:

> People are not interested in ideology: they are looking for practical improvements in public services, and greater security, both economic and physical. We have to convince them on the issues of basic concern to them: health, education, crime and the economy. We cannot win the election through private health insurance and being tough on asylum-seekers.[92]

Significantly, however, the logical consequence of the message was surely contradicted by Maples' insistence that 'the size of government' should remain a clear dividing line with Labour: 'if a Conservative government cannot reduce the tax burden', he declared, 'then it will not deserve re-election'; the 'tax guarantee' (which promised that taxes would fall as a share of the nation's income over the term of the next parliament) must stay. In other words, of course the Party must stick to the bread-and-butter stuff, but it had to promise jam tomorrow, come what may. Even the pragmatists, it appeared, kept the faith.

One step forward into modernization, two steps back into the comfort zone

Ironically, however, the other victim of Hague's mini-reshuffle was very much an ideological torch bearer. Continually undermined by briefing from his own side concerning his so-called 'Vulcan' image among voters, John Redwood was replaced as Environment spokesman by Archie Norman, one of the architects of Hague's organizational reforms. Norman, however, was privately worried about the populist policy direction pursued by the leadership and was to become increasingly drawn to Portillo, who wasted no time making waves. Just two days into his new job, the latter not only committed his Party to accepting the independence of the Bank of England but also pledged, equally sensationally, that it would not repeal the minimum wage. Behind the scenes, Portillo was even manoeuvring his colleagues into scrapping Maude's tax guarantee – the centrepiece of the Party's 'Common Sense' promises announced only a few months previously but which Portillo (a former Chief Secretary to the Treasury after all) regarded as 'economically illiterate'.[93]

While some were supportive of Portillo's plan to scrap the guarantee – even Widdecombe, a right-winger, thought anything that suggested the Tories were bound to cut spending was electoral suicide – others were predictably horrified. Lansley and Collins saw it as the thin end of the wedge for the kind of party they wanted to see Hague leading. 'If the Conservative Party does not stand for tax cuts', asked Collins, 'then what does it stand for?' – a question that, some would suggest, summed up the shrunken, more-Thatcherite-than-Thatcher vision that so hobbled the Tories' response to New Labour after 1997.[94] Hague was likewise urged to stand up to Portillo (who by the summer was privately threatening to resign on the issue) by Coe, Platell, and Osborne and John Whittingdale, Thatcher's former Political Secretary, who was now serving as Hague's PPS. In the end, knowing he simply couldn't risk losing Portillo, Hague backed down, even though he was evidently concerned that by doing so he might endanger his own position as leader.[95] His attempt to cloak his retreat under an announcement that the Party was definitely committing itself to restore the married couple's tax allowance made little difference, not least because Portillo's supporters were not shy about briefing the media about their 'triumph' on the tax guarantee.

Interestingly, however, anyone hoping that Portillo's move might presage a generally more centrist approach, rather than simply ridding the Party of a policy which many regarded as economically idiotic and politically unsalable, would have been disappointed. The dropping of the tax guarantee was accompanied by a clear refusal on the part of both Hague and his Shadow Chancellor to match a step-change in public spending by a Labour government now planning – in the run-up to an election – to show voters that its self-styled prudence was about to pay off in massive across-the-board increases, especially in health and education. The option of accepting the increases and focusing the Party's fire on how a Labour government would inevitably use them less efficiently and effectively than a Conservative administration – one that Portillo was later to adopt – was at that stage rejected. Maude may have been able to do it back in 1998 before the breathtaking scale of Labour's largesse became apparent, but matching it now would be seen, especially on the right of the Party, not so much as political calculation as capitulation to social democracy running rampant. Instead, Portillo and Hague argued that the proposed increases – except where they related to the NHS – were 'unsustainable' and that, by increasing spending 'by a smaller proportion than the growth of the economy as a whole', they would have more scope for tax cuts.

What looked, then, at first glance like a victory for those opposed to the idea that the Conservatives must maintain 'clear blue water' between themselves and Labour actually ensured (just as Blair and Brown had hoped) that the water would be clearer and bluer than ever – and more than deep enough to drown in. Portillo might be more 'touchy-feely' on social questions, but when it came to the economy he appeared to have moved little further than the leader he was supposedly so determined to usurp. Neither he nor Hague could therefore do anything to prevent Labour making the obvious point that, since it was promising to increase public spending over and above economic growth while the Tories were promising that, under them, increases would not outstrip it, they were in effect committing themselves to spending cuts. Less technical, but just as damaging politically, was the charge that people could no longer believe a word the Tories and their leader said. Responding to Blair's accusation at Prime Minister's Questions that the new Tory policy would mean 'fewer nurses, fewer teachers, fewer police and fewer hospitals', Hague tried attack as the best form of defence, comparing Cabinet divisions over the single currency to the Tories' clear-cut commitment to rejecting it. 'Oh,' retorted Blair, 'so he is going to keep the pound. Is that a "guarantee" or just something he intends doing?'

Given the difficulties Hague faced taking the fight to Labour on public services and the economy, it was hardly surprising that he and his advisers fell back on the populist approach that they had begun to cobble together before they were blown off-course by the avalanche of bad news surrounding Archer and distracted by the need to accommodate Portillo. At the Party's 2000 Spring Forum in Harrogate, Hague laid into Labour for wantonly ignoring 'the values, expectations and opinions of Middle England'. The Tories would stand up for what Hague took routinely to calling 'Middle Britain' and the 'Mainstream Majority' – those apparently abandoned and betrayed by a government presiding over stealth taxes, rising crime, and immigration, obsessed with minority rights, and in thrall to the European Union. The speech was of course music to the ears of those around Hague who believed, like Amanda Platell, that his colleagues should 'Let William be William' – a politician more comfortable (and easier to sell to the electorate) when he returned to his (and his Party's) emotional comfort zone.

The problem was that such a message, while it provided great copy, risked drowning out what little Hague and his colleagues did or said to try to reassure people and influential pressure groups of their moderation on other – arguably more important – issues. Portillo, for instance, used his speech at Harrogate to insist that the Conservatives were committed to state education and the NHS – a message that was picked up by one or two journalists as 'a bid to rebrand the party' and 'to steal Labour's clothes'.[96] But – partly because of anxiety within Hague's media team to avoid headlines that cut across Hague's populist themes – the Shadow Chancellor got hardly any coverage. Hague – as if to confirm Platell and Wood's fears about getting out of the comfort zone – fared even worse when he tried some reassurance of his own. A few days after Harrogate, he had addressed the Royal College of Nursing conference (the first Tory leader to do so in living memory) and reiterated his Party's promise to match Labour's health spending. They could trust him because he had 'the NHS in his bones', because he was someone who always used the NHS himself. Under the next Conservative government, there would 'be no privatisation, no retreat to a core service, no compulsory health insurance'. Unfortunately all the Tory leader got for his efforts was an emergency resolution taken immediately after his speech that showed over 80 per cent of delegates were still 'unreassured' that the NHS was safe in Tory hands and a *Sun* headline which told voters all they needed to know by declaring 'Nurses don't trust Hague'.

Hague, then, found it much harder to get coverage – and harder still to get positive coverage – on non-Tory issues. Instead of seeing this as evidence (dovetailing with what was coming out of ICM's private opinion research) that the Party had to do even more to reassure voters of its good intentions on topics like health and education, his inner circle took it as confirmation that such topics were best avoided. And that inner circle was as influential as ever. True, the Tory leader tried in early 2000 to play down internal and media criticism that his so-called 'closed-door set' (Wood and Platell plus Coe, Osborne, and Finkelstein) had trapped him in what had become known as 'the bunker' by holding a once-weekly strategy meeting that only his senior colleagues in the Shadow Cabinet (plus Rick Nye, head of research) attended. But inevitably he still spent more time with his non-elected advisers, who joined the politicians in the events-led tactics meetings that took place almost every morning.

Hardly surprising, then, if tactics, especially media tactics, sometimes drove, or even became what passed for, strategy. This clearly worried some Shadow Cabinet members: David Willetts, for one, asked his colleagues, 'Is there anything we will not do to get three paragraphs on the front page?' [97] In fact, so difficult did things become that, occasionally, instead of developing policy and then trying to get good headlines for it, Wood and Platell would come up with the headline first and then go see Lansley and Collins hoping 'they'd be able to flesh out the policy that went with the headline'.[98] The *Telegraph* and the *Mail* were (probably rightly) assumed to be the papers most read by Conservative Party members at all levels. Given this, and given the understandable need for validation of a man who was openly derided by the public in poll after poll and focus group after focus group, securing good headlines in those papers in particular became, as one of Hague's Shadow Cabinet colleagues later put it, like getting 'a fix of approval'.[99]

Hague's fix was most easily achieved by linking hard-line messages on immigration, law and order, and Europe to breaking news stories. It was no fun being labelled 'Billy Bandwagon' as a consequence but it was better than being 'Billy No Mates' – especially when the leader was, as many Shadow Cabinet members suspected, worrying as much about hanging on to his job as he was about the outcome of the upcoming election.[100] As a result, Hague followed up his populist speech at

Harrogate with a string of calculatedly controversial interventions. One week, following the life sentence handed down to Tony Martin, a farmer who famously killed a man who had broken into his home, Hague was making clear where his sympathies lay by calling for a law-change to protect people defending their property against burglars. Next, he was suggesting the number of applications for asylum, many of which were bound to be 'bogus', represented 'a flow that is out of control' – 'the dictionary definition', he reminded people, 'of a flood'.[101] Although such interventions were easily justified as a duty to express the concerns of 'the Mainstream Majority', which, if ignored by their elected representatives, would end up fuelling support for extremist alternatives, they were predictably condemned by what Hague took to calling, in textbook populist fashion, 'the liberal elite'.

Equally predictably, both commentators and reporters saw Hague's initiatives as part of what they routinely referred to as his attempt to appeal to the Tories' 'core vote' – a move supposedly designed, firstly, to get disproportionate numbers of those voters to the ballot box at a time when Labour supporters had little incentive to turn out and, secondly, to shore up Hague's position within his own party by appealing to it in ways that his most obvious challenger, Michael Portillo, now refused to do. This take on Hague's populism was by no means wholly wrong: both of those motives played a part. But it failed to recognize that hard-line stances were also intended to 'reach out' way beyond the core vote to people who may have sympathized with Labour on the economy, health, and education but for whom it would never be able to do enough on crime, immigration, and Europe.[102]

Just like academic observers, the practitioners realized – even if only implicitly – that politics is at the very least two-dimensional. Running horizontally is a socio-economic dimension, with state at the left pole and market at the right. Running vertically is a dimension with authoritarian at the top and libertarian at the bottom. Voters belonging to the so-called 'chattering classes' – liberal lefties, if you like – are located in the bottom left (and libertarian) quadrant. Dyed-in-the-wool Thatcherites are located in the top right: to them, a free market in economics is fine but not in morals. Those whose economic liberalism extends to social and moral issues are located in the bottom right quadrant. But the bulk of voters are almost certainly in the top left quadrant – slightly to the left on the economy and the welfare state, but believing in harsh treatment for criminals (and welfare cheats), as well as controls on immigration. The Conservatives under Hague gave up (almost before they started) on appealing to this largest group of voters by trying consistently to project a change of heart and direction on the economy, health, and education; instead they hoped to detach them from Labour by appealing to their authoritarian instincts, as well as to their scepticism about European integration (which either formed a third dimension or one that many politicians believed could be collapsed into the second libertarian–authoritarian dimension).

This might not have been pretty – not least because Labour politicians, especially under Blair, tried to reduce their vulnerability by talking tough on crime and asylum and not appearing too enthusiastic about Europe. And its effect was always going to be limited by the Conservatives' refusal to move palpably leftward (or at least into the centre) on socio-economic issues. But, as an electoral approach, it probably had considerably more going for it (as Thatcher had herself demonstrated) than the mix of tolerant inclusivity and low-tax free-market capitalism purportedly proposed by Portillo and other 'post-Thatcherites'. Theirs was an appeal directed to the bottom right quadrant on the two-dimensional diagram, which clearly contains the smallest number of voters. Indeed, if one looks at British election surveys, less than 10 per cent of voters at the time could be fitted into this box: most liberals on social issues are also left-wing, while most voters who would describe themselves as left-wing are not liberals.[103] Indeed, trying to combine self-consciously and heavily promoted live-and-let-live positions on social issues with 'dry' policies on the economy would appear to be a fool's errand. If moving to the centre on the state–market dimension was out of the question for Hague and co., then it clearly made much more sense to rely on the Thatcherite mix of neo-liberalism and authoritarian populism.

In less highfalutin terms, that mix also made more sense as a means to rescue Hague from the prison of public ridicule in which his early PR gaffes (along of course with his famous speech as a teenager to the Conservative Party Conference) had hitherto trapped him, threatening both his leadership of the Party and its chances of winning at least a few seats back from Labour. As Nick Wood put it,

All this 'Concede and Move on' stuff wouldn't save Hague from execution. It wouldn't gain us a single bloody vote. What we had to do was . . . to transform William's image. If you think about how he was portrayed by, say, Rory Bremner [the impressionist and satirist] in his time as leader, Bremner used to portray him as a little boy sitting in a high chair with his feet two feet off the ground. He was a figure of ridicule and fun – and weak, not up to it, a child trying to do a man's job. . . . By the end Hague was this skinhead driving a taxi, doing endless u-turns in the middle of the road. That's fine by me. I'd rather have him as a skinhead taxi driver than an object of ridicule. . . . We worked essentially to portray Hague as the voice of middle England . . . and generally transform his image from weakness to strength. 'Concede and move on' was not a splash headline in the *Sun*, or the *Daily Mail* or the *Daily Telegraph* and it wouldn't lead the *Ten O'clock News*. It might get you on *Newsnight*, but no-one watches *Newsnight*.[104]

False dawn

The argument that 'skinhead Conservatism' stood some chance not just of mobilizing the core vote but also connecting with voters who were simply unwilling to give the Tories a hearing on public services was superficially reinforced by real election results. In May 2000, the Conservatives picked up 593 council seats and 16 councils – more than expected – and Hague made it clear in media appearances and briefings that he would not be deflected from his tough stance. Yet the Tories' share of the vote on a nationwide turnout of just 29 per cent was, at 38 per cent, still a long way short of what they would need at the general election likely to take place in a year's time. Moreover, Hague's foot-soldiers had performed less well than on average in some of the key Southern seats Labour had captured from the Conservatives in 1997. Worse still, the Lib Dems managed to overturn a huge Tory majority in a by-election held on the same day in Romsey – an upset that suggested that the tactical voting that in 1997 had helped turn a comfortable victory for Labour into a landslide was still very much in operation. All in all, it looked as if the Conservatives could only do well when turnout was exceptionally low and Labour supporters utterly apathetic or disillusioned – conditions that were unlikely to be repeated at a general election. As the *Sun*'s veteran political editor, Trevor Kavanagh, warned 'This was NOT a Tory triumph'.

Hague had been saved in 1999 by election results that could be spun as giving the lie to opinion polls. Fortunately for him (but unfortunately for his party perhaps), warnings that this time he shouldn't be let off so easily were drowned out by opinion polls that appeared to show that one of the longest post-election honeymoons in British political history was finally coming to an end. Nothing was going right for the government. The Millennium Dome, a paltry 75 pence increase in the state pension, and Labour denying Ken Livingstone the chance to fight its corner in the London mayoral contest seemed to confirm the impression (captured by Labour's own research) that Blair was a spin-obsessed, out-of-touch control freak who was failing to deliver much beyond 'stealth taxes'. So too did the slow hand-clap reception given to the Prime Minister by, of all people, the Women's Institute. Hague had predicted in his first speech as leader back in 1997 that the voters' views on Labour would progress through 'fascination, admiration, disillusion and finally contempt'. At last it appeared to be coming true. A MORI poll in early June cut Labour's lead to just three percentage points: for an opposition that for so long had flatlined on 30 per cent while the government recorded ratings just shy of 50, 38 versus 41 was little short of sensational.

But the Tory 'recovery' evaporated like dew in the summer sun. This was partly in the face of Labour's massive increases in spending on health and education – a move which, in the light of the Conservatives' stubborn insistence that they could still find savings to finance tax cuts, was reinforced by an August poster campaign showing scissor cut-out marks around three of seven health service workers shown, along with the slogan 'Tory health policy. Cut here, cut there, cut everywhere.' But Hague had also been subject to press and public ridicule in the second week of August in response to his boast in an interview with the upmarket lads' mag *GQ* that as a teenager he had sometimes drunk fourteen pints of beer a day. By the end of August MORI had Labour back on 51 per cent and the Tories down at 29 per cent, with Hague's satisfaction rating dipping alarmingly and Blair's moving up once again; more ominously, if Labour's spending splurge on health and education was in part an attempt to enthuse its 'core support' or 'heartland' as well as assuage public opinion more generally, it seemed to have done the trick – at least as many Labour as Conservative supporters were saying they were certain to vote. The tiny minority of Conservative MPs who had openly criticized the Party's populist approach – Ian Taylor, for example, had earlier warned that being 'defined by who we hate – the euro, the EU, asylum-seekers, gays and criminals' would not be enough to win a general election – looked like they might have a point after all.[105]

Depressingly for Hague, muttering about the Tory leadership began again, and some felt able – perhaps unwisely in the long term – to voice thinly veiled criticism in public. David Davis had been a Whip and a minister under Major, but, after backing Ken Clarke, was not invited to serve in Hague's Shadow Cabinet and had therefore opted for the Chairmanship of the influential Commons Public Accounts Committee. In an interview in the wake of the MORI poll, he recalled how Labour in opposition had kept the pressure on the Conservative government in July and August 1996 and wondered (in a manner that could only have made him more enemies among his senior colleagues than he had already) why Hague and co. weren't doing the same.[106]

Defeated mayoral candidate Steve Norris, now a Party Vice-Chairman with a brief to improve relations with (and membership among) ethnic minorities and young people, piled on the pressure over the same weekend by criticizing his party for clinging to what he saw as its outdated social attitudes. The Tories had at the end of July 2000 made much once again of their blocking in the Lords the government's attempt to repeal Conservative legislation (known as Section 28) that prevented local authorities 'promoting' homosexuality. This stance had already prompted the defection of a minister (and former Director of Communications), Shaun Woodward, who crossed the floor at the end of 1999, claiming that his party had 'lurched further and further to the right, to the point where it was impossible for me to stay' and, for good measure, 'The Tories want to shrink the NHS to an emergency-only service with people forced to take out private insurance for all other care.'[107] And while it may have reflected the traditionalist views of grassroots members, the defence of Section 28 proved the last straw for a wealthy (and gay) Conservative supporter, Ivan Massow, who in a blaze of highly contrived publicity left a party which, he claimed, had 'become less compassionate, more intolerant and, frankly, just plain nasty'.[108]

As well as opining that this had to change, and speaking just as Shadow Minister of Health Liam Fox was suggesting patients' lives were being put at risk by the poor communication skills of foreign-born NHS doctors, Norris also declared that the Party should mind its language on race and asylum too. When Labour predictably piled in to accuse the Tories of exploiting fear, encouraging prejudice, and failing to adapt to the multicultural reality of modern Britain, the Conservatives' reaction was fronted, with characteristic aggression, by Tim Collins, claiming that 'On asylum, William Hague is speaking for the mainstream majority of people.' [109] Whether his reaction was really as 'furious' as it was described in the press is doubtful: getting Labour to talk about an issue 'owned' by the Conservatives was, after all, exactly what Hague's advisers wanted. Indeed, it was to become the main thrust of their election campaign in the coming months.

At the end of the summer of 2000, however, talk was once again turning to whether Hague was really the right man to take the Party into the upcoming contest, and had opinion polls continued to suggest that the Party was still going nowhere, he might have been in serious trouble once again. Although Michael Portillo's star had waned (particularly at Westminster, where his failure to make any headway against Brown contrasted sharply with Hague's occasional besting of Blair), he and other Shadow Cabinet members had at least hoped that a pre-Conference retreat in mid-September might allow them to force a shift away from the populist strategy. But, as luck would have it, the polls suddenly turned sharply in the Tories' favour as the government failed to stop a spectacular illegal fuel blockade mounted by commercial drivers (described by Hague in a TV interview as 'fine upstanding citizens') protesting against what they claimed were excessive taxes on fuel. Indeed, according to MORI, which had brought such gloom just a fortnight before, the Conservatives were actually in the lead for the first time since the summer of 1992. Instead of a wholesale rethink of the Party's electoral strategy, the retreat turned into a concerted attempt by Hague and others to bounce a reluctant Portillo into sanctioning a call for a substantial cut in fuel duty.[110]

In the event, the Shadow Chancellor's agreement was seen as too little too late. As far as Hague was concerned, it also came at the cost of him promising that the 2000 Conference in Bournemouth, rather than being another bang on the populist drum, would supposedly pitch the Tories as a 'One Nation' party – inclusive, in-touch, concerned with the inner cities, determined to 'reach out' and focused on improving, not privatizing, public services.[111] It seemed, then, that the 'mods', as the media had taken to calling those frontbenchers who agreed that the party needed to tone down or at least dilute its strident populism, had at last gained the upper hand. Lined up against Portillo, Maude, and Norman – and Tim Yeo, David Willetts, and John Bercow, the future Speaker of the Commons – were those (labelled, with depressing inevitability, the 'rockers') who believed the Party should stick to the traditional Tory issues on which it apparently had a guaranteed lead over the government. Included in this group were Widdecombe, Duncan Smith, Redwood, Lansley, and Collins. Among those in the supposedly 'muddled middle' were Hague himself, Party Chairman Michael Ancram, and Chief Whip James Arbuthnot, who had apparently agreed to ensure that at Conference their traditionalist colleagues would be singing from the same, slightly more tolerant, hymn-sheet.[112]

In the event, however, the 'rockers' refused to stick to the 'mod' script and 'the muddled middle' were unwilling, and perhaps unable, to do much about it. Portillo, ranging (without autocue or lectern) way beyond his Treasury brief, made a speech insisting that the Party had to be an inclusive organization that stood up for all people, irrespective of their sexuality or ethnicity. Even before he spoke, there had been tension because briefings had ensured the media focused its attentions on his plans to boost private healthcare and tear down 'the Berlin wall' that separated it from the NHS rather than emphasize the Shadow Chancellor's attempt – yet again – to reassure voters that the health service, like other core public services, was safe in Tory hands. And almost as soon as Portillo had finished speaking, more briefings ensured that his headlines would be stolen by trailers for the more hard-line contribution due to be delivered the next day by Ann Widdecombe. The Shadow Home Secretary was still thought to be sufficiently serious a threat to Portillo as Hague's successor that the former's close journalistic ally, Michael Gove, had witheringly compared her in that morning's *Times* to the irredeemably naff seventies tipple 'Blue Nun' – the kind of 'cheap hock' that 'makes the party go with a swing, but is designed primarily to appeal to older customers', too much of which 'renders one increasingly ridiculous'.[113] It came as no surprise, therefore, that the so-called 'mods' leapt in after Widdecombe's speech, which promised a criminal record for anyone caught in possession of cannabis, to admit to smoking the stuff in their youth. Those admissions, along with the media's incredulity and police disquiet over her plans, completely undermined – and were probably intended to undermine – any leadership ambitions Widdecombe might have been harbouring.[114]

Trying to have it both ways

Hague's own speech at Bournemouth in 2000 was not a move to the centre. No Conservatives (apart from a tiny handful of 'One Nation' pamphleteers like MPs Damian Green, Ian Taylor, and Stephen Dorrell) were seriously proposing that, not least because anyone on the frontbench who did so was in serious danger of losing his or her job.[115] Instead, Hague was trying to have it both ways. The now traditional themes (criminals, asylum-seekers, Brussels, supporting marriage) were there, but, as agreed with the 'mods', so too were inner-city estates, ethnic minorities, and the rest. As per *Believing in Britain* – the draft manifesto endorsed by 99 per cent of the paltry 17 per cent of members who bothered voting on it just before the Conference – there was, Hague asserted, no contradiction between the two impulses, just as there was apparently no contradiction between the Party's promises to spend as much as Labour but somehow tax people less.[116] The speech, especially when compared to the previous year's populist tub-thumper, fell between two stools. That it also fell flat was not lost on Hague or on those in his inner circle arguing there were no headlines, or votes, in the 'touchy-feely' approach advocated by Portillo and Maude – a conviction that may have led to accounts appearing in the press of the ear-bashing received by the two during a meeting of the Thatcherite 'No Turning Back' group, thus souring relations still further.[117]

Hague (like Blair, ironically enough) was conflict-avoidant when it came to man-management – an individual trait that, as well as meaning he chaired rather than really drove meetings, often saw him commit to a course of action in which really he had no faith but which at the time seemed the best hope of keeping the peace. After the fiasco over the 'No Turning Back' leak, Hague felt obliged to accede to Portillo and

Maude's insistence that they be given control of election strategy, while Collins and Lansley would handle day-to-day campaign tactics and timetabling and Wood and Platell stick to their media role. Meanwhile Widdecombe, along with Iain Duncan Smith, would be kept so busy touring the country during the campaign that they would be unable to exert much influence. Hague also gave the impression that he would place less emphasis on issues like keeping the pound, asylum-seekers, and tax cuts and fight the election on the slogan 'compassion that people respect'.

Doubts as to whether the Shadow Chancellor and Foreign Secretary really had prevailed over those arguing the Tory leader was better advised to stick to his populist guns were only heightened when the media was briefed on the Tory campaign team. Although Portillo and Maude (and Norman) would be central to the Tories' election effort, so too would Widdecombe and Duncan Smith, who was later drafted into Hague's Strategy Group at the beginning of the New Year, partly as a counterweight to Portillo and Maude. Meanwhile, Lansley would be sharing the key position of election coordinator with Ancram, with Collins – another right-winger – playing a central operational role. Although Finkelstein and Nye were not (as per some press reports) thereby 'marginalized', their advice clearly counted for less than it had done and they were not part of the inner circle around Hague – a circle that, apart from Lansley and Collins, still included Hague's Chief of Staff, Seb Coe, his PPS, John Whittingdale, his media people, Platell and Wood, and (until he departed to fight and win a seat in parliament) George Osborne.

Playing the race card?

It came as no surprise to some inside the Conservative camp, therefore, that in the run-up to Christmas 2000 Hague was back on what had become familiar and, he continued to hope, fertile territory. After ensuring that Maude and Portillo were kept out of the loop lest they veto his plans, the Tory leader made a heavily trailed speech claiming that the Macpherson Report on the Metropolitan Police's handling of the death of black teenager Stephen Lawrence had been seized on by 'the liberal elite' in order 'to brand every officer and every branch of the force as racist', thus contributing directly to 'a collapse of police morale and recruitment and . . . to a growing crisis on our streets', with constables now so scared of being accused of discrimination that they were wary of using stop and search powers. Intended to provoke the government into attacks that could be further exploited to remind voters that it was apparently keener on political correctness than cracking down on crime, the speech inevitably landed Hague in hot water with some of his 'mod' colleagues.

The New Year, however, brought some comfort to those in the Party who hoped that the Conservative campaign might still attempt to engage Labour on the territory that voters cared most about – crime and asylum, of course, but also the schools and hospitals that were a bigger priority for swing voters in what the Party's pollster, ICM, called 'Pebble Dash Subtopia' and 'Green Belt Expansion'. Now that donations and loans had at last begun to flow in advance of an imminent election, the Party could finally afford to pay for a series of hard-hitting posters dreamed up by Rick Nye. These challenged Labour's ability to deliver real improvements in public services, reminding people that they'd paid the taxes but asking where were the nurses or teachers or police officers. However, the polls – unsurprisingly given the time-lags involved – refused to shift at all, suggesting, even to those who thought it worth trying an assault on Labour territory, that it was too little, too late.[118]

To many in Hague's inner circle, most obviously Tim Collins, this simply confirmed what they had asserted (and Hague had suspected) all along. The main message of the opinion research conducted by ICM – namely that the Party had to improve its devil-take-the-hindmost image and work night and day to make up big deficits on those issues that, along with the economy, really decided elections (health, education, and pensions) – was all very well perhaps. But, assuming it would ever have been possible for a party in charge of public services for 18 years to suggest their failings were all down to a government in office for just four, it was simply not practicable at this stage. Better instead to exploit the few issues on which the Party already enjoyed leads – immigration and asylum, law and order, and the euro (if not Europe as a whole).[119] Nor should it forget, Hague's advisers argued, the power of tax, which had, after all, delivered in 1992, not least because it had distracted attention from issues that Labour 'owned', competing on which would apparently be 'suicidal'.[120]

In a post-election report, however, ICM's Nick Sparrow could 'only conclude that a decision was taken to ignore the research' advising against going hard on tax cuts and the euro. 'Indeed', he continued, 'the campaign looked to be only slightly influenced by the research; very largely it depended on political dogma.' Inasmuch as it was used, he felt, the Conservatives 'treated Market Research as an add-on, to be used to gauge reactions to campaign themes already launched'. Of course, ICM were paid for what they did. 'Nevertheless, it is somewhat disheartening to have expended so much energy on research to find the conclusions have had so little bearing on the strategic thinking.' Perhaps he and his colleagues had not been persuasive enough, but 'one could argue that many in the party, from William Hague down, were obsessed with their own agenda particularly on the euro, convinced like Michael Foot in 1983 that the answer to negative polling evidence was to shout even louder'.[121]

To those around Hague, then, the quicker the Party got off Labour's territory and back on to what they saw as a more profitable populist track, the better. Not very reluctantly, and once again without bothering to get buy-in from his senior Shadow Cabinet colleagues, the Tory leader agreed. In a speech made at the Party's Spring Forum in Harrogate in the first week of March 2001, Hague (possibly inspired by his new speechwriter, *Telegraph* leader writer and Tory MEP Daniel Hannan) suggested that, under a second-term Labour government, Britain would become a 'foreign land'. He also promised voters no less than eight times in the same speech that 'We will give you back your country.' While Hague insisted his remarks referred to the pernicious influence of the EU, journalists claimed they had been led to believe by briefing from Nick Wood that he was talking too about the impact of immigration.[122] Prior to the speech, the *Express*, for instance, quoted 'a senior Tory spokesman' to the effect that 'Mr Hague is manifestly not a racist. He is conveying the message of Britain becoming a country where its people feel uncomfortable, where people feel alienated by political correctness.' Hague's message, in true populist fashion, was apparently '"trust the people". They are right about tax, about crime and about asylum. They want something done about it.' He knew that

'People feel nervous and ill at ease in their own country. The people's instincts are right and William Hague trusts the people. He is placing himself squarely as the champion of popular opinion.' [123] At that stage, few people in Britain had heard of 'dog-whistle' politics – the use of words and phrases which, while insufficiently explicit to get the politician using them into serious trouble, are nevertheless well understood by those voters he or she is targeting. This, however, was an early example.

Yet while Hague's message went down a storm with his audience and with the *Daily Mail*, the *Sun* (no stranger itself to exploiting xenophobia but beginning to swing in behind Labour) suggested that the Tory leader had, despite his denials, allowed his speechwriters to 'flirt with extremism', albeit of the 'clever' and 'coded' variety, all of which 'left a nasty taste in the mouth'.[124] Possibly perversely, the strength of the negative reaction, particularly from the government, only encouraged those in the Tory high command who were apparently keenest on the populist strategy: as Andrew Lansley loyally told a journalist: 'Labour wouldn't attack us for jumping on bandwagons unless they feared that we were getting through. We just have to hold our nerve.' [125] In the meantime, however, Hague had to endure criticism bordering on contempt by some liberal Conservatives outside Shadow Cabinet. For those of like mind inside it, the whole thing was just another depressing example of Hague's repeated tendency to apparently accept the validity of their argument about the need for a more moderate, balanced approach and then, after being 'yanked back' by the entourage in the Leader's Office, to go off and do the exact opposite – and, worse, to do it without giving them any advance warning that he had changed his mind.[126]

Worse still, by raising doubts about his Party's attitudes towards foreign and ethnic minorities, Hague effectively gave himself no choice but to sign, on pain of being accused once again of pandering to prejudice, a Commission for Racial Equality (CRE) pledge committing politicians not to 'play the race card' during the election campaign. The cross-party pledge blew up in Hague's face, however, when a row ensued over the refusal of some Conservative candidates to sign – a row made worse because the media got hold of remarks by Tory MP John Townend about Britain's 'homogenous Anglo-Saxon society' having been 'seriously undermined' by 'Commonwealth immigration' and more recently by illegal immigrants calling themselves asylum-seekers. It also got hold of an internal memo which, by reminding candidates 'to avoid using language which is likely to generate racial or religious hatred', implied that some of them might be tempted to do so. Townend then declared that Labour seemed to think that the British were a 'mongrel race' and called for the CRE to be abolished, thereby negating the supposedly reassuring signal sent to ethnic minorities by Hague's visit to multi-ethnic Bradford and provoking the ire of black Conservative peer John Taylor. In the end, Hague managed to get Townend to apologize for his 'ill-chosen words' and persuaded Taylor (who called Townend's apology 'meaningless and worthless') not to act on his threat to resign from the Party on the eve of a general election. But the impression created was not a positive one: even if the Tories weren't a bunch of closet racists, they looked divided and ill-disciplined.

Trouble at the top

In 2001, as in 1997, most of those at the top of the Conservative Party thought it would lose the upcoming election, and some of them – or at least their supporters at Westminster and in the media – were already manoeuvring for the leadership contest that would probably occur soon after it. In mid-April, just before the race row really began to heat up, polls were published suggesting that the Conservatives, still well over 20 percentage points behind Labour, were heading for another landslide defeat and that Hague, who less than 20 per cent rated as making the best Prime Minister, was even more unpopular than ever. At the same time, the media reported that 'Michael Plotillo', as the *Sun* dubbed him, was already working hard to maximize his chances of winning any post-election ballot. As so often, there was, behind the headlines, both less and more than met the eye. Neither Portillo nor Maude was actively seeking to undermine Hague, but they could both perhaps have done more to silence their characteristically zealous acolytes, who were more than happy to mix it – preferably anonymously – in the media.[127] Clarke might have jumped in quicker to deny rumours that he would endorse Portillo, although doing so would have run the risk of making it too obvious that he still wanted the leadership. And Hague him-self could perhaps have intervened to stop those fiercely loyal to him overreacting. That said, the problems were not merely imaginary. Nor were they just about individual ambition. They might not have been fiercely ideological, but they did arise from differences over strategy and tactics which, because the Party leader was unable to insist on his chief lieutenants doing his bidding, inevitably impacted on the Tories' ability fully to take the fight to Labour.

An obvious example was Portillo's evident reluctance to bang the drum for tax cuts as hard as Hague would have liked. The Shadow Chancellor now clearly thought it best to avoid talking about the economy on the grounds that it would only benefit Labour.[128] Even highlighting the £8 billion worth of tax cuts that the Tories were proposing, he believed, risked undermining their claims to care just as much about public services as Blair and Brown – especially as media reports at the height of the plotting fever in mid-April suggested his deputy, Oliver Letwin, couldn't be trusted not to float the idea of restricting spending in future in order to finance a rolling programme of tax cuts. In the event, Portillo's concerns turned out to be well-founded when, at the start of the election campaign proper, Letwin was comically forced into hiding after obliging Hague and Portillo to cope with the fall-out from his boast to the *Financial Times* that the Tories were in fact planning on £20 billion rather than £8 billion of tax cuts in the hope that they could reduce the state's share of the economy from its current rate, 40 per cent, to 35 per cent. These sorts of figures could only be delivered by spending much less on public services than the Party had committed itself to just days earlier in its manifesto, *Time for Common Sense*, the writing of which had been taken off Andrew Lansley and given to David Willetts (helped by Danny Finkelstein and Greg Clark) after the early stages of preparation had descended into bickering.

The episode, indeed, is a cautionary one for academics who subject such documents to laborious coding procedures in order to pronounce with apparently scientific precision on where the parties that produce them stand on a left–right scale. Such an exercise (the same one, note, that suggested Labour in 1992 was considerably more left-wing than it was in 1987) allows some to assert that the Conservative Party in 2001 (and, indeed, in 2005) made a significant move back to the centre compared to its position in 1997 – an assertion supposedly backed up by pointing out that the billions promised in tax cuts represented 'an almost imperceptible' percentage of national income.[129] But however 'hard' the data thus produced, it cannot be a valid measure because it fails to factor in the extent to which, in the real world, parties are defined by what they talk (and by what they are forced to talk) about, not what they write in documents that only a tiny minority of even their own members bother to read – whose authors should be seen not as authoritative voices but simply as the best crafters of compromises cobbled together with an eye to heading off an internal row rather than actual implementation.[130] The Conservatives in 2001 were still a party associated with tax cuts that would damage the public services that were most important to voters. And the vast majority of the latter cared more about (and understood) the fact that those cuts ran into the billions in absolute terms than the relative percentage of national income (or 2 per cent of government spending) the Conservatives' official figure represented. Letwin's hint that they would not in fact leave it at that only served to reinforce the impression that the Tories were ideologically beyond the pale and still had a long way to go before they could be trusted by the two-thirds of voters who, the polls said, were (a) more interested in extending health, education, and welfare than keeping taxes down and (b) refused to believe that 'a Conservative government, by saving money elsewhere, could combine tax cuts and increased spending'.[131]

In short, the Conservative Party in 2001 was a long way away from the average voter on crucial socio-economic issues and had managed neither to make nor to convey significant progress onto the hallowed centre ground. Standing pat, however, seems to have been popular with the grassroots. In a survey of Conservative activists conducted some two months prior to the election being called, YouGov found that, even though most thought Hague was performing poorly and should step down after an election that most of them already considered a lost cause, they were definitely not for accommodating the public's preferences. As the *Observer* reported, 'Asked whether the party should shift to the left – the centre ground where most political experts believe elections are won and lost – only 8 per cent of Tory activists surveyed agreed. More than a third thought the party should shift more to the right with over half saying that Hague's present tone should be maintained.'[132] There was simply no pressure from below for the kind of change that the Party needed to make.

The Letwin episode also indicated that the discipline and coordination that Lansley and Collins were supposed to bring to the Tory campaign were not all they might have been. As we have seen, this was nothing new: similar problems occurred in both 1992 and 1997. Like then, things were made more difficult by the Conservative leader being unable to oversee the campaign from HQ personally because he needed to be seen touring the country, even if, incredibly, he somehow only managed to visit just one school and one GP surgery during the entire campaign. But they were almost certainly made worse by the continuing tension in the aptly named War Room between Portillo and Maude and what they saw as the Tory leader's entourage – tensions which were typified by the row over Hague's decision (withheld from them until it was too late to change it) to have Margaret Thatcher appear alongside him at an election rally.

At the rally, Thatcher did not, as some had feared, express her well-known antipathy to the multicultural society that Portillo and others insisted had to be embraced or at least accepted, though she did go further on the single currency than Hague would have liked, ruling it out forever. But her appearance merely served to remind voters (by no means all of whom shared grassroots Tories' passion for the former Prime Minister) that the Party had not really changed very much. Her presence, and her humorous reference to a billboard advertising the film *The Mummy Returns*, reinforced the impression that Hague himself (whom two-thirds of respondents in a pre-campaign Gallup poll agreed came over as 'a bit of a wally') was simply not up to the job of awakening what one mischievous observer called 'that slumbering dragon, the party faithful' – now 'less like a fighting phalanx of fanatics than a mere mythical beast of heraldry: crossed blue rinses, with rampant pound signs'.[133] And for some of Hague's supposed supporters in the party in the media the contrast between the glorious past and the mediocre present was almost too much to bear.[134] This must have been particularly galling: after all, in early December, just before the Macpherson speech, a Central Office source admitted – apparently in all seriousness insisted the initially incredulous journalist – that 'We read the *Daily Mail* editorial one day and make it our policy the next.'[135] Ever since, Hague had been giving that paper, and probably the majority of his party, most of what it wanted.

Banging the drum: the 2001 campaign

This was particularly true when it came to Europe. Indeed, resisting the single currency was to be a key part of the Tories' platform in the election – the 'last chance to save the pound'. The leadership even negotiated a tacit agreement that allowed candidates (some of whom were facing a UKIP challenge) to rule out the euro forever. Superficially, this made little sense. First, polls suggested that only a small minority of voters regarded it as an important issue, particularly when seen side-by-side with issues such as the NHS, education, and the economy. Second, Labour was seen as having the best policy on Europe, not least because it would let people make up their own minds on the euro in a referendum. Third, even Conservative supporters were apparently confused as to the precise stance of their preferred party – had it ruled out adopting the euro forever or temporarily, and was it going to give the people a say or not? And lastly, a two-thirds majority of people surveyed after the election believed that the Party had focused too much on the issue.[136] It is possible to argue, however, that there is another side to the story – one consonant with the approach advocated by Hague's inner circle.

According to some of Hague's advisers, Europe was worth the time and effort spent on it in the campaign for two reasons. First, it helped divert media (and, it was hoped, voter) attention from Labour issues on which the Tories, even if they overstated the extent to which the electorate agreed with them on Europe, were even further away from most people's preferences. Second, it may have helped minimize the flow to UKIP of people who would ordinarily have voted Conservative – something some Tories were so worried about that they made freelance attempts to persuade the smaller party to stand aside in constituencies fought by Conservative Eurosceptics.[137] Yet, while it is true that UKIP picked up a tiny 1.5 per cent of the vote at the general election, and while there is some evidence that the Conservative Party's focus on its signature issues worked in the sense of setting the media agenda, it was never going to be enough.[138] Simply because they were the issues that the media seemed happiest talking about did not guarantee that the Tories' positions on them were discussed uncritically or that more voters were turned on to the party than turned off it as a consequence. Nor did the fact that those issues were talked about necessarily mean that the media's (and therefore the Party's) priorities became the voters' biggest concerns. Evidence for even the indirect influence of the media – namely its ability not so much to tell voters what to think but what to think about – is limited and highly contested by researchers: whom you eat your cornflakes with in the morning, for instance, may well be more important than what you read, watch, or listen to while you're eating them.[139]

Thus the Conservatives in 2001 undoubtedly managed to grab headlines but they failed to grab votes. For instance, Labour's early-release scheme had, according to the Tories' first Party Election Broadcast, led to violent sexual offences that otherwise would never have occurred. That claim had earned valuable media attention, even if some of it was critical of what seemed like a desperate homage to the infamous Willie Horton ads that supposedly destroyed George Bush Senior's opponent in the 1988 US presidential contest. So, too, did Hague going to Dover to promise that a Tory government would ensure Britain became 'a safe haven, not a soft touch' by holding asylum-seekers in secure 'reception centres' – a stunt encouraged not just by Tory MPs telling Central Office that immigration and asylum were going down well on the doorstep but by the news that the Party's relentless focus grouping of swing voters (not, note, 'core' supporters) suggested that they, too, wanted to hear some tough talking on the issue.[140] But although the two campaigns probably served to reinforce the Party's long-term lead on both crime and immigration, as well as making those issues slightly more important to voters, they could not lift either of them above those that counted most and on which Labour (as the Party's pollster told it again and again) enjoyed massive leads. And at least one of the two issues – immigration – might have done the Party as much harm as good. Its rise up the agenda may have helped win a few votes (though not as many as the Party needed). But, as with the euro, it also provided its opponents with yet another chance to brand it as extreme, obsessive, and old-fashioned.

In other words, even the issues that the Conservatives 'owned' had a flipside: they went down poorly with some groups of voters while reminding even those with whom they went down well of things they didn't like about the Party. Moreover, they caused morale-sapping and distracting rows behind the scenes – and not just between members of the Shadow Cabinet and Hague's inner circle. Half-way into the election campaign, for example, an argument between the latter and the men in charge of the Party's advertising and polling even spilled into the papers. Ronnie Duncan of Yellow M and Nick Sparrow of ICM had been dismayed by the Tory leadership's decision to move away from Rick Nye's floating-voter-friendly campaign on public services (built around Nye's 'You've paid the tax, so where are the nurses/teachers/ policemen' posters) and onto the so-called 'core issue' of Europe.

But if Sparrow was frustrated, he wasn't entirely surprised. As Hague moved through his leadership, and especially when Andrew Cooper left in the summer of 1999 and Danny Finkelstein was moved sideways, the Party's pollster found himself confronted by 'a sort of cabal of real insiders who weren't particularly listening to anybody' and who were determined to act as gatekeepers for their increasingly beleaguered boss. The number of face-to-face meetings he had with Hague (never frequent) dried up almost completely, despite Sparrow's efforts to make direct contact. Even had Hague been privy to the findings of the focus groups and the polling, however, Sparrow doubted whether it would have made much difference, given the right-wing, populist instincts Hague shared with those closest to him. In Sparrow's view, arrived at after working not just for Hague but also his immediate successors, the tendency towards preference-shaping (trying to convince voters to see things your way) rather than preference-accommodating (adapting your policies to their views) is almost innate and therefore the default option:

> It's a fight between pragmatic politics and ideology. . . . Why does any-body go into politics in the first place? You go into politics because you think you know best, because you've got ideas that you feel passionate about and you want to implement them. . . . So to find out that swing voters and the people you've got to appeal to aren't actually concerned about the things you're concerned about – and, inasmuch as they are, they see things another way – must be hard.[141]

It is far-fetched to suggest that the Conservative Party that lost the election of 1997 was capable – ideologically, institutionally, and individually – of moving as far to the centre as it needed to in order to stand any chance of seriously troubling Labour in 2001. However, that does not mean that the Party was somehow bound to have headed off as far over the horizon as it did. The idea that Hague seriously tried to 'reach out' before collapsing back into a 'core vote' strategy is wrong: he was never really convinced that a move to the centre could or should be effected and he always hoped that a populist strategy would be a popular one. Nevertheless, what academics would call 'a critical juncture' occurred in the spring of 1999. As Hague's deputy came under attack, the leader and his team could perhaps have made up their minds to tough it out and tack more closely and consistently to their Labour opponents. They could have concentrated the Party's efforts on the bread-and-butter issues that decided elections, even admitted that some of the things they were proud of about its record since 1979 should be subject to scrutiny and correction in the light of changed circumstances and the obvious preferences of the majority of the electorate. But, because they were convinced their ideological instincts resonated (even if only below the radar) with the electorate and because they believed they had to keep the Party (particularly the party in the media) onside lest Hague risk losing the leadership, they chose instead to appeal to voters via their pocket-books and their pet peeves. As a result, they little had realistic alternative by the time the election came round in 2001 to fight it the way they did. It was too late to do anything else. As one of those involved later confessed, 'The truth of the matter is simply that, in the final campaign, you are only able to mobilize pre-existing prejudices in your favour, and we had a small number of positive prejudices that we could mobilize.'[142]

At the height of the election campaign of 2001, the *Independent* was (rather belatedly) passed a copy of 'Kitchen Table Conservatives' by 'Tory officials' who apparently believed the Party was 'paying the price' for failing the tests the paper had supposedly set, especially when it came to neutralizing the Party's negative reputation on public services.[143] In fact, the Tories did not so much flunk those tests as choose not to take them. To have done so would have meant a risky and above all consistent move onto Labour territory that would have provoked a wave of internal and media criticism. This could have overwhelmed a leader who began badly and grew weaker as he went on – a leader who anyway was a Thatcherite and surrounded himself with people who were either of like mind or simply convinced that populism was the only approach that stood a realistic chance of keeping their boss in the leadership and eroding Labour's majority. To them, an authoritarian appeal was worth trying not simply because it might mobilize a 'core vote' that would therefore turn out in higher numbers than New Labour's rather less committed coalition, but because it might be able to pull that coalition apart, attracting to the Tories those voters whose vaguely centre-left preferences on bread-and-butter issues might be trumped by their strong feelings on crime, Europe, and immigration. That the only alternative on offer seemed to focus on a social liberalism shared mainly by voters who would not have dreamed of voting Conservative while the Party continued to talk of tax cuts financed by vaguely defined savings in public expenditure meant it, too, stood little chance of success – especially as its main advocate turned out to be less of a class act than many had hoped. In any case, a change in leadership was never seriously contemplated, not least because when it was talked about something (superficially reasonable local and European election results, government troubles, a fuel crisis) always contrived to turn up and suggest that Hague might be on to something after all.

In fact Hague's populist approach failed to pull apart Blair's cross-class support and even to mobilize appreciably more Conservative supporters to go out and vote than their supposedly more apathetic Labour counterparts. And, inasmuch as it managed to create 'clear blue water' between the parties, its influence may have been negative rather than positive. A survey in February 2001 found that more than two-thirds of voters saw the parties as 'much of a muchness' but also that those planning to vote Tory were less likely, at 30 per cent, to detect 'really important' differences between the parties than the 36 per cent of Labour supporters who could do so.[144] This figure (especially when one remembers that 50 per cent said they would be voting Labour and only 29 per cent Conservative) suggests that the Party's strategy may have been not merely useless but actually counterproductive. By that stage, however, Hague's team were way beyond telling. As one apparently confident member of that team told journalists being shown the Party's supposedly state-of-the-art call-centre and direct-mail operation just before the election, 'We've spent four years ignoring the opinion polls. We keep hearing we are wrong to make our pitch on our chosen issues. Any doubters on our side really should know better.'[145]

4

'SIMPLY NOT UP TO IT'

IAIN DUNCAN SMITH, 2001–2003

The 2001 election was an unmitigated disaster for the Tories. Their campaign made things so easy for their opponents that one Labour strategist claimed it had been like 'machine-gunning a corpse'.[1] Even worse, they had managed to poll 1.2 million fewer votes than they had in 1997 and almost six million fewer than in 1992. The Conservative vote share was 31.7 per cent – only one per cent up on 1997. The Party clawed back only nine seats and managed to lose eight – a net gain of just one which left Blair's massive majority virtually untouched. The Conservatives remained becalmed in their suburban and rural heartlands, while Labour, which won 412 seats on just under 41 per cent of the vote, maintained many of its 1997 gains in the South and held on to its heartlands in the North. The gap between the parties was of course magnified by an electoral system that punishes parties which build up big (but pointless) leads in safe seats and rewards those whose votes are more thinly (but efficiently) spread. But that problem wasn't going to go away: experts calculated that the Conservative Party would need a lead of more than 11 per cent over Labour next time in order to win an overall majority of just one seat.

Writing after the election in the *Telegraph*, Andrew Lansley and Tim Collins, both of whom had been instrumental in the populist approach that had characterized Hague's campaign, sought to convince fellow

Tories that, far from being 'time wasted or thrown away', the years after 1997 had 'given us firm foundations on which to build'.[2] Not all of their colleagues were persuaded by this self-exculpatory whistling in the dark. A handful of them even set up a tiny ginger group, Conservative Mainstream, dedicated to the idea that 'success for the Conservative Party depends on it being a moderate, pragmatic, and realistic voice on the centre-right of politics' – a message summed up by one of their number, Andrew Tyrie, in a provocative pamphlet called *Back from the Brink* which also laid into the idea that the election had been anything other than a disaster. By the time it was published, however, in December 2001, its author's colleagues had a more pressing concern, namely the fact that, at least on the evidence of opinion polls and parliamentary and media performances, they had been landed with a loser for a leader.

The 2001 leadership election I: the party in parliament

William Hague had privately set himself the target of 240 to 260 Conservative seats – a Labour majority of around 50.[3] When it became clear that he had come nowhere near meeting this goal, he resigned. Few beyond his inner circle mourned his passing, and even some of them thought he had to go: the speculation that had helped undermine his authority for so long would only have intensified, and had he not jumped, he would almost certainly have been pushed. As some of his colleagues feared, however, his departure, like John Major's, prevented the Party from carrying out a political post-mortem. Ideally, it needed to work out why its policies and marketing scared off voters or simply failed to convince them. It needed to work out why its expensive technology – the 'Geneva' call-centre operation – spewed out political intelligence that proved pretty useless. And it needed to work out why its supposedly new and improved party organization was overstretched and, in the words of one expert, 'crashed on its first proper outing', leaving the party in the country, to quote one venerable veteran, 'weaker than at any time since the general election of 1945'.[4] Instead, the Party once again plunged headlong into a leadership contest that this time would see the ultimate decision given to ordinary members after MPs had narrowed the field to just two candidates – a process which (perhaps predictably) provided more heat than light, involved more character assassination than cool analysis, and ultimately gave the Tories more problems than it solved.

The 166 Tory MPs returned to Westminster in 2001 were not very different from their predecessors either in terms of their individual and institutional backgrounds, their ideas, or indeed their interests.[5] The average age of a Conservative MP fell, but only from 50 to 49. All were white. Not surprisingly, since the Party failed to choose even one woman as a candidate in any of the seats in which the incumbent was standing down, 152 (or 91.5 per cent) of them were male. Indeed of the 38 new Conservative MPs only one was a woman. Unlike Labour MPs, only a minority of Tories had any experience of local government and only a handful had a connection by birth or upbringing with the constituency they represented. Like Labour MPs they were overwhelmingly middle-class professionals, but more solidly so and from the private rather than the public sector – lawyers, bankers, farmers, and a handful of soldiers and journalists, as well as, of course, a smattering whose only career had been in politics, working for the party in jobs that they had always hoped would lead to them becoming an MP one day. As for ideas, the new intake were, for the most part, like most of those they joined at Westminster – convinced Thatcherites, only more so. Academic research suggests that the proportion of free marketers had risen from 56 per cent in 1992 to 68 per cent in 1997 and 73 per cent in 2001, while Eurosceptics now made up 90 per cent of the parliamentary party – up from 58 per cent in 1992 and 85 per cent in 1997.[6]

Of the five candidates whose names went forward into the parliamentary ballot that would decide which two MPs the membership would be allowed to choose between, only three stood a serious chance. The better-known of the two less likely contenders, the emollient Michael Ancram, Chairman under William Hague, would have been a stop-gap at best. His message that the Party needed time to think rather than rushing headlong into change as a knee-jerk reaction to defeat might have had more appeal had it not come from someone so involved in that defeat – especially as his campaign manager, Tim Collins, had a fair claim to be one of its architects. David Davis, on the other hand, had the advantage of not having served under Hague. But his reputation as an over-ambitious schemer with a small but fiercely loyal group of admirers meant that he remained personally distrusted and disliked by many of his parliamentary colleagues, some of whom resented him harping on about his council house background and his 1970s stint in the territorial equivalent of the SAS, others of whom had never forgiven him for helping to whip the Maastricht Treaty through the Commons.

Of the three candidates in with a serious shout, two were high-profile heavyweights. Michael Portillo, although Shadow Chancellor, had made it abundantly clear throughout his tenure that, although still very much a Eurosceptic, he was uncomfortable with much of Hague's approach – a stance that had not endeared him to some of his Shadow Cabinet colleagues. But he still had some appeal on the right of the party, not least among those who combined liberal economics with a more liberal outlook on matters moral and social. To others, however, that kind of outlook was precisely what they found off-putting, especially when taken together with Portillo's confessions that he had had 'some homosexual experiences as a young person'. Some even regarded Portillo as tantamount to a traitor to the Thatcherism they had once shared. Yet to MPs in the centre and on the left of the Party he was still regarded with suspicion, not just because of his Thatcherite past but also because of the efforts of his fan club both within and without Westminster to try to ensure that as many potential supporters of his would be standing as candidates at the 2001 election.[7] For his part, Portillo was (not altogether privately) unsure whether, in his heart of hearts, he really wanted the job – so much so, indeed, that he had to be persuaded to run by colleagues.[8] Consequently he made it clear (perhaps too clear) that if he were to win the leadership, it would have to be on his terms rather than as a result of him tacking and trimming in order to attract the votes of those who failed to appreciate how much the Party needed to change.[9]

Ken Clarke, on the other hand, had no doubts about his desire to do the job but was unsure whether, as the Party's leading Europhile, he had a realistic chance of being chosen. By focusing on his business activities and joining the nascent cross-party campaign for the single currency, he had done nothing to improve his chances compared to 1997 other than ensuring that he was untainted by association with Hague's failure. When he eventually decided to stand, however, he was savvy enough to ensure that his campaign would be managed by Andrew Tyrie, who, despite being heavily critical of Hague's populist approach in *Back from the Brink*, was not associated with the Party's pro-European left. Clarke's campaign also benefited from its single-minded focus on meeting MPs and conveying a simple message to them, namely that he could win the next election. Opinion polls confirmed that he was twice as popular with the public as Michael Portillo and four times as popular as the only other genuine contender, Iain Duncan Smith.

Duncan Smith, or IDS as he was known, was a Maastricht rebel with no ministerial experience and a traditionalist 'rocker' on all the social and moral questions on which Portillo was seen as a 'mod'. In Hague's Shadow Cabinet he had tended to lend his support to the populist approach and operate in harness with Ann Widdecombe, out of whose shadow he stepped after the drugs débâcle at the 2000 Conference finally put paid to her leadership ambitions. A convinced Eurosceptic who played a full part in rebellions over Maastricht and other European legislation, he was a favourite with Margaret Thatcher and with Norman Tebbit, who noted pointedly that Duncan Smith was a 'normal family man with children', although to be fair IDS himself was determined to protect his family's privacy to an extent that would later come to frustrate those working to improve his media image. Few, however, took his candidacy seriously. Even many of those who promoted it assumed he would lose but, by standing, would establish the strength of support for socially conservative and economically right-wing ideas within the parliamentary party and thereby constrain Portillo.

Duncan Smith's biggest problem was that he was not renowned among his colleagues for being the sharpest knife in the drawer. This applied especially to those MPs who were familiar with his military career or who had bothered to look at his less than impressive academic record – something which may account for his relative lack of support among the 46 per cent of Tory MPs who had been to Oxford or Cambridge.[10] Moreover, his rebellious behaviour during the 1990s meant that some of those working in the Whips' Office at the time (and quite a few of those who had bitten their tongues and stayed loyal to the Conservative government) were convinced that Duncan Smith neither should nor could lead the Party. More generally he was seen by many MPs as an unthinking, reactionary right-winger. The comments of one who served under both Major and Hague sum up all these concerns nicely:

I can't think of a good thing to say about Iain. I mean I really can't. He's not a bad bloke. He's not stupid but he couldn't be a Cabinet minister. He'd be a liability because he's got these gut instincts which drag him off without really thinking about things. He's not very bright. He's not very loyal either.

As it turned out, however, the 'anyone but Clarke' and 'stop Portillo' camps turned out to be much larger than the small group with a grudge against Duncan Smith. Clarke picked up most of his votes from the Tory left, such as it was, and pro-Europeans, most of whom were one and the same. But he also gained some support from right-wing traditionalists (like Ann Widdecombe) who believed that he was the only realistic alternative to a social liberal like Portillo. The latter's appeal clearly went wider than his fellow 'modernizers' on the economically liberal right (such as Francis Maude) but included many on both the Tory left (Stephen Dorrell, Tim Yeo, and Damian Green) and some on the right who saw him as an election-winner. Portillo's problem, however, was the belief among many fellow MPs that his apparent obsession with changing the party's image and making it more inclusive and representative – characterized by one MP as 'weed, women, and woofters'[11] – was neither their kind of Conservatism nor a stance that would win over an electorate that was to the left of the modernizers on economic issues and well to the right of them on social issues. They were also aware that Portillo's gay past had gone down like a lead balloon with many ordinary grassroots members, who simply would not vote for a man guilty of such 'deviancy' – the term employed by a disappointed and distrustful Norman Tebbit. And just in case they wondered whether it was only their own constituency activists who agreed with the *Telegraph* that the Party would never look 'normal' if run by someone whose view of the world was 'brittle, oversophisticated, childless', they could turn to a 'survey' of 300 constituency party chairmen in the *Mail*. For all that its questions were loaded, it suggested a clear majority were unhappy at the prospect of Portillo as leader.[12]

Portillo's enemies believed that the most effective way of de-railing any attempt by him to make the Party more moderate across a range of issues was to focus only on a narrow (and probably not even the most important) part of his agenda – one that they could caricature as pro-drugs, pro-gay, pro-women, and pro-minorities.[13] Given academic research which estimates that the proportion of Tory MPs who shared Portillo's social liberalism had, if anything, fallen markedly between 1992 (when it was put at 30 per cent), 1997 (18 per cent), and 2001 (13 per cent), this made a lot of sense.[14] But Portillo's problems went beyond this. True, some people were simply prejudiced: one MP recalled being told by a colleague that he wasn't going to vote for Portillo because '(a) he's gay and (b) he's a foreigner'. But many who weren't were none-theless worried that there might be more revelations about his private life still to come out. They were also worried about his performance in the Commons as Shadow Chancellor: anyone, they reasoned, who could be bulldozed by Brown would almost certainly be beaten by Blair. These concerns only increased after Portillo's disappointing showing on the BBC's *Question Time*, at the parliamentary party hustings, and in front of the parliamentary press gallery – all of which suggested to many that he simply wasn't hungry enough. To these reservations were added the tactical mistakes of what Ann Widdecombe cruelly dubbed Portillo's 'little band of backbiters' – their initial attempt to strong-arm career-minded MPs into their camp by suggesting the election was a done-deal, their over-reliance on other *Portillistas* who had, by fair means or foul, been secured safe passage into the House of Commons, their implying Thatcher's endorsement when it was not forthcoming, and their failure to persuade their candidate that he had to take a less 'take me as I am' and a more accommodating attitude to potential supporters.[15]

The first and second rounds of parliamentary voting only confirmed Portillo's fears that the Party was unconvinced it needed to change even in the wake of a second massive defeat. The first ballot (in which he got 49 votes to Duncan Smith's 39 and Clarke's 36) resulted in a tie for last place between Ancram and Davis. Their insistence on a re-run, after which they both dropped out, had the important effect of delay-ing proceedings sufficiently to allow MPs, and the rest of the country, to see Channel Four broadcast a secret video diary by Hague's Head of Media, Amanda Platell, which was heavily critical of Portillo's behaviour in the run-up to the election. The delay also gave MPs a few more days to take the temperature in local associations, which were, by and large, swinging against Portillo. The re-run second round saw Portillo add only one extra vote compared to the three each that went to Duncan Smith and Clarke.

In the third and final round, Portillo netted only three extra votes. Clarke picked up 20 – enough to see him finish in first place. Duncan Smith picked up 12. Although his support was limited almost entirely to Eurosceptic and socially conservative economic liberals, and although he did not impress colleagues who had served in government, he did rather better than Portillo in picking up votes among older as well as younger MPs, among MPs who had not been to Oxford or Cambridge, and among both longer-serving parliamentarians and relative newcomers. This was enough to see him edge out Portillo by just one vote – a vote Portillo might easily have had if only he had been prepared to do the conciliating and the stroking his campaign team urged on him or even just to rule out the idea of all-women shortlists for candidate selection.[16] If some saw this as a tragedy for the Party, not least because it meant that it would fail to change sufficiently to put it back in electoral contention, the man himself did not:

> I knew that I wanted to make these huge changes . . . and I thought if I get a big mandate for that, it's possible. If I get 80 MPs voting for me, that's great. But as it became clearer and clearer that I was in the 50 territory, I knew the thing was hopeless, that with that sort of mandate the thing could not be done. And so I'm afraid – it's kind of a let-down for people who supported me – I was relieved to lose.[17]

That he lost was a perfect example of the interplay between institutions, ideas, interests, and individuals. Had the voting been conducted in an arguably more rational way – for example, by allowing those voting to express a second preference – then IDS may well have fallen by the wayside. Ideology mattered too: academic research suggests that nine out of ten of Tory MPs were Eurosceptic, seven out of ten were economically liberal, and eight out of ten were socially conservative: the two 'best candidates', unlike the eventual winner, could not tick all three boxes.[18] And while interests are a grey area – MPs are reluctant to discuss who offered which Shadow Cabinet job to whom – they clearly counted for something. The very vagueness of Clarke's pitch, plus his reassurance that Eurosceptics would make up a majority of his Cabinet, was helpful. Few took seriously IDS's attempts to woo pro-Europeans into his Shadow Cabinet, but his offer of a job to David Davis may temporarily have swung some of his ultra-loyal supporters. The fact that Portillo had attracted support from many who had served in Hague's Shadow Cabinet made it difficult for his team to persuade ambitious backbenchers that there would be room for them anytime soon.[19] And individuals clearly mattered. Ken Clarke made it through to the membership ballot not because of what he stood for but because of who he was. If Michael Portillo had not been who he was, and had he perhaps shown a little more hunger and a little less honesty, he would have gone through with him.

The 2001 leadership election II: the party in the country

Because Portillo did not make the parliamentary cut, the Party's grassroots were now obliged to plump for one of two apparently polar opposites. Should they succumb to the robust charm of an ideologically flexible big-hitter with presumed voter-appeal who, contrary to their instincts, would head for the centre ground and possibly re-open the Party's options on 'Europe'? Or was it to be the supposedly right-wing 'headbanger', who might have been 'one of us' on Europe but who might fail to command the respect of the colleagues who knew him or the electorate who had never heard of him? What from the outside looked like a dilemma, however, turned out to be no contest. Some 86 per cent of Conservative Party members told ICM in August that Europe was very or quite important in determining their vote.[20] It also figured (at 37 per cent) much higher up their list of priorities than either health (at 28 per cent) or education (at 6 per cent), suggesting those priorities were some way off those of voters in general and that they were less like the electorate as a whole than the grassroots members surveyed (more representatively) back in the early 1990s.[21] Some 58 per cent thought it likely that Ken Clarke would split the Party, whereas only 18 per cent thought the same of IDS, who, notwithstanding his record of parliamentary rebellion against John Major, was seen as more loyal than an opponent who had shared a platform with Blair – a move that saw him called a traitor to his face.[22] True, 52 per cent thought the Party had a chance of winning the next election under Clarke, but the figure for Duncan Smith was 75 per cent. If he was good enough for Margaret Thatcher (and indeed for William Hague, who also endorsed him), then he was good enough for them.

Iain Duncan Smith was not only closer to the instincts and attitudes of the grassroots, he had also had far more contact with them. While IDS had personally visited well over 100 constituency associations just before and just after the general election, his rival had preferred to nurse his business interests and then to drum up support at Westminster rather than in the party in the country. Once the August truce the two had agreed to was over, Clarke, like IDS, went out 'on the stump', but it was too little too late. He had little opportunity to engage Duncan Smith in direct debate and, when he eventually did (on BBC's *Newsnight*), he underperformed. In any case, a hostile party in the media ensured that Clarke was continually on the back foot while IDS was given a relatively easy ride, notwithstanding the revelation that one of his campaign staff was not only father to the leader of the far right British National Party but the husband of the BNP candidate who had stood against Duncan Smith at the general election – a tale that lent credence to the frank admission by some senior Tories that there was 'endemic racism' among the Party's rank and file.[23] In the event, IDS picked up the endorsement of the *Mail on Sunday*, *Sunday Times*, *Sunday Telegraph*, *Telegraph*, and *Sun*. Clarke was backed only by the ailing *Express* and (perhaps surprisingly) by the more robust *Mail*. These newspaper endorsements were not decisive but they were probably important since Central Office's decision to deny the candidates access to members' contact details prevented Clarke (who unlike Duncan Smith didn't have the constituency contacts to get round the ban) from making much in the way of direct contact with them.

The Conservative Party issued just over 400,000 papers for the 1997 membership ballot that retrospectively endorsed William Hague's leadership. But only just over 328,000 were eventually sent out for the 2001 contest. Such shrinkage was an indictment of the managerial and organizational reforms that were the hallmark of Hague's first year in the job, although no-one could be quite sure since, incredibly, it emerged that Central Office still had no accurate national register (one of the central purposes of Hague's reforms) and was obliged to issue thousands of extra ballot papers in response to complaints. On the other hand, no-one could moan about turnout, as they had done when Hague had put questions of policy and organization to the grassroots: 79 per cent of members voted. When, after a day or two's delay occasioned by the September 11 attacks, the results were announced, they showed that 61 per cent (155, 933) of members plumped for IDS and only 39 per cent (100,864) went for Clarke.

On probation from the off

That the margin of victory was so large surprised everyone, even convincing one of Clarke's campaign team that the Party was now so 'full of nasty old people' defined by their 'hatred of gays, blacks, successful women and the EU' that it could no longer be reasoned with.[24] It did not, however, fool the bookies, who immediately lengthened the odds on the Conservatives winning the next general election from 3/1 to 7/2 and shortened the odds on them finishing third behind the Liberal Democrats from 16/1 to 12/1. This seemed a little premature, but there was a widespread feeling, inside as well as outside the Party, that the protracted and sometimes nasty leadership election had done the Conservatives few favours – indeed, no sooner had it finished than some were demanding the rules be changed to ensure a shorter process and more choice next time round.

Whether a different set of rules really would have produced more variety among the candidates is questionable, however. Europe aside, anyone looking for differences in kind rather than degree would have struggled. All the contenders had claimed the Party needed to stop talking to itself and to start talking to the voters about the bread-and-butter issues they cared about, particularly public services like health and education. To a greater (Portillo) or lesser extent (the rest), they had all spoken too about the need to revamp the Party's image so it looked and sounded more like the kind of outfit ordinary people could not only vote for but perhaps even join. All had promised some kind of policy review, identifying in particular the need to engage with, rather than run away from, or simply promise to spend as much as, Labour on public services.[25] And all had maintained they would select their frontbench on individual merit rather than on ideological loyalty.

Duncan Smith's new team, however, appeared to give the lie to all this. Admittedly, he was perforce deprived of the talents of Messrs Maude, Portillo, and Clarke, all of whom refused to serve. But not one of the Tory MPs most closely associated with the Clarke campaign (Tyrie, Curry, Maples, and Taylor) was given a job. IDS announced that his Shadow Chancellor would be Michael Howard, albeit assisted as Shadow Chief Secretary by the more liberal John Bercow. His Shadow Foreign Secretary, Michael Ancram, while no Europhobe, was certainly a sceptic. His successor as Party Chairman was David Davis, a thoroughgoingly Thatcherite right-winger. True, Oliver Letwin was appointed Shadow Home Secretary, but his credentials as a 'modernizer' were (as was the case with virtually all those thus labelled) more to do with his views on personal morality than his low tax-low spend/ private good, public bad thinking on economic policy and public services. The same went for Duncan Smith's campaign manager, Bernard Jenkin, who went to Defence, and for Hague's PPS, John Whittingdale, at Trade and Industry. Meanwhile, one of the architects of Hague's populist approach (and another Thatcherite true-believer), Tim Collins, was made Shadow Cabinet Office Minister. Some rather more moderate characters were appointed to Shadow Work and Pensions (David Willetts), Culture (Tim Yeo), and Transport (Theresa May, who was one of just three women in a team of 25). But Health was given to the right-wing former GP Liam Fox. Indeed, the only appointees who could definitely be described as being on the left of the Party were IDS's Europhile friend Quentin Davies, who was sent to Northern Ireland, and, shadowing Education, Damian Green. Finally, the choice of Eric Forth as Leader of the House and David Maclean as Chief Whip did not suggest a move into touchy-feely territory, while the announcement that the zealous Eurosceptic Bill Cash would be Shadow Attorney General prompted one anonymous former party official to claim the Party had 'handed over control of the asylum to the lunatics'.[26]

Many of those who complained were of course finding it difficult to reconcile themselves to their champions having lost to IDS. But some MPs were not so much aggrieved as anxious about the image created by the appointments: Duncan Smith might want to take the fight to Labour on health, welfare, and education, but many of those he had chosen would be seen, thought one, 'as the nasty, hard right' who would 'put spending cuts before people's needs and services', making them an easy target for the government.[27] Others made it clear that IDS was going to have to work hard to earn their support. As Steve Norris, trotted out by the media as a beacon of moderate Conservatism, put it, 'Iain Duncan Smith says he understands the need to make the party decent and a party that we can like again, and I am ready to help him do that. But I have warned that if he drags the party off to the right, then I and thousands of supporters will go. He is on probation, if you like.'[28] Some critics, however, were less bothered about ideological direction than electoral success: almost incredibly, less than a week into Duncan Smith's leadership, one Shadow Cabinet member was prepared to go as far as telling journalists, albeit anonymously, that 'If he can't pull this around in two years, he could be out.'[29]

Softer image, same old solutions

Stung by criticism of his Shadow Cabinet choices, Duncan Smith moved swiftly to try to show critics he was not necessarily the Neanderthal of their nightmares. He struck a small but supposedly symbolic blow for gender equality by refusing membership of the Carlton Club on the grounds that it did not accept women as full members. And, although his choice as Chairman, David Davis, ruled out any move towards introducing quotas for women in candidate selection, Duncan Smith insisted that the Party not oppose the passage of the Sex Discrimination (Election Candidates) Bill, which saw to it that parties could legally impose quotas, or indeed all-women shortlists, if they wanted to. Then, to try to put paid to the lingering accusations of racism which had dogged his leadership campaign, Duncan Smith obliged three backbenchers to quit the anti-immigration Conservative grouping, the Monday Club – a move announced on the eve of the Party Conference and followed within a week or so by Davis hinting he might expel the Club's members from the Party if it failed to 'clean up its act'.

True, these were largely symbolic moves, while one of IDS's first substantive acts was to make it clear that the Party would 'never' sign up to the single currency under his leadership. With that out of the way, however, a determined attempt was made to downplay the European issue. It was made clear to Shadow Cabinet ministers that they should avoid it, and those who could not had to clear their speeches with either

Ancram or Howard, both of whom, along with Maclean and Letwin, were seen as forming what passed for an 'inner (Shadow) Cabinet' in the first few months. This *omertà*, combined with the strength of feeling among many of the Tories' 36 MEPs, also put Duncan Smith off trying to insist they withdraw from the largely federalist EPP–ED group in the European Parliament after his demands for even more independence were swatted aside in Strasbourg.

Meanwhile, in his first press interview as leader, he argued that the Conservative Party, far from being some kind of 'strange quirky sect that doesn't need to be involved with the health service or education', was 'desperate to be part of – and catch up with – the way that people live their lives in modern Britain'.[30] 'The truth is,' he insisted, 'that we are a Right of centre party, but there's a big difference between being Right of centre and being extreme.' He conceded that 'we have allowed ourselves to be characterised as a party that literally knew the price of everything and the value of nothing' – a perception he was determined to change. This didn't mean repudiating Mrs Thatcher, but it did mean moving on. 'Thatcherism is a valuable part of our past. You don't reject it – you learn from it. . . . But the battles are different. In the 1970s, the economy was shot to hell, the trade unions were over-powerful, state-owned industries had encroached into all the areas they shouldn't. Now, the challenge is to take on the public services.'

Here, however, was the problem – the reason why Duncan Smith represented not a transcendence of Thatcherism but a desire to resume where it had left off. The solutions he claimed to be interested in – insurance and voucher schemes – were exactly the kind of radical-right proposals which some sections of the party in the media were longing to see make a comeback.[31] But they – and Liam Fox's declaration that it was 'time to end the serfdom of the NHS monopoly' – were the very last thing the electorate wanted to hear from a party they already believed was neglectful of or even hostile to the services they relied on and regarded with considerable affection.[32] Forcing the Party to forget about immigration and Europe in order to focus on those services, while necessary, would be pointless or even counterproductive if the policies the Party came up with involved reforms that Labour could easily portray as wholesale or partial privatization. One of the reasons, after all, that Hague had shifted the focus away from such issues was not simply that they played to Labour's strengths but that this was inevitably so while he insisted on continuing to flirt, first, with tax cuts that undermined Tory claims to match Labour spending and, second, with structural reforms that brought the market into domains where the vast bulk of voters were convinced, rightly or wrongly, that it had no place.

For Duncan Smith effectively to dismiss any attachment to services funded and provided by the state as 'dogma' or 'ideological baggage' that had to be dropped if standards in the UK were to match those of its continental neighbours was foolish or at least foolhardy. Claiming that a revered institution like the NHS had 'always been a Soviet-style command-and-control organisation', increased spending on which was 'like pouring water into a colander', was equally silly.[33] And his refusal, in a high-profile television interview just before Christmas 2001, to rule out a Conservative government making people pay to see their GP was, electorally speaking, insane. True, the Tories could point out that Labour was belatedly beginning to see the merits of involving the private and voluntary sector in service provision and capital funding. But this missed the political point that voters were prepared to accept such developments from a party whose fundamental commitment to the NHS and state schools they took as read and which was, once again, promising to increase spending (and if necessary taxes) to improve them. For the Conservatives to do the same simply reinforced the suspicion that they continued to see health and education, in the words of a Tory peer who announced he was leaving the Party just after its first conference under IDS, as 'anomalous statist leftovers in a market economy'.[34]

Moreover, it was frankly far-fetched to believe that the electorate's enthusiasm for radical reforms of healthcare and education would be enhanced by Duncan Smith's promise, in his first Conference speech as leader, to make the Tories a more inclusive, 'nicer' party. By the same logic, Labour, whilst in opposition in the 1980s, should have closed its membership to all but white, privately educated heterosexual males and thereby persuaded voters of the merits of further nationalization, the extension of trade-union power, and unilateral nuclear disarmament. Admittedly, the belief that the Conservative Party could change its fortunes by becoming less white and more feminine, as well as by softening its rhetoric to emphasize its caring and 'compassionate' side, also remained integral to the strategy advocated by those 'modernizers' who had supported Portillo for the leadership and in some cases refused to serve under Duncan Smith. But Francis Maude and Archie Norman, for example, also seemed to understand by that stage that there needed to be a closing of the ideological as well as the image gap between the Tories and Labour – a conviction that fed into their initiatives to promote fresh thinking inside the Party. These, they claimed, were 'post-factional', but many more traditional Tories would come to see them (not without reason) as some kind of ideological insurgency.[35]

Institutional tinkering

William Hague had been so keen to push through organizational change that policy was essentially allowed to drift for a year or more. And in the end his reforms had had only limited success in tackling the Party's underlying structural flaws. Constituency associations had largely preserved their traditional autonomy, making it difficult, former Treasurer Michael Ashcroft complained publicly, for the centre not only to communicate directly with ordinary members but also to allocate resources – money, agents, the best candidates – more rationally, namely from safe seats towards more marginal prospects.[36] Duncan Smith's determination not to waste his time in the same way was not necessarily wise: problems like these would not go away of their own accord. But it was understandable. Firstly, he was determined to persuade people that the Party was spending every waking hour re-thinking its policies rather than looking inward – an impression reinforced by the much-publicized creation of a beefed-up Policy Unit headed up by his own adviser, Greg Clark.[37] Secondly, he had only just been elected by the very people who might have been most resistant to any attempt to erode constituency autonomy. Given this, modernizers placed little faith in their new leader's aspiration to boost the number of women MPs – one backed up, it seemed, by little more than exhortation. Similar scepticism greeted the announcement that Central Office would be reviewing the Party's 'approved list' of candidates with a view to weeding out those who had proved a disappointment or had views (on race, for instance) that did not fit with the new 'tolerant' image Duncan Smith was keen to promote.

IDS did, however, have more room for manoeuvre at Westminster, deciding to move the Leader's Office back to the House of Commons from Central Office in Smith Square on the grounds that its location there had encouraged the 'bunker mentality' and lack of accessibility that, according to many MPs, had characterized Hague's regime. He also made some interesting, even counter-intuitive, personnel changes. His predictable promotion of Nick Wood, Hague's press man, to the Head of Media role was counterbalanced by the appointment of an acknowledged *Portillista*, Mark MacGregor, as Chief Executive and the announcement in late January 2002 that the face of Business for Sterling (the anti-euro campaign group), Dominic Cummings, would become the Party's Director of Strategy. Modernizers also welcomed the announcement that the Party, via Vice-Chairman Shailesh Vara and a revamped Conservative Future (created in 1998 to replace both the Young Conservatives and Conservative Students), would be trying to boost its support and membership among the under thirties. Others, however, were less pleased – and not just because they had had problems with MacGregor in the past. As one MP who happily voted for Duncan Smith put it, his appointment (and to a lesser extent that of Cummings) suggested that the Tory leader had chosen 'to pander to the Portillo faction' and 'appease the centre and left of the Party' with 'political correctness' – something he would come to regret because 'if your own supporters feel that you've moved off of where they are to appease people who aren't really on your side, you end up getting no respect'.

The ability of the Party to pay for all this new thinking and new talent was also greeted with some scepticism, though this time on all sides. Rather unusually, the beginning of IDS's leadership was not hobbled by massive debt because Michael Ashcroft's parting gift as Treasurer had been to secure a one-off donation of £5 million from billionaire American-turned-UK-citizen John Paul Getty II. IDS was also helped, ironically, by the fact that the new statutory limits on election spending had meant that, at the 2001 election, the Conservatives spent over £12 million less than the £28 million it spent in 1997. Since then, however, donations had been few and far between. Fortunately, the famously Europhobic retail entrepreneur Stanley Kalms had finally agreed to step into the breach and replace Ashcroft, but there was little he would be able to do to tackle what once again had become a chronic gap between the Party's income and its outgoings, estimated at the end of 2001 to be running at around £300,000 and to be so serious that its auditors were supposedly reluctant to sign off its accounts. A small reduction in staff agreed by the Party Board in January 2002 helped, but money was to remain a continual worry throughout Duncan Smith's time as leader.

'No cop in the Commons', no traction in the country

In his first big speech to the 1922 Committee, IDS promised an 'intelligent opposition' that knew it had four years to overhaul Labour and would base its appeal on becoming a 'credible government-in-waiting'. The suspicion was, however, that this move away from the dispatch box repartee and headline chasing that had characterized the Hague years owed less to a genuine belief in the power of calm critique and competence than it did to making a virtue out of necessity. Following a few weeks in which Duncan Smith was given the benefit of the doubt, the media – Tory, Labour, whatever – unanimously decided, to quote one scribe writing after the Tory leader had yet again 'lurched from cough to over-prepared insult via agonising pauses', that he was simply 'no cop in the Commons'.[38] This shortcoming might be dismissed by those close to the Tory leader as unimportant, but in their heart of hearts they knew that having a leader who could at least compete on equal terms at Prime Minister's Questions (PMQs), while not a sufficient condition for Conservative victory, was probably a necessary one. The contrived jousting provided soundbites that stood at least a chance of impacting on the majority of voters who knew little and cared even less about politics. It also contributed mightily to the morale (or lack of it) of Tory MPs – those who ultimately held the fate of their leader in their hands. The extent to which parliamentarians (and indeed supporters in the country) die inside when they see their leader stumble, fall, and fail yet again cannot be statistically measured, but it should not be ignored.

Duncan Smith's poor performances in the Commons did at least mean that the media was prepared to pay some attention to those Tories who were judged to being doing well. One such was Oliver Letwin, whose forensic dissection of Labour's anti-terror legislation – plus the fact that Letwin had himself been the victim of an (albeit rather comic) robbery a few days before he made a major speech on crime – ensured largely favourable coverage (from both left- and right-wing commentators) for his attempts to re-orientate Tory policy on law and order so that it combined traditionally tough sentences with a new focus on community prevention.[39] Letwin even felt confident enough to argue (rather less convincingly perhaps) that rejection of a private member's bill to introduce civil partnerships on the grounds that it would undermine marriage did not mean the Tories were unconcerned about the myriad examples of legal discrimination faced by homosexual couples.

This kind of thing, along with, for example, Duncan Smith's rather precipitate call for a fully elected Second Chamber, was intended to project the impression that the Conservative Party was moving with the times. But there were always limits and simultaneous attempts to reassure the right, especially on the economy and public services. In the same set-piece interview in which IDS observed, for instance, that his four children (the oldest of whom was a teenager) had no memory whatsoever of Mrs Thatcher, he also asserted, firstly, that, although the Party had to change, it must not 'change against itself', and, secondly, his continued conviction that

> the British people are over-governed and too much of their responsibility is being taken away from them and too much is being spent by government on the things that it wants to do. The corollary is that if we get less government, people will have to pay less taxation but they will have more to spend on the services they choose.[40]

The new leader could point at the end of January 2001 to some polling evidence, however, that voters were picking up his signal that the Tories were changing, with ICM for the *Guardian* suggesting slightly more voters now inclined to see the Party as friendly to public services than they had been a year or so previously. On the other hand, it was clearly premature to talk of a transformation in its image: 45 per cent of respondents thought of the Conservatives as right-wing when only 20 per cent put themselves in that category. Even more worryingly, the Tories continued to trail Labour by 45 points to 30, with their leader's approval rating, while better than Hague's, still miles behind that of the Prime Minister. Indeed large numbers of voters as yet had no opinion about him or even failed to recognize him – something his more measured, less aggressive approach would do little to change in the short term.

This lack of traction presented the Conservatives with a dilemma. One response was to start acting like a conventional opposition again and dedicate their time to generating and exploiting damaging news stories in order to chip away at the reputation of the government and, in particular, the Prime Minister. The other was to regard the above as a distraction and a displacement, avoid anything that would allow Labour to portray IDS as a swivel-eyed extremist, and instead continue to focus on incremental changes that would over time help the party reposition itself as a credible government in waiting.

Duncan Smith (along with people like Oliver Letwin, David Willetts, and Damian Green) initially appeared to favour the long game. However, unable to resist pressure to think more short term and act more aggressively, he suddenly – and probably unwisely – switched gear at the end of January 2002, using an emotive individual case to highlight defects in the NHS. The ensuing furore over 94-year-old Rose Addis initially put Blair under pressure and got Duncan Smith some admiring headlines and plenty of airtime. But then his judgement was almost immediately called into question when it transpired his office had neglected to ask the hospital concerned for its side of the story before he stormed in and, according to Labour, began criticizing hardworking frontline staff in order to prepare the way for NHS privatization under a future Tory government. A MORI poll taken in the immediate aftermath of the affair suggested that the proportion of respondents (54 per cent) who in December had no view either way about IDS had now dropped to 42 per cent. Unfortunately, however, most of those who had now made up their mind about him were not impressed: 25 per cent were satisfied with his performance but 33 per cent (up from 25 per cent) were not. Meanwhile only 27 per cent said they would vote Tory.

Helping the vulnerable . . . but not the NHS?

At the end of Duncan Smith's first six months as leader, Margaret Thatcher, it was revealed, was sadly suffering from health problems which all but guaranteed she would play no further part in public life. She had, however, managed to complete her last book, *Statecraft*, and its main message – that the UK should think seriously about undoing the mistake it had made in participating in European integration – was made much of by Tony Blair, who predictably inquired whether Duncan Smith would be distancing himself from her views. Equally predictably, perhaps, the Tory leader refused to follow the advice of Tory modernizers that the Party seize the opportunity to (in the words of one of them who had earlier been a big fan) 'demythologise Margaret Thatcher, to blow the cobwebs off its Miss Havisham, setting her past achievements in context while defining how it has set itself free from the ossified parody of greatness she has become'.[41] To have done so would have outraged many of his own MPs and, judging from a *Times* survey of association chairmen, the majority of the Party's activists.[42] In any case, Duncan Smith saw no need to repudiate Thatcher explicitly when, urged on by his new Director of Strategy, Dominic Cummings, he was in any case about to launch the next phase of his plan to reposition the Party.

In the run-up to the 2002 Conservative Spring Forum, Conservative spin doctors briefed that Duncan Smith had been so humbled by his visit the previous month to the rundown Easterhouse area of Glasgow that he was now determined to see the Tories become the champions of 'the vulnerable' – those at the very bottom of the pile who had been let down by Labour's top-down welfare solutions. This should not, it was stressed, be taken as some kind of swerve to the left – as Chairman David Davis put it, it was about 'focusing Right-wing policies in such a way as to make sure they help everybody'.[43] But it could be sold as a counter-intuitive departure. True, some in the Party found it hard – at the time anyway – to believe that Duncan Smith's damascene discovery of poverty (something he hadn't really mentioned during the leadership contest) was anything but opportunistic. But Ken Clarke, who confessed that he had been 'horrified' at the 'quite appalling' speech given by Hague at the same venue the year before, was full of praise: although it would take 'more than one weekend to persuade people that the Conservative Party is heading back in a more sensible direction', the speech, and indeed IDS's conduct of the leadership so far, had left him, he claimed, 'surprised and delighted'.[44]

Those were not the adjectives most Tories would have used, however, to describe their reaction to the news, which emerged a week after the Forum at Harrogate, that their Health Spokesman was planning truly radical surgery for the NHS – and that the transcript of an illicit recording of him admitting to it was splashed all over the resolutely hostile tabloid, the *Mirror*. It was bad enough that Liam Fox had confirmed to a fringe meeting of fellow medics that he was determined to move away from an exclusively tax-financed system towards insurance and what he euphemistically called 'self-pay'. But worse, he had outlined the four-step strategy by which he intended to get there. Step one was to show voters that the NHS was failing – was this what Rose Addis had been about? Step two was to persuade them it could never work. Step three was to begin a public debate on alternatives. Step four would see the Party reveal its support for these in its election manifesto.

To the Labour government, suffering the first signs of serious internal dissent over Iraq but hoping that the massive injection of funding for the NHS to be announced in its forthcoming Budget would help it in the local elections in a few weeks' time, this was manna from heaven: indeed, Blair, Brown, and Campbell were convinced that winning the argument on this question was going to be crucial to Labour's success from then on until the next election.[45] For the Tory leader, especially after the Shadow Cabinet had just decided (after some argument) not to support the government's plans openly to raise extra revenue to finance NHS improvements, it was a PR disaster. Post-Budget polling, at least, suggested that an overwhelming three-quarters of voters – including the majority of Conservative supporters, most of those who thought they would be worse off as a result of the tax rises, and even those who weren't confident they would feed through into better healthcare – believed Brown was doing the right thing. In the run-up to Harrogate, an ICM survey had caused a flurry by suggesting Duncan Smith was closing the gap with Labour. In the wake of the Budget, the Tories were back down under 30 per cent, 16 points adrift. The Party's former Head of Media, Amanda Platell, despite being accused of knowing nothing about politics, could see the writing on the wall already: Duncan Smith simply lacked 'the charisma necessary for a modern politician' – after all, 'The meek and the bald do not inherit the earth'; in a year's time he would be 'irreparably damaged' and replaced, either by David Davis or by Michael Howard.[46]

'Hague all over again'?

There was little, surprise, then, when at the May 2002 local elections – the first big electoral test for IDS – the Party performed poorly, taking around 32 per cent of the vote nationally compared to Labour's 35 per cent. Moreover, where voters rejected the government they seemed more ready to transfer their loyalty to the Lib Dems – or some bizarre fringe candidates – than to the Conservatives. The media, as well as noting the failure of David Davis to play the normal role of Chairman and front up on election night, suggested Shadow Cabinet members were privately prepared to give their leader only one more year before ditching him in the summer of 2003. Then, without warning, Duncan Smith was thrown straight into a row which undermined his message that the Party was changing its ways. Soon after the votes were counted it emerged that Shadow Rural Affairs Minister Ann Winterton had told an embarrassingly racist joke at a private function. This, plus rumours that some kind of high-level discussion had been needed before IDS sacked Winterton from the frontbench, and the fact that Tory MPs had to be ordered by pager not to speak to the media about the incident, suggested that the Party still had 'issues' when it came to race. Duncan Smith's next move, however, spoke volumes about both his lack of individual judgement and his increasingly apparent inability to pursue a consistent strategy, especially when it conflicted with his own ideological convictions.

Instead of moving swiftly on, IDS decided to pen (or have penned for him) a piece for the nation's biggest selling daily, the *Sun*, which insisted, in the words of its title, 'It is not racist to debate immigration' and launched into a tirade against Labour's failure to deter and deport asylum-seekers. And he followed it up a couple of weeks later by a similar effort that added a complaint that the government had been duped by its European neighbours on the issue.[47] To some of those who worked with him these outbursts were an accurate reflection of his real, still rather strident, views on such issues – views which tended to surface as the 'compassionate Conservatism' symbolized by 'helping the vulnerable' failed to gain the traction he hoped for. To others close to him, however, such views were all of a piece with the 'High Tory' patriotic communitarianism that (not unreasonably given that the plurality of British voters lean slightly to the left but are also nationalistic and authoritarian) they believed could (and should) be a vote-winner.[48] But whatever Duncan Smith's motivation (and however much it was balanced by his playing in a five-a-side football tournament designed to highlight the plight of asylum-seekers), his suddenly opening fire on such issues sat strangely with attempts to tone them down in favour of counter-intuitive themes that would convey a sense of change as well as reposition the Party.

As such, it brought him into conflict with those in the Shadow Cabinet who, like Oliver Letwin, saw such forays not only as an unwarranted interference in his Home Affairs brief but as politically counterproductive. Other unnamed frontbenchers expressed similar concerns to the media: 'This is Hague all over again,' claimed one. As such it was particularly alarming to Director of Strategy Dominic Cummings, who was determined to keep the Party on message – and therefore off issues like immigration and asylum – however much the party in the media (notably the *Mail*) approved of Duncan Smith's tough talk. However, any attempt to shift back onto more inclusive territory was also undermined when, after a stormy meeting in early May, the Shadow Cabinet agreed to oblige Tories at Westminster to vote against a government bill that would allow unmarried couples (and therefore homosexual couples) to adopt children – a line that then, all too obviously, had to be softened to accommodate a significant number of MPs (inside as well as outside the Shadow Cabinet) who objected to it.

Anger at this messy climb-down, combined with frustration at the lack of traction in the opinion polls being achieved by the Party's promotion of a more 'caring–sharing' and 'inclusive' image, soon boiled over. In early June, one of those most strongly identified with the makeover, Dominic Cummings, gave a provocatively frank media interview during which he warned the Party against trying to piggy-back on the No campaign in any referendum on the single currency. Not only would it undermine Duncan Smith's attempts to persuade voters that the Party was no longer obsessed with the issue, it might actually produce a Yes vote. 'It is difficult', he said, 'for some [Tories] to accept – but nevertheless true – that for many people, just about the only thing less popular than the euro is the Tory Party.' [49] This prompted outrage among many Conservative MPs and (just as predictably) drove much of the party in the media wild, with one livid right-wing columnist, already lamenting Duncan Smith's evident desperation to 'appear nice and cuddly and caring', despairing at what he saw as 'crazy losing-side psychology amounting almost to self-hatred'.[50]

Mixed messages

These views were reflected inside the Shadow Cabinet and at Central Office. Some (Oliver Letwin, Damian Green, Tim Yeo, John Bercow, and, more surprisingly perhaps, Chief Whip David Maclean) were of course sympathetic to Cummings' 'helping the vulnerable line' but were angry that his careless talk played (like the gimmicky suggestion that Tory MPs take a week off to volunteer in schools, hospitals, and charities) into the hands of the advocates of a more adversarial stance. So, too, it was felt, did the modernizing refusenik Francis Maude, who in late June 2002 formally launched C-Change, the ginger group which (along with the think-tank Policy Exchange) aimed 'to modernise the Conservative Party and to ensure that it reflects the realities and complexities of contemporary Britain' by holding provocatively titled debates like 'Tory Culture – right but repulsive?'[51] This was exactly the kind of thing that infuriated some of those closer to IDS, who were also concerned that trying to change the Party's image would prevent it from aggressively exploiting its ongoing advantage on issues like Europe and immigration – a concern shared by Michael Howard, and especially David Davis and Eric Forth, whose contempt for focus groups and the like was well known. To them, and others like them, elections were won and lost by going after the government and getting on with policy.

This traditional view, of course, conflicted with the idea that Duncan Smith initially seemed to have bought into, namely that there should be a moratorium on policy until the public could be persuaded that the Party, to use his own words, was no longer 'Nasty. Extreme. Strange' – 'brand decontamination' *avant la lettre*. As one Shadow Cabinet Minister confided to a journalist, 'If we come up with a good idea, because it is the Tories who are promoting the idea, then it will be contaminated. Any idea we advocate is at risk of automatically being regarded as a bad idea.'[52] And of course it could be stolen. Those unconvinced by this strategy, however, had a point. For one thing, the Party could not allow

itself to look as if it were operating in a total vacuum, utterly bereft
of ideas. Nor could it avoid responding to events and to government
initiatives. As the man most often charged with the latter, and as someone who sympathized with both sides of the argument, Duncan Smith
oscillated between them: as Nick Wood, who worked for him as well as
his predecessor, observed, 'He struggled strategically – went through a
very similar phase to Hague, you know, some modernizing, some not
modernizing, bit of this, bit of that.'[53]

The resultant confusion and lack of message discipline was illustrated
when, in mid-July, having spent a good nine months signalling that
public services might have to take priority over tax cuts, Duncan Smith
and Howard suddenly announced they would be dropping the Tories'
election commitment to match Labour's spending on education as well as
health. The party in the media was predictably thrilled. But the rationale
put forward by IDS and Howard (that the money Labour was going to
spend would not result in the kind of improvements the public expected)
ignored the advice of the Party's opinion pollsters, who agreed with this
line of attack but only if it was made on the basis of the Tories spending
the same amount of money as Labour, only better.[54] Rejecting this meant,
to the government's obvious delight, that any criticism the Conservatives
made of the two services the public most cared about could easily be
countered by asking them (endlessly but nonetheless effectively) how
precisely they planned to improve those services by spending less.

That the Tory message was, by the summer of 2002, both confused
and confusing was hardly surprising given the arguments over both
ideas and individuals going on (but only theoretically) behind closed
doors. For one thing, Michael Howard, clearly the Party's best parliamentary performer, could reasonably object, as Shadow Chancellor, to
having policies virtually decided for him by an automatic commitment
to match everything that an increasingly less prudent Gordon Brown
decided to do. For another, there was mounting tension with David
Davis, seen by some close to Duncan Smith – already frustrated at their
boss's increasing tendency to match each modernizing move with something for the traditionalists – as sabotaging their attempts to change the
Party's image.

The pressure on Duncan Smith to show he was firmly in charge of
a party genuinely committed to change by turning on those who were

less than committed both to him and to modernization finally became overwhelming. Right at the end of July, the Tory leader relieved Davis of the Chairmanship, after he had spent less than a year in post, as part of a reshuffle and reorganization of his private office that ended up being so messy that it shook what little confidence Tories (whatever their ideological views) still had in those supposedly in charge. Exactly who said and did what to whom would have passed the bulk of the public by. But the extensive media coverage did enough to convey the impression that the Tories, renowned since the 1990s for infighting and indiscipline, were (to quote a tabloid that generally prided itself on being a politics-free zone) 'once again heading up that brown, smelly creek, having left the paddles at home'.[55]

The one positive note, at least for the modernizers, was that Davis had been replaced by Shadow Transport Secretary Theresa May, the 45-year-old product of a state education, widely regarded as both approachable and capable but possibly best known for her fashion sense – 'Think Diana Rigg meets Sybil Fawlty,' as one media profile put it.[56] But the impact of the decision was dulled by carping that her appointment as the first woman to hold the post of Chairman in the Party's history was 'sheer tokenism' – and probably not helped by Duncan Smith telling a reporter (though hopefully only in jest) that he had chosen May 'Not just for her leather jeans, although that's part of it.'[57] Equally depressing was the fact that May had clearly not been given permission to go any further than Davis in obliging constituency associations to broaden candidate selection. Likewise, the highly choreographed declaration of support offered by the leadership to frontbencher Alan Duncan after he became the first sitting Tory MP publicly to acknowledge he was gay was slightly marred by the unease easily uncovered by journalists at the grassroots and expressed by old warhorses like Norman Tebbit, who insisted on warning that 'Despite the ramblings and spoutings of the over-excitable and scarcely rational children in Central Office, the nation is not possessed by an overwhelming urge to fill the Shadow Cabinet with 25-year-old black lesbians and homosexual, asylum-seeking Moslems.' Duncan Smith, he warned, must 'raise his game, end the petal-plucking "they love us, they love us not" introspection of a twice-defeated party, and set out the red meat of politics – the principles and policies on which he would govern'.[58]

True, whatever modernizers might say, Tebbit as a living reminder of the glory days of the 1980s, could not simply be dismissed as some kind of dinosaur. Indeed, one of the difficulties any Conservative leader had after 1997 (in marked contrast to Blair after 1994) was that critics from the old guard could not be written off as a bunch of losers who were barely worth listening to. Yet to a leader determined to drive change – a leader confident that he could, or at least had to, take his party with him – antediluvian comments like these might have presented an open goal. But Duncan Smith, now being given under a year to turn things round or face the chop, refused to shoot, let alone score. Instead, he judged it best to keep quiet and continue his holiday in Italy whilst letting it be known that the Party would be speeding up its policy process and coming up with some specifics. In the meantime, a few tasters – all designed to appeal to the right – were provided by some tough talk on school discipline, the proposed EU Constitution, and promising to bring back hunting with dogs.

The attempt to assuage some of the frustration expressed by Tebbit and his sympathizers in the media was somewhat undermined, however, by briefing that Duncan Smith was about to approve 'a radical revamp' of the upcoming Party Conference, to be held that year in Bournemouth. This revamp, it was said, had been inspired by the 2000 Republican Convention, at which George Bush was projected as a new kind of 'compassionate conservative' – an example that a number of IDS's advisers, in particular Cummings, MacGregor, and Nye, were keen to follow. Apparently, non-party experts and professionals would address delegates in order to show that the Tories were 'opening their eyes and ears to the outside world'. There would be a series of 'outward looking' debates with themes like 'helping the vulnerable' and 'public services first' and little or no room given to Europe. Most of the action would take place in the afternoon and evening, with mornings devoted to 'reaching out' via visits to public services and community projects.[59] This would link in to Duncan Smith's heavily trailed foreword to a new book on 'compassionate conservatism' edited by Tory MP Gary Streeter. It was hoped that its title, *There is Such a Thing as Society*, would, like a speech he gave in mid-September at Toynbee Hall, send out a pretty clear 'post-Thatcherite' signal.

But just as it looked as if the Tories might almost make it to (if not through) Bournemouth in reasonable shape, the Party's Director of Strategy, Dominic Cummings, resigned after only eight months in the job. The 30-year-old had got up the noses of Tory traditionalists almost as soon as he had arrived – and not just for his determinedly casual dress-sense and allegedly astronomical salary. Yet far from having 'captured' IDS, in the way that some of his enemies claimed, Cummings had come to realize that he was never going to be able to get the Tory leader to go far enough or fast enough and that therefore the modernizing project was doomed to a series of half-measures, superficial initiatives, off-message statements and all-too-obvious compromises with those who had never bought into it. For his part, Duncan Smith, who, according to people who worked closely with him, had a tendency to be ridiculously keen on people until they proved themselves 'disloyal' by daring to criticize him, seemed relieved to see him go.

The nasty party

Fortunately, Cummings (who had apparently been driven mad by his boss's legendary disorganization) had agreed to go quietly.[60] In any case, news of his departure was quickly forgotten as Tory MP-turned-bonkbuster-novelist Edwina Currie spilled the beans about her adulterous (if now rather ancient) affair with John Major – a story that, to some, explained the former Tory leader's reluctance to fire colleagues whose personal lives became the talk of the tabloids, as well as his exaggerated concern about what the papers were saying about him. Such stories, of course, were not merely amusing. They were a damaging reminder of the 'sleaze' that did the Conservative Party so much damage in the 1990s. Things got even worse when its 'house magazine', the *Spectator*, edited by Boris Johnson (now a Tory MP as well), published a well-sourced article laying bare the agony of a party torn between modernization and traditionalism and increasingly convinced it could not recover until a leader now widely regarded as 'not up to it' was ditched.[61]

Just as damaging were the pre-Conference polls. An NOP survey splashed in the Tories' house daily, the *Telegraph*, showed not only that they were now on just 28 per cent but that IDS (on 11 per cent) was languishing in third place behind the Lib Dem leader, Charles Kennedy, in the best Prime Minister stakes. The Conservative-supporting *Mail* also had bad news: its survey of 100 constituency chairmen revealed that 44 of them did not think IDS had been a success, while 30 of them thought he should be replaced.[62] How far IDS still had to go in turning round voters' views not just of himself but of the Tories was underlined by a YouGov poll published by the *Telegraph* on the day delegates travelled down to the South Coast, which suggested some 86 per cent of those questioned (and 68 per cent of those who would vote for the Tories) thought they were 'not yet ready for power'. Nearly two-thirds thought the Party was 'much the same' as it had been under Thatcher and Major. And while they recognized that it was less likely now to 'go on too much about Europe' (which suggests that the one element of Duncan Smith's strategy applied with anything approaching consistency was beginning to have an impact), they clearly did not buy his stuttering attempt to reposition the Tories as the champions of 'the vulnerable' – a claim which some 70 per cent found implausible. Most voters continued to believe the Party was 'out of touch with modern Britain', in particular when it came to understanding and representing the interests of women.

Judging by the extent to which those who lived in the 'world of brooches and regimental ties, . . . pork pies and potted meat' that was supposedly the typical Tory association continued to prefer white middle-class male candidates over the relatively small number of women available for selection, this was unlikely to change any time soon.[63] Rumour had it, though, that the Party was secretly planning to force associations to choose from a 'gold list' of specially selected candidates and parachute women, ethnic, and gay candidates into safe seats ahead of 'straight white men'.[64] Clearly, the plan (apparently drawn up in February) had not been adopted, although it bore some similarity to a C-Change pamphlet called *Do the Right Thing* by Andrew Lansley, who, free from frontbench responsibilities, was now openly embracing some of the ideas he had rejected when working under Hague. But its leaking to the media on the eve of the Conference – a gathering of those it had supposedly been designed to hoodwink – suggested that people were beginning to play very dirty indeed. Bournemouth was awash with talk of plots to replace IDS and already being billed as his last chance. No wonder the Tory leader's new nickname among his colleagues was, the press reported, 'In Deep Shit'.

Theresa May, the new Party Chairman, saw it as her responsibility to get her leader – and her party – out of it. Instead she made things worse. In a speech drafted in part by the Party's modernizing Chief Executive, Mark MacGregor, May reminded her audience that 'Twice we went to the country unchanged, unrepentant, just plain unattractive. And twice we got slaughtered. Soldiering on to the next election without radical, fundamental change is simply not an option.' Conservatives had to stop the internal feuding, face up to the fact that they were seen as 'the nasty party', and commit to embracing, and looking like, twenty-first-century Britain instead of hankering after 'some mythical place called Middle England' and descending into 'Punch and Judy' politics, 'glib moralizing', and 'hypocritical finger-wagging'.

Media reaction to May's speech – at least until the right-wing columnists (and Norman Tebbit) got to work on it – was largely positive. Predictably enough, the *Times* (by now, according to the Party's Head of Media, Nick Wood, 'a wholly-owned subsidiary of the modernisers'), praised her 'courageous and impressive' effort, relieved that it provided a 'stark contrast to the swivel-eyed partisan hyperbole offered by Tim Collins', the hard-line Shadow Transport Secretary.[65] But even the best-selling tabloid, the *Sun*, for example, praised the way May 'took the blue rinse set by the scruff of their necks and rammed some sense down their astonished throats'.[66] In Bournemouth itself, however, those who applauded did so out of duty rather than any great enthusiasm – just as they did when, later on in the week, Caroline Spelman told them 'there is such a thing as society' and David Willetts promised that 'the Tory war on lone parents is over'. Most delegates were left bruised and rather confused. Were they to take May's medicine even though many of them wondered whether beating themselves up about how awful they (still) were was (a) really fair and (b) really the best way to get voters to like them? Or should they instead go with David Davis, who declared, in a thinly veiled but well-received rejection of such masochism, that '[n]ow is not the time for us to lose heart', since, 'for people to believe in us, we have to believe in ourselves' and 'not be afraid of saying what we know to be true'?

Duncan Smith was left with the unenviable task of squaring the circle. Warning people not to 'underestimate the determination of a quiet man', he suggested both that the Party had rediscovered the courage of its convictions and that it was leaving the past behind. The inconsistencies were glaring: here he was talking about moving on when briefings by his aides on the eve of the Conference suggested (in no uncertain terms) that the policies the Party would unveil during the week would be about pressing on with the unfinished business of the Thatcher years.[67] And the policies themselves, detailed in a document pulled together by Greg Clark called *Leadership with a Purpose*, also suggested the Party wanted it both ways: it sought to reassure people that no-one (and especially, *à la* Bush, no child) would be 'left behind', but it also seemed bent on rolling back the state and rewarding those who sought independence from it. Rather than appealing to the worst-off, or to those who believed they needed to be helped (the real target audience), many of the flagship policies, particularly in health, education, and care for the elderly, seemed directed at wooing affluent voters by subsidizing them to go private or doing away with means-testing.

Duncan Smith's hopes, then, that 'Leadership with a Purpose' would silence his critics (he was overheard at a reception telling workers from his constituency that he would 'personally post it to all the bastards who have been stabbing me in the back') were unlikely to be realized. Instead, talk immediately turned to the extraordinary allegation by Norman Tebbit that a shady group of modernizers and Europhiles calling itself 'The Movement' was urging Duncan Smith to expel his lordship from the Party to create 'a Clause IV moment', knowing full well that this would lose IDS the support of the Thatcherite right and make it easier for them to bring in a leader more to their tastes. May was eventually forced to issue a denial that any such plan had been considered – allowing the ingenious peer to demonstrate, firstly, that the modernizers had not 'won' the week after all and, secondly, that there was still room in the Party for people whose views on just about every truth the modernizers held to be self-evident were, to say the least, unreconstructed.[68]

'Unite or die'

After Bournemouth, Duncan Smith began a tour of the provinces to 'take his message to the country'. Unfortunately, he also found time to drop into Westminster to deliver a couple of performances at PMQs that were so embarrassingly inept that they had MPs wondering how long it could go on like this, especially when opinion polls suggested the Conference had actually decreased support for the Conservatives.[69] A meeting of the 1922 Committee saw backbenchers lay into Theresa May's speech as not only an insult to them and their activists, but also a propaganda gift to Labour – like Cummings, they argued, she had 'done a Gerald Ratner', self-destructively rubbishing her own 'brand' much as the disgraced jeweller had done. There was no way now that her proposals to have associations pick candidates from a centrally composed list designed to maximize the selection of women and ethnic minorities would ever see the light of day under Duncan Smith; instead she was reduced to trying, with the help of an academic expert, to level the playing field by encouraging constituencies to adopt a more business-like set of selection criteria.[70] IDS also bowed to pressure from right-wingers within the Shadow Cabinet like Davis, Howard, and Fox not only to follow Tory peers in rejecting adoption by unmarried and gay couples when that bill returned to the Commons in November, but to issue a three-line whip ordering all Conservative MPs to do the same.

With dismayed backbenchers beginning to brief the media on attempts to gather the 25 signatures needed to trigger a leadership election, and polls showing his approval rating in negative territory even among Tory voters, Duncan Smith's priority was now not to alienate those MPs who had initially supported him as a man of the right. With their backing, at least, he was probably safe for a while: getting rid of him now would only precipitate a leadership contest in which none of the alternatives (Clarke, Davis, and perhaps even Portillo) looked capable of winning with a clear majority, an outcome that could lead to another damaging and protracted contest for the votes of grassroots members, who (if surveys were to be believed) were in no mood to dump him just yet.[71] It was a mess but a mess no-one knew how to get out of, leaving IDS as leader, quite literally *faute de mieux*.

But knowing he was probably safe in the leadership for a few months yet did not mean that Duncan Smith was any better able to control his party. Once again, he was forced to climb down on the three-line whip he had promised right-wingers against the controversial adoption bill when it became clear that a significant number of Tories would not accept his authority on this issue, obliging the Chief Whip, David Maclean, to inform the 1922 Committee that absence from the vote would be tolerated. In the event, over 30 Tory MPs, including a couple of impressive new entrants, David Cameron and George Osborne, stayed away. So did members of the Shadow Cabinet. However, one frontbencher, John Bercow, resigned so he could protest against the party line and seven other members of the parliamentary party, including Portillo, Clarke, Maude, and Lansley, joined him in voting against it.

The Conservative leader's reaction to this mini-rebellion was extraordinarily oversensitive – and utterly self-defeating. He was hardly one to talk when it came to parliamentary disloyalty and in any case had created the problem by trying to whip MPs on what many saw as a 'conscience issue'. It was also becoming apparent that the Lords would now let the bill pass. Yet Duncan Smith allowed himself to fall prey to suspicions that supporters of Clarke and Portillo (who in Bournemouth had held a joint fringe event sponsored by Conservative Mainstream and the modernizing C-Change) were plotting to overthrow him and install the bloke-ish former Chancellor in his place. At a hastily convened press conference, the Tory leader claimed that, for some of those who had gone against the party line, the previous night's vote 'was not about adoption but an attempt to challenge my mandate to lead this party'. He was therefore issuing a 'simple and stark' message to Conservatives to 'unite or die'.

Duncan Smith's melodramatic statement was a mistake in so many ways – 'a five star fuck up', as one Shadow Cabinet member memorably put it.[72] It revealed once again the confusion at the heart of his strategy: if he really were committed to what he called in his statement 'the necessary and sometimes painful process of modernization', then why had he sided with the traditionalists on such an iconic issue? The statement also drew attention to his lack of authority but gave no hint that he knew how to deal with the problem beyond appealing over the heads of his parliamentary party to a wider membership he hoped were still supportive. Finally, the chaotic manner in which the statement was announced and then delivered to the media (who were not allowed to ask questions) guaranteed that the whole thing would be written up (and, worse, broadcast) as bizarre, even surreal. It left Duncan Smith looking not just weak but a laughing stock – a phrase that comes up again and again whenever Tory MPs recall the IDS years. One sketch-writer went even further, calling Duncan Smith 'the first Conservative leader in history to turn himself into a suicide bomber'.[73]

Not surprisingly, the polls only got worse. In December 2002, notwithstanding a sustained onslaught against sleaze in Number Ten and divisions between Blair and Brown over the euro and university tuition fees, ICM had the Tories on just 27 per cent – their lowest showing for four years and only four points ahead of the Lib Dems. Leaked focus group findings on both IDS ('unelectable, not normal, no character, patronizing') and his party ('clapped out', 'a joke') were, if anything, even more damning. Speaking at the end-of-term meeting of the 1922 just as the media had decided to recycle an old story about his having exaggerated his educational achievements, Duncan Smith called for 'steady nerves and steely determination'. Among his audience, however, nerves were anything but steady and the only people possessing anything like steely determination were those who had now made up their minds that IDS just wasn't up to it and would have to go. The problem, still, was finding the right individual and overcoming the institutional barriers to a swift transfer of power.

When it came to the first part of the problem, the most commonly touted successors to Duncan Smith by the end of 2002 were Clarke and, some way behind him, Davis. The only other name in the frame was Michael Howard. His relationship with Duncan Smith was not a close one.[74] The Tory leader was slightly intimidated by his Shadow Chancellor's forensic intellect – a gift that ensured Howard was the first holder of that post since 1997 to come anywhere near besting Gordon Brown in the Commons, thereby throwing into even sharper relief Duncan Smith's poor performances in that arena. IDS was also well aware that Howard did not, at that stage anyway, buy into the idea that the right-wing instincts they shared were best suppressed to help the Party project an image more in tune with modern Britain. Despite this, however, the two had rubbed along reasonably for fifteen months. This changed dramatically just before Christmas 2002 when Howard felt obliged to stamp on off-message hints made by Duncan Smith in a newspaper interview that the Tories would be promising tax cuts at the next election. Whether those hints were the result of IDS accidentally letting slip his Thatcherite heart's desire or were simply an attempt to shore up his support on the right and in the media was a moot point. But they were also an unplanned move onto Howard's territory and risked blowing all the effort he had made to curb his own enthusiasms on tax and spending for the greater good of the Party.

The disagreement was of course blown out of all proportion by the media, but it was significant. First, it encouraged talk that Howard was interested once again in the leadership – a prospect that was routinely raised in the almost invariably flattering profiles of him carried in the media from then on. Second, it reflected, once again, the Party's ambivalence over fiscal policy and public services. It had become clear since the summer that the Tories did not agree with Labour (and, insofar as the polls were right, the public) that the UK, at least for a while, was going to have to commit as much money as was necessary to do something about health and education. So what, then, was it proposing? Was the Conservative Party willing, as Howard continued to claim, to put tax cuts on the back burner? Or did it believe (as his deputy, Shadow Chief Secretary to the Treasury Howard Flight, openly insisted) that there was so much waste in the public sector that a Tory government could cut spending by up to 20 per cent and thereby deliver both better public services and tax cuts – a claim which most voters, as was well known, thought too good to be true? Attempts by IDS to make his position clear left nobody any the wiser and, as Flight had done, merely gave Labour yet another opportunity (which it accepted with its customary alacrity) to accuse the Tories of wanting to take an axe to health, education, and even policing.[75]

The contretemps between Howard and Duncan Smith also illustrated, once again, the problems at the heart of the latter's leadership. Some of these were to do with IDS as an individual: as someone who worked closely alongside the Tory leader noted, 'Iain was someone who really needed intellectually strong people around him, and the people who could have perhaps supported him and made things work better were the very ones who were excluded because he felt insecure', with Howard being the perfect example. Equally important, however, was the ideological (and therefore the strategic) problem. The Tory leader, either because he didn't really believe in wholesale change or because he believed he could not hold on to his job without throwing the occasional bone to the right, was no more capable than some of his errant colleagues of the message discipline and consistency that projecting change required. Floating tax cuts as he did at the end of 2002 not only cast even more doubt on the Party's commitment to public services, it also drowned out, for instance, the announcement that the Tories would not seek to privatize the newly renationalized Network Rail – a policy born of necessity but one which a more savvy leader might have seized on to distance his party symbolically from its ideologically driven past.

The confusion created by the floating of tax cuts prompted yet another round of damaging stories about Tory divisions but provided ample opportunity for those who wanted rid of Duncan Smith to try to precipitate his demise by confiding (off the record but nevertheless in no uncertain terms) what those who worked at Westminster really thought of him. The anonymous comments of one frontbencher were unusually explicit but not unrepresentative; they also provide an insight into one of the reasons the parliamentary party did not move to replace IDS as quickly as it might have done:

> The real problem is that Iain is not that bright and is very naive. He simply hasn't got the intellect or the charisma. To be brutal, he hasn't got anything going for him. The worst thing is there is nothing we can do about it. He is a damaged product and he refuses to take advice. There is a universal view on this among MPs. It is not just a few rebels; the mood and morale can be summed up as desperation and frustration. . . . It is now a matter of when, rather than if, Iain is replaced as leader. . . . But we will have to wait for the grass roots to rebel. None of us can be seen to do it. And I think that will start happening after the local elections in May, when we fail to make an impact.[76]

If ever proof were needed that institutional change at one level of the Party – namely the move to involve ordinary members in choosing the leader – could affect behaviour at another level, this delay in acting would provide it.

Into the bunker

As 2002 turned into 2003, the Conservative Party could look back on a year that had gone from bad to worse. Even if, as alleged by Stephan Shakespeare, the pollster and former campaign manager for Jeffrey Archer, newspapers hostile to the Tory leader (he picked out the *Times*) were spinning polls to accentuate the negative and eliminate the positive, their findings were still worrying.[77] Panicky MPs were beginning to wonder if the Liberal Democrats might one day make good on their promise to push the Tories into third place – a nightmare scenario that prominent modernizers like Francis Maude had been warning about since the summer of 2001. Now even the most sceptical academic observers had to admit that such a realignment could no longer be dismissed as fantasy politics. The Lib Dems were actually closest to the voters on many issues and getting better and better at winning seats, while Labour seemed determined not only to hog the centre ground but to expand it both to the left – on tax and spending – and to the right – on law and order, asylum and immigration, university tuition fees, and military action overseas.[78]

The government's tough line on asylum and immigration – personified by the plain-speaking Home Secretary, David Blunkett – was particularly problematic for the Tories. Immigration was 'their' issue; not to run with it, especially when high-profile cases of asylum abuse and government mismanagement were in the news, was surely the waste of a golden opportunity to get onside with the public, take the fight to the government, and enthuse their loyal supporters? On the other hand, picking up the proverbial pitchfork and flaming torch and rushing to join the party in the media on one of its periodic witch hunts risked espousing policies that, while they went down well in the proverbial *Dog and Duck*, were unrealistic, extreme, and internally divisive – as was amply demonstrated by an embarrassing semi-public spat in January 2003 between IDS and Oliver Letwin over the former's off-the-cuff call to detain asylum-seekers as potential terrorists and criminals. A hard line was also strategically questionable. The Party's big lead on asylum and immigration did not, modernizers pointed out, translate into boosting its overall support because it was mostly preaching to the converted and to less educated, less well-off people who would, if they bothered to vote at all, nonetheless continue to vote Labour while it delivered the goods on welfare and the economy. Secondly, responding to media anxiety about asylum and trying to outbid a Labour government already prepared to go much further than some of its liberal supporters would have liked, took the Conservatives back into 'nasty party' territory and Hagueite headline chasing. Calling for prison ships and withdrawal from the UN's 1951 Geneva Convention would blur the image of change and the more measured tone the modernizers were so desperate to project in order to tempt (often better-off and better-educated) voters who were beginning to turn away from Labour but were turning instead to the Lib Dems.

In any case, the main reason for Labour's plummeting popularity in the New Year of 2003 was, according to opinion polls, the increasing likelihood that the country would join a US-led invasion of Iraq. The Conservatives, however, could do nothing to capitalize on this. The Liberal Democrats remained sceptical and were therefore in a position to articulate the concerns of a substantial proportion of voters – something which only increased the threat that they then appeared to pose to many Tory MPs, who were very aware that disquiet about being dragged into war was shared by both their constituents and their activists. Duncan Smith, however, left his party absolutely no room for manoeuvre. Before engaging in any serious discussion of the issue in Shadow Cabinet, the Tory leader – whose own time in the army meant he saw himself as something of an expert on defence matters – made it crystal clear that he shared Blair's concerns about Saddam's weapons of mass destruction and would support military action to pre-empt their use. Indeed, as early as November 2001 on a visit to Washington he had let it be known that he, like his hawkish contacts in the American administration, thought Iraq might have to be next on the list after Afghanistan. But even if IDS had had his doubts, it would still have been almost impossible for a party whose brand was built on assertive nationalism and anti-appeasement to have opposed military action, especially once the armed forces began their build-up in the Gulf. Many Tory MPs, then, might have supported Blair (as David Cameron put it at the time) 'grudgingly, unhappily, unenthusiastically', but support him they did.[79]

Yet even had IDS not been predisposed to back military action against Saddam, he might well have been too distracted to ask the penetrating questions that, for example, the Tories' former leader, John Major, thought needed to be asked about Iraq. Once again the causes and the consequences mixed the ideological, the institutional, and the individual. Having fallen out with one of his two counter-intuitive picks for key jobs at Central Office, Dominic Cummings, Duncan Smith was busy falling out with the other, Chief Executive Mark MacGregor, over the decision of the party in London to reject his favoured candidate, the model-turned-businesswoman Nikki Page, and give Steve Norris another shot at the mayoralty. When the Tory leader failed in a behind-the-scenes bid to get Page's candidacy reconsidered, he became convinced that MacGregor had not only stitched things up but was operating at the heart of some sort of *Portillista* fifth column dedicated both to undermining his leadership and to preventing the Party returning to pressing home an attack on tax and asylum that, according to his reading of the opinion polls, was beginning to pay off. So, on a day when the media was preoccupied with wrangling over Iraq at the UN and the upcoming anti-war demo, and without bothering to consult either the Party Chairman or the Party Board, Duncan Smith secured MacGregor's resignation.

MacGregor's departure, along with that of Rick Nye, the Party's Director of Research, who had been instrumental in the 'helping the vulnerable strategy', fanned concerns that the Tory leader was now taking most of his advice from right-wing familiars like Bernard Jenkin and Owen Paterson and had become increasingly distant not just from modernizers like Oliver Letwin but moderating influences like Chief Whip David Maclean. In December, the Party had announced the creation of a new post, Senior Director of Communications, and that it would be filled by Paul Baverstock, an executive with the communications company founded by Thatcher's iconic adviser, Tim Bell. In his train came Stephan Shakespeare of YouGov, the pioneer of internet-based polling in the UK. He, like Baverstock, was sceptical about the electoral impact of modernization. And, at a purported £20,000 per month, his polls were thought by some (including apparently MacGregor and Nye) to lend expensive but unwarranted support to the belief that traditional Tory issues (tax, crime, immigration, Europe) were the way to go. They certainly seemed to show a smaller gap between the Tories and Labour than the research done by other companies, prompting some in the Shadow Cabinet to regard them as little more than a 'costly comfort blanket'.[80] Duncan Smith appeared not only to be cutting himself off more than ever from the Shadow Cabinet but to be moving into the bunker with some new best friends.

The even nastier party?

In fact, like Jenkin and Paterson, some of those now accompanying Duncan Smith were old and very loyal chums. Indeed, one of them,

Barry Legg, had already been lined up as a replacement for MacGregor. Between 1992 and 1997, Legg, like Duncan Smith, had been a notably Eurosceptic, right-wing Tory MP who had worked on John Redwood's leadership campaign against John Major in 1995 and was rumoured to have considered joining UKIP. Legg, apparently, would combine the post of Chief Executive of the Conservative Party with being Chief of Staff – essentially an adviser-cum-gatekeeper – to IDS. However, only the second of the two posts was in the leader's gift since the appointment of the Chief Executive was, strictly speaking, a matter for the 17-member Party Board, on which the voluntary party – the party in the country – had substantial representation. By not even consulting the Board before appointing Legg, Duncan Smith risked alienating the constituency representatives whose presumed loyalty was one of the main reasons why Tory MPs (who were also worried about appearing to stab him in the back while the country was at war) were staying their hands before the local elections.

Things spun rapidly, damagingly, and even comically out of control. Angry board members demanded and were given a meeting to discuss the situation. In the chair would be Theresa May, who was no more pleased than they were and who, rumour had it, an embattled Duncan Smith was now planning to replace with John Redwood, prompting the classic *Sun* headline, 'The Vulcan returns (but how long will IDS Klingon?)' The members of the Board who met with May instructed her to convey their unhappiness to Duncan Smith, to warn him to stop his office briefing against her and others, and to re-consider Legg's dual appointment – a message that, to the fury of the Leader's Office, was of course leaked to the media. Possibly even more seriously, Portillo broke his silence to claim, in a widely splashed interview with the BBC, that May's position had been made impossible, that the wounds of the past week were utterly self-inflicted and represented 'a narrowing of the party', and, most witheringly, that trying to make yourself look tall by standing in short grass was anything but a sign of strength.

Portillo's barb predictably provoked Duncan Smith's office to return the compliment: Portillo was 'self-indulgent to the point of madness', a 'cancer' destroying the Conservative Party. Duncan Smith's opponents bit back: the Tory leader was 'a dead man walking'. IDS's office then orchestrated a move to get the Party's 60 or so newly selected candidates to write to the *Telegraph* in support of their leader. Even the Chief Whip took the unusual step of penning an article for the same newspaper reminding his charges that 'There is no messiah waiting in the wings who will command more support in the party than Iain.'[81] Meanwhile staunch leadership loyalist, and Shadow Agriculture Minister John Hayes was reported as having accused prominent critic (and former Head of the Cats' Protection League) Derek Conway of acting as a spokesman for Portillo, claiming he'd 'gone from pussies to bums'.[82]

To most voters, of course, the slights and the slurs – and the ins and outs – were meaningless. But the bare bones of the story told them all they needed to know. An opinion poll published in the *Telegraph* at the end of February and in the wake of the chaos triggered by the shenanigans at Central Office suggested that, although the Labour government was in a mess, twice as many people thought the Lib Dem leader Charles Kennedy would make the best Prime Minister as thought the same of Iain Duncan Smith. Just 15 per cent of respondents (and only 37 per cent of Tory voters) thought IDS was 'proving a good leader' of the Party. Some 54 per cent of respondents (up from 41 per cent) characterized his leadership as 'weak and ineffectual', with 58 per cent (and 43 per cent of Tory voters) saying the Party should dump him. But Duncan Smith was not the Party's only problem. Over half those questioned said they would be 'dismayed' at the prospect of its forming a government, while an incredible 82 per cent of respondents (and even the majority of Tory voters) said the Conservatives gave them 'the impression of being confused and lacking in any clear sense of direction'.

To many Tory MPs Portillo's intervention looked like the act of a man trying to fire the starting pistol for a leadership race, albeit one in which, like Geoffrey Howe in 1990, he himself now had no intention of entering. In fact, Duncan Smith's job, as most of his potential challengers (and their frustrated supporters) continued to conclude, was safer than it looked – for both ideological and institutional reasons. Any challenger breaking cover in the run-up to a possible war and local elections would get it in the neck from ordinary members, who, if a survey of them published on 23 February in the *Sunday Times* was anything to go by, were lukewarm about a contest and overwhelmingly supportive of sticking with the Party's core values rather than embracing a modernizing agenda. In such a context, even MPs might vote to give Duncan Smith the benefit of the doubt and, under the rules, he would then be safe from the prospect of another challenge for a whole year. Institutional considerations aside, the two individuals most widely tipped as challengers also had good cause to think a longer game might benefit them. Davis was unsure he had enough support in the parliamentary party to make it through to the membership ballot he thought he could win, and was also increasingly convinced that it might be better to avoid having to lead the Tories into an election that was in all probability already lost. Clarke was unlikely to make a move unless and until it became obvious to the Party that, notwithstanding his pro-European stance, he was its only realistic chance of avoiding electoral meltdown. Moreover, he was well aware that, as one of only 13 Tory MPs who voted against war with Iraq at the end of February and one of only 18 who opposed an attack on the eve of the invasion in March, he had put himself even further (and possibly permanently) offside with most of those whose support he would need.

Going into the Tories' 2003 Spring Forum, then, Duncan Smith had yet another breathing space. Clearly influenced by one of his advisers, Tim Montgomerie, founder of the Conservative Christian Fellowship and soon to be appointed his Political Secretary, Duncan Smith talked of 'the and theory of politics': it was possible, he argued, to present voters both tough and tender, policies that would help the vulnerable but also crack down on crime and asylum and provide 'fairness for the backbone of this country' – the hard-working, hard-pressed middle classes who would, it was hoped, be tempted by the signature offer of a subsidy for private healthcare to be called the 'patient's passport'. For the minority of Tory MPs who attended, probably of more import was the C-Change meeting (attended by Portillo and MacGregor) at which Andrew Cooper, formerly of Central Office but now of Populus, the polling company, told his audience that an election held tomorrow would see four members of the Shadow Cabinet lose their seats to Liberal Democrats. This sobering thought, modernizers hoped, might grab the attention of a party that, in their opinion, still failed to grasp how much it needed to change in order to have any chance of challenging Labour. Indeed, so concerned was Cooper that in February 2003, together with the modernizing Tory journalist Michael Gove, he had put together a presentation packed with polling evidence intended to shake the Party out of its complacency and took it round the country.[83] This C-Change 'roadshow' not only laid open the facts but also provided a roadmap back to political success that was in effect the next stage on from the recommendations Cooper had delivered to Hague back in 1998 and 1999.

To say that Cooper and Gove were prophets crying in the wilderness would be an overstatement. Clearly some people were listening: indeed, their prescription provides a point-by-point prediction of the strategy that David Cameron would employ after winning the leadership in 2005, even if at that stage Cameron didn't 'get it' quite as much as his friend George Osborne, who was likewise involved in prepping Duncan Smith for PMQs.[84] But back in the spring of 2003, most people in the Party had what they saw as much weightier matters on their mind. Having backed the call to go to war, there was little that the Tories could do but share the relief of most of the country as US and British forces blitzkrieged their way to Basra and Baghdad. They also had to watch as support for Blair's performance, like support for military action in general, initially skyrocketed while Labour's lead over the Tories returned to double figures. That said, most Conservatives (along with the media) thought Duncan Smith had had 'a good war', while the run-up to it did much to deflect attention from the denouement of a long-running dispute within the Party over the repeal of Section 28 – one also defused by Duncan Smith this time allowing MPs to abstain if they objected to an attempt (which he and many of the right-wingers on the frontbench supported) to reinstate it.

Out of the woods?

William Hague's leadership had lasted longer than it might have done because he was able, on several occasions, to hang on to, and then point to results in, 'real' elections that supposedly gave the lie to poor opinion poll ratings. So it was no surprise that IDS hoped to pull off the same trick at the local elections in the spring of 2003, primarily by depressing expectations so that even a very average result could be spun as surprisingly good. For a few months the estimated gains given out by Central Office were laughably low (as low as 30 out of 10,000 seats being contested), but by the beginning of April the Party settled on a figure of between 200 and 400. In the event, the Conservatives performed, if not spectacularly, then at least in a manner which could be spun as respectable progress. On a notional share of the national vote of 35 per cent compared to Labour's truly woeful 30 per cent, they made gains of around 600 seats, becoming for the first time in years the largest party in local government. There were, however, some worrying losses, particularly for certain key individuals – Shepway Council, the boundaries of which matched Michael Howard's Folkestone and Hythe constituency, fell to the Liberal Democrats, for example. Duncan Smith's talk of a 'spectacular' victory also ignored the worrying news that the Lib Dems polled around 30 per cent, even if their share did not translate into seats because (and this was comforting) it increased most in safe Labour seats. And it ignored the fact – also conveniently forgotten under William Hague – that little could be extrapolated from such a low turnout. Moreover, the Conservatives' performance at the devolved elections in Scotland and Wales suggested they were far from making a serious comeback.

Nevertheless, the results were enough to stymie an immediate leadership challenge, particularly when the post-election opinion polls suggested that the Tories, without rising much on their own account, were within touching distance of the government. The latter, after all, was in serious trouble over Iraq as it became increasingly evident that no WMD would be found and that the peace would be much harder to win than the war. Blair was also in hot water with his party over plans to give NHS hospitals more autonomy and introduce 'top-up' fees for higher education (both of which the Tories, allowing their enthusiasm for defending the supposedly embattled middle classes to trump their ideological principles, voted against). But Duncan Smith was not out of the woods. His most pressing problem was institutional, but was bound up, too, with individuals and interests. The Party Board was going to insist that Barry Legg, whose role in the Westminster City Council 'Homes for Votes' scandal was now the subject of intense scrutiny, be stripped of the Chief Executive post and a proper appointment process started – a demand that had the support of Conservative Treasurer Stanley Kalms, whose relationship with Duncan Smith had deteriorated markedly as a result of the arguments over Legg's payoff and the near-insolvency of the Party. Neither the fact that Legg was prevailed upon to go quietly after less than 80 days in the post of Chief Executive, nor the fact that Kalms was also eased out, could disguise the reality that the grassroots, or at least their representatives, had forced the hand of the leader in a manner unprecedented in Conservative history.

The local election results and the faintly encouraging opinion polls published in their wake had, for those pushing for change in the Conservative Party, another unfortunate result. The post-election 're-launch', dubbed 'A Fair Deal for Everyone', was designed to show that the Party had not forgotten about 'the vulnerable', even if it believed that both they and the middle-class 'backbone of Britain' would be better served by freeing them from dependence on the state and encouraging 'civil society' to undertake some of its functions. This, in the supposedly trendy lower case lettering on the backdrop behind Duncan Smith, would apparently deliver '. . . opportunity and hope and value and potential and service and prosperity and public services and community and reassurance and opportunity . . .'. The same went for a high-profile restatement of the party's commitment to the inner cities made in late June and to drug rehabilitation schemes in July. Behind the scenes, however, Duncan Smith and many of his advisers were convinced that the apparent uptick in the Party's fortunes must have had something to do with his Christmas and New Year initiatives on tax, crime, and, of course, asylum and immigration.[85] Moreover, he was now tempted to build on that 'success' and play the one card the modernizers had so far managed to persuade him to keep firmly at the bottom of the deck – Europe.

With the exception of one or two very brief forays, Duncan Smith had maintained radio silence on the EU from the moment he took over as leader. True, the topic reminded his party of why they picked him, making it a tempting resort for a leader in trouble. But it also reminded voters of the bad old days under both Major and Hague and distracted from the Party's efforts on other issues. It also brought forth the familiar accusation from Blair that the Conservatives ultimately wanted to get out of the EU altogether – accusations that were difficult to deny given their leader's continued equivocation on the issue.[86] So it came as something of a surprise in early May 2003 when Duncan Smith, hoping to exploit the obvious divisions between Blair and Brown on the issue, suddenly called for an immediate referendum on the euro and then moved on to call for one on the EU's proposed Constitutional Treaty.

This line was predictably (and, for IDS personally, usefully) criticized by Ken Clarke, who, abandoning any lingering hope he had of going for the leadership in the near future, took to the airwaves to indicate his disdain. But, even more predictably, it went down a storm with the party in the media, with the charge led by the *Mail*, which organized a staggeringly large (and presumably fantastically expensive) poll revealing widespread public support.[87] Not to be outdone, the *Telegraph* went on to praise an address made by IDS to Eurosceptic parties in Prague as 'possibly the most coherent Conservative prospectus for Europe since Margaret Thatcher's Bruges speech'.[88]

Amazingly, especially for those who remembered how ineffective and counterproductive an issue Europe had been for Hague, it seemed, just for a while, as if all this (along with the Party's opposition to university tuition fees and its promise to come up with 'a fair deal for drivers' by increasing the speed limit on motorways to 80 mph) might be working. At the end of June 2003, Duncan Smith's favourite pollster, YouGov, put the Tories, on 37 per cent, ahead of Labour, on just 35 – their first lead in any opinion poll (discounting the blip during the fuel crisis in 2000) for 11 years and one that held up in its July poll as well. Meanwhile those around the leader were cheered up by the news that Dougie Smith, one of the organizers of C-Change, Francis Maude's modernizing ginger group, was leading a double life running a business arranging high-class orgies – a revelation that drastically curtailed Tory MPs' willingness to associate their names with the project. In any case, the mood among those MPs as they prepared for the summer recess seemed palpably more positive. And Duncan Smith was even beginning to put in the odd strong performance at PMQs, aided no doubt by the voice and presentation-skills coaches on whom the Party was reported to have lavished a six-figure sum. The only cloud on the horizon – and then only for a prescient and principled minority – was Duncan Smith's calling for and (in a manner of speaking) getting a judicial inquiry into events surrounding the decision to go to war in Iraq.

'Wabbling back to the Fire'

The Hutton inquiry, however, would take time. For a few weeks, it seemed, the Party was on the up and Duncan Smith, whose office talked about 'a tipping point' having been reached, was safe. Apart from Labour making a big comeback in the polls, there was only one thing that the disaffected could think of that could still lead to his removal before a general election, namely a big by-election defeat by the Lib Dems in a safe Tory seat. Unfortunately such an event had stubbornly refused to materialize, and few were investing much hope in a contest that had just been called in the Brent East constituency of a Labour MP who had died in June. It looked, then, as if they were finally going to reconcile themselves to making the best of a bad job even if (as was the case when Health Spokesman Liam Fox demanded that all immigrants be tested for HIV and TB and Duncan Smith himself let fly once again on asylum) it involved having to stand idly by as the leader and his lieutenants reverted now and then to tabloid-pleasing type.[89]

There was, though, one other possibility – a reshuffle, which, if as badly botched as his first, could cause both backbenchers and frontbenchers to turn against Duncan Smith. Few dared hope, however, that even he was that foolish. Yet their hopes were soon raised when ill-advised briefing from the Leader's Office suggested, once again, that he was thinking of moving Theresa May out of the Chairmanship and Michael Howard away from the Treasury brief. Moving May was not going to be as costless as some thought: the rumours prompted leaks about strained relationships between Central Office and Duncan Smith's team which allowed opponents of the latter to re-create the (hardly inaccurate) impression that, as one anonymous source put it, 'The whole thing is a shambles.' [90] Meanwhile, moving Howard could only mean one thing – that IDS was concerned about being outshone by a man whose name had, since the New Year, increasingly come to be mentioned (not without encouragement, some claimed) as a possible successor. Such a strike would be so transparent as to make it terribly risky. This was highlighted almost as soon as the idea was mooted when Howard appeared on TV to opine that, notwithstanding another YouGov poll putting the Party four points ahead of Labour, 'we need to be much further ahead'. It became even more apparent when the *Telegraph* suddenly opened up its letter pages to correspondents wondering 'Should he stay or should he go?' – 'an astonishing development,' wrote one columnist, 'akin to *L'Osservatore Romano*, the semi-official Vatican newspaper, encouraging a debate on "the Pope, is he really that infallible?"' [91]

Given the risks, Duncan Smith sensibly decided against a reshuffle. Rather less sensibly, he decided that the Party should adopt a relatively low profile over August, thereby prompting predictable criticism that he was doing nothing beyond allowing Labour to stew in its own juices: 'Where on earth are the Tories?' asked a frustrated *Mail* at the beginning of September. Worse, the first polls to come out after the summer break suggested that Labour had regained its lead (if indeed it had ever really lost it). Equally worrying were signs that Duncan Smith's internal enemies were beginning to build up the Brent East by-election into a test of how far the Party had really come – just as it was becoming apparent that the Lib Dems' decision to pour resources into the seat, in which they finished a very poor third at the general election, might pay off. The Tory candidate, a local Asian woman and a nurse, should have been the candidate of every Tory modernizer's dreams, but she was proving a big disappointment. Unfortunately, however, the Party was preoccupied with its new big idea, 'a decentralized state' that would 'trust the people', set out in a policy document called *Total Politics* – although quite how this was supposed to set the public's pulses racing was anyone's guess. Meanwhile, IDS, though he did visit Brent, was busy trying to make up for his quiet summer by calling loudly and repeatedly for the resignation of Defence Secretary Geoff Hoon, as well as Tony Blair, over the manipulation of intelligence in the run-up to the Iraq war.

When the Shadow Cabinet gathered at its now traditional pre-Conference get-together in Buckinghamshire in the week before the by-election, then, any confidence that its members may have been able to summon up before the summer recess had evaporated. Lynton Crosby was flown in from Australia to explain how the rather humdrum John Howard had been able to beat the much slicker Paul Keating in 1996. But few believed they could repeat the trick under Duncan Smith. And worryingly for IDS, some of his so-called 'colleagues' were obviously doing nothing to stop their boosters in the Commons briefing journalists that a bad result in Brent East would trigger a leadership crisis. Certainly only a handful put any faith in an upcoming conference on 'Compassionate Conservatism' being the launch-pad for a successful autumn. This was especially the case after Duncan Smith's keynote speech suffered a pre-emptive surgical strike from Portillo, who turned up on a Sunday morning sofa TV show to note, not unreasonably, that, though 'the Conservatives have now fully recognized what it is that interests people', there was 'still a hankering to talk about the old agenda and maybe still a lack of complete conviction about talking about the new agenda'. Certainly there was a striking disconnect between Duncan Smith's claim at the conference that he had 'refocused' his party's attention onto 'Britain's left-behind communities' and the fact that it looked like doing pretty badly in Brent, a prototypical inner-city constituency.

In fact, the Conservatives did worse than pretty badly, suffering a defeat with implications not only for the Party as a whole but, just as importantly, some key individuals. To borrow from the *Mirror*'s headline on the morning after the night before, the Labour Party was humiliated, but the Tories were annihilated. The Lib Dems, who had picked up a paltry 11 per cent of the vote in 2001, took the seat from the government with a share of almost 40 per cent on a swing of nearly 30 per cent achieved by a lethal combination of hard work, supreme opportunism, a highly personable young candidate, and both apathy and anti-war feeling among government supporters. That the Tories took just 16 per cent, down from 18 per cent in 2001, in a constituency in which they had won 37 per cent of the vote in 1992 mattered less than the fact that they were beaten into third place by 'the yellow peril'. As many Tories at Westminster knew only too well, only three of the 50 Lib Dem targets at the next election were held by Labour MPs. And the *Sunday Express* piled on the pressure with a post-Brent poll that purported to show that 'even with a swing in key seats to the Liberal Democrats just half as big as last Thursday's, . . . 13 members of the Shadow Cabinet would be out of a job'.[92] The list of names it helpfully provided included both men (Howard and Davis) who by that stage were best placed to take over if IDS were dumped, plus the Chief Whip, the Party Chairman, and one or two MPs whose hopes of becoming leader some time in the future were not utterly unrealistic.

Some in the party in the media were keen to blame the woman the *Mail* referred to as 'the deeply unimpressive party chairman, Theresa May', for the poor result. But for most this was a pathetic attempt at deflecting responsibility from the real problem. A *Telegraph* leader spoke for many Tories at Westminster and beyond when it cited the lack of 'flair' shown by Duncan Smith as the main reason for why the Conservatives had ceased not only to be the natural party of government but the natural party of opposition as well.[93] This tendency to blame the individual is understandable and not wholly misguided, but it misses so much, underplaying not just institutional constraints but also the ideological realities that many in the Party were still seemingly incapable of facing. Survey research indicated that the Conservatives' attempts to signal change, partly because they were continually undermined by a tendency under pressure to revert to Thatcherite type, had confused voters – but they didn't seem to have fooled them.

Detailed polling by Populus, released at the start of the party conference season but conducted before Brent East, revealed that not only did the majority of respondents not trust the Conservatives to run the country, or even to cut taxes, they also failed to detect any sign that they had changed for the better since 1997. Nor did they think they were any more centrist. Asked to place themselves and the parties on a left–right scale running from one to ten, 46 per cent put themselves dead centre on five, with 25 per cent claiming to be to the right and 20 per cent to the left. The average was 5.17. When it came to the two main parties, voters placed Labour at 4.94, some 0.23 points from the average voter. They placed the Tories at 6.21, some 1.04 points from the average voter. Interestingly, when it came to so-called 'swing' or 'floating' voters who confessed that they may well change their minds before the next election, the gap between the average self-placement (4.95) and where they put the Tories (6.18) was, if anything slightly bigger (1.23 points), with Labour (which they located at 5.10) only 0.16 points away and, significantly, located to their right.[94]

The same was true, indeed slightly more so, for AB voters from the professional and managerial classes, who put themselves at 5.11, Labour at 5.13, and the Tories at 6.78. Support for the Conservatives among this social group was running at only 29 per cent, well down from the estimated 56 per cent who had backed them in 1992. It was this figure that particularly worried modernizers. Indeed it was one of their guiding principles that the Party could not construct a winning electoral coalition without majority support from this expanding part of the population – people who, especially in the younger age groups, were as concerned with quality of life as standard of living, were liberal on moral issues, and more relaxed than most about Europe and immigration, the benefits of which they felt more than other social groups. Unless people like this could feel good about voting Conservative, unless the Party could pass what one modernizing commentator called 'the dinner-party test', then it would never recover.[95] Moreover, as a few fellow modernizers had at last begun to realize, being nice to gays and ethnic minorities wasn't going to be enough.

Although both Clarke and Lansley (who had moved an awfully long way since his days working under Hague) pleaded on the Conference fringe for an end to talk of tax cuts so the Party could focus on regaining trust on health and education, this more general argument was made most eloquently by a less high-profile MP who had voluntarily confined himself to the backbenches. In a newspaper article published mid-Conference, Nick Gibb argued:

> The whole thrust of Conservative policy development since 1997 gives the impression that our thinking ceased in the 80s. We remain fixated by the internal market and privatisation. Privatisation turned round Britain's failing, uncompetitive nationalised industries in the 80s, but it is not the solution the public are looking for when it comes to education, health or the fight against crime.
>
> The answer to the problems in the public services is not for politicians to wash their hands and leave it all to the invisible hand of the market, or gradually let some patients and parents exercise choice. The answer is for politicians to face up to the responsibilities they have to ensure that schools, hospitals and the criminal justice system are properly managed and deliver high quality services to all.
>
> . . . Our party needs to develop a new agenda for the state, for how it would run public services within the state sector more successfully. It's no good putting our hands up and saying the state can never run education or health properly. If that's our view then we become irrelevant in an election which is about electing a group of people to ensure that those state sector services are properly run.[96]

Typically, however, there was little or no appetite among the delegates for this deeper debate – the one that, arguably, the Party should have started in 1997, if not before. Previously it had been crowded out by arguments between socially liberal modernizers and authoritarian traditionalists, or simply suffocated by the Thatcherite consensus. This time, it was buried not just by speculation over Duncan Smith's position but by a scandal supposedly got up by those bent on getting rid of him.

Of the party in the media, even the most charitable were billing Conference as Duncan Smith's last chance: it was 'make-or-break', 'do-or-die' time. Others – sometimes more in sorrow than in anger – were insisting that a leader who was 'simply not up to it' would have to go.[97] Successors were also being touted, most commonly now Michael Howard. The Shadow Chancellor not only openly contradicted his leader's now apparently firm commitment to tax cuts but was joined on stage by his famously attractive wife as he acknowledged the applause that followed his speech to Conference – something only supposed to happen to leaders. Indeed, it was even said that Blackpool was basically about checking with the grassroots before MPs installed Howard as a stop-gap. Meanwhile, a bizarrely testosterone-fuelled interview given by Duncan Smith to the *Telegraph* on the eve of the Conference alarmed rather than reassured those travelling up to Blackpool.[98]

As the Conference delegates gathered, the media at last took the plunge into a story that had been doing the rounds at Westminster concerning Duncan Smith using his parliamentary allowance to employ his wife Betsy in a secretarial capacity for over a year after he became leader – a post that afforded him unlimited administrative and clerical support from the Party. Despite the Tory leader's public threat to sue, this, plus the disagreement with Howard, a swathe of depressing pre-Conference polls, and tales of plots to unseat the Tory leader before Christmas, suggested that things really were beginning to slide away from IDS. He had won and retained the leadership because no-one else, it seemed, could do better. Now the Party seemed to have reached the conclusion that no-one could do any worse. Nothing would happen at Conference, confided MPs to journalists, but on their return to Westminster, knowing now that their frustrations were shared by many ordinary members, they would gather sufficient signatures to persuade Duncan Smith to 'do the decent thing' or, if he didn't, to force a vote of no-confidence. Just in case any MPs were still worried about incurring the wrath of the grassroots by triggering a contest, it was also made clear that their names (in theory at least) need never be publicly revealed. In any case, a YouGov poll of Conservative members showed most of them believed the Party had made a mistake in electing Duncan Smith and almost half thought he should be replaced right away.

The Tory leader's only chance, it seemed, was to take the Conference by storm in his closing speech. Pulling off a trick like that, however, was always going to be hard for a poor public speaker like IDS. And his task was made all the more difficult by Blair – the benchmark for many Tory MPs – managing during Labour's Conference the week before to triumph over what everyone had predicted would be his most hostile audience ever. In the event, the Tory leader's speech – best remembered for the line 'the Quiet Man is here to stay and he's turning up the volume' – was a hyperbolic rant. Blair and his government were several times branded 'liars' and 'corrupt'. The word 'anger' appeared again and again. And references to recently launched and re-launched policies on public services and pensions were drowned out by tub-thumping stuff on crime, immigration, and, in particular, tax and Europe, provoking Michael Gove (still a journalist but shortly to become a Tory candidate) cruelly to recall Kipling's lines: 'The Dog returns to his Vomit and the Sow returns to her Mire, And the burnt Fool's bandaged finger goes wabbling back to the Fire.' [99]

In the Conference hall, the speech earned Duncan Smith 17 patently stage-managed standing ovations, including eight minutes' worth of applause at the end. But it was painful, excruciating, peevish, even pathetic. Moreover, it clearly wasn't going to be enough to save him, notwithstanding a poll rushed out by YouGov that contrived to show the Tories galloping ahead of Labour and people warming to IDS. Within hours of his finishing, Chief Whip David Maclean was on the BBC with a message for the plotters that, far from being the put-down some took it to be, was effectively a come-on. 'My message', he declared, 'is simply this: on Monday go to Michael Spicer [Chairman of the 1922 Committee] with your 25 letters and we can lance the boil that way.'

Endgame

As MPs returned to Westminster, it became obvious that Duncan Smith was not going to be able to contain what, with crushing inevitability, came to be called Betsygate, especially once the Parliamentary Commissioner for Standards announced he would be launching an inquiry. Some blamed the modernizing former Chief Executive Mark MacGregor. But one of those at the eye of the storm, Vanessa Gearson, could not simply be written off as a disgruntled or mischievous ex-employee.

Yes, she had served as Chief of Staff to IDS, but she was now Deputy Director of Organization and Campaigns at Central Office, as well as a Conservative parliamentary candidate, and therefore quite well known to many Tory activists. Meanwhile, Duncan Smith's threat to sue failed to translate into legal action, leading many to jump far too quickly to the conclusion that there must be some truth in the allegations. At the very least, the whole thing hinted at a private office that was chronically chaotic. The final straw for many MPs, however, was the Tory leader's intemperate reaction when questioned about the affair in a number of television appearances – performances that seemed to confirm once and for all that he lacked whatever qualities were needed to lead Her Majesty's Opposition, let alone to be Prime Minister.

Smelling blood, Duncan Smith's most determined critics closed in for the kill. For the majority of Tory MPs, however, the obstacles – institutional and individual – that had prevented his removal for nearly a year now still seemed daunting. The membership as a whole had elected him and had the right to elect any successor. Many, though not necessarily all, of those members (as shown in a survey by the *Times* of 80 chairmen in the Party's most marginal and most winnable constituencies) had a residual loyalty to their leader – one shared, it seemed, by those at the very top of the voluntary party, two of whom, Don Porter and Raymond Monbiot (President and Chairman of the National Convention), wrote to the *Telegraph* to dismiss calls for a contest. This loyalty might result in a backlash against any MP discovered to be among the 25 needed to trigger a vote of no-confidence, particularly in the (admittedly unlikely) event that Duncan Smith survived it. It was therefore proving difficult to reach that magic number, even though it became apparent that the total could be reached cumulatively via individual letters to Michael Spicer, Chairman of the 1922, rather than by presenting him with a round robin. What made it even harder was the fear that a vote which ended in Duncan Smith's removal would lead to a leadership contest which could (a) drag on for months and (b) result in the membership choosing, once again, an MP (David Davis?) who did not command the support and trust of most of his colleagues.

Fortunately for Duncan Smith's opponents, Conservative MPs were not the only key players who by this stage had decided something had to be done. They were joined by men who were – perhaps characteristically

– less concerned with the institutional niceties and the individual considerations that made change so tricky to achieve. The Conservative Party supposedly promotes the interests of industrial and especially finance capital.[100] Yet only rarely do representatives of those interests feel the need to intervene personally, let alone publicly, in its affairs. The removal of Iain Duncan Smith, however, was one of those occasions in Tory history where money talked rather than simply whispered, and where people listened and acted, at least in part, on its advice.

Relatively speaking, the Party was not in financial trouble under IDS. Things had been worse under Major and Hague, and Labour was finding it even harder to raise funds. The Conservative Party had an estimated 50,000 members (out of a total of over 330,000) who now paid their subscriptions direct to Central Office rather than to their constituency association. Equally significantly (if rather embarrassingly for a party supposedly so hostile to state featherbedding) it could also rely annually on around £4 million of taxpayer subsidies provided for its parliamentary work and for its policy activities. It had also reduced its bank overdraft, thereby cutting interest payments. Underneath these apparently healthy figures, however, there was a problem. An increasing proportion of the Party's income was coming not from donations but from loans which were not always interest-free and which, theoretically at least, would have to be repaid. The Party was also finding it very difficult, as always, to cut its expenditure to match its income. Moreover, donations were beginning to drop off as donors began to despair of serious progress in overhauling Labour. Very few of them, however, were outwardly critical of the Party: merchant banker Robert Fleming, who gave over £200,000 to the Party in 2002, and who in December of that year publicly expressed his dissatisfaction with the leadership, was the exception who proved the rule. Most of those who shared his feelings simply gave less or stopped giving altogether.

By the autumn of 2003, it was common knowledge that the Party's two former Treasurers, Michael Ashcroft and Stanley Kalms, had drastically reduced their financial aid, though neither had chosen to criticize Duncan Smith publicly. Indeed, Ashcroft had stuck up for the Tory leader, admitting, however, that there was some unhappiness among donors, many of whom were also understood to have a low opinion of David Davis based on their contact with him during his time as

Chairman. On the other hand, the effort put into drumming up loans by Kalms' successor as Treasurer, George Magan, meant that the Party was far from imminent collapse. However, with an election looming, it was clear to most MPs – even to those who took no more than a cursory interest in the Party's finances – that, unless a new and unexpected source of finance came along, the Party was going to need to bring its former donors back on board.

On 22 October, these money men, whom Duncan Smith had never exactly gone out of his way to butter up, made their move. Speaking on BBC radio's agenda-setting *Today* programme, the spread-betting tycoon Stuart Wheeler, who had famously given £5 million to the Tories under Hague, declared that previous donors were unwilling to give 'a sausage' to the Party in the current circumstances and that 'the case for changing the leader' was now overwhelming: he was 'weak', 'terribly bad at communicating', and simply not a potential Prime Minister. Without explicitly threatening to withhold his money, Wheeler made it obvious that none would be forthcoming until Tory MPs took action. It was therefore 'almost their duty to have these 25 letters and get the thing going', although he confessed it would be 'desirable, if possible, that a change . . . be made without a battle'.

The only way to do this – and it had been obvious for months now – was for the Party at Westminster to agree on just one candidate, thereby avoiding a membership ballot. And it had been obvious for weeks now that the only possible contender for such a role was Michael Howard. Although the latest opinion poll taken by ICM suggested that 26 per cent of people would be less likely to vote Conservative with him as leader and that only 19 per cent would be more likely to do so (figures that were only marginally better than those for Davis), many Tory MPs, irrespective of their ideological leanings, had come to believe that his experience, authority, and parliamentary ability would at least 'stop the rot'. What was needed now was someone who, though he might not inspire affection, would at least engender respect rather than ridicule.

Tory MPs were therefore heartened by the findings of a Populus focus group for the *Times* – now utterly implacable in its desire to see Duncan Smith gone. None of the other likely contenders rated with the participants, either before or after they were shown clips of them; Howard was not only recognized by some of the group, he was also taken seriously. The fact that he was older than the competition was not mentioned by those taking part, and among MPs the fact that Howard was 62 was not seen as a hindrance. Indeed, for those who did not share his right-wing views it was a positive advantage: he could lead the Party to a respectable defeat at the next election and then be replaced once they could agree on a younger standard bearer. David Davis, who was anyway widely disliked and distrusted, was 54 and would therefore have a better claim to be allowed to stay on if he could improve on the Conservatives' showing at the last election. Howard's right-wing views would also help to win over the grassroots members, who might otherwise resent Duncan Smith's passing and perhaps hanker after Davis.

Although Howard's fans in the parliamentary party began to canvass their colleagues, the man himself, as was his wont and knowing (à la Heseltine) that 'he who wields the knife never wears the crown', played the straightest of straight bats in public. Indeed, even as fellow MPs were approaching him as the best, if not the only, man who could bring a sense of discipline and authority back to the Party, he toured broadcast media studios to call for loyalty to the leader.[101] In those same studios, however, Wheeler's message was effectively reinforced by Michael Ashcroft, who told the BBC that he and Wheeler could hardly be expected to give anything to 'a gaggle of squabbling losers' but that the money would flow once 'unity of purpose' was achieved. In private, Ashcroft then met with Howard, at the latter's invitation.[102] In public, his line was endorsed over the next few days by other millionaire donors like John Madejski, Tom Cowie, Irvine Laidlaw, and Michael Bishop.

Key parliamentary players were now breaking cover too. David Maclean, the Chief Whip, had worked with Michael Howard for several years at the Home Office and had run his leadership campaign in 1997. In 2001, when Howard did not stand, he had decided to take an active role in Duncan Smith's leadership bid and had genuinely hoped that he would turn the Party's fortunes around. But he had been disillusioned for months, was concerned about his seat, and was actively seeking the views of discontented MPs.[103] Maclean held a meeting with Duncan Smith to inform him that support was draining away and that he would almost certainly face a vote unless he resigned. Then, in a highly unusual move, he appeared in the media effectively to confirm that such a meeting had taken place. At a meeting of the Shadow Cabinet later that day, Duncan

Smith, who had put in another underwhelming performance at PMQs, made it clear that he would have to be voted out rather than go quietly. Inevitably news of his remarks leaked immediately, forcing a number of MPs, who had hoped he might be prevailed upon to fall on his sword, into the realization that they would have to write to Spicer. Remarkably, this was now the advice coming from the Whips' Office, Maclean having decided not only that Duncan Smith would have to go but that he would have to be pushed. In private, one MP who was openly trying to get rid of the Tory leader was approached by a Whip and asked 'Why don't you guys just get on with it?' In public, a statement from the Office stressing its 'total loyalty' to IDS only served to stress how bad things had got.

A weekend survey of 120 constituency chairmen by the BBC revealed that three-quarters of them were professing confidence in Duncan Smith. But it was too late. Long-term critic (and Davis supporter) Derek Conway had gone public with his letter to the Chairman of the 1922 and urged others to follow him. Unwisely, the Tory leader issued a back-me-or-sack-me statement. By suggesting that he would regard any failure to muster 25 signatories by Wednesday 29 October as a mandate to carry on until the next election – something he had no right to do – he may well have encouraged some waverers to heed Conway's call. By Tuesday afternoon, although only two more (Francis Maude and John Greenway) had gone public with their intentions, 41 MPs had written to Michael Spicer to trigger a confidence vote.

On the morning of the vote, the *Times* carried an article by Duncan Smith pleading for his MPs' support. That the main argument he made for being kept on was a negative one – to avoid another leadership contest – only served to remind his colleagues how few positive reasons there were for sticking with him. And his assurance that his conversations with backbenchers over the last few days had left him with 'a deeper understanding of the shortcomings of the past two years, and of what needs to be done to address them', simply reinforced how long he had already had to get it right, as well as how out of touch and incapable of improving he was.[104] The fact that almost the entire frontbench expressed support for a statement backing Duncan Smith from Howard, Davis, Ancram, Letwin, and May made no difference. Everyone knew they were going through the motions.

The result of the vote came through in the early evening: 75 MPs had supported their leader, but 90 had expressed no confidence in him. It was not the humiliation some had feared – possibly because some MPs belonging to one of the parliamentary party's centre-left dining clubs voted for IDS in the vain hope that he might cling on for a few more months, during which time their colleagues would come to see Ken Clarke as the only man who could save them from oblivion. Even so, it was a clear-cut result: Iain Duncan Smith was finished. According to Nick Wood, the man Duncan Smith had appointed as the Party's Head of Media, IDS was, during his tenure as leader, 'often vitriolic about Tory MPs', complaining they were 'idle, selfish, vain and pathologically ambitious' – so much so that 'they were virtually impossible to lead' and 'turned on any leader who failed to deliver the goods pretty much overnight'.[105] The tragedy for the Party was that they had taken so long after turning on IDS to actually get rid of him.

To say that the 777 days Iain Duncan Smith served as the Conservatives' leader were a complete waste of time would be too harsh. He might, ironically, have done the Party some good by being so bad. Off the record, a number of Tory MPs compare him in this regard to Michael Foot, with one of them (who confesses that his attitude at the time was simply to 'put the padlock on the door and wait for better times') even going so far as to thank IDS for so discrediting 'knuckleheaded, bovine, right-wingery' that even those sympathetic to such an approach finally began to wonder whether it would do the trick. More positively, Duncan Smith did begin to point the way, albeit fitfully, towards a concern for the less well-off that would play a part in the repositioning of the Party after the 2005 general election. What he did not do, however, was to put the Tories in a position where they stood any chance whatsoever of winning that election. Worse, he had presided over a party that at times had descended into institutional chaos, a party that was unable to call on the services of many of its most talented individuals, a party that eventually lost the confidence of the economic interests that funded it, and a party whose ideas were still some way away from the preferences of the electorate whose votes it needed to return to power. In so doing, he all but obliged the Conservatives to turn to a politician who was no more likely to help them achieve that aim – at least in the short term – than he was himself.

5

LIKE MOTHS TO A FLAME
MICHAEL HOWARD, 2003–2005

Michael Howard was elected unopposed to the leadership of the Conservative Party on 6 November 2003, his willingness to accept the job not simply a consequence but also a condition of his colleagues' finally getting round to dumping IDS. He had the support of the party in the media, most importantly of the *Telegraph*, the *Mail*, and the *Sun*, whose reliably right-wing columnist Richard Littlejohn helpfully reminded readers that at the Home Office Howard 'cut crime, banged up villains, tackled illegal immigration and put noses out of joint'. Choosing a politician, he suggested, was like hiring a lawyer: 'do you want someone everybody likes, or a ruthless bastard who takes no prisoners?'[1]

Assuming the crown

With IDS out of the way, Michael Howard was able to engineer an immediate show of support from MPs who seemed to embody the widespread backing for him across the parliamentary party – Oliver Letwin (socially liberal), Stephen Dorrell (less Europhile than he once was but still on the centre-left of the Party), and Liam Fox (a Thatcherite who had agreed to be Howard's campaign manager even before the vote of confidence in IDS was held). Within a couple of days of what one of

Howard's supporters called this 'conscious attempt at shock and awe', his team was able to release a list of 89 MPs, from across the Party, pledged to support him, showing he could already command over half of the Tories sitting in parliament. What united them was the need for a leader who could command respect rather than provoke laughter – someone who looked as if he could actually run a government, even if there was little likelihood of him actually being called on to do so. As one brutally honest MP put it, 'Many of us who hate everything Michael Howard stands for politically will back him because we are tired of being embarrassed.'[2]

Howard, though, might not have become leader – at least so quickly – had it not been for the failure to act of the only Tory MP who could possibly have represented a threat to him in the event of a contest spilling out from parliament into the party in the country. David Davis's reasons for not standing are not, however, hard to fathom. For a start, he calculated that he would run a poor second to Howard in any parliamentary voting. This would make it difficult not only to turn things round in a membership ballot but even to justify forcing one when it was so clear that the Party needed to pull together as quickly as possible. By pulling out, even without securing a deal to secure particular Shadow Cabinet posts for himself and his supporters, he hoped to earn the gratitude of relieved colleagues and a reputation for putting the Party first that might stand him in good stead in any contest that took place after a general election. He did not believe, anyway, that the Tories could win that election, and knew that he would need to work hard to maintain the majority of just under 2,000 votes that had already made him a target of what the Lib Dems were calling their 'decapitation' strategy. He also knew that leading the Tories would be difficult for anyone who, like Duncan Smith, had won a majority in the party in the country but had failed to command the clear support of his parliamentary colleagues from the outset. In any case, there was no guarantee that Davis would make it through the parliamentary stage of a contest. Indeed, there may well have been a move among some MPs hostile to him to get Tim Yeo to stand, turning the parliamentary stage into a left–right contest that might well have seen Davis lose out to Howard as the right's candidate while Yeo got enough votes from modernizers to push him into second place.

There was inevitably some concern about a Howard leadership among modernizing Tories and the few remaining MPs on the centre-left. Personally, he was reasonably well liked. He was also given some credit for appearing to understand that the Party had to put maintaining support for public services above calls for tax cuts. For all that, though, his record as a hard-line Home Secretary and a staunch Eurosceptic in the Major government, plus his more recent record in stiffening Duncan Smith's opposition to a more socially liberal Conservatism, did little to suggest that he would make the kind of changes they felt were necessary. It was to address these lingering doubts that Howard gave what effectively became his first speech as leader. Speaking at the Saatchi Gallery, a setting deliberately chosen to emphasize the new rather than the old, and with a text in part drafted by 'the modernizers' moderniser', Francis Maude, Howard gave the by now standard promise (made and swiftly broken by both Hague and Duncan Smith) not to indulge in point-scoring opposition for opposition's sake. He also echoed them word for word by promising there would be 'no no-go areas for a modern Conservative Party' and to 'trust the people'. He also promised, however, to 'look forward not back', by showing, among other things, that the Party understood 'how younger people aspire to live their lives' and that it needed 'to preach a bit less and listen a bit more'.

Some who knew Howard were amazed, if not altogether convinced, by the Saatchi Gallery speech. Even someone heavily involved later confessed himself 'gobsmacked that he bought the whole thing', while another Tory MP commented, 'I rather wonder to this day whether Michael had read it before he made it. As he was reading out, he must have thought "Bloody Hell! Am I really saying this?" because it was so deeply un-Michael.' [3] Yet a careful reading of the speech suggests that rather than saying much that he didn't believe, Howard had (characteristically) chosen his words rather carefully, on this occasion in order to press as many buttons as possible without offering any hostages to fortune. His words, as opposed to the atmospherics, involved no departure from the policies produced under Duncan Smith – policies which most of the Party was still convinced were popular and only waiting to be better sold by a better leader.

Howard may have expressed his intention in his Saatchi speech to 'lead this party from its centre', but it was clear that this did not mean leading it *to the* centre – the political space where the vast majority of voters were located. Indeed, there was enough red meat sprinkled in the salad to provoke one astute observer to wonder whether there wasn't quite a bit of 'dog-whistling' going on – it might have been too subtle to allow modernizers to call him nasty, but there was reassurance enough for right-wingers keen to hear it.[4] Certainly, the new leader's first big interview, with the *Sun*, in which he stressed Europe and asylum as well as his long-term aspiration to deliver tax cuts, suggested to many that he was the same old Michael Howard. This, according to the man himself, might not have been completely accurate, but he was nevertheless constrained in the extent to which he could convincingly reinvent himself:

> I was always a bit torn. I accepted a large part of the modernizers' thesis intellectually. But I had . . . great difficulty putting it into effect fully because I was, after all, very closely associated with the previous Conservative government. . . . Another factor which is crucial in this is that I didn't have much time. . . . Everyone knew there was likely to be an election in 2005.[5]

This was undeniably true, yet it suggests Howard may have underestimated his room for manoeuvre. In the eyes of the overwhelming majority of his colleagues at Westminster, he had, simply by taking over, stopped his Party from becoming 'a laughing stock', prevented 'meltdown', and pulled it 'back from the abyss'. As a result, as one of them put it, 'He could have signed up the Tory Party in 2005 to a programme for the nationalization of steel. He could have led it anywhere. . . . He was the most powerful leader in the modern history of the Tory Party at that moment – by a mile.' The reason he chose not to push that power as far as he might have was ultimately down to ideology. Another Tory MP summed it up perfectly: 'At heart, Michael Howard is a highly capable, but very old-fashioned, strongly right-of-centre Conservative politician who was not well-placed full-heartedly to lead the Party back to the centre ground.'

The Conservatives' euphoria at having ditched Duncan Smith and being led by a 'grown-up' politician blinded them, temporarily at least, to this big disadvantage. Moreover, Howard was not only an instinctive right-winger. He also had baggage: he was a reminder of two of the most unpopular governments in history – Margaret Thatcher's last administration and John Major's attempt to follow on from it – and he was associated with one of the Tories' most catastrophic policy failures, the Poll Tax. 'Grip', 'gravitas', and 'discipline' were at that stage crucial to Conservative MPs but they were not enough for voters. According to ICM, in the first poll published after Howard took over, Labour was on 39 per cent, and the Conservatives on 31 per cent. Next into the field, Populus put the Conservatives on exactly the same figure, and revealed that just over half of all respondents thought changing the leader was unlikely to see them do any better. Two-thirds thought that Howard's role in the Major government made it 'very important for the Tories to show that they [had] really changed' since then. That said, polls taken a few weeks into Howard's leadership suggested the Tories' fortunes were improving and, possibly even more crucially as far as MPs were concerned, that the Liberal Democrat threat was falling away as 'two-party politics' began to reassert itself.

Different men, similar measures

Michael Howard's inheritance was far from golden – as one of his advisers put it in an interview, if the Party had been a dead parrot under Hague, all that was left after Duncan Smith was the cage. Howard's first appointments were to the Leader's Office. As Chief of Staff, he brought in the ultra-experienced Stephen Sherbourne, who had worked briefly for Heath and was Thatcher's Political Secretary between 1983 and 1988. As his own Political Secretary, Howard appointed his special adviser at the Home Office, Rachel Whetstone, who, like Sherbourne, left a position in public relations. Howard then announced he was going to reduce Central Office's existing eleven departments to three: press, research and marketing, with the first overseen by Guy Black, who had worked as a special adviser in the Major government before spending over a decade outside Tory politics. Black would also serve as Howard's Press Secretary – a dual posting deliberately designed to improve coordination between the Leader's Office and Central Office and one in which he would be assisted by George Eustice, formerly of the anti-euro No campaign.[6] The appointment proved a good one. Black, a widely respected operator who, as former Director of the

Press Complaints Commission, knew not only the editors but also the proprietors of all the papers that counted, was almost immediately able (mainly by not playing favourites and doing the basics right) to stop Central Office leaking like a sieve in the way that it had done under IDS.[7]

Conservative Research and Development (appropriating the old abbreviation CRD) was once again to have a life of its own on the grounds that its desk officers, because they had been co-located with press officers, had been too preoccupied with helping the Party's media effort to do much policy work.[8] Greg Clark, Duncan Smith's head of policy, was to be its Director and David Willetts its Chairman, charged not so much with rethinking IDS-era policies as trying to weave them into a more coherent whole. George Bridges, who had served as Assistant Political Secretary to John Major, was later brought in to provide the CRD with a sharper campaigning edge and, according to those who worked there, further improved both its morale and its productivity, measured by the 'political hits' achieved by the ammunition they provide for frontline politicians. Marketing was to be run by Will Harris, formerly an adviser to Tory London mayoral candidate Steve Norris, but who also had extensive experience in commercial branding. The Department would also cover polling as well as advertising and member services. Harris swiftly curtailed the Party's relationship with YouGov, the internet pollster that had provided Iain Duncan Smith with what (to his critics at least) were overly optimistic results in his last year as leader.

Appointing a Shadow Cabinet was of course slightly more difficult. Ken Clarke and William Hague chose not to serve, though, along with Major, they did agree to join an advisory council, which attempted to meet every two or three months.[9] Michael Portillo was offered a post but declined it, announcing he had already decided to stand down at the next election. Short of stars, Howard made a virtue of necessity by reducing the size of the Shadow Cabinet in order to try to make it more of a meaningful directorate of 12. His first decision on its personnel was perhaps the most innovative. Theresa May was replaced by two Co-Chairmen. Veteran ad man Maurice Saatchi would be mainly tasked with 'sorting out' Central Office, which would move out of Smith Square to more modern, less labyrinthine accommodation. Meanwhile,

Howard's campaign manager, IDS's Shadow Health Secretary Liam Fox, would take a front-of-house role communicating with the media and rallying the grassroots. Both were thoroughgoing Thatcherites, although whether that would help them through the inevitable demarcation disputes that splitting the role would involve was another matter.

Similar disputes were also a risk for those tasked with particular portfolios. It was difficult to see, for example, how Tim Yeo, supposedly in charge of both health and education, was going to be able to answer for the Tories on such huge (and hugely important) subjects; but it was equally difficult to know where his responsibility ended and those of the 'Shadow Secretaries', Andrew Lansley (Health) and Tim Collins (Education), began. Moreover, it allowed Labour to argue that the Tories cared so little about two such vital public services that they believed just one man could run them, albeit with the help of two juniors who, it claimed (wrongly in Lansley's case), were still convinced Thatcherites. The presence of David Curry, a pro-European who had resigned in protest at Hague's harder line on the euro, provided some balance, but he was stranded in what some saw as a backwater and given way too much to do in shadowing Local Government (including Housing), the Regions, Northern Ireland, Scotland, and Wales.

Apart from Curry, who anyway stepped down within months, John Bercow, and David Willetts, there was little room made for MPs on the centre-left of the Party and those most associated with modernization. Damian Green, the only clearly centre-left element in Duncan Smith's Shadow Cabinet, was demoted from Education. And, in spite of the useful backing they provided for Howard's leadership bid, Stephen Dorrell and Francis Maude were not brought in, the latter because it was feared that his inclusion (like that of John Maples) might have seen Duncan Smith refuse to go quietly. In fact, most of the latter's overwhelmingly right-wing team were kept on the frontbench, albeit outside the newly slimmed-down Shadow Cabinet. Included in the latter, however, was David Davis, who took on the newly expanded role of Shadow Home Secretary, out of which Oliver Letwin was promoted to Shadow Chancellor in charge of a Treasury team that still included the thoroughgoing Thatcherite Howard Flight. David Maclean, who as Chief Whip had attracted accusations that he had failed to show sufficient loyalty to the outgoing leader, was reappointed to his post, as was Michael

Ancram. All this meant that the ratio of men to women increased (from 27:3 to 12:1) and that Howard's core team could initially only boast one woman, Theresa May, now at Environment and Transport. Things improved slightly in the spring, however, when Caroline Spelman was promoted into the Shadow Cabinet to replace Curry. Lower down the pecking order, this move led to David Cameron's installation as Shadow Spokesman on Local Government Finance, though both he and George Osborne were retained by Howard to help him prepare, just as they had helped IDS prepare, for PMQs.

Howard's first few, highly combative, appearances in that spot suggested that his talk of a more measured and constructive opposition was predictably little more than hot air. Howard knew the importance of commanding the House and was prepared to do whatever it took to do so, especially if it distracted from stories that might otherwise have reflected poorly on his own Party. For example, his much-reported retort to Blair in early December 2003 that 'This grammar school boy is not going to take any lessons from a public schoolboy on the importance of children from less privileged backgrounds gaining access to university' helped bury the bad news that his newly appointed Shadow Chancellor had finally admitted he could not expect to do that job and hang on to his six-figure salary from Rothschild's. The marked contrast in the Commons with the leader they had dumped contributed to the widespread feeling among Tory MPs that they had made the right decision.

Their confidence was confirmed by news that wealthy Tory donors, including those who had helped do for Duncan Smith by signalling their lack of confidence, were coming back on board. Howard announced the formation of a new Conservative Party Foundation that aimed to put the Tories' long-term finances on a firmer footing by hiving off some of their income into a fund that could not be spent on day-to-day expenses or election costs, but almost more important was the impressive list of those fabulously wealthy members of the great and the good who would serve on it.[10] He could also point to large donations coming in from Leonard Steinberg (about to be recommended for a peerage along with two other prominent donors, Stanley Kalms and Irvine Laidlaw) and Stuart Wheeler. Indeed, when figures were released in the New Year by the Electoral Commission, they showed that 94 per cent of the total amount donated to the Party in the final quarter of 2003 came in after Duncan Smith was deposed at the end of October.[11] Clearly, a proportion of this step-change was accounted for by ordinary members responding generously to a letter soliciting their help sent out by Howard when he first took over. Large donations and loans, however, would remain vital because whatever the new leader did for his Party, he did not bring in many, if any, new members.[12]

But while the institutions had been tinkered with, the individuals swapped around, and the interests brought back on board, many of the ideas – or at least the policies – went unaltered. A number of Tory MPs, for example, were hoping for a switch to supporting Tony Blair in his battle against his own backbenchers on university top-up fees, not only on the grounds of parliamentary tactics, but because they regarded Duncan Smith's decision to oppose them as an intellectually indefensible act of opportunism which put the continuation of middle-class subsidies before the long-term viability of UK higher education. As Howard used media interviews to stress the need to cut the number of students on what he called 'Mickey Mouse courses' rather than charge fees, however, it rapidly became clear that no such switch would be forthcoming. The new leader had, in fact, considered one, but decided it would smack of inconsistency, especially when the Party had already dispatched to the nation's universities thousands of Tory coffee mugs imprinted with the Party's pledge to scrap top-up fees, promising there was 'no small print' attached! The same went for health policy. In private, Yeo and Lansley tried to use the Party's own opinion research to persuade Howard to allow them to drop Liam Fox's 'patient's passport', which would involve the government subsidizing the cost of private medical treatment. It was not going to help in practice, they pointed out, and the punters hated it too. To Howard, however, it made ideological sense and getting rid of it would lay him open to charges of inconsistency. So it stayed.

Howard's assumption of the Tory leadership, then, did not mean all the Party's policy problems disappeared, let alone that it would move swiftly to distance itself from either its recent or its ancient past. This applied even where consistency meant the continuation of confusion, as was the case with taxation and spending. When Duncan Smith had been leader and Howard Shadow Chancellor, they had on several occasions appeared to contradict each other as IDS, under the influence of advisers and anxious to shore up his position, had emphasized tax cuts while Howard stressed caution. The only thing they were clearly united on was their decision, in 2002, to scrap the Party's promise to match Labour's spending on health and education, even though to some more centrist Tories the pledge remained a necessary, though not sufficient, condition for neutralizing Labour's massive leads on the issues.

On taking over as leader, Howard had, predictably enough, not renewed the matching pledge: not only did he believe Labour's massive increases were profligate, but evidence was emerging in opinion polls (particularly the internet polling done by YouGov for the *Telegraph*, which was running hard on a supposed middle-class 'tax revolt') that voters, concerned that public services were failing to improve, were beginning to feel hard done by. However, he had once again refused to promise tax cuts, claiming that public services would have to come first. And yet in his first party political broadcast to the nation, Howard stressed the need to do something about taxation, even going so far as to commit the Tories to Maurice Saatchi's gimmick that 'Tax Freedom Day' (the point in the year on which the average taxpayer could be said to stop 'working for the government') should be made a bank holiday. He also argued that there was no necessary contradiction between tax cuts and spending on health and education, since the cuts would increase economic growth, which would then provide a Tory government with more money to spend. This was not necessarily a misleading argument but it was a complex one – and one which, the Party's own opinion research suggested, was going to be difficult to sell to voters, many of whom (especially in the light of Labour's stealth taxes) were sceptical about the ability of either of the main parties to maintain spending at the same time as offering people a genuine cut in taxation. Oliver Letwin, the Shadow Chancellor, on the other hand, sounded a note of caution, telling the *Telegraph* in early December that 'We will not go to the polls at the next election saying that we will reduce the tax bill.' Just hours after he had spoken, however, what the paper called 'senior figures' stepped in to reassure readers that 'There is a belief in the party that we will be able to achieve sensible expenditure savings and use them for attractive, socially responsible reductions in the burden of tax.' [13]

Looking up

Given the evident confusion on tax, it was understandable that the word did not appear in a full-page newspaper advert, also emailed to Party members, which the Tories released on 1 January 2004. Purporting to be Michael Howard's personal political credo, it was written with the help of Jeremy Sinclair, about to become Creative Director at M&C Saatchi, and clearly owed much to Maurice Saatchi's belief that the Tory leader had to present himself as a conviction politician, as well as to John D. Rockefeller, Jr's 1941 'I Believe' declaration printed on a plaque outside the centre which bears his name in New York. The pledges were mocked by some, but praised by others for being authentically conservative in their distrust of the state and its 'armies of interferers', as well as its rejection of the politics of envy and its approval of individual aspiration and national sovereignty. Whatever, it represented fantastic value for money since the discussions that followed it saw it repeated again and again without the Party having to pay a penny in further advertising costs.

The credo provided a platform for a New Year campaign against the government launched by a signed article in the reliably populist *News of the World*, in which Howard solicited readers' contributions to a dedicated interactive website (*www.cutredtape.org*):

> Every time you feel like Victor Meldrew – you 'can't believe' you've just been fined for paying your car tax late because you were ill, that the NHS won't let your sick mother be treated in a hospital near you because it is 'against the rules', that your neighbour won't report a crime because 'there is no point' – then I want to hear from you.[14]

He also announced that he was commissioning the business 'troubleshooter' David James to conduct a review of government waste that would isolate 'unnecessary' spending that might be squeezed in order to finance tax cuts without inflicting hardship on 'frontline' public services. The same distinction was highlighted in another signed newspaper ad trying to show public-sector professionals that they were valued by the Tories but also asking them to send in examples of the profligacy and regulation that supposedly drove them mad. The New Year also saw Howard put himself, Hague-like, onside with populist media campaigns to renew pressure on the government to give homeowners the right to use lethal force against burglars, to blame the Ministry of Defence for failing to provide adequate body armour for British troops, to reverse the government's decision to downgrade cannabis from Class B to Class C, and to get rid of speed cameras, which were supposedly raising cash rather than saving lives.

Howard's authoritative aggression seemed to resonate with voters as well as with the party in the media: by mid-January, his personal rating, as measured by ICM, was +14. This compared very positively both with the -15 enjoyed by the embattled Prime Minister and the -22 IDS had been on just before he was deposed. Some polls even suggested the Tories were now edging ahead of Labour, particularly those conducted by YouGov – the polling company many of IDS's enemies had affected to disbelieve but now seemed more than happy to trust. Buoyed up by these figures, some of the right-wingers Howard had appointed were beginning to make their personal preferences for a return to a more Thatcherite agenda increasingly obvious: Co-Chairman Liam Fox, for instance, made a strong plea in a speech at Central Office in mid-January for a return to Thatcherite principles, or what he dubbed 'liberation Conservatism'. More moderate Conservatives were worried that this was playing into Labour's hands but were wary of rocking the boat so early on.

Indeed, in public, anyway, there was initially only one lone voice raised, albeit implicitly, against the new, more assertively right-wing strategy – and even then it was from a politician who no longer had anything to lose. Writing just after the release of Howard's credo, Michael Portillo set out what was effectively the alternative strategy for the Party and one which, interestingly, now went way beyond the characteristic support by modernizers for socially liberal measures and more representative faces. Instead, it advocated a wholesale move onto the centre ground where, in the absence of a Labour Party so incompetent or so left-wing as to rule itself out as a serious contender, elections, Portillo concluded, had to be fought. In order to do this, he declared, the Party had to demonstrate that it had changed, and this meant more than market-testing policies, more than broadening candidate selection and adopting a less strident, 'Labour-bashing' tone. It also meant waking up to the fact, for example, that just as Labour in opposition had praised the police and the armed forces in order to neutralize the widespread impression that it was 'anti-police' and 'anti-defence', the Tories had to do everything in their power to counter the conviction that they were 'anti-NHS'. Forget the criticisms, the radical reforms; the Party would do better simply 'to parrot how much we love the NHS'. Just as importantly, it should 'do away with the whole debate about cuts in tax and spending' by committing the party to stick to Labour's spending plans on the grounds that 'there's no hope of implementing party policies unless the party is elected, and to be elected it must be trusted'. If arguing all this meant his colleagues would accuse him of 'pushing for an anaemic election manifesto', Portillo pleaded guilty.[15] It was a mark of how semi-detached and powerless he now was that no-one in or close to the leadership even deigned to respond, even if, privately, some of Howard's younger advisers worried that the Party's policy on tax and spending, and the NHS, was simply too complicated and therefore vulnerable to attack.

Not everything, however, was going Howard's way. He had invested heavily in the Hutton Report criticizing Blair, even suggesting the Prime Minister might have to go. But when, at the end of January, Howard and Cameron (who was tasked with tracking the inquiry) finally came to see the full Report, just six hours or so before Hutton delivered his verdict live on TV, they realized that all their work had been for nothing and, worse, that their upping the ante was now bound to backfire. Obliged to accept the Report's conclusions, however, they had chosen to soldier on rather than simply admit defeat, allowing Blair to wipe the floor with his opposite number in the Commons: 'Yesterday [the day the top-up fees legislation squeaked through] was a test of policy . . . and he failed it. Today is a test for his character and he failed that too. What he should understand is being nasty is not the same as being effective, and opportunism is not the same as leadership.' So bad was it that Howard was hissed as he gave his speech and literally booed as he finished it – a surprisingly rare thing even in the cockpit that the Commons becomes on such occasions. All his planned appearances on the media after the debate were cancelled and the next day Howard got his first taste of the kind of off-the-record criticism from colleagues that had become a daily occurrence for his predecessors. The media reaction was even more brutal – especially in the *Sun*, which Howard had done so much to cultivate but which was always going to revel in a Report that found the BBC wanting.

Tory nerves were steadied, however, when opinion polls, far from suggesting Howard had got it wrong, showed most people agreed that Blair was to blame and that many thought he should resign. Even more important for morale, the week after Hutton saw the publication of the first non-internet poll – conducted by NOP for the *Independent* – to put the Tories ahead of Labour (albeit by just 1 per cent) since Howard had taken over from Duncan Smith. It also showed that nearly half those questioned thought Howard was doing a good job. This was a far greater proportion than had said the same of his predecessor, who, a day or so after the poll was published, appeared in 'An Audience with Iain Duncan Smith' at the Liverpool Philharmonic Hall in front of just 63 paying punters and 533 unsold seats. Howard was also given some credit by the party in the media for throwing his support behind a campaign led by the *Express* and the *Mail* which, by focusing on gypsy 'benefit tourists', forced Blair to announce that citizens of the EU's new member states would have their access to UK welfare payments severely restricted.[16] In fact, far from following the logic of its free-market ideology, Howard made it clear that his Party (which under IDS had raised no objections to government plans) now wanted to follow the majority of member states which were not merely limiting benefits to citizens of accession states but shutting them out of their labour markets altogether.

This newly protectionist line was opposed by business groups like the British Chambers of Commerce but did fit with Howard's belief that there was still mileage for the Tories in the immigration issue. He knew it had to be handled carefully, but he also knew he would be helped by the fact that (as he was to stress in a speech on 'the British Dream' in February) he came from a Jewish family that had fled to Britain between the wars – a background that had already been brought up when, just a few weeks after taking over, he had pleasantly surprised many liberals by condemning a draconian plan floated in the Queen's speech that the children of asylum-seekers who refused to return home might be taken into care. Liberals also found it difficult to criticize Howard when, in February, he chose to highlight immigration in a much-trailed visit to

Burnley, scene three years previously of race riots. In a textbook move, Howard attempted to insulate himself from the inevitable accusations that he was 'playing the race card' by stressing his family background and claiming (as Hague and IDS had done) that his main concern was to show voters tempted by extremist outfits like the BNP that the Conservatives – although not of course the government – were committed to addressing their concerns about asylum-seekers and illegal immigrants. Howard also earned the respect of liberals – at least initially – for his swift decision to withdraw the whip from Ann Winterton, the Tory MP who had been sacked by IDS in May 2002 for telling a racist joke, when, just a few days after his trip to Burnley, she refused to apologize for treating an international audience to a gag making light of the recent deaths of 20 Chinese migrant workers in Morecambe Bay.

Howard also hoped that he could similarly finesse Europe. He recognized – at least in the first few months of his leadership – that the Party must not appear obsessed with the issue, however important he felt it to be. Along with an acknowledgement that the Conservatives' de-regulatory, pro-business agenda would be best served by Tory MEPs continuing to belong to a larger party group in Brussels and Strasbourg, this led him to abandon any flirtation with the idea that they should leave the EPP–ED group – much to the chagrin of hard-core Eurosceptics. Labour accusations that the Tories' position on Europe would ultimately end in withdrawal also meant that Howard needed a policy that would reinforce his sceptical credentials at the same time as projecting a more positive vision. This he attempted to do in Berlin in February by flying the idea of a 'made-to-measure' rather than an 'off-the-peg' Europe, whereby states that wished to go further towards federalism be allowed to do so with the quid pro quo that those who wished to repatriate powers be allowed the same freedom. This 'live and let live, flourish and let flourish, . . . modern and mature approach' could be spun as a welcome shift to more Euro-friendly media and voters while being capable of a completely different interpretation in Eurosceptic quarters. Hence, the *Independent* welcomed it as 'notably pragmatic in tone', while over at the *Sun* Howard was a 'Euro crusader' who had 'opened up clear blue water between himself and Tony Blair' by making clear 'his distaste for, and sorrow at, the way Europe is heading'.[17]

Too clever

As exemplified by his much-hyped 'British Dream' speech made at the beginning of February 2004, the new Tory leader thought there was a moral as well as a political case for lower taxes: 'Only when the state is small', he insisted, 'will people be big.' This dovetailed with 'the trust the people' message that Duncan Smith had begun to develop, but actually went further. Under IDS, the notion that the Tories could square their aspirations for tax cuts with their claim to safeguard front-line services by eliminating billions of pounds of waste had to be floated by ideological outriders like Howard Flight. Under the new regime, however, it quickly became part of the standard spiel.

Indeed, a few days after his speech, Howard was standing in front of hundreds of cardboard cut-outs of Sir Humphrey (the Whitehall mandarin from the vintage TV comedy *Yes Minister*) to announce his pledge to freeze civil service recruitment from day one of a Tory government. Then came a media presentation by Oliver Letwin, the Shadow Chancellor. The Tories, he promised, would reduce the state's share of national income from 42 to 40 per cent over six years, thereby freeing up some £35 billion that would otherwise have been spent by the public sector in order to pay down government borrowing and/or (in the long term) reduce taxation. The NHS and education, as well as pensioners (for one year only), would see spending increases, he insisted, but only as part of a reform programme that would see schools and hospitals compete for pupils and patients. Transport, defence, and criminal justice would be the losers, although apparently funds would be found by cutting down on (wouldn't you just know it) bogus asylum-seekers' benefit claims to provide the extra 5,000 police officers whom Howard had promised a few days earlier.

The modesty of Letwin's ambition – this was surely about slowing social democracy rather than slashing and burning – inevitably attracted criticism from those inside the Party who wanted more clear blue water and had been under the impression, especially after listening to, say, Saatchi and Fox, that they were going to get it. But the more immediate political problem with Letwin's move was that it was too clever for its own good. Indeed, it risked looking like a smoke-and-mirrors job, offering something for nothing – a pitch that was routinely rejected by focus groups and impossible to encapsulate in a convincing soundbite. Worse, the £35 billion figure, although it was insufficient to impress those who wanted to seriously shrink the state, could be (and was) easily seized on by Labour as the total worth of a Tory cuts package that could be then set against its 'cost' in terms of doctors, nurses, teachers, soldiers, military hardware, police officers, roads, whatever. Nor was that level of exposure on spending balanced by anything specific on tax cuts: all the pain was there but there was little obvious gain. Then there was the issue of the areas that looked set to lose out – clearly not everyone in the Tory team was reconciled to the new strategy, with those shadowing International Development and Defence going so far as to make their concerns public.

Notwithstanding these arguments, and reservations about Howard's sudden and seemingly opportunistic decision to withdraw Tory support from the Butler inquiry on the use of intelligence in the run-up to the Iraq war, the Party went into its Spring Forum in Harrogate in good heart – and in much bigger numbers, with an estimated turnout of 1,500 compared to the 300 who had trooped up to see IDS the year before. It also travelled north determined to make the most of two controversial policies that had been developed under Duncan Smith, the so-called patients' and pupils' 'passports'. Tim Yeo (despite his private misgivings) now announced that the Party would extend the former scheme to certain chronic conditions and announced that the education voucher, originally limited to parents of pupils in inner cities who wanted to get their children into a better state school or schools set up by parents or charities, would gradually be rolled out to cover the whole country. There were even hints that it might be further extended to allow the voucher to be spent at existing independent schools with fees not far above its estimated worth (around £5,500) – a policy which would have effectively reinstated the 'assisted places' scheme abolished by Labour in 1997 and applied it to all children, not just the academically able. Howard's speech may, in contrast, have been virtually devoid of specific policies but was no less ideological, offering 'a choice between Labour's third-term tax rises and lower taxes under the Conservatives' and claiming it was time '[t]o let the sunshine of choice break through the clouds of state control'.

This went down a treat with most of his audience. But it was also lapped up by Blair and Brown, who were happy to use the latter's post-Harrogate Budget to contrast what they saw as Howard's shift to the right with their claim that they were using the fruits of economic growth (and their own inquiry into waste led by Peter Gershon) to build better public services for the many rather than give away tax cuts to the few. Arguably it was the lack of an immediate post-Budget poll boost for Labour – as well as David Davis's successful campaign to force the resignation of Immigration Minister Beverley Hughes over yet another asylum crisis – which blinded the Conservatives to the long-term logic and proven superiority of the government's strategy. But, just as unforgivably, they also allowed themselves to be distracted by an all-too-familiar but nonetheless fatal attraction.

Moths to a flame

The surprise election, in the wake of the Madrid bombings, of a Socialist government in Spain meant that the EU Constitutional Treaty, which Labour had thought it had kicked into the long grass, was suddenly a live issue once again. Howard could hardly do nothing: this was a serious threat to UK sovereignty and an issue on which Blair stood to lose both public and media support. Accordingly, at the Party's Welsh Conference in April, he launched a petition for a referendum on the Treaty. Speaking at the same conference, the Party's Co-Chairman, Liam Fox, played the nationalist card by wrapping the issue together with the hunting ban and Lords reform to claim that 'Labour are truly the most un-British government we have ever had and Tony Blair has to be the most un-British prime minister we have had.' Fox also made it clear that the Party's internal polling was helping to drive a shift of emphasis away from public services towards immigration, crime, and Europe – the issues Hague had focused on in 2001. 'William', he said, 'had many of the right issues – it was just the wrong election.' 'Politics', he claimed, 'has now shifted.' As a result, it would be 'amateurish' not to focus on immigration, crime, and, of course, Europe, which he claimed was 'roaring up as an issue'. In fact, he promised, the Party was 'going to turn the European elections this summer into a referendum on a referendum.' [18]

Seeking to turn up the volume again on Europe risked a return to territory that did not so much divide the Party now as confirm that underneath it was still obsessed with an issue that to most voters was nowhere near as important as more bread-and-butter concerns. Quite how Fox and others had come away with the impression that this was no longer the case is a mystery. It could not have been, as he claimed, the Party's own survey work. Nick Sparrow, the head of ICM, which had won back the contract to conduct polls and focus group research for the Conservatives, made it perfectly clear that Europe was nowhere near as important to voters as the Party thought it could and should be, and would only cause it grief. Indeed this was one of the factors behind ICM's decision to end its relationship with the Conservatives in April 2004. Sparrow had objected to being instructed, firstly, to ask what in his professional opinion were loaded questions designed to provide the answers the leadership wanted and, secondly, to do more polling and focus groups in the hope of getting different answers to the ones he was already getting.[19]

Like moths to a Thatcherite flame, those around Howard just could not seem to help themselves, no less prone than other Eurosceptic Tories (as Michael Portillo, hardly a Europhile himself, put it) to 'think that Europe is their secret electoral weapon, despite an abundance of evidence that it is their curse'.[20] As a result, they fell into an obvious trap, indeed exactly the same one as they had fallen into over the single currency. Valuing long-term electoral success over short-term political embarrassment, Blair executed a screeching U-turn and agreed to hold a referendum. Howard, on a high having persuaded the *Express* news-papers to come home at last to the Conservatives, could not resist the urge to crow but knew his fox had been shot.

Incredibly, the Tory leader proceeded (though only in private) to flirt with the idea of upping the ante by calling for a referendum on a funda-mental renegotiation of the UK's membership of the EU, but was talked out of it by, among others, Cameron and Whetstone.[21] Going that far would surely have increased rather than reduced a risk that the hand-ful of pro-Europeans left in the Party had been pointing to for some time. By relentlessly associating the EU with all sorts of threats, such as unlimited immigration from Eastern Europe and an end to British control of criminal justice, foreign and defence policy, the Tories were in danger of creating the ideal conditions for a populist party that could claim to have not only the interests of the people at heart but also, in calling for outright withdrawal, the courage of its convictions. Worse, such a party already existed: indeed, evidence increasingly suggested that the UK Independence Party (UKIP) was now better resourced, better funded, and better advised than ever. Moreover, it was soon to be given extra visibility by the recruitment of the outspoken, perma-tanned daytime-TV heart-throb Robert Kilroy-Silk, by opinion polls suggesting it might improve on the 7 per cent it took in the 1999 European elections, and by Michael Howard having to withdraw the whip from four Conservative peers who expressed their support for the party.

For the European elections, of course, it was highly probable (and some would argue quite proper) that the Party would pay a lot of attention to EU issues. Like Hague in 1999, Howard (and the new Head of Campaigns, David Canzini) planned to do well not by turning the contest into a protest vote against a mid-term government but by fighting on European issues that would, it was hoped, mobilize more Conservative than Labour voters. This time, however, the Party's programme, which promised to keep Britain out of 'a country called Europe', was even more sceptical. Along with the claim that they would bring an end to the gravy-train lifestyle enjoyed by many MEPs (which backfired when the Party was forced to drop one of its MEPs who had made unjustified expense claims), the Tories claimed that once in government they would abolish around 25,000 directives, repatriate control of Britain's fisheries, and even hold 'a referendum on any future treaty agreed by the EU which would transfer significant powers from Britain to Brussels'. The Tories also made much of their view that the proposed Constitutional Treaty would hand over control of asylum policy to the EU.

Labour, however, used the European elections as a chance to roadtest its attack on Howard as a throwback associated with the extremes of the eighties and the economic failures of the early nineties, in particular the Poll Tax and 'a million unemployed'. It launched its campaign with a poster picturing Howard, Thatcher, Major, Hague, and Duncan Smith with the slogan 'Britain is working. Don't let the Tories wreck it again.' Its first television broadcast of the campaign featured footage of Poll Tax riots, house repossessions, and Howard in his various ministerial roles, accompanied not by a voiceover but by Simply Red's version of the soul classic 'If You Don't Know Me By Now' – a technique that was to be repeated at the general election a year later, albeit with a change of soundtrack to Barbara Streisand's 'The Way We Were'.

Such a negative, personalized approach was of course condemned by Central Office, which (rightly) suggested that the government, already torn apart by renewed speculation about a leadership challenge, was rattled by recent opinion polls suggesting the Tories were matching or had even overtaken Labour. But those same polls, while suggesting Howard was seen (by men if not by women) to be as good a bet for PM as Blair, also revealed net agreement with the statement that the Tory leader was 'too associated with past Tory governments and their failures to be a credible prime minister' – which is exactly why Labour (which later on in the campaign put out a poster of Howard with the tagline 'Poll Tax. Cuts. Splits on Europe. No Change There Then') had decided to play him the way they did. As Alastair Campbell later put it in an article purporting to give the Tory leader some much-needed strategic advice, 'The key question . . . is whether voters look at Mr Howard and see something better than they have, or better than what he delivered in Government before. It's one of those where to pose the question is to get the answer.'[22]

Labour's other line of criticism against Howard – that he was opportunistic – also risked sticking, not least because it resonated with some on his own side. This became increasingly apparent as the Tory leader grew more determined that his predecessor's support for the war in Iraq should not prevent him (quite reasonably perhaps) from expressing public disquiet on the issue, even to the extent of seeming to distance the Conservatives from a US administration reeling in the wake of revelations about the mistreatment of prisoners in Abu Ghraib.[23] This move – made against the advice of some in Howard's inner circle – was too much for some in the parliamentary party, a number of whom were prepared to criticize him (albeit off the record) in the media for what they regarded as a ham-fisted and even slightly shameful attempt to reposition the Party. Nor did Howard escape criticism from the party in the media, particularly in the *Telegraph*.[24]

As the European elections approached, however, the Conservatives were less concerned about seeking advantages than stemming potential losses. In the third week of May, a YouGov poll suggested that UKIP was set to take nearly 20 per cent of the vote on 10 June. This shocked

all three main parties but the Tories most of all since, as the party closest to UKIP on the ideological spectrum, they were widely thought
likely to suffer worst if it did well. The CRD responded by sending
candidates a 14-page briefing paper on UKIP (leaked to the media)
which belittled the party as a home for 'Little Englanders' and for
'cranks and political gadflies'. Howard's own response was to make a
speech (heavily spun as 'hard-hitting') at the start of June emphasizing
the Tories' Eurosceptic credentials and urging people not to vote for a
party that was on the fringe and lacked the clout to deliver. His attempt,
in so doing, to suggest that the Tories were now the mainstream option
between a Europhile and a Europhobe extreme was potentially a useful
one. However, inasmuch as Howard's words registered with voters at
all, they probably served only to raise UKIP's profile. They also put the
Tory leader in the farcical position of having to deny in media interviews
that any of his MPs backed withdrawal from the EU when it was plain
that some of them did.

Howard, by going so hard on Europe since April, had played with fire
and was now getting burnt. He therefore needed something, anything,
that would deflect attention back to the government. The most obvious candidate for this role was increasing unrest in the road haulage
industry over rising fuel prices – the very same issue that had helped
William Hague to his one and only month of opinion poll leads back in
2000. And, like Hague, Howard seemed prepared to endorse the kind of
action that, had it been perpetrated under a Conservative government
– especially with him as Home Secretary – he would have condemned
outright. Commenting on a possible repeat of the go-slows and block-
ades of 2000 by truck-drivers and farmers, Howard empathized with
their anger and emphasized their right to protest. It was wholly understandable, but it once again played into the hands of opponents (not all
of them outside the Party) determined to portray him as a serial opportunist. As a result of the criticism, Howard made it clear that he did not
support action that prevented people 'going about their business', which
then led the government to level the obvious criticism that the Tory
leader, as on tax and spend, wanted it both ways.

As polling day for the European Parliament elections approached,
Labour pressed on regardless with a campaign that highlighted the consequences of what it claimed (to Letwin's fury) would be Conservative

cuts in health and education – a campaign that barely featured either the Prime Minister or Europe. The Tories, however, could not avoid the latter as they scrambled to avoid UKIP eroding their vote so badly that Howard – who had travelled over 8,000 miles campaigning across the country – risked doing worse than Hague had in 1999. Faced with calls for him to adopt an even more sceptical line, while Europhile ex-ministers like Curry and Taylor talked about their Eurosceptic colleagues reaping what they themselves had sown, Howard chose to remind voters how Margaret Thatcher had been able to say no to Brussels without leaving the EU. The Labour leadership, not for the first time, could hardly believe its luck. It had spent the entire campaign trying to convince the country that Howard, as well as being an opportunist, was a Thatcherite dinosaur, and here he was doing its work for it! Underneath the headline messages that UKIP was going to do well, the opinion polls also suggested that Labour's disciplined, focused, relentlessly negative attack was beginning to pay off. Howard's ratings were beginning to go backwards, and any lead that he had helped give his Party was fast disappearing. Labour was still more trusted on the economy and the NHS, and voters were beginning to sense some improvement in education as well as healthcare.

Local elections were held on the same day in early June as those for the European Parliament, but the results emerged much sooner. On the face of it, they looked reasonably good for the Conservatives. Extrapolating nationally, the Party won 37 per cent of the vote to the government's miserable 26 per cent – a figure so low that Labour was beaten into third place by the Lib Dems. However, there was little genuine cause for celebration, especially when the result was compared with, say, the local elections of 2000, when Hague had won a notional 38 per cent to Labour's 29 per cent only to lose the following year's general election by a landslide. Worse, however, was to come when the European results were announced. True, Labour did appallingly badly, taking just 22.6 per cent of the vote nationally – its lowest share since 1918. The Lib Dems were also disappointed by their 14.9 per cent. But the Tory result – 26.7 per cent of the vote – was 9 per cent down on its performance under William Hague in 1999 and the worst the Party had obtained at a national election since 1832. It was rendered all the more wounding by the fact that UKIP had won 16.1 per cent.

As post-election polls revealed that 45 per cent of UKIP voters had supported the Conservatives in 2001 (as opposed to 20 per cent who had supported Labour), Tory MPs were called to a special post-election meeting. Many feared it would be hijacked by hardline Eurosceptics demanding that the leadership toughen the Party line in order to respond to the UKIP challenge. Bill Cash was already in the media, claiming the result was 'a historic turning point' and calling for the Tories 'to move to a fundamental renegotiation of the treaties' so as to 'save the United Kingdom'. And Ken Clarke, of course, had already weighed in on the other side, warning his Party that to 'start chasing after Robert Kilroy-Silk's vote would be a complete disaster'. Michael Howard, however, had other ideas. Telling his MPs that he was 'not interested in presiding over a debating society', and calling them to show 'self-discipline not self-indulgence', he made it clear European policy would not be changing and announced a mini-reshuffle. Yeo was moved sideways to Transport and Environment to replace May (who was given the new post of Shadow Minister for the Family). His two deputies, Lansley (Health) and Collins (Education), were promoted into the Shadow Cabinet, Howard having decided that his experiment with a small team had not proved a success. Meanwhile, Willetts kept Work and Pensions but handed his role in policy coordination – a job that involved writing the manifesto – to Cameron. Although the latter would formally remain outside the newly expanded Shadow Cabinet, he was now routinely referred to in the media as a rising star – the 'golden boy' of the 2001 intake and, indeed, a future leader.

Right to choose

Anxious to shift the focus from the European elections, Howard then went onto the offensive on policy with a campaign he hoped would simultaneously appease those critics who blamed the losses to UKIP on the Party not delivering enough red meat and those who argued it needed to talk about public services. A big advertising blitz featuring doctors and nurses tied up in red tape accompanied the announce-ment that the Tories had now decided to invest another £49 billion per year by 2009–10 to introduce what Howard called (in a deliberate echo of Thatcher's 'right to buy') 'the right to choose' into health and education – services which, he claimed, were currently 'trapped in a time warp'. In fact, the whole thing was little more than a repackaging and rebranding of Letwin's plans for public spending and the complicated patients' and pupils' passports that had so confused voters, many of whom, Tory focus groups revealed, assumed they were going to be helped to go abroad for better treatment and education. Nor was it well coordinated with Health and Education spokesmen Lansley and Collins, thereby giving the government a golden opportunity to tell the electorate what the Tories were apparently intending to do before they had time to present their plans in their own terms. Blair was left with an open goal at PMQs and, as usual, he took his chance: 'If you want the debate to be, between now and election day, who cares for Britain's National Health Service? . . . come on and have it. . . . We want the NHS better. You want to wreck it.' A few days later, he had sorted his soundbite: the Tories, he claimed, were offering 'not a right to choose, but a right to charge'.

This hurt Howard badly. Not only had he gifted Labour the chance to tap into well-known voter concerns about the Tories' intentions for the NHS, but he risked losing the one big advantage he had over IDS, namely his ability to get the better of Blair in the Commons – something that means little to the electorate but counts an awful lot to the troops at Westminster and beyond. Indeed, for the first time since his misjudged reaction to the Hutton Report, his colleagues were beginning to whisper their concerns to journalists. As is often the case, however, their complaints at this stage were aimed more at those who surrounded (and supposedly isolated) the leader than at the leader himself. In the firing line were 'trust fund Tories' who lived in places like Notting Hill, with one recently promoted MP singled out for particular attention: 'Nobody,' claimed one backbencher, 'disputes that Cameron is a bright young chap. But he and his circle seem to have Howard eating out of their hands. The trouble is that an expensive education does not always instil either common sense or a feel for the concerns of ordinary people' living in 'Middle Britain'.[25]

In view of this, it was somewhat ironic that the Conservatives' relaunched plans for education, which followed hard on the heels of those announced on health, still seemed bent on trying to give everyone the benefit of an expensive education courtesy of the taxpayer. Dissatisfied parents would now be given a voucher worth £5,500 which they could use to get their child into another state school or, as long as the fee charged was no more than the value of the voucher, into private education. According to Collins, this would 'get middle-class parents, who at the moment feel they can only get a decent education by sending their kids to an independent school, back into the state system' – a bizarre claim given that an estimated 93 per cent of children were currently educated by the state and one that suggested the Conservatives were guilty of imagining that everyone else did (or could afford to do) as they did. Likewise, Howard's pledge that selective state grammar schools would 'survive and thrive' suggested, since only 164 out of nearly 3,000 secondaries in England and Wales were grammars, that it was disproportionately concerned with a small (and supposedly fortunate) minority rather than the vast majority of pupils. So while the party in the media loved the repackaged policies, with the *Mail* declaring they might turn out to be 'a real vote winner', many Tory MPs were not so sure, especially after they saw their leader roasted over them by a re-animated Prime Minister: 'The fact is,' sneered Blair as Labour MPs roared him on, 'that where your policies are coherent they are reactionary and divisive. Where they aren't reactionary and divisive they are utterly incoherent.'

In short, Howard was finding, just as Hague and Duncan Smith had found, that there was little point in taking on the government on education and health unless and until the Conservative Party stopped making it so easy for Labour to suggest it was pretending to be able to deliver more for less at the same time as holding on to the 'private good/public bad' attitudes that had supposedly characterized the Tories under Thatcher. Indeed, while those attitudes continued to shine through everything it did and said on public services, any attempt to neutralize Labour's lead on them would not just be in vain but actually counterproductive. Merely talking about the issues voters were most interested in was not the same thing as fighting the government on the centre ground. The problem, though, was ideological: these Thatcherite views were deeply held by the leader and the majority of his parliamentary party, if not necessarily by ordinary members, the bulk of whom were almost certainly reliant on state-provided services. Indeed, instead of stopping the 'right to choose' in its tracks, Letwin and others were allowed to move straight on to the next stage – called (in a straight lift from the Sainsbury's supermarket ad campaign) 'good government costs less'. Worse, many Conservatives continued to believe (and were encouraged by the party in the media to believe) that the government's perceived vulnerability on issues of supposed Tory strength – immigration, crime, tax, and Europe – would see the Party through in the end.

Little wonder, then, that, instead of urging their leader to plough on with public services, many MPs hoped Howard would get back onto Tory territory as soon as decently possible, especially as more and more polls were suggesting that any gains they had made under him had now disappeared and the Party was back to the levels of support it had registered in the darkest days under Duncan Smith. A Populus poll for the *Times* on 6 July might be discounted by right-wingers as a modernizing stitch-up, but it showed that Conservative support, which had run at 34 or 35 per cent in the first six months of Howard's leadership, was now at 29 per cent, with Labour on 33 per cent and Blair (and Brown) easily beating Howard in the 'best Prime Minister' stakes. Even worse, as a clutch of by-elections loomed, the Lib Dems seemed to be creeping back into the mid-twenties.

Howard's response was to ease up on policy for a while and focus on trying to project himself as a personality, not least to counter Labour's caricature of him as the Thatcherite 'Mr Poll Tax' and consummate opportunist. His appearance on BBC Radio Four's *Desert Island Discs* – the chance for a cosy chat to the accompaniment of eight pieces of music chosen by the interviewee – was extensively trailed (and even reviewed) in the media, which played up his fascinating family background under headlines like the *Express*'s 'My family's Nazi death camp hell'. His appearance – along with his glamorous wife, Sandra – on the daytime ITV show *This Morning* was similarly trailed and no less undemanding. The first question (*sic*) from host Fern Britton ('We're so unused to having a British politician with a beautiful and a very supportive and a big positive, er, person to have by your side') was not exactly challenging. But at least it showed the three million who were watching that Howard (apparently a demon at ping-pong but hopeless at DIY) was a human being – and obviously (as the Tory leader himself admitted) a 'very lucky' guy.[26]

'Doing a William' – or an Iain?

Tens of thousands of civil servants who would supposedly lose their jobs to make way for the £1.7 billion of savings offered by Letwin's 'good government costs less' initiative were no doubt already looking forward to the general election, which most commentators assumed would take place in the spring of 2005. The voters of Leicester South and Birmingham Hodge Hill, however, were going to be able to have their say in the summer of 2004. The Conservatives were under no illusions that they could take either seat from Labour but they were desperate not to see a repeat of their disastrous showing in Brent East and therefore poured resources into their campaign. The leadership, via the Chief Whip, David Maclean, and Andrew Mackay, the MP Howard had tasked with ensuring the Party upped its game in by-elections, even demanded that its parliamentarians and candidates spend ten hours or more in each constituency, with Howard himself paying five visits to both. But all was in vain: not only did the Lib Dems leapfrog the Tories to take Leicester South on a 21 per cent swing, they did the same in Hodge Hill, although the even bigger swing of 27 per cent they achieved there was insufficient to prevent Labour winning a narrow victory. The Conservatives, this time without the excuse of a poor campaign, finished third in both seats and with a reduced share of the vote – from 23 to 20 per cent in Leicester and from 20 to 17 per cent in Birmingham. If any Tories still believed, even after the disappointing European elections, that they could still pull things round, then these results crushed the spirit of all but the most optimistic. An NOP poll for the *Sunday Express* conducted on the day after the by-elections put Labour on 37 per cent, the Lib Dems on 24 per cent, and the Tories on 26 per cent.

Desperate times unfortunately prompted desperate measures. Before the by-elections, Howard had put in a well-judged performance in his initial response to the Butler Report on the use of intelligence on Iraq. Speaking to the media the weekend after them, however, he strayed back onto the dangerous territory he had moved into over Hutton – an attempt seemingly to distance the Conservatives from a decision to go to war which, under IDS, they had so clearly favoured, even pushed for. Although insisting he would still have voted for war on other grounds,

Howard revealed that, had he known then what he knew now about the weakness of the case for war, he would not have voted for it.

Howard was trying to satisfy both those in his inner circle who were urging him towards a more robust, almost anti-war stance and those counselling caution. The result was the worst of all worlds. Not only did it do nothing to help embarrassingly strained relations with the US Republicans, it looked too clever by half, allowing Labour once again to shift the debate on the Butler Report away from the government's own very serious shortcomings and onto Howard, now apparently plumbing 'new depths of opportunism and hypocrisy' – a charge which a number of Tory MPs were prepared to concede publicly (though anonymously) was damaging. As Blair put it in another vintage performance, 'The public respect politicians who were for the war, or against the war. But not politicians who were for and against the war in the same newspaper article.' Howard was reduced, as IDS had been a year earlier, to borrowing from Elton John, asking, 'Why is it that for this Prime Minister, sorry seems to be the hardest word?', which contrasted badly with Blair, who was happier copying a rather more successful Tory leader when he suggested the House 'rejoice' that Iraq had been liberated from the tyranny of Saddam. It was brutal but effective – so much so that Nick Robinson, then ITN's political editor, confessed, 'I felt impelled to leap from my ringside seat to jump into the ring and stop the fight'.[27]

The failure to nail Blair on Iraq, plus of course the by-elections and the gloomy opinion polls which followed weeks of sustained emphasis on public services, inevitably led to speculation as to whether Howard should now shift back to the so-called 'Tebbit trinity' of Europe, immigration, and tax, with 'law'n'order' thrown in for good measure.[28] The official line was to scotch suggestions that Howard intended to 'do a William' and push the populist button. At the last PMQs before the recess, however, it was back to the future. All of Howard's allotted questions were used to talk about the government's failure to curb crime, while the Tory leader promised his backbenchers at the 1922's end-of-term meeting that he would be turning up the heat on the issue. The ground was further prepared by the party in the media, starting with the reliably right-wing George Pascoe-Watson of the *Sun* suggesting that, since '[a]ides say Mr Howard is unlikely to beat the PM on the economy, public spending or foreign policy', he should start 'waging a one-man crime war on Mr Blair'.[29]

The summer blitz began in August with a photo-op with Mayor of Middlesbrough Ray Mallon, the former policeman whose forthright views on crime had seen him christened 'Robocop', and continued with a speech that could have been cut-and-pasted from any number of tabloid leaders over the years. 'The distinction between right and wrong has been lost in sociological mumbo jumbo and politically correct nonsense' – a phenomenon which was also, Howard claimed, preventing police officers doing anything about the fact that crime was now so 'out of control . . . that women fear intimidation from hooded youths as they walk home at night [and] couples stay in rather than run the gauntlet of binge drinkers'. By relieving police of the need to record stop-and-searches to allow ethnic monitoring, by increasing their numbers by 40,000, by the ending of the government's early-release tagging scheme, and by beginning a prison-building programme without limit, a Tory government would 'stand up for the silent, law-abiding majority, who play by the rules and pay their dues'. The latter were also promised (at various points during a summer in which Howard and his team were determined not to repeat Duncan Smith's masterly inactivity of the previous year) an end to the 'asylum shambles' and 'the compensation culture' created by the Human Rights Act, and (just in case they had missed anyone with a grievance) help for those objecting to, among other things, wind farms, speed cameras, and mobile phone masts.

The party in the media (which, incidentally, had always objected to the Human Rights Act since it might make it more difficult to pry into people's private lives) was predictably pleased with this return to populist form, especially on crime. To the *Sun*, such initiatives would 'raise a cheer in every decent home in Britain'; the *Telegraph* believed Howard's commonsense policies 'should help reverse the recent decline in Conservative fortunes'; and the *Mail* claimed the Tory leader was 'pushing at an open door' and, '[d]espite the condemnation of the chattering classes, he should turn up the volume.' Whether this was altogether wise, however, was highly arguable. For one thing, Blair could follow Brown in continually asking where the money was going to come from. For another, the Prime Minister had only recently announced a raft of criminal justice measures sold as a commitment to favour victims' rights over those of criminals' and even as an attack on the flipside of the permissive society of the sixties, which was the bugbear of many a traditionalist Tory. 'People', noted Blair in his speech, 'do not want a return to old prejudices and ugly discrimination. But they do want rules, order and proper behaviour. . . . They want a community where the decent law-abiding majority are in charge; where those that play by the rules do well and those that don't get punished.'

Blair's talent for running a Labour government but talking like a Tory politician, his ability to deliver on a centre-left agenda in a style that still resonated with Middle England, if not the media that claimed to represent it, was infuriating. This did little for democracy, perhaps, in the sense that it made it ever harder, polls suggested, for voters to tell the difference between the two parties. Nor, the same surveys showed, did it wipe out the Tories' leads in their traditional areas of strength. But it probably did enough to render them relatively harmless to Labour, which could then rely on lingering suspicions about the Conservatives' intentions towards public services, as well as doubts about their competence, unity, and capacity to understand ordinary people, to see the government through another general election against an opponent that many voters still saw as stuck in the past.[30] The government could also take comfort that voters appeared, at last, to be more willing to believe that its policies on public services – policies increasingly wrapped in the rhetoric of choice and efficiency as well as investment – were beginning to make a difference.

Notting Hill and beyond

For anyone interested in the institutional culture of the Conservative Party and the small world constituted by the individuals who operate in it, however, the summer of 2004 was not simply a time of ideological inertia and the repetition of old mistakes. It provided the first faint glimmer that it might not always be that way. Before Howard could start on his campaign against crime and political correctness, he was obliged to try to control an argument which burst into the open after a newspaper article alleged that Chief Whip David Maclean had been tasked with getting rid of MPs labelled 'bed-blockers' – 'old suntanned faces' who were supposedly failing to pull their weight at Westminster.

Not surprisingly, some of those named reacted furiously. Angriest of all was backbencher Derek Conway, whose willingness to speak out against Duncan Smith's leadership and to champion the cause of his friend David Davis (also accused of performing 'below par') had made him untold enemies. Conway went straight onto the BBC to denounce the whole thing as a setup by what he called 'the Notting Hill Set' – a group identified the previous month by the *Spectator*, which had named David Cameron and Howard's Political Secretary, Rachel Whetstone, part-time Saatchi adviser and former Central Office staffer Steve Hilton, Nick Boles from the modernizing think-tank Policy Exchange, who had achieved a modicum of publicity as one of two openly gay candidates, and the columnists Edward Heathcoat Amory of the *Mail* and Alice Thomson, in whose paper, the *Telegraph*, the 'bed-blocker' story, co-written by her friend George Trefgarne and Jonathan Isaby, appeared.[31] Various follow-up articles named George Osborne, Michael Gove, the modernizing *Times* journalist who had just beaten Hilton to the safe seat of Surrey Heath, Ed Vaizey, a speechwriter for Michael Howard, also selected for a safe seat, and George Bridges, who, following the departure of the Head of Marketing, Will Harris, in the wake of 'right to choose', had become a key figure at Central Office.

Some Tories (and by no means only those hostile to Cameron and co.) claim that this spat shed the first light on what was, in the words of one of them, 'a very well-organized, very well-executed, very professional' take-over of the Party by a clique determined to exploit the essentially patronage-based system that continues to characterize the Conservatives in order to achieve change. Taken as a whole, the group was probably less a tight-knit conspiracy than a number of overlapping circles united by a grudging admiration for Blair and, in some cases, a spell in Central Office in the sometimes dark days of the late eighties and early nineties.[32] The individuals involved were resented by a number of MPs at Westminster because of their supposed influence over the leader – one much exaggerated since, unlike some of his predecessors, he was very much his own man (a chief executive rather than a chairman) and, inasmuch as advisers like Cameron and Whetstone did influence him, it was far more about pulling him back than egging him on. Those in the Notting Hill Set were also resented because of their socially liberal views and their ready access to, and promotion of each other in, the media – efforts which reflected, many suspected (not altogether wrongly), the beginnings of a bid for the leadership after the next election. Alice Thomson, for example, had recently penned an article which, while apparently praising what Michael Howard (helped of course by many of the above-named) had done since he took over, also noted that they were 'desperate for power. It doesn't matter to them that they may have to go through another leader, as the young Tony Blair did, before they get there. They will drag their party back to the top. Their target is not the next general election, but the one after that.'[33]

Anyone looking for clues about how the next-election-but-one might be fought would have done well to read a dispatch by one of the Notting Hill Set from the Republican Convention in New York. The trip was largely billed as an attempt to pour oil on troubled waters (and to secure a version of their sister party's voter identification software) by Co-Chairman Liam Fox. But among those making it was George Osborne. In a newspaper article, Osborne recalled how inspired he had been when, as part of the Hague team, he had seen George Bush recast the Republicans as the party of 'compassionate conservatism' and 'deliberately steered clear of the obsessions of his . . . activists' in favour of 'a conservatism for the 21st century: interested in social problems, not just economic ones; concerned with the vulnerable, not just the well-off; accepting of cultural change; relaxed rather than shrill'. Now Bush's re-election campaign was like 'getting a masterclass in politics' and could teach the Conservatives a thing or two about the importance of projecting optimism about the country's future and about the need, having tossed some red meat to party activists, to focus relentlessly on 'the things the uncommitted voters are interested in: jobs, education, healthcare and security'.[34]

The 'bed-blocker' controversy was not, then, merely a silly-season story of petty jealousy and class-snobbery (inverted or otherwise). It exposed tensions which had existed as soon as, if not before, Howard had taken over. It was just that, in typical Tory fashion, they had been largely suppressed while there was some hope that he might yet improve upon the Party's chances of recovery, only leaking out at the end of June 2004 with the criticisms of the 'trust fund Tories'. These tensions certainly involved individuals. But they also revolved around the Party's policy and strategy in the run-up to the general election and, since that election would almost certainly end in defeat, around who would succeed Howard and the direction in which they would take the Conservatives thereafter.

For the moment, though, Howard was going nowhere – literally and metaphorically. Despite the summer blitz, the polls suggested the Tories were not merely becalmed but doing worse under his leadership than they had been doing at the same point the year before under IDS. Since it was, in his opinion, far too late to row back now even if he had wanted to do so, Howard pressed on, making yet another set-piece speech – inevitably billed as a 'fight back', in which he promised that 'Whenever there is a conflict between political correctness and common sense, I stand firmly on the side of common sense.' Unfortunately, however, this black-and-white view, with all its depressing echoes of the Hague years, could not be extended to the Party itself, some parts of which were behaving in a way that made the leadership wonder whether a little more political correctness might not be such a bad thing. In early September, Howard had to intervene personally to prevent the constituency association in Falmouth from deselecting its candidate, a gay barrister, who had run into trouble by supporting action against some of its members (later dismissed and disqualified) for promoting UKIP – a stand which had seen both him and his family subjected to some pretty vicious homophobic abuse. Howard's intervention proved that he took seriously the need to stamp out discrimination, but the fact that he had to get involved at all (and the sheer nastiness of some of the stuff quoted by the media) indicated that it remained a serious problem for the Party.

Equally serious, but not taken anywhere near as seriously since May's departure as Party Chairman, was the fact that even the limited progress she had made on getting more women into winnable seats had stalled. By the spring of 2004 it had become a standing joke that the Tories' top 20 target seats had selected more men named Philip (three) than women (two) and, as the *Times*' Mary Ann Sieghart sadly reported, only 17 per cent of Conservative candidates were women, compared with 16 per cent at the last election. When the paper returned to the subject in December (with no cooperation, note, from Central Office), it calculated that in the 15 Tory seats where the incumbent was standing down at the next election, only two women had been selected, that is,

7.5 per cent (compared to Labour's 79 per cent in seats where its MPs were retiring). Meanwhile, all of the three women due to stand down were going to be replaced by men. More broadly, of the 31 seats where, in 2001, the Conservatives had finished second and were within five or less percentage points of the winner, only three (or 10 per cent) had chosen women.[35]

Whatever the reason – the fact that constituencies had a stereotypical view of what represented a 'good' candidate, the fact that the men with whom women were competing were more familiar with the process because they were already networked – women were still losing out, especially in winnable seats. And, although the Party's Vice-Chairman for Candidates (a clearly frustrated Trish Morris) was still doing her best, there was little or no interest in the issue at the top of the Party, either from the leader himself or from his two Co-Chairmen. Nor was there any real pressure within the parliamentary party: the only MP to raise the question publicly in the run-up to the election was Julie Kirkbride, concerned that two women candidates in Yorkshire had apparently been hounded out of their seats. If anything, the Party hierarchy paid more attention to isolated incidents of purported racism in candidate selection than to what was the biggest barrier to the Conservative Party looking more like the people it wanted to represent.

'Juices flowing'

Howard, perhaps understandably, had rather more pressing concerns: time was running out and he had to concentrate on trying to hit the government where it hurt. In September, this turned out, with the help of a hysterical media, to be hospital-acquired infections (like the notorious MRSA) – an issue which Howard himself felt particularly strongly about since his mother-in-law had died after catching one, but which the Party's research also showed was a concern for many voters. Suggesting the government had let the problem get worse, and promising that a Conservative government would make controlling these infections a priority, offered a neat way to show the Party cared about the NHS at the same time as criticizing the way the government was apparently strangling it with targets and red tape. After all, the cutting of both (in education as well as health) had become something akin to a Conservative cure-all – a solution for real problems that would simultaneously silence all those awkward questions about how the Party planned to boost spending and cut taxes.

It was in this context that Howard announced that he was rearranging his frontbench. The reshuffled Shadow Cabinet was to contain 17 members, including David Cameron, who would continue in his role as policy coordinator. Further down the food chain, Cameron's close friend George Osborne replaced arch-Thatcherite Howard Flight as Shadow Chief Secretary to the Treasury, while arch-modernizer John Bercow was replaced at International Development by Alan Duncan – a departure that prompted a deliciously blow-by-blow newspaper account that did little to increase confidence in the Tory leadership.[36] The real news, however, was that Howard was bringing a blast from the past back into frontline politics: John Redwood was to head a newly created portfolio covering deregulation. This really was an extraordinary decision: to the extent that voters would even register the change, any votes Redwood's presence might leach from UKIP, and any weight it would bring to the attack on red tape, would surely be outweighed by what even Tory MPs suggested was the propaganda advantage it handed to a government desperate to remind voters of the mad and the bad old days. The centrist Damian Green, who returned to the backbenches, only made things easier for Labour by admitting in an interview that the reshuffle was divisive and looked very much like 'a shift to the right' – not, in his view 'a sensible approach' because 'If we only concentrate on the issues that get the juices flowing of our hard-core supporters then we will be left only with our hard-core supporters.'[37]

That the Conservatives were about to shift to an almost wholly populist appeal was obvious but (just as it was when Hague and Duncan Smith had done the same thing) the motivation was not simply to shore up the leader's support and to mobilize the Party's core vote. This was important, but so was the belief that traditional Tory strengths could be used to woo back floating voters even though the economy was apparently doing well and in spite of the fact that the Party was not yet trusted on health and education. This may have represented the triumph of hope – and ideology – over experience, but it was not utterly irrational. Both public and private polling were still picking up some scepticism about whether increased public spending was achieving gains commensurate with the tax rises levied to pay for it, as well as rising anxiety about crime and immigration – issues on which many Labour voters had views every bit as illiberal as their Tory counterparts.

That said, the stress on such issues was thought by the leadership to be particularly important in terms of winning back voters from UKIP, many of whom, the Party's research suggested, were channelling their essentially xenophobic views into the socially more acceptable cause of Euroscepticism. Indeed, when Howard made a big set-piece speech on immigration on 22 September – right in the middle of the Lib Dem Conference – the similarities between his words and a speech that UKIP icon Robert Kilroy-Silk had recently made at a gathering of his own party were so exact as to attract accusations of plagiarism – a charge most vigorously pursued by the inveterately hostile *Mirror*, which cruelly but effectively invited readers to spot the difference between a couple of choice passages.[38] Howard, as always, stressed his own immigrant background and praised Britain's existing ethnic minority communities, and even took out extra insurance, first, by ensuring he was flanked during the speech by a couple of the Party's handful of ethnic minority candidates and, second, by attending, a few days later, a big meeting of Britain's Sikh community. But while there was a cautious welcome even in liberal quarters for his following Kilroy in floating an Australian-style points system – an idea whose time had come – many migration charities (and the UNHCR itself) were predictably alarmed by his suggestion that the 1951 UN Convention on Refugees might be ditched. Equally predictably, it was the party in the media that was most enthusiastic, agreeing that it was, as the title of the *Express*'s leader put it the next day, 'time to close the gates'.

The party in the media also warmed to the hints that the Party began to throw out about tax cuts. Saatchi and Fox had been trying for months to persuade Howard and Letwin that the Party should promise something on income tax but, apart from the possibility of tinkering with the threshold for higher-rate taxpayers, they were reluctant. For one thing, they believed it might be better to wait until nearer an election so they had a better idea both of government borrowing and of the overall savings that David James' review of government waste would come up with once completed. The Party's opinion research also counselled caution: voters still saw a trade-off between public services and tax cuts and were also sceptical about the Conservatives' ability to deliver the latter. It had, however, indicated scope for promising to reduce specific taxes, like inheritance tax and the stamp duty paid on house purchases, which were generally regarded as unfair. With a week or so to go before the Party Conference, the leadership therefore began to brief that it was indeed planning to announce something along these lines in Bournemouth, hoping that it would help the Party grin and bear its way through Labour's Conference in Brighton and a by-election in Hartlepool in which the Conservative candidate stood absolutely no chance.

Labour's Conference kicked off, as usual, amid predictions (once again confounded) that this year there really would be blood on the carpet (most of it Blair's) and a slew of opinion polls. The most detailed of these (by the increasingly respected YouGov) showed why, despite the shine having long since come off the government (and especially the Prime Minister), Labour and not the Conservative Party was still on course to win the general election. For one thing, Labour was seen as closer than any other party to almost every identifiable section of society apart from 'the countryside', which it was thought to have alien-ated by the proposed ban on hunting with dogs – a measure which the Tories opposed but which was supported by 60 per cent of the elector-ate (although by only a third of Conservative voters). Furthermore, Labour's running of the economy was widely seen as a strength, while there was less and less criticism of the government for not delivering on public services. Finally, Labour's leader was seen by voters as being slap-bang in the middle of the political spectrum where the vast majority also located themselves (the average voter was two points to the left of zero, Blair was four points to the right). True, Labour MPs were seen to be 25 points (and Gordon Brown 22 points) to the left of dead centre, but their Conservative counterparts (and Michael Howard himself) were seen to be 52 points to the right.

Probably because the Hartlepool by-election was held just after its Conference and because it mounted a negative but effective local campaign in a constituency without an ethnic minority population that cared deeply about Iraq, Labour managed to hold off the Lib Dem challenge. The Conservative candidate, however, finished a highly embarrassing fourth behind UKIP with a vote share of just under 10 per cent, less than half what his predecessor got at the general election in

2001. According to those Tory MPs brave enough to face the media the next day, the result was 'disappointing' (Liam Fox), 'a bummer' (Boris Johnson), or 'fucking awful' (Nicholas Soames). It did not, though, send those unhappy with the direction in which the Party was headed scurrying off to brief the media against the leadership. A combination of renewed self-discipline and fatalism, plus the fact that Labour was no longer likely to sweep all before it, meant that Howard was safe until the general election, even though, in objective terms, he was doing no better than his predecessor.

Anyway, not all the news was bad. Tony Blair announced that the next election would be his last as Labour leader. This was bound to cheer the large number of Tory MPs who, while they detested Blair, had convinced themselves that Labour was unbeatable as long as he remained at the helm. In the meantime, polling suggested it was going to be difficult for Blair, now so widely distrusted, to pull his party up towards the 40 per cent share of the vote that would see Labour maintain its current overall majority: as long as the Conservative Party could stay above 30 per cent and the Lib Dems below it, it might still reduce the government's majority to under three figures.

Reports from the UKIP Conference in Bristol were also encouraging. First, increased media interest in the party meant that readers and viewers finally got to see just how strange some of its members really were or were at least made out to be.[39] Second, UKIP members rejected the idea that their candidates stand aside in favour of Tory MPs who expressed support for leaving the EU. Given the fact that many sceptical Conservatives feared for their majorities and polls were suggesting that over a third of their voters favoured local deals with UKIP, this could have caused a great deal of trouble for the Tory leadership. Even better, the decision led to Eurosceptic millionaire Paul Sykes, who had been impressed by John Redwood's return to the Shadow Cabinet, announcing he was no longer going to bankroll UKIP. His aim, after all, had been to use the party to nudge the Conservative Party towards withdrawal, not to 'kill it', as Robert Kilroy-Silk (whom William Hague had once invited to join the Tories) now wanted to do. Third, it looked as if Kilroy-Silk's audacious bid for the leadership was going to end in failure and recrimination. The Conservative Party, in contrast, could try to pick itself up by staging a show of unity and purpose in Bournemouth.

Once again, Conservative conference-goers were not short of opinion polls that showed what a difficult position the Party was in. A Populus poll published for the *Times* on day one put the Party on just 28 per cent (with Labour, fresh from its Conference, on 35 per cent). Howard's ratings were now lower than Duncan Smith's had been at the same point the previous year. Although, the Party was seen as more competent and capable than it had been the year before, the proportion thinking the Conservatives would do a good job of running the country was, at 38 per cent, even lower than in 2003. Just over half of all respondents did not think the Party had changed for the better since 1997 and about the same proportion said that the Party didn't seem to stand for anything. Nearly 60 per cent also thought that John Redwood's return in particular was 'a sign that the Conservatives lack fresh ideas and are stuck in the past'. When it came to what the Party could do to get more people to vote for it, the poll revealed that the gimmicks that well over two-thirds of the Party's existing supporters were convinced would help it recover (more police and prisons, tax cuts, opposing the EU) found favour with considerably less than half of those not currently planning to vote for it.

In short, the ideological blinkers were still on. The tendency among loyal Conservatives to assume, wrongly, that the quintessentially Thatcherite policies that continued to excite them would enthuse everybody else was still alive and well over seven years after they had been comprehensively rejected by the electorate. While voters saw the Party as stuck in the past, many Tories, in parliament, at Central Office, in the country and in the media, remained convinced that the best way to recover was to go back to it. Whether this had anything to do with the fact that only one in ten ordinary members was under 35, while two-thirds were over 55, is a moot point.[40] But the response of the high command was not to try to re-educate their supporters – something they could hardly have done in the time available and with the leader they were saddled with even if they had disagreed with them (which for the most part they did not). Instead, they simply told those supporters it would be alright on the night. The results of its own private polling by Opinion Research Business, claimed Fox and Saatchi, showed that the Party was on course to win 103 of the 130 Labour seats it was targeting, apparently turning an 11 per cent Labour lead at the previous general election into a Tory lead of 4 per cent.

Mixed messages

As the Conference opened, it was clear that the designers at least had taken the need to appeal to twenty-first-century Britain to heart. The set was all bare metal, white leather armchairs, and plasma screens. But set against this minimalism was a plan to emphasize the Party's human face by showing, between debates, short video-grabs (or 'idents') of members of the Shadow Cabinet recalling their first kiss, talking about their favourite films and holiday destinations, how they liked to relax, and the last book and CD they had bought – a technique borrowed from TV station Channel Four. Each Shadow Minister, following the thinking of David Cameron, would speak to resonant themes rather than dry-sounding departmental briefs. They would also come on stage to Junkie XL's 2002 remix of Elvis Presley's 'A Little Less Conversation' – a track already used by Nike in its advertising and picked in order to illustrate what Cameron decided should be the Party's main message, namely (in what was probably an unconscious echo of Ted Heath's 1966 election slogan) 'less talk, more action'.

Cameron in particular had digested the findings of focus groups and opinion polling analysed by Steve Hilton and George Bridges over the summer, which showed, as he explained in an interview, that 'the big problem in politics at the moment is disillusion, cynicism and apathy. People . . . feel so let down by a government that promised the earth – wonderful phrases, and grandiloquent language.' The problem was those feelings had led them to distrust the Tories, too. The Party's response to this, argued Cameron, had to be to convince people that it had a realistic, practical leader who would not promise the earth but instead offer the electorate a modest and therefore credible 'timetable for action' – a concept suggested by Steve Hilton. This would be out-lined for each area by each Shadow spokesman and then confirmed in a deliberately short pre-manifesto which would project a Conservative government as one that would do what it said on the tin. This not only allowed the Tories to show they were listening but dovetailed with their leader's belief that politics should be about tangible delivery rather than 'the vision thing'. It also reflected the fact that those working closely under and alongside Howard realized, like Hague's advisers, that it was probably better to have their leader – especially because he was going to feature so heavily in the Party's media coverage at the forthcoming election – try to sell something he was comfortable with rather than run the risk of being seen as inauthentic.[41]

While it had the advantage of turning what Howard and Letwin saw as the necessity of not promising too much on tax into something approaching a virtue, the problem with this approach was that (as people like Maurice Saatchi were arguing) it was more about achieving presentational discipline than providing political vision; it risked appearing small-minded rather than inspiring. Just as seriously, it also relied on the policies selected to radiate the sense of a party that, in Cameron's words, was 'credible, decent, tolerant, sensible, moderate', rather than plunging it even further into the clear blue water of which, at least in his opinion, there was already 'enough . . . to drown in'.[42] Yet the right-wing populist policies that had been inherited from IDS and the initiatives developed since – crystallized in the so-called 'ten words to remember' (school discipline, more police, cleaner hospitals, lower taxes, controlled immigration), plus an eleventh (accountability) – were simply incapable of doing that. And even if they had been, prominent right-wingers like Fox, Redwood, Davis, and Collins would not have been willing or able – judging from their hard-core Conference contributions at least – to sell them. The same went, of course, for Howard himself. Little wonder, then, that Gregor Mackay, former Press Secretary to William Hague, thought it all sounded terribly familiar: 'They're going to make the same mistake we did in 2001,' he predicted. 'They start off fishing in the sea for votes and they end up poking around in a puddle outside their front door.'[43]

The only publicly voiced criticism of Tory strategy from within the Party proper came in a satirical newspaper column from Michael Portillo, who was not simply retiring but exiting stage left:

> There now follows a quiz. If you were a Tory spin doctor, and you knew that before the conference Howard's score was plus 52 (that is people consider him to be twice as far to the right as Labour MPs are to the left) would you want to use the party gathering to a) move towards the centre or b) move to the right?
>
> Question two. According to opinion polls Labour has shed up to 10 percentage points (one quarter of its votes) since 2001. In an

important number of seats, the Liberal Democrats came so close behind the Conservative MP at the last election that if just a proportion of the Labour voters there decided to switch to Liberal Democrat the Conservative would be defeated. So, if you were the Tories would you a) try to persuade former Labour supporters to vote Conservative or b) direct your efforts to attracting UK Independence Party voters?

Question Three. The Liberal Democrats presently have 55 seats in Parliament and are winning by-elections quite frequently. The UKIP has no seats, and Europe is their single issue. As Hague discovered, Europe is not voters' top concern at general elections. Understanding that, if you were a Conservative strategist would you a) counter the Liberal Democrats by focusing on public services or b) repulse UKIP with more aggressive language about Europe?

If your answer to any question was a) you clearly do not understand the Tory Party. Do not blame yourself; in truth, it is difficult to comprehend.[44]

Law and disorder

Shortly after the Conference, the Conservative Party announced that it was appointing the Australian political consultant Lynton Crosby as its new election supremo. This was a huge help in institutional terms, instilling a much needed sense of professionalism and co-ordination of effort from the very top to the very bottom of the Party. By appointing Crosby, Howard helped ensure a degree of 'joined-up opposition'. On the other hand, his decision virtually guaranteed that the Conservatives' appeal to voters would be a highly ideological one. Crosby, after all, was renowned for no-holds-barred campaigns on populist issues, and Howard almost immediately launched into what he claimed was the government's plan quietly to surrender control of Britain's borders to Brussels. A week or so later, Howard was telling ITV's top-rated politics show that 'a small and crowded island' like Britain could not be expected to shoulder 'a wholly disproportionate burden' and that the Conservatives planned to cap asylum at around 20,000 per year. A YouGov poll duly confirmed the Tory lead on the issue, but also showed that Labour was either extending its lead or narrowing its deficit on every other issue, while it remained four points ahead of the Conservatives overall. Once again, the only Tory MP willing publicly to question the course the Party was on was one who had nothing to lose, in his case because he had just been returned by Howard to the backbenches. It spoke volumes that John Bercow's criticisms, instead of being debated, were immediately jumped on as signalling a possible defection to Labour.

Immigration was not the only tabloid favourite Howard planned to campaign on. After a brief and rather unconvincing foray into 'family-friendly' policies and the release of the first of the Party's consultation on tax reductions, journalists were briefed that it was planning to tighten a legal loophole that made it possible for travellers to establish camps on private land without planning permission, thereby securing admiring headlines for a supposed 'war on gypsies' in the selfsame papers (the *Mail* and the *Express*) which had been running outraged stories on the issue for weeks. The problem for Howard, however, was that Labour was determined not to cede law and order – and now the battle against terrorism – to the Tories. Indeed, it believed it might even be able to outflank and divide them, announcing legislation cleaning up neighbourhoods, battling drugs and organized crime, and bringing in ID cards – a measure that it knew would split the Conservatives almost as much as it would outrage some of its own backbenchers. Howard, a fan of cards and anxious not to be seen as soft on terrorism, managed, however, to avoid too much embarrassment by allowing his MPs to abstain. He was then able to turn the tables on Blair by offering support for a private member's bill that would offer more protection to householders using force against home intruders – a move which Blair countered by agreeing to set up an urgent review of the issue and promising to support a change in the law if it was deemed necessary. Howard made the most of the U-turn at PMQs, prompting cheers from Tory backbenchers who were enjoying what, in recent months, had become the increasingly rare pleasure of seeing their man triumph in the Commons. But, in truth, they were merely back at square one. Joining self-styled crusades by right-wing newspapers no doubt helped them retain their lead on law-and-order issues. But because Labour either pre-empted or followed their calls for action, that lead was never going to be wide enough to guarantee them victory even in the unlikely event that they could ensure the election was fought on that issue and that issue alone.

This to-ing and fro-ing on law and order (like the lurid media coverage of the lives and loves of their colleague Boris Johnson) at least gave Tories at Westminster something to think about other than who might take over from their leader if (but probably when) he lost the next election. Of great interest in this regard was the announcement that David Cameron would be responsible for policy in a small team dedicated to general election planning which would also include Crosby and George Bridges, who would now run what was effectively a re-creation of the old 'War Room' melding research and media. Some – including MPs who hoped they might have a shot at the leadership themselves after the election – went so far as to claim (not without a hint of bitterness) that it was 'now an accepted piece of knowledge that Michael has anointed David as his successor'.[45]

Others were not quite so certain, noting that both Cameron and Osborne (who was also expected to play a high-profile media role in the election) were bound to be wary of repeating William Hague's mistake of taking on the leadership too early in their careers. There were also differences of opinion as to whether Howard could or should stay on after the election, thereby allowing the new boys to play themselves in. And this was bound up with the institutional question of how any successor would be chosen. When, for example, it became apparent in mid-November that the 1922 Executive (with Howard's approval) was planning to try to change the rules so as to restore the final say to MPs, it was clear that support for such a move would come from those who believed the wider membership could not be trusted to elect an electorally appealing pragmatist. On the other hand, those hoping to replace Howard quickly with another right-winger would oppose such a move, believing it was in their best interest to have the contest take place not only swiftly but under the existing system. Wherever individual MPs stood on this question, however, most were agreed that the role given to Cameron by Howard suggested their current leader was not intending to hand things on a plate to, say David Davis or Liam Fox, with whom, ideologically speaking, he would seem to have more in common.

Davis, of course, never expected any favours and was relying on his own efforts, though he could do little to stop the sniping against him by his rivals and their friends in the party in the media.[46] Fox, however, was doing less well. The sharing of the Chairmanship with Saatchi was not proving to be a successful experiment: who was supposed to do what had never been clear and was even less clear after the appointment of Lynton Crosby. The Australian was not very impressed by what he had found on his arrival and made little secret of the fact. Saatchi was dismissed as 'twenty years out of date', while the voter-identification system ('Voter Vault') that Fox managed to get from the US Republicans was nowhere near as impressive as the hype surrounding it. Moreover, Crosby, whose speciality was motivating his staff and zeroing in on swing voters in marginal, but winnable, constituencies, was, not surprisingly, unimpressed with the idea that the Party spread its limited resources over the 167 seats that Saatchi had claimed at one stage to be targeting. The leaking to the media of his criticisms led to Saatchi and Fox demanding, and getting, an apology and then circulating an email (also leaked) to all at Central Office (now renamed Conservative Campaign Headquarters or CCHQ) to publicize, rather pathetically perhaps, the fact Crosby had said sorry.

Widespread concern that all was not well at CCHQ was only made worse by the drip-drip of stories pertaining to the dire state of the Party's finances. Only a few months after Howard had announced the new Conservative Party Foundation composed of aristocratic and plutocratic philanthropists, it had become clear that the idea behind it – trying to ring-fence some of the Party's donations to prevent them being spent on day-to-day expenses – was not going to work. For one thing, people at all levels of the Party were unhappy about the setting up of the fund in the first place. For another, those expenses (mainly staff and opinion research costs) were running at such a high rate that the Party needed every penny coming in to pay for them. It had been unable to negotiate the quick sale of (nor find a tenant for) Smith Square before it moved in (at huge expense) to its refurbished offices in Victoria Street – a location it would eventually abandon for a more permanent base at Millbank in any case. Although the Party could probably count on donors stumping up to help it fight an election, it was clear that it was also going to have to dip into both its substantial overdraft and whatever reserves it could muster. It was also clear that much of the money pledged would come in the form of loans, some of which might eventually be converted into donations but a proportion of which would have to be repaid in the long term. Meanwhile, it was obvious that something was not quite right when one of those who had given the Party considerable amounts of money, former Treasurer Michael Ashcroft, had so little confidence in its target-seats strategy that he had decided to set up his own parallel system of funding. Indeed, he even opted to commission his own opinion research in the belief that CCHQ (not for the first time) was going with polling and focus groups that told the leadership what it wanted, rather than what it needed, to hear.

But the Party's internal problems were not, of course, merely institutional. They were also ideological. Conservative MPs, especially on the right of the Party, were unconvinced by Letwin's argument that he could not commit to tax cuts, at least until Brown had delivered what was bound to be an election Budget. During a meeting at the beginning of December, after Letwin had presented his thinking, some MPs voiced their concern (both to him and the media) that the tax cuts they wanted to see should be pledged sooner rather than later: waiting until March when the election was almost certainly due at the beginning of May would make them harder to sell to voters, not least because Labour would condemn them as last-minute opportunism. A Populus poll on public attitudes to tax and spending, however, suggested they were all wasting their time: voters, it appeared, did not want to be taxed any more but valued the public services their money was spent on and were not crying out to be taxed less; nor did they believe 'the party of low taxation' would be able to deliver on its promises anyway. Little wonder that the leadership of that Party, while ideologically convinced of the need for tax cuts and prepared to carry on floating them as a possibility, was less inclined than some of its more determined followers to see them as a magic bullet. Some, including Cameron and Hilton, believed that making big promises on tax, however carefully costed and supposedly funded by cutting waste, risked undermining what little progress the Party had made in neutralizing Labour on health and education. It would also simply run into the wall of voter scepticism that, focus groups suggested, routinely greeted promises of tax cuts by any party. In any case, there were other issues – notably immigration and asylum – which had greater resonance with voters across the board.

Raising the temperature

Howard kicked off the Conservatives' near-term campaign with a much-trailed speech accompanying the 'rolling release' of the Tory manifesto. In classically populist terms which recalled the rhetoric of both Hague and Duncan Smith, he promised to turn things around for 'the forgotten majority, the people who make up the backbone of our country', who had been 'neglected and taken for granted by Mr Blair', who had 'asked them to trust him and when they did . . . let them down'. The message of course went down well with the majority of the party in the media, which praised him for having 'spoken up loud and strong in defence of Middle Britain', although there was some concern that this did not add up to the kind of 'ideological framework' which had apparently helped Mrs Thatcher into Number Ten and would not be matched by specifics on (surprise, surprise) tax cuts.[47] There were therefore high hopes for the imminent release of the final report by businessman David James on reducing government waste, which would hopefully allow the Party to explain how it would match or even out-spend Labour on health and education at the same time as offering tax cuts and financing recent promises on policing, prisons, defence, and (in the light of the Asian tsunami) overseas aid.

Labour characteristically got its retaliation in first, in this case via the exquisitely timed defection of retiring Tory MP Robert Jackson. Jackson – a Ken Clarke fan – had general complaints: the Conservatives were seen as obsessive and fanatic and had lurched 'inexorably' and 'in an eerie way' to the right, making it impossible for them to build the kind of broad-based coalition that the country (and victory) required. He also thought Michael Howard had only 'two registers. One is scorn and the other is anger'; worse, after wobbling on Iraq, the Tory leader had managed to alienate the Americans as well as the Europeans. But Labour's newest recruit was also prepared to be specific about his former party's forthcoming report: 'The waste thing', he claimed, 'is a fig leaf which is used to avoid talking about the practical implications of cutting taxes and spending.'[48] He also pointed out that the Rayner review for Mrs Thatcher's government had resulted in a reduction of 0.4 per cent of total public expenditure – a figure which suggested that the James proposals, which amounted to a cut of some 8 per cent, were totally unrealistic.

Taken as a whole, James' recommendations involved cutting over 230,000 public-sector posts and closing down 168 public bodies, which would lead to savings totalling around £35 billion, some £23 billion of which would be ploughed back into public services, including the recruitment of 40,000 new police officers and the provision of 20,000 extra prison places. Rather confusingly, however, it was not entirely clear whether the overall figure included the £21.5 million already identified by the government's own review of waste by Peter Gershon, and closer examination of the figures that were made available suggested that by the end of the decade the state run by a Conservative government would still be spending some 41 per cent of GDP as opposed to 42 per cent under Labour. Still, claimed Howard and Letwin, James' savings would allow them to reduce borrowing by £8 billion and make around £4 billion worth of tax cuts, though the latter would not be announced until after Brown's Budget on the grounds that he would simply steal any ideas he liked and trash those he did not. The fact that this occasioned no public hint of disappointment or frustration from MPs on the right of the Party, however, probably said less about their true feelings than the discipline which Howard and Maclean had managed to instil – a discipline reinforced by Crosby, who was now emailing each and every Conservative MP a daily campaign bulletin of lines to take.

The leadership's underlying uncertainty about its tax and spending proposals was reflected in its evident determination to move back swiftly onto surer ground. Insisting once again that it was not racist to want to impose tougher controls – an accusation that the Tories constantly claimed was being laid at their door – Howard and Davis once again launched into immigration. The latter, they claimed in interviews and a full-page ad in the *Sunday Telegraph*, was 'unlimited' under Labour, which was allowing 'a city the size of Peterborough' to settle in the UK every year. A Conservative government would adopt the 'common sense' solution of turning back all those who pitched up at British ports and airports to claim asylum and instead take 15,000 people a year from UNHCR camps around the world (although the UNHCR, for its part, warned it would refuse to cooperate with any country that pulled out of the 1951 Convention). With the exception of (literally) one or two modernizing 'holdouts' at the *Times*, the party in the media was predictably pleased and was happy to note that Tory policy would inevitably bring it into conflict with European law. The *Mail* spoke for the rest when it claimed Howard, 'the proud son of Jewish immigrants, deserves much credit for courageously refusing to accept the orthodoxy of our smug liberal elite who want to suppress real debate on this issue', while 97 per cent of *Sun* readers apparently backed Howard's 'curb on migrants'.[49]

Labour, which for all its problems had not forgotten the importance of message discipline, was careful not to get drawn in too deep, leaving it largely to representatives of what the *Telegraph* (among others) liked to call 'the race relations and human rights industries' to respond directly. And Blair played things in the Commons with customary skill. Having issued instructions to his troops not to attack on the issue, he used the attempt by the Tory leader (now helped by Michael Gove as well as Cameron and Osborne) to link Europe and immigration in order to reinforce Labour's now familiar attack on Howard: 'I am not accusing you of being a racist,' he assured him. 'You are not a racist; you are just a shameless opportunist.' The first opinion poll to be published after this push on immigration suggested this was a line which resonated with the public, with only 36 per cent of respondents agreeing that Howard 'genuinely believes immigration should be limited', while 58 per cent believed he was focusing on the issue because he 'desperately wants to win votes for his party'. Meanwhile a MORI poll showed the Tory leader's satisfaction rating at only 22 per cent was (a) only two points above Michael Foot's in 1983, (b) 12 points behind Neil Kinnock's in 1992, (c) below William Hague's in 2001, and (d) as bad as Iain Duncan Smith's the month before he was replaced.

Such figures made it certain that the Government would continue to focus as much on Howard personally as on his policies, although even some Labour supporters were unhappy with posters on its website that, according to some Tories at least, were (by superimposing mugshots of Howard and Letwin onto flying pigs) offensive to Jews and implicitly linked Howard with negative Jewish stereotypes like Fagin and Shylock. Given the depressingly long half-life of anti-Semitism in the population as a whole (surveys suggested that nearly one in five believed Jews had 'too much influence' in Britain and would not want a Jewish Prime Minister), it would be difficult to argue that they were making something out of what they knew to be nothing. On the other hand, it would be just as difficult to argue that Conservative strategists, and the party in the media, were unaware of the fact that branding any visual representation of Howard by Labour as anti-Semitic would make things harder for the government to run a negative, personalized campaign against him. Political correctness could sometimes come in handy, even for the Tories.

The heightened atmosphere also meant that there was more interest than there might have been in the Conservatives' campaign posters released a day or two later. The 'handwritten' text on the posters (each of which was accompanied by the same tagline 'Are you thinking what we're thinking?') included: 'I mean, how hard is it to keep a hospital clean?', 'What's wrong with a little discipline in schools?', 'Put more police on the streets and they'll catch more criminals. It's not rocket science, is it?', and, most controversially though by no means originally, 'It's not racist to impose limits on immigration'. To the critics this was Australian-style dog-whistle politics – nothing you could actually label prejudiced but people who were would get the message and vote accordingly. Labour, however, took it as a cue formally to announce a much-trailed 'five year plan' to curb what the new Home Secretary, Charles Clarke, suggested were abuses of traditional 'British hospitality' towards immigrants, one aspect of which – a points-driven system – was (not for the first time) a direct lift from the Tories. And, when the Tories in turn upped the ante by insisting a Conservative government would make all immigrants coming to the UK for more than a year undergo screening for HIV/AIDS, hepatitis, and TB in order to protect public health and access to the NHS, Labour, true to form, said it was already considering such checks.

As well as trying to neutralize as far as possible the Tories' advantage on asylum and immigration, Labour continued to revive memories of the last Conservative government by making the most of official papers on Black Wednesday in 1992, made available under the Freedom of Information Act. Ordinary voters did not of course read them, and probably very few even glanced at newspaper stories about them. But the ensuing row did of course mean that they saw all the old footage of the City in chaos as Norman Lamont jacked up interest rates to 15 per cent and blew at least £4 billion in one day. Unfortunately, the few million viewers who tuned in to watch a BBC film on Howard, *No More Mr Nasty*, were likewise treated not only to a glimpse into the Tory leader's home and family life but also footage of those parts of his ministerial career that he might have preferred voters to forget.

The burning desire to 'humanize' Mr Howard, which led to him being joined on stage (US-style) at the Tories' Spring Forum by his children and grandchildren, was understandable. But to have cooperated in the documentary – 'not so much a hatchet job as a smirk-packed hour spent poking at the Tory leader with a stick', as one commentator put it – was, on balance, probably unwise, not least because it gave the BBC a chance to show the satirist and impressionist Rory Bremner doing Howard as Dracula and summing up his policies as 'Less tax. Less blacks.' [50] On the other hand, the swift decision to have Howard do a soul-searching personal interview with the ever-sympathetic *Mail* in which he admitted that his grandfather might have been an illegal immigrant was a smart move that allowed the Tory leader to put a positive spin on a story that would otherwise have been a pre-election scoop (and possibly a damaging one) for Howard's biographer, Michael Crick. Even then the fanatically pro-Labour *Sunday Mirror* had a field day after its own research showed Howard's father was only allowed into Britain after the intervention of a sympathetic Labour MP.

Harping on the familiar

Having gone about as far as they thought they could go on immigration – the BNP leader, Nick Griffin, admitted the Conservatives would 'make a significant hole in our vote' with what he saw as 'a definite move on to our turf' – the leadership surprised everyone by moving on to tax.[51] Letwin's initial reluctance to promise anything until after the Budget eventually gave way in the face of arguments from colleagues that this would give the public insufficient time to appreciate the offer and might also run the risk of being labelled opportunist. Accordingly, Howard committed a Conservative government to giving every household containing a pensioner a discount on their Council Tax – a gift that would swallow over a quarter of the £4 billion tax cuts the Party was promising but a worthwhile one given that over-55's (who were already being targeted by its costly promise to move away from means-testing pensions) constituted about one third of those most likely to vote.

Staying with senior citizens, Howard then used the plight of an individual pensioner – Margaret Dixon, who had an operation for surgery postponed several times – to highlight problems in the NHS. This was a risky technique: both Duncan Smith and Howard had used it before and had it blow up in their face when, as almost inevitably occurred, the details of the cases in question turned out to be a lot more complicated and the Party's exploitation of them came under critical media scrutiny. Even more importantly, the 'war of Margaret's Shoulder' also focused public attention on an issue – health – on which Labour had a commanding lead. And it gave the Prime Minister, in his speech to Labour's Scottish Conference on 4 March, a chance to take time out from exploiting draconian legislation to paint the Tories as soft on terrorism in order to trot out exactly the kind of stuff on health that they found so difficult to counter:

> To say our NHS today is worse than it was in those Tory years, to see Michael Howard who sat for ten years in that Cabinet as they cut it, starved it of resources, sneered at its values – to see him take the case of someone in pain and use it to run down and denigrate the whole of our NHS, should make any decent right-thinking person turn away in disgust. . . . How dare the Tories claim nothing has changed for the better in Britain's NHS since a Labour Government took it back from them. . . . I say this to the people of Britain. Shortly you will make a choice. Rightly the NHS and its future will be at the heart of it. If you believe the NHS today is worse than it was when Mr Howard and the Conservatives ran it, don't vote for me. Vote for him.

That the Conservatives, of their own volition and out of their own eagerness, gave Blair a chance to run that line yet again suggested that the discipline instilled by Lynton Crosby on the Tory campaign, while undoubtedly valuable, was possibly less iron than many liked to think. Howard's advisers could point to research that suggested that the Party came out of the episode reasonably well. But even they acknowledged privately that this was a long way from the new kind of politics he had promised in his Saatchi Gallery speech. Moreover, ranging onto Labour territory – even if the Party could score a short-term hit by doing so – was, some believed, ultimately counterproductive.

More immediately worrying, however, was Brown's Budget. While careful not to be so generous as to be billed as an irresponsible pre-election giveaway, it was also clearly targeted at pensioners (Council Tax discounts, higher pension credits, and free bus travel), as well as working families (increased tax credits) and people buying homes (cuts in stamp duty) or inheriting them (inheritance tax thresholds raised). Howard's soundbite response that this was a 'vote now, pay later' Budget was well crafted, and his reply to Brown's speech well delivered. But they were just words in the face of deeds – deeds, moreover, that, post-Budget polls suggested, reinforced the impression that, even if it might tax people more than they would like, this was a government capable of safeguarding economic prosperity and public services at the same time as helping those in need. Moreover, the Budget marked a decision on the part of the Prime Minister and Chancellor to suspend their feuding at least temporarily in order to defend their project against a common enemy – one they now claimed (with considerable poetic licence but no less eye-catchingly) wanted to cut £35 billion from public services.

The ensuing argument over 'Labour's lies' about Tory plans for spending reductions was not, however, one that the leadership, knowing the truth was complex, felt able to win. Accordingly, it returned to the grid with signed adverts in Sunday newspapers which teed up a speech by Howard promising, once again, that the Tories would take action against illegal occupation of land by what he (with admirable political correctness) labelled travellers but what the party in the media (which had re-ignited its campaign on the issue) called gypsies. Given the numbers of caravans involved, this did not seem like an issue that would affect many voters, and even those it might touch were likely to be in rural areas that were already Tory strongholds. But it was apparently a big enough deal for the BBC television news to lead on the story – a vital performance indicator for the Tory campaign team, for whom 'travellers', like asylum-seekers and illegal immigrants, were simply another out-group that they could target in polite tones, knowing their supporters in the media would amplify their words in more direct language. 'We will jail the gypsy invaders insists Howard' (*Express*) and 'Howard: I'll boot out gypsy cheats' (*Star*) were just some of the headlines that accompanied the Tory leader's pledge. Even those modernizers who felt distinctly queasy about the whole thing had to admit that Howard had 'sunk to the occasion in a ruthlessly competent manner'.[52]

The effect on the Party's morale of this frenetic, and frankly successful, headline seeking was electric: few thought in their heart of hearts that they could win, but many – buoyed up by a leaked internal report purporting to show how the polls routinely overstated Labour's leads – were actually beginning to believe they might seriously eat into the government's majority. But there was an opportunity cost. Firstly, screaming headlines may have done wonders for the morale of activists and candidates, but they crowded out the Party's message on matters that might have shifted more votes, such as its claim that Labour would have to put up taxes. Secondly, campaigning on immigrants and gypsies was not so much a toot on the dog-whistle as a blast on the foghorn. Everyone could hear it and it warned all sorts of people not to do anything that might let the Conservatives back in again.

In short, for every voter the strident stances attracted another was repelled, sometimes to the point where those who had lost faith in Blair and were tempted not to bother voting or to switch to the Lib Dems stayed loyal to Labour because of what they saw as the 'nastiness' of the Tory campaign. Populus polls taken at the beginning and end of March confirmed the suggestion that there was a class distinction operating in this respect: the Tories picked up support in the lower social groups but lost support among those with higher income and status; the Party was failing the proverbial 'dinner party test'. The same research also suggested to some that the tone of the Tory campaign was tarnishing its overall brand, stranding it in 'nasty party' territory. Voters were asked whether they agreed with a policy without being shown which party it belonged to and then asked the same question when the policy was associated with a party. If the party was Labour, the measure of agreement was unaffected. If the party was the Conservatives, support for the policy dropped significantly – especially amongst so-called 'swing voters'.

Down to earth with a bump

It was these 'swing voters', of course, that the Conservatives were keen to target with what by that stage was practically the only shot left in their locker – the £2.7 billion of tax cuts they had still not allocated. Letwin's complex calculations had, naturally, come in for criticism from opponents, with both Labour and the Lib Dems arguing that the savings made could not possibly be achieved, or not at least without cuts in frontline services. Given the importance of rebutting this, it was absolutely vital that everyone in the Party stuck to the script.

There were already signs that this was not going to be easy. There had been a tricky moment when John Redwood had confided in a Channel Four interview that the £12 billion of putative savings not allocated to frontline services but to tax cuts and debt reduction was 'just the down payment' and that more would be forthcoming 'over the lifetime of the Parliament . . . if all goes well'. This clearly contradicted Letwin's assurances that his figures related not to 'the first Budget', as Redwood stated, but to the next five years. A clarification was issued, however, and it seemed to do the trick. So, too, later on in March, did the resignation as the Tory candidate in Tony Blair's Sedgefield constituency of Danny Kruger, think-tanker, *Telegraph* leader-writer, and CCHQ adviser, who had rather rashly claimed, 'We plan to introduce a period of creative destruction in the public services.'

By the end of March, however, pre-election fever had built to such a pitch that the leadership could not keep the lid on things when the *Times* – the paper that had already fallen out badly with CCHQ – was handed a tape-recording of comments made by an MP to a private meeting of the Thatcherite Conservative Way Forward group. Howard Flight, now a Deputy Chairman of the Party, seemed to suggest that the Tories were promising moderation but were intending to pursue a much more radical agenda once Michael Howard made it to Number Ten. The James review, he assured his audience, had been 'sieved for what [was] politically acceptable', while the 'continuing agenda' would have to wait until after the Party won power, since 'whatever the fine principles, you have to win an election first'.

Flight had gone beyond expressing a widely shared aspiration that the Conservatives would be less timid in government than in opposition, and had allowed the Party's enemies to suggest that there was some kind of secret plan just waiting to be put into operation after the public had been fooled into voting in a party that, fundamentally, had never really changed. Within a couple of hours of his being confronted with what had happened, Howard forced Flight to resign as Deputy Chairman, had him issue an apology, and had CCHQ put out a statement to the effect that his words 'did not represent the policy of the Conservative Party'. By the next day, however, clearly anxious that Flight had undermined the Party's carefully constructed claim to deliver what it promised and to promise only what it could deliver, Howard went even further.

He withdrew the Whip from the errant MP and declared he would no longer be the Tory candidate for Arundel and South Downs. 'We will not', he declared, 'say one thing in private and another thing in public. Everyone in my party has to sign up to that. If not, they're out.'

Given how difficult John Major had found it to prevent constituency parties from reselecting MPs who were clearly causing the Party massive embarrassment, it was testament to Howard's personal authority (note his use of the term 'my party') that Flight's association did not make more of a fuss. The fact that the leadership, by removing the whip, had rendered Flight ineligible (as per a rule change agreed by the Party Board in March 2004) for the Party's approved list of candidates (a condition of being adopted as a candidate under the 1998 constitution) gave the officers of the association no choice. After a few days of speculation about a local revolt and a legal challenge from Flight, they knuckled under for the good of the Party and, with an election only weeks away, swiftly selected another candidate, Nick Herbert, whose homosexuality represented something of a departure but whose views on public-sector reform and spending did not.

The party in the media was gloomy but largely quiescent. However, the reaction in the parliamentary party to Howard's 'nuclear response' was one of alarm. Save for a handful of MPs who may have seen it as some sort of ersatz 'Clause IV moment', most regarded depriving a colleague of his seat for shooting his mouth off at a private meeting of true believers as over-the-top, with some (not for the first time) blaming Howard's Political Secretary, Rachel Whetstone. Even those who saw the advantage in having a leader who could now be portrayed as ruthless and brutally honest wondered if he might not have overdone it. Howard's reaction was bound to give the story legs and spun by Labour as proof that the Party had something to hide and was punishing the man who let the cat out of the bag. Flight's dismissal also set a worrying precedent: would the same brutal treatment be handed out to others who stepped out of line in the future? Given the extent of these concerns, it was, once again, a testament to the discipline Howard (and Maclean) had instilled at Westminster that almost nobody in the parliamentary party was prepared to be quoted by journalists on the issue, either on or off the record.

Not only did the Flight furore take some of the pressure off the government over revelations concerning the legal advice it received prior to the Iraq war, it also cast a shadow over anything the Conservatives tried to announce in the immediate aftermath. For instance, what would otherwise have been welcomed as a sign that they were beginning to wake up to the need to help working women juggle their job and child-care – a plan to improve maternity pay and subsidize more informal methods of childminding fronted by the camera-friendly Cameron – was all-too-easily dismissed as a desperate attempt to distract from the Party's problems. It also overshadowed the launch of the Party's defence policy and its plans to set up a new border police force and provide 24-hour surveillance at all of Britain's ports. Given all this, CCHQ's attempt to make a story out of the 'dirty tricks' used (supposedly by a blind German student, no less!) to tape Flight's speech – an effort which merely prolonged the agony and merely confirmed how damaging the Party thought it had been – was amateurish in the extreme.

By the time the election proper got going, the die was cast. If the Conservatives had failed to neutralize Labour's leads on health and education, they still hoped to win the support of a group of voters who were more likely to turn out than any other with promises of 'respon-sible' tax cuts targeted at older people (with £1.7 billion of income tax cuts for pensioners added to the £1.7 billion cuts in their Council Tax that was announced in the pre-campaign period). They also hoped to do everything they could to distract attention from the economy – Labour's trump card – and onto issues that they themselves 'owned', notably immigration and asylum, which polls suggested were more important to the electorate than in 2001. As in that election, this was not simply a 'core vote' strategy aimed at mobilizing loyal supporters and preventing drift to UKIP but an attempt at 'wedge politics' – the promotion of issues that divide the supporters of your opponent. As in 2001, the Tories' tracking polling and focus group research sug-gested considerable public sympathy for their relatively hard line. And, as in 2001, of course, immigration was not the sole feature of the Conservatives' campaign, although it stretched credibility for Party strategists to claim, after the election, that the heavy focus on it had been down to the media rather than Howard, especially as it later emerged that Howard and Crosby had planned to return to the topic by raising abuses of family reunion from the Indian sub-continent, with this being aborted only at the eleventh hour after a plea from Cameron.[53]

Some scepticism is also merited when it comes to another key claim, namely that Crosby's decision to focus not just on issues like immigration but also on target seats resulted in the Party winning the so-called 'ground war'. For all the use of voter identification software and state-of-the-art call- and campaign-centres like the one in Coleshill Manor in the West Midlands, the evidence that the Party did appreciably better in its official target seats is patchy at best, although arguably more successful was the private initiative directed by former Treasurer Michael Ashcroft (which boosted spending in the two years running up to the election by candidates lucky enough to have benefited from his largesse). More generally, the campaign as a whole – symbolized by what Michael Portillo memorably dubbed their 'Victor Meldrew manifesto of moans about modern Britain' – did the Tories no favours.[54] The concentration on certain signature policies made it easier for Labour to portray them as immoderate and even obsessive. Polls showed that the Conservative campaign was judged to be the worst of those mounted by the three main parties and that 'on every major issue Labour improved its position relative to the Conservatives, even on issues where it was at a disadvantage'.[55] The gap between Howard and Blair also widened – to the disadvantage of the Tory leader and, given what voting studies now say about the increasing impact of leadership evaluations on vote choice, the Party as a whole.[56]

That said, Labour won its historic third consecutive majority on a much reduced share of the vote and with a majority down to double rather than triple figures, having held on to only around seven out of ten of its 2001 voters and losing the rest mainly to abstention or the Lib Dems. The Conservatives held on to nine out of ten of their voters from 2001 and the UKIP threat failed to materialize – a tribute perhaps to the Tories' right-wing offer.[57] They also won marginally more votes than Labour in England, even if they ended up winning 93 fewer English constituencies than the government. But they gained just 32 extra seats on a share of the vote that increased by less than one percentage point compared to 2001. There were still only 198 Tories entitled to sit in the Commons – fewer than the 209 MPs who sat on the Labour benches after the *annus horribilis* that party experienced in 1983.

For any political party, a change of leadership is a critical juncture – one which presents the possibility of a new departure, a chance to get out of the rut in which it may be stuck. Clearly there are constraints. No leader starts with a canvas that is absolutely blank. And each one has baggage, as well as debts that must be repaid, and sometimes even scores that need settling. Nevertheless, replacing the individual at the top offers parties one of the few opportunities they have to signal and achieve change, both ideological and institutional. Within the limits imposed by his own reputation and the colleagues he needed to reward and keep on board, Michael Howard could have done pretty much what he wanted with the Tory Party in November 2003. He chose to tackle what he saw as the Party's most urgent problem – the public's impression of it as a divided and rudderless outfit that could not lay a glove even on a Prime Minister widely regarded as slippery. But he either left policy much as he found it or else extended and emphasized its rightward, authoritarian thrust, forgetting all about the 'compassionate' conservatism on which his predecessor focused and creating more 'clear blue water' than ever.

In so doing, Howard did the Tories some damage but also did them a favour or two. He failed to move the Party out of the ideological and institutional rut in which it had been stuck since the early 1990s, meaning it had almost as far to go after 2005 as it had after 1997 and 2001. On the other hand, he prevented it slipping into third place behind the Lib Dems. He also tested to destruction the idea that it could win power on a platform of populist promises and taking up where Thatcher left off. And, because ultimately he valued competence more than complete agreement with his own ideas, he picked out for preferment individuals who realized that something simply had to give.

6

'COMETH THE HOUR, COMETH THE DAVE'

THE LONG LEADERSHIP CONTEST,

MAY–DECEMBER 2005[1]

In the immediate aftermath of the 2005 general election, the Conservative Party leadership was purportedly put up for sale on eBay by one 'mike-howard'.[2] It was, he admitted, in 'poor condition', 'rarely used in recent years, and in need of major restoration'. Yet, he went on,

> [t]here is a slim chance . . . [of] rejuvenation but this would take a brave person and would require action now. Gypsies need not apply.
>
> Unfortunately this item comes with the baggage of a small, but potent membership list; so if you are a progressive, socially inclusive, fair minded, outward looking, normal sort of person, then do not apply.
>
> No reserve as urgent sale required.
>
> PS. Can deliver to Notting Hill.

The whole thing was of course a spoof. But it was indicative of the low regard in which the Party was held by some after what was widely characterized as a nasty and negative election campaign. It also hinted, however, at an equally widely held suspicion, namely that Michael Howard, who announced he would be stepping down once new rules were put in place to restore to MPs the final say over the choice of leader, had already decided who should succeed him.

Post-mortem

If the author of the spoof was under no illusions about the scale of the task facing Howard's successor, many Conservatives were more sanguine. According to one member of the party in the media, Howard was 'nothing less than the saviour of the Conservatives' who, 'through sheer power of will, . . . brought the Tories back from the precipice' and was 'rewarded with a magnificent result on Thursday'.[3] The Party had, after all, avoided the meltdown that might have occurred under IDS. It was clearly in no danger of being overtaken by the Lib Dems. It now had 33 more seats than in 2001. It welcomed 55 new recruits (49 men and six women) to the Commons, most of whom were in their thirties and forties and only three of whom had been MPs before. It could even boast the first black man ever to grace the Conservative benches in the Commons. Yet in reality there was still a mountain to climb and, though Labour had fallen from the summit, it was by no means clear that the Tories had even reached base camp.

Two pollsters who had previously worked with the Party, Andrew Cooper (of Populus) and Nick Sparrow (of ICM), were so anxious that it not fall into the trap of believing that all that was needed was one more heave that they both produced reports intended to puncture any complacency and to suggest what needed to be done if the Tories really were to stand a chance of winning in 2009/10.[4] Cooper's report, produced for the modernizing ginger group C-Change, showed that the Party's vote share overall masked the fact that it had actually lost support in Labour-held seats and in those regions (the West Midlands and the North) where it simply had to win seats to form a majority. It was also doing as badly as ever among key groups of voters, especially the growing educated middle class and women, many of whom (like the majority of voters) thought the Conservatives' campaign was 'mean, nasty and negative'. Indeed, between 1992 and 2005 Tory support fell by 13 points to 32 per cent among women, by 18 percentage points to 36 per cent among AB voters, and by 16 points to 26 per cent among 25–45 year olds. Populist policies would not win these people back. Moreover, of the 31 seats gained at Labour's expense, the majority had gone Tory as a result of Labour voters switching to the Lib Dems and other parties rather than to the Tories themselves. The Party had a core vote that shared its values, but it would never be big enough to win it a majority. Worse, if it were listened to, the Party would not make the changes needed to get back into contention: 79 per cent of Tory voters thought the Party was 'on the right track to get back into power before long' but only 28 per cent of those who hadn't voted for the Party agreed.

Sparrow's report likewise made it clear that disillusionment with Labour had not translated into support for the Conservatives. Indeed, they had played an already poor hand badly, and had only been saved further embarrassment by the relatively low turnout, which meant that the tendency for their support to be concentrated among the elderly and the affluent had not hurt them as much as it might have done. It also suggested that the campaign focus on immigration and asylum had got the Party noticed but it did not sway many votes, most of which were decided on bread-and-butter issues (health, education, and, above all, the economy) and on who would make the best Prime Minister – areas where Labour enjoyed solid leads. Just as importantly, it concluded that the Party's problems went way beyond its policies: most voters didn't understand the detail of the latter and weren't sufficiently interested to try to find out more; they simply saw them as confirmation that the Conservatives were not a brand they wanted to have anything to do with. The only way forward was to present new policies or at least to repackage old policies in such a way that they were seen as genuinely relevant to, and workable in, the world as it was now rather than in the eighties or nineties. The only way that could be done was by a leader who represented and was totally dedicated to conveying change.

Quite how the Party was going to find such a leader was a mystery since it first had to decide how it was going to conduct the contest to replace Howard. This was not going to be easy. The outgoing leader's announcement that he was hoping to change the rules was immediately criticized by supporters of David Davis as being a blatant stitch-up aimed at preventing their man coming into what they regarded as his rightful inheritance. To those outside Davis's fan club this seemed a little rich. One of the reasons Howard had gone so quickly, they believed, was because just a few days before the election he had got wind of a move by

Davis supporters – one they denied making – to collect the signatures needed to trigger a vote of no-confidence unless he went of his own accord. Howard himself maintained that he stepped down because he thought it unlikely that the public would elect as Prime Minister a man who would by then be nearly 70, while his attempt to change the rules was the fulfilment of a clear promise he had made to do so, the beneficial by-product of which would be to stop the Party rushing into a contest before it had time to think properly and thereby storing up problems for whoever was elected leader.[5]

The delay meant that, in marked contrast to 1997 and 2001, those thinking of entering the contest had the means, motive, and opportunity to try to define, either in speeches and interviews or in newspaper articles, where the Party had gone wrong and what it had to do next, thereby helping the Tories to conduct something like the post-mortem they had previously avoided. Indeed, the days following the election saw a rash of such interventions by politicians like Malcolm Rifkind, Tim Yeo, and Damian Green, all of whom thought they might stand some chance being drafted as a moderate, centrist alternative to the assumed frontrunner, David Davis.

Of course not everyone who entered the debate, often on similar lines, could be dismissed as simply setting out his stall for the leadership contest. John Bercow, for example, could afford to be more outspoken than many in laying into Howard's campaign emphasis on immigration as 'at best obsessive and at worst repellent' and in laying out a modern-izing agenda that no longer concentrated simply on social liberalism but focused on spelling out 'a Tory vision of economic efficiency and social justice' and 'pitching to the centre ground where elections are won and lost'. Health and education policies which made it obvious that 'we think that the best way to improve public services is to offer people an escape route from them' were 'a counsel of despair', benefiting an affluent minority while 'the majority understandably concludes that the party has given up on them'. As well as supporting (and having politicians who actually used) the public sector, the Conservative Party needed to stay firm in its support for civil liberties and to eschew 'Punch and Judy politics'. It also needed 'decisive action from the top to make the party think, look and sound more like the country we want to govern'.[6]

Howard was reportedly furious with Bercow. Yet his new Shadow

Cabinet, although it included just two women (Caroline Spelman and Theresa May) out of a total of 22 members, suggested that he understood where he was coming from. The big winners, George Osborne (shadowing the Chancellor), David Cameron (shadowing, at his own request, Education), and Francis Maude (made Party Chairman having served his time for crimes against Tory traditionalism and helping to topple IDS), had all worked closely with right-wing traditionalist leaders but did not necessarily share their politics. The first two were clearly being given the chance to show their paces in time for a leadership contest in the early autumn, although Osborne (who had never been personally very popular with many of his fellow MPs) – to the disappointment of Michael Howard, who considered him the more ruthless campaigner – apparently decided almost immediately that his chances of becoming Prime Minister were greater if he waited things out this time around. But Maude's appointment was just as significant.

Everyone interested in the leadership, of course, was paying lip-service to the need for change. Even David Davis, who clearly still believed that events would prove that the 'timeless principles' the Party had offered at the election were right, had the chutzpah to claim he had believed in modernization 'even before the phrase became fashionable'.[7] But Maude, who had had to put up with being written off as a doom-and-gloom merchant for telling the Party year after year what it didn't want to hear, was the real deal. And judging from a post-election piece published together with the impeccably centrist Stephen Dorrell, the new Chairman was not likely to resile from his modernizing views. The Tories, Maude and Dorrell claimed, had to take the Lib Dem phenomenon seriously if they were to snatch from them the mantle of the main opposition to Labour in urban Britain. That meant them appealing to 'One Nation Middle Britain' by sounding authentic in their desire to improve health, education, and pensions, looking like they were glad to be living in the twenty-first century, and being genuinely interested in environmental issues.[8] Speaking after his appointment, Maude was happy to reiterate his view that the Party had 'serious problems'. The key to winning again, he insisted, was 'to identify those problems with absolute stark honesty, not delude ourselves, not persuade ourselves that it is all fine, understand what the negatives are and then apply yourself completely single-mindedly to removing them'.[9]

As part of that process, Howard rather bravely – and probably help-fully – decided to set up a series of weekly forums for his MPs where the parliamentary party could meet together and chew over the election and future directions, helped by presentations on polling and policy from staff at CCHQ.[10] Part of the rationale, admittedly, was the hope – forlorn it turned out – to encourage errant colleagues like Bercow to let off steam in (relative) privacy rather than in the pages of the broad-sheet newspapers. But in the course of so doing he saw to it that MPs were confronted with evidence that the Conservative brand (as it was now increasingly labelled) remained so tainted that it continued to put voters off even those policies with which they agreed. This was testa-ment to the fact that, whatever his own instincts and however belatedly, Howard was coming round to the idea that some kind of step-change had to take place, as well as to the idea that those who were reluctant to agree needed to be persuaded.

Rules of the game

The key to achieving that ideological departure was institutional: the Party would buy itself time to think by altering the rules by which Howard's successor would be chosen. The proposed new system was set out just two-and-a-half weeks after the general election, when the Party Board approved a document entitled *A 21st Century Party*.[11] The system was controversial since it not only involved restoring the final say on the leadership to Tory MPs but was bundled together with proposals that would give the Party Board powers to reconfigure (and even dissolve) constituency associations, as well as diluting their influ-ence on the National Convention, which henceforth would be the only means through which ordinary grassroots members would have even an indirect say in choosing the Tory leader.

Those who were reluctant to see the Party change ideologically still held out some hope that they could scupper Howard's plans to delay a contest by mobilizing disquiet about the new rules and tapping into lingering resentment against his supposedly high-handed treatment handed out to one of their former colleagues, Howard Flight, before the election. Most MPs were pleased that the proposals restored the final say on the leadership to the parliamentary party: many of them, after all, had been pressing Howard to do this almost as soon as he became leader.[12] They were disappointed, however, that they only got to see the proposals after they had been approved by the Party Board. And they resented the proposal that the National Convention would get to rank the list of candidates and that its first choice would apparently be given a guaranteed place in each parliamentary ballot, including the final one. It did not help that the leadership rules were presented together with a package of reforms designed, in many members' opinion, to make it easier rather than harder for the leadership to get troublesome MPs and candidates disciplined or even deselected (à la Flight). MPs also thought it silly (not unreasonably) to make approval of the new leadership rules conditional on approval of wider institutional changes: if the voluntary party did not like the latter and voted against them, then the parliamentary party would be stuck with the current system for electing the leader.

As a result, Howard came in for severe criticism at a meeting held to discuss the changes – so severe, in fact, that there was some talk of him having to step down in the face of a motion of no-confidence before they could be put in place. Concerned lest this plunge the Party into a precipitate contest, a chastened Howard immediately made it clear he had no intention of going immediately, but also admitted consultation on the rule changes 'could have been better handled'. MPs would now get the chance to vote on a range of compromise proposals in the next few weeks, while the decision to bundle the leadership rules into a package of reforms was apparently not set in stone. All this appeared to do the trick. Supporters of David Davis (who had to be careful not to be seen to be knifing Howard and was unsure anyway he would win an immediate leadership contest) backed off – for the moment at least.

Setting out their stalls

Whatever the bookies said about him being frontrunner, David Davis knew he was not going to find things easy. To get where he had from his working-class beginnings had required tremendous self-belief and single-minded ambition. In a Tory politician from a more conventional background such qualities might have been admired or at least discounted as the inevitable by-products of a private education. But, in Davis's case, they had earned him a reputation as a lazy but arrogant know-all, a charmless, calculating, and egotistical chancer, unpopular even with those who shared his Thatcherite and morally conservative views. This reputation was only enhanced when early on he allowed his lieutenants, who appeared to some MPs to be already 'measuring the Whip's Office for curtains', to repeat the mistakes of the *Portillistas* in 2001 by trying to strong-arm MPs into supporting him as the only way to secure the favour of the candidate who was supposedly bound to win. Realizing that this was going to backfire, Davis called the dogs off and instead tried to go about mounting a convincing claim to be the Tories' unity candidate. He also had to persuade people that, as well as a proven ability to take out government ministers, he had the ability to communicate a coherent, positive vision. Consequently, Davis needed time just as much as the man who, next to Ken Clarke, many already suspected might be his most serious rival – David Cameron.

Institutionally, and as an individual, Cameron was close to Michael Howard. Ideologically, however, the two were further apart than many realized. The fact that Cameron put together the Party's 2005 'Victor Meldrew manifesto' said much more about his phrasemaking, his ambition, and his 'feline disposition to insinuate himself with the current in-crowd' than it did about his political philosophy, which tended towards classic Tory pragmatism and scepticism.[13] A report from the fringe of the Tory Conference in the early autumn of 2004 made this obvious:

> 'How can the Tories win again?' is . . . the question on most lips. . . . David Cameron, rising hope of the soft, pragmatic Tories, had a try in a single-sentence response at a lunchtime event yesterday: 'By emphasising the Conservative values that the vast majority of the British public share, by turning them into Conservative policies – and by showing how we would put them in to action.'. . . Cameron yesterday pointed to some of the things they have to do to begin to get closer to the middle ground: avoid creating artificial differences with Labour; avoid monomania on Europe or anything else; concentrate on shared values; be prepared to modernise; and always acknowledge in policy 'that there is a "we" as well as a "me"'.[14]

The same report noted wistfully, however, that 'there is a gulf between knowing roughly what to do and having a serious opportunity to do it'. And even those who worked in Westminster were all-too-ready to assume in the summer of 2005 that Cameron would not get that opportunity any time soon.

Like Liam Fox, Cameron trailed Davis badly in a YouGov opinion poll of Conservative Party members and voters released on the first day of June: Davis was the first or second choice of 54 per cent of members, with 30 and 24 per cent naming Cameron and Fox, respectively. Nevertheless (and this was clearly not the case when it came to Ken Clarke) there was no widespread feeling against the new Shadow Minister of Education. Moreover, three-quarters of members claimed they valued 'the ability to reach out beyond the party membership to attract more support among voters', while almost two-thirds mentioned 'the ability to articulate a clear vision of the party's future' – an encouraging finding for someone like Cameron, who was a good communicator and not afraid to talk about a general direction. And, while a new leader would be expected to be tough on immigration and Europe, only just over a third of members thought he needed to be 'committed to cutting taxes drastically and to reducing greatly the state's role in society'. The poll also made it clear that there was no enthusiasm to see Howard go quickly and very substantial approval (71 to 23 per cent) of plans to return the choice of leader to Tory MPs. In short, inasmuch as those MPs cared about the opinions of the grassroots, the poll suggested that Howard's timetable should be stuck to and that David Davis would be a popular choice; but it also hinted that Liam Fox and, in particular, David Cameron couldn't be written off.

The same could not be said, however, of Malcolm Rifkind or any of the other MPs – Alan Duncan, Damian Green, Andrew Lansley, and David Willetts – who were considering a crack at the leadership. Yet their attempts to get themselves noticed during the phoney war that resulted from the delay to the contest while the rules were sorted were nonetheless useful. Typically, of course, some took to it with more gusto – and more thought – than others. The most obvious example, predictably enough, was David Willetts, who received good notices for a speech to the Social Market Foundation whose synthesis – he called it 'grown-up Conservatism' – of some of the points raised by modernizers like Bercow with a more traditional Tory belief in the power of civil society seemed to set the agenda for candidates with more chance than he ever had of actually winning the contest.[15]

With the prospect of an immediate leadership contest receding, Willetts' intervention, plus the desperate desire of some of the new intake to be seen to take ideas seriously ('localism' being the flavour of the month), other, more serious contenders felt increasingly obliged to debate ideas as well as do the numbers. There were even signs that the frontrunner, David Davis, was willing to signal where he stood, even if it seemed to be a long way from Willetts and virtually indistinguishable from what the Party had offered the electorate since 1997. Although he claimed to understand that 'one last heave' would not be enough to win the next election, he seemed to think that task could be accomplished by nodding to social liberalism and then offering pretty much the same as last time, only more so.[16] As usual, this kind of thinking ignored the wide and continuing gap between Tory voters and voters generally. Polling suggested that a third of both groups were attracted by bigger cuts in taxes and public spending. But less than half as many voters overall (18 to 41 per cent) thought the Conservative Party need only 'stick to its guns and put over its existing ideas more strongly', while nearly twice as many (43 to 22 per cent) believed that it needed 'to change significantly, get more in touch with life in modern Britain and become more moderate'.[17]

Davis was of course aware that he had to appeal across the Party, albeit from the right, and therefore sought to stress his belief that a smaller state and lower taxes would actually benefit 'the weakest in society' by attacking the dependency culture that had supposedly brought social mobility to a halt: 'The test of the success of Conservative policies', he claimed, 'is what they do for the disadvantaged, for those on the outside and those who want to make the most of their lives.'[18] Here he was in good company, just outclassed and outbid. Liam Fox, although no less convinced than Davis that the Party could shape public preferences rather than accommodate them ('Smart politicians do not move to the centre – they move the centre'), had better soundbites, using a television interview, for instance, to stress the need to fix Britain's 'broken society'. David Cameron, on the other hand, while equally comfortable tapping into some traditional 'High Tory' preoccupations with family

and community cohesion, was also able to portray himself as a politician open-minded and pragmatic enough to drop those aspects of the
Conservative offer that hadn't delivered results at the last election.

Cameron, who also had the advantage over his two rivals of being
able to call movingly on his own experience and empathy as the father
of a severely disabled child, set out his stall in tones that suggested he
had been listening much more carefully than they had – and not just to
Willetts but also to Duncan Smith, who, though still an MP, was also
now the head of a think-tank dedicated to proving that the centre-left
did not have a monopoly on social justice. 'Conservative compassion',
claimed Cameron, was needed to rebuild 'a stronger society' via a stress
on family and 'a Government that looks at society from the bottom up.
That recognises that . . . we are all in it together, with a mutual responsibility to care for those who would otherwise get left behind.' [19] A few
weeks later he declared: 'We do think there's such a thing as society, we
just don't think it's the same thing as the state' – an implied (but only
implied) break with Thatcherism which, though it became something
of a trademark for the young pretender, was an outright lift from the
IDS days.

Notwithstanding the above, or the Euroscepticism that gave him
such a huge advantage over Clarke, Cameron's main appeal, of course,
was individual rather than ideological. This had long been recognized
by cheerleaders like Bruce Anderson, who predicted in his *Spectator*
column as early as July 2003 that Cameron would be leader. But now
others were beginning to share his opinion – some of them in unexpected quarters. One such was Peter Preston, former editor of the
left-leaning *Guardian* newspaper and an acute analyst of politics and the
media on both sides of the Atlantic. He asked himself who the ruthless
Republican strategist Karl Rove would pick if choosing a Tory leader to
go up against the man who was clearly going to take over from Blair by
the next election. The answer, he wrote, was obvious:

> [I]t means David Cameron because he ticks most of the non-Gordon
> boxes. Sharp enough on detail to cope? Absolutely. Flexible enough
> on policy to settle in the middle ground? Yes. Affable and witty and
> open enough to make PM Brown seem too dour by half? A liberal-
> seeming chap? More ticks. Young enough to take two shots at the top

and mould a party in his image? Of course. Does it matter that he went to Eton? Well, Blair's public-school Englishness didn't do him any harm against John Major. . . . A touch of the toff could even come in useful.[20]

But it was not just commentators on the centre-left who liked what they saw. In the Tory media, any enthusiasm for Cameron was largely confined to those who believed that the route to electoral recovery was to recapture the centre ground. Indeed, he was routinely dismissed as Blair-lite by pundits in the *Mail*, the *Express*, and *Telegraph* who believed the Party must have the courage of its Thatcherite convictions. Yet Matthew Parris, one of the sharpest members of the party in the media but not a 'modernizer' and definitely no fan of Blair, made up his mind early on that the Tories must choose the younger of 'the two Davids' – and not because of what he thought but because of who he was. He did not know Cameron well – and might perhaps have qualified his remarks if he had talked to those journalists who had dealt with Cameron during his time out of politics as an apparently ruthless PR flack for Carlton Communications. But what he knew about him had persuaded him that, at least in his public life,

[h]e is completely without swagger yet never without command. He has the courtesy of a leader. He treads softly. He does not rush to judgment yet leaves you in no doubt he exercises judgment. He is the most well-judged potential Tory leader we have seen in years.

He is not a hater. He is not a plotter. But he shows a worldly under-standing of a party in which others are. He can be circumspect. He can stand back. He knows how and when to withhold comment. He knows how to listen. He is not impatient to advertise his opinions. Yet with all this he manages to convey the impression of a lively mind and an openness to the opinions and stories of others.

He comes across outstandingly in interview and on the media. He seems sympathetic.

He is smug-free. He never crows or scores points. You feel he is talk-ing to voters who hope the best years of their life lie ahead, rather than those resentful that the best years of their lives are behind them. He is a child of this age, not the last.[21]

The rules of the game – again

Any gratitude Tory MPs felt towards Michael Howard for bringing the Party back from the brink to which IDS had driven it was, by the middle of June 2004, wearing very thin indeed. At a meeting to approve one of six options for a new set of rules to elect the next leader, Howard was joined by just three of his MPs in backing the Party Board's original proposals. The majority instead supported a 'compromise' option whereby, after an initial secret ballot at Westminster, the grassroots would be informally consulted on all those names getting more than 10 per cent support before MPs voted again themselves.

As negotiations with the Party Board on this proposal began, anxiety began to build about the parliamentary party being seen to snatch back the democratic rights of ordinary members. A letter to the *Telegraph* claiming 'members deserve more than an ill-defined consultation mechanism' was signed both by modernizers like Theresa May, Andrew Lansley, and Michael Gove and right-wing traditionalists like John Hayes and Edward Leigh, who had just announced the formation of what they were calling 'Cornerstone' – a network of around 30 MPs keen on a 'faith, flag and family' approach, many of whom had stuck with IDS to the end.[22] Outside parliament, it was IDS's former Chief of staff, Tim Montgomerie, who was leading the campaign to maintain the democratic rights of ordinary members, mainly via a website he had set up called ConservativeHome.

Tory MPs, however, were in no mood to be magnanimous when they were asked to consider both a counter-offer on the leadership rules and a legally binding code of conduct which the Party Board wanted all candidates to sign. On the code (which allowed CCHQ to dismiss candidates who, say, falsified their CVs or attracted embarrassing media coverage), MPs insisted that it not apply to sitting members. On the rules, they voted 127–50 for a system whereby MPs, after a two-week 'consultation process' with their constituency associations, would report back to the Chairman of the 1922, who would then 'assess their findings' and identify two top candidates, in order of preference – a ranking they would bear in mind when voting.

This system was given the nod by the Party Board in early August but it still needed approving in September by a specially convened

'Constitutional College' made up of just over 1,100 MPs, MEPs, peers, association chairmen, area and regional officers, members of the Party Board, and other senior members of the voluntary party. Approval required at least 50 per cent of all those eligible to vote to say yes, and, of these, 66 per cent of both the MPs and National Convention members had to approve the proposal. This was by no means a foregone conclusion. The new rules would be opposed not just by ConservativeHome but by its founder's former boss, Iain Duncan Smith, who mounted a spirited and convincing defence in the media of ordinary members' right to choose.[23] The battle was also waged by a newly launched campaign, called 'A Better Choice', led by Barry Legg, who, after being effectively forced out of his post as Chief Executive by the Party Board in 2003, now had every reason to give it a bloody nose. That the Board recognized things would be tight was obvious when it confirmed that the Constitutional College would be asked to vote only on the leadership rules and not on the other structural changes suggested by *A 21st Century Party*.

Beneath the froth

While this institutional wrangling was going on, the individual and ideological sparring continued. Even the former Tory leader, John Major, entered the fray, arguing that the Tories could win again 'only if we embrace the changing nature of the world as it is today, and capture the non-ideological heart of the British voter' – something which (whether he recognized it or not) he had failed to do after 1990. The kind of campaign fought in 2005 – one that, in his words, had seen both parties 'sinking to the level of who could best out-bigot their opponent' – did not represent the way forward. Nor did a reliance on old nostrums: the Tories only won elections on a right-wing platform in the eighties because Labour was un-electable; the road recommended by 'the ideological Right of the party' would lead only to 'perpetual opposition'; instead the Party had to 'reclaim support from the centre to win'.[24]

A not dissimilar message, albeit one backed up by masses of opinion poll evidence paid for from his own pocket, came from Michael Ashcroft. Certainly no fan of Major, who had after all replaced a Tory leader he very much admired, Ashcroft had long been an institutional modernizer but had become increasingly persuaded that the Party needed to change ideologically too. In the self-published and handsomely illustrated *Smell the Coffee: a Wake-up Call for the Conservative Party*, the former Tory Treasurer, now back on the Party Board, ripped into the approach pursued by the leadership at the general election. Lynton Crosby was praised for belatedly forcing the Party to focus on a smaller group of target seats. However, his campaign's emphasis on immigration came in for particular criticism: it appealed most to less affluent, less educated voters who carried on voting Labour regardless or didn't bother to vote at all, but it actively put off more well-heeled, well-educated people. More generally, research showed voters thought the Tories were out of touch and didn't believe they cared about the problems or shared the values of ordinary people – impressions that only grew more negative as their campaign progressed. Policy, according to Ashcroft, was also a problem: over three-quarters of non-Tory voters thought the Party should concentrate on developing policies to improve the NHS and other public services, not help a minority to escape them. So, too, was personnel: nearly half of the same group thought the Party should involve more women, young people, and ethnic minorities so it looked more like modern Britain.

Such moves would mean nothing, however, argued Ashcroft, unless they contributed to an overhaul of the Conservatives' largely negative brand image – a problem first identified a few years before by IDS and illustrated, as had become commonplace since, by pointing out the difference (estimated at 15 percentage points for 'swing voters') between people's views on policies when they were labelled Tory and when they were not. The Party also had to realize that its 'real core vote' was not a shrinking group of xenophobic nostalgics determined to protect their own interests but 'the election winning coalition of professionals, women, and aspirational voters' that had put them in government for most of the twentieth century. To mobilize them it had to change, and not just superficially. 'The problem', concluded Ashcroft, 'was not that millions of people in Britain thought the Conservative Party wasn't like them and didn't understand them; the problem was that they were right.'

Interventions like this strengthened Cameron's case, not least because they convinced even some right-wingers that the policies they favoured hadn't a chance of being sold unless the Party could somehow convey a sense that it was changing. But it also presented him with a problem or two. He had to be careful not to be seen buying too whole-heartedly into such a critique, not only because he had been at the heart of the general election campaign but because many of those whose votes he was after took such exception to what, in essence, was an attack on both their competence and their ideas. So while he was willing to signal, as he did in one television appearance, that perhaps the Party may have focused too much on crime and immigration, he also took the opportunity provided by some outspoken comments from Malcolm Rifkind (who, despite having no chance whatsoever, had decided to run for leader) to observe, 'You don't get anywhere in life by trashing your brand.'

This kind of stuff was vital because Cameron's only realistic rivals were not those running to his left. A media desperate to inject some colour into the process may have enjoyed speculating that Ken Clarke's imminent entry into the race would damage Cameron. But in reality, this was highly unlikely. Clarke's one big positive – his presumed appeal to voters – could be dismissed as reflecting little more than superior name recognition. And it was simply insufficient to outweigh so many negatives in the eyes of most Tories. Even if he did admit to (sort of) getting it wrong on the single currency, Clarke was a Europhile in a party whose MPs, activists, ordinary members, and financial and media backers were overwhelmingly Eurosceptic. He had refused – and continued to refuse – to serve in any other frontbench capacity except leader. He had made little or no effort to cultivate support in the parliamentary party during the IDS and Howard years, and many of those who might have backed his bid were now signed up to other candidates. He was still a director at British American Tobacco, whose activities in selling its products in developing countries made him vulnerable to attack. He was still determined to rake up his opposition to a war that most Tory politicians supported. And he was still convinced that the only thing fundamentally wrong with the Conservative Party was that it had been stupid enough not to put him in charge. The media might have talked up his chances, but one or two of his closest friends were honest enough to tell him, 'You simply cannot win.'[25]

The real contest, then, beneath all the froth, was still between a young pretender with little ideological baggage and few enemies – David

Cameron – and an old bruiser – David Davis – who, despite his claims to be a 'One Nation' Tory, was still a Thatcherite at heart, who had enemies aplenty, and whose campaign seemed, even to some insiders, to be distinctly second-rate. Indeed, it was becoming obvious to anyone who thought about it hard enough that, with only 21 public declarations and an estimated 41 undeclared pledges according to the *Telegraph* on 19 August, the frontrunner was not as far ahead as he should have been if he truly was as unstoppable as his campaign team claimed – claims which, along with their complacent refusal of offers of help from some younger MPs who feared things weren't going to be quite that easy, did not help Davis's cause. Nor did his careless, even dismissive treatment of the right-wing traditionalists loosely identified with the Cornerstone group. Some of them, he assumed, would be bound to vote for him as the best-placed right-winger and he was anxious that too enthusiastic an endorsement from them might put off more centrist and liberal MPs. Others, he knew, remained personally loyal to IDS and considered themselves 'High Tories' rather than Thatcherites, so they would never vote for him anyway.[26] All this presented Cameron with an opportunity, as long, that is, as he could carry on reassuring the right at the same time as inspiring the moderates and the modernizers.

While refusing to get into the game of trying to match Davis's promises on tax cuts, Cameron did nothing to discourage George Osborne from talking up the possibility that a government led by him might introduce a flat tax. He himself, though, concentrated on 'values' rather than policies – more often than not values that would resonate with the right-wing 'Cornerstoners', who might otherwise vote for Fox. In a Foreign Policy Centre speech in late August, for example, Cameron not only reiterated his backing for the Iraq war, but also criticized public bodies that, by providing so much interpretation and translation for ethnic minorities, undermined Britain's 'shared national culture'. And in a speech right at the start of September he argued for a focus on 'family, community, country', on 'quality of life', on making Britain 'a more civilised place to live'. At the same time, however, he expanded the range of issues that such concerns should cover to include issues that younger voters apparently cared so much about – childcare, plus 'the environment, urban space, culture and leisure'.[27] Cameron's claim to understand these desires – 'I know this is how young people feel because this is how I feel' – may have been a stretch for someone approaching 40, but it was not one that Davis (57), let alone Clarke (65), could hope to match.

Liam Fox, who, at 43, also had what passed for youth in the Tory Party on his side, could not be discounted by Cameron but, in fact, was more of a threat to Davis. The Shadow Foreign Secretary was as much of a state-educated Thatcherite as the Shadow Home Secretary, interested in healing Britain's 'broken society' but standing on a manifesto he summed up as 'sound defence; keeping more of what you earn; less government interference in people's lives; a sense of family, community and respect for the law; Britain controlling its own destiny'.[28] He could of course claim to be younger, more dynamic, and less divisive than Davis, and had spent more time than he had visiting constituency associations as Party Chairman. But to anyone looking for a candidate able to reach out to those who had declined to vote Conservative in 2005, Fox was no better a bet than Davis. If anything, he came over as being even less interested in trying to reach out than his right-wing rival, telling an interviewer just after the launch of his campaign,

> We need to break away from some of the nonsense about inclusiveness. There are lots of voters out there who do not share our basic perceptions and never will. You will never please all the voters, so we should be speaking to people who share our aims about society and Britain's role in the world. There are some people who will never agree with us however nice we are to them.[29]

Fox, though, did give himself one advantage over Davis by announcing that he would insist on something Hague and IDS had failed to achieve – making Conservative MEPs leave the EPP–ED group in the European Parliament. This went down well with the party in the media and allowed him to tap into an ancient grievance against the Shadow Home Secretary over his role in whipping through the Maastricht Treaty. Davis, still believing he would win and not wanting to promise something he knew would be difficult to deliver, did not follow suit. Cameron was less complacent and therefore had fewer compunctions: whether he believed it was realistic or not, he matched Fox's pledge. After all, the strength of his position lay in the fact that he combined

Fox's youth, his Euroscepticism, and his concern with 'the broken society' with Clarke's willingness to accept voters as they were rather than
as the Conservative Party wanted them to be. And just as importantly,
he was not David Davis.

Blackpool

On 27 September, Francis Maude was obliged to announce that the
proposed changes to the system for electing the Party's leader had failed
to achieve sufficient support. After all that, the contest, which would
kick off in earnest at the forthcoming annual conference at Blackpool,
would be conducted under the same rules that elected Iain Duncan
Smith. MPs, predictably enough, had given the changes the required
two-thirds majority: 132 had voted for and 53 against. But in the
National Convention support for the changes had run at only 58 per
cent, well short of the votes needed. Four-and-a-half months had been
spent on a project that had run into the sand and humiliated Howard,
while earning Maude the enmity of many grassroots activists and the
derision of many in the party in the media. Barry Legg, then, had got
his revenge on the Party Board, and in a noble cause.

On the upside, however, the hiatus had – as was intended – given
others, especially Cameron, time to establish themselves as credible,
or at least visible, opponents to David Davis. Just as importantly – as
Howard had also intended – it had provided the time and space the
Party desperately needed to think (if not necessarily to come to any firm
conclusions) about the hole it had fallen into and what it needed to do
in order to get out of it and avoid falling into it again next time round.
Indeed, even David Davis had got round by now to promising not to
repeat the mistakes of recent election campaigns.

In fact, it was this move on Davis's part, together with rumours that
Fox (who had shrewdly championed the continuation of grassroots
involvement) had more pledges than many had expected, which convinced Cameron that his appearance at what was now being billed as
the Tories' 'beauty contest' in Blackpool would have to be even bolder
than he had originally envisaged. As a result, his campaign launch at
the end of September turned into a dress rehearsal for an all-out bid,
urged on him by George Osborne, to sell himself as the only candidate

genuinely willing and able to make the changes the Party needed to make in order to win. True, he took some stick for serving smoothies and playing ambient music. But the positive reaction of journalists to his performance – delivered without notes and much more impressive than what they heard from Davis at his more conventional (and much less expensive) launch the same day – made it all worthwhile, and it was Cameron's picture rather than Davis's which appeared on the front page of the *Telegraph* the next morning.[30]

It was easy to portray David Davis as the favourite as delegates made their way to Blackpool. But it was foolish nonetheless. Davis had indeed picked up many pledges and not all of them from MPs on the right of the Party. David Willetts and Damian Green, for instance, decided to sign up not simply (as some suggested) because they were concerned they would lose out if the Party 'skipped a generation', but because they believed (on the 'Nixon to China' principle) that a figure from the right was best placed to drag it towards the centre.[31] Other centrist MPs were also convinced that Davis had moderated but retained the killer instinct that would be needed to take on the right; as one MP who supported him put it, 'If anybody was going to shoot the headbangers at the side of the road it was going to be him.'[32] However, the gap between the figure of 55 parliamentary supporters Davis named at his launch and the 16 Cameron could muster at his disguised the fact that, after nearly five months, the so-called shoo-in had reached a ceiling rather than a critical mass.

Given all the incentives to attach themselves to a man whose victory was supposedly near-certain, the fact that 143 Conservative MPs had refused to back Davis publicly should have given more people pause for thought. Certainly, while Cameron himself remained nervous, there were those in his campaign team who were now more convinced than ever that Davis was eminently beatable. Andrew Robathan, an experienced ex-army man from the no-nonsense right, had taken over 'running the book' from fellow ex-soldier Hugo Swire, who, like Robathan and the MP for Bexhill and Battle, Greg Barker, had supported Cameron from the very start. After another look through his list of those who were supporting all the candidates persuaded him that there were simply too many MPs hostile to Davis (and his parliamentary lieutenants) to mean the frontrunner could win, and certain that Clarke had no chance, Robathan decided he should have the courage of his calculations. He rushed off to the bookies to place a few hundred pounds on the young pretender at what he rightly regarded as the ridiculously good price of 14–1.[33]

If Tory MPs were paying as much attention to polls as they normally did, then Cameron was also better placed than many outsiders assumed. A YouGov survey for the *Telegraph* did little for Cameron directly but did emphasize the dilemmas and drawbacks posed by his two main rivals: a substantial minority of Conservative Party members were viscerally opposed to Clarke, while Davis, although he attracted much less opposition, was not thought likely to boost the Party's electoral fortunes. Meanwhile a MORI poll for the *Sun*, also conducted on the eve of the Conference in Blackpool, suggested that neither Clarke (definitely not the *Sun*'s favourite) nor Davis would make much more of a dent in Labour's lead than the much less well-known Cameron. More striking still was an in-depth study of voters who had not voted Tory but would consider doing so, conducted for the *Guardian* by ICM, which polled them after showing them footage of each candidate in action: on balance, Cameron outperformed both Clarke (jovial but divisive) and Davis (competent but dull), especially when pitted against Gordon Brown. The public, and probably most ordinary party members, might not have realized it, but the youngest candidate in the field was now in pole position.

The Conference opened with Chairman Francis Maude doing what to anyone who had been listening to him for the last four years was his usual turn, delivering a message that would also have been familiar to anyone who'd read Ashcroft's *Smell the Coffee*. The Tories shared the same values as voters – 'honesty, generosity, respect for all, compassion, fairness' – but had managed to convince them that it cared mainly 'about the well-off, not the have-nots'. Electoral progress was predicated on the Party changing to reflect twenty-first-century Britain, a largely urban country where many took multiculturalism, gender equality, and a relaxed (or at least a tolerant) attitude to moral matters for granted. Judging from the audience reaction, it was not what delegates wanted to hear – and the man who had tried to strip party members of their voting rights and interfere in their associations was not the man they wanted to hear it from. But even if they listened in silence and applauded only half-heartedly, they could hardly fail to understand his message.

Intentionally or not, all this was the perfect warm-up for Cameron's speech the next day. The Party and the media had been told – by a figure whom few warmed to and in tones that were largely negative – that the Tories had a problem. Cameron, a charismatic speaker who sold change as something positive, came over as the solution. More than any of the other candidates, he understood, possibly because of his commercial PR experience, that his appearance had to be a pitch not a speech.[34] His mission was to persuade the Party, without notes and, more importantly, without beating it up, that he understood its problem and could supply the solution – 'a modern, compassionate Conservatism [that] is right for our times, right for this new generation, right for our party and right for our country'.

Like Ken Clarke (whose own speech, a knockabout affair which emphasized his electoral and governmental credentials, also went down well), Cameron found time to criticize Labour and particularly Brown. But what was also apparent was that here was a man who understood that Blair, by showing that it was possible to combine a vibrant economy with a high-spending commitment to social justice, had (as Thatcher had done before him) altered the terrain on which the opposition had to fight. The Conservatives had to realize New Labour had won voters over, not simply fooled them. This did not mean it was unbeatable, but it did mean that it would have to be beaten at least in part on its terms. To win, the Tories would have to show that they were genuinely committed to more effective delivery rather than just to doing things on the cheap. They would have to blend aspiration and compassion, and project not only modernization but moderation too. And if all this weren't enough, Cameron was sufficiently media-savvy not only to invite his yummy-mummy wife onto the stage with him after the speech but also to give her pregnant belly a paternal pat. It all combined to create, as intended and as one of his team had been hoping for from the very beginning, 'a JFK moment'.[35]

The reaction in the conference hall, reflected by the evening's television news coverage, was enthusiastic, even electric. The reaction in the next day's print media was equally positive – and in all the right places. Writing in the *Sun*, the man sometimes referred to as 'Rupert Murdoch's representative on earth', Irwin Stelzer, compared Cameron's optimistic effort to the 'Morning in America' message that had helped Reagan win over American voters in 1979. Just as importantly, the *Telegraph*'s leader praised Cameron: while it regretted that he seemed keener on 'reinforcing the state health and education systems rather than radically transforming them', it noted that he also believed in 'low taxes, family stability and national sovereignty' and praised him for realizing that it was 'necessary to cast these policies in the idiom of the voters' and 'in language of decency and compassion'.

By performing to such acclaim, Cameron (and to some extent Clarke) set the bar very high for the man whose declared support among MPs (now in the mid-60s) was still apparently more than that of all the other candidates put together. David Davis knew he was no platform speaker – coaching and watching videotapes of acknowledged masters like Reagan and Clinton had made no difference. But his desire to be seen all around the Conference meant that, although he did rehearse his speech, he was simply too tired to make the most of a text that in any case suffered from being written by a trio of talented individuals (Nick Herbert, Damian Green, and Paul Goodman) whose collective effort sadly turned out to be less than the sum of their parts.

Moreover, many people in the Party were willing Davis to fail. They included modernizers who winced at his busty supporters in their 'It's DD for me' tee-shirts, as well as implacable enemies from way-back-when.[36] Just as importantly, his ill-wishers also included many in the media, Tory and otherwise. Davis's relationship with them was poor. It was not just that he, unlike his main rival, had little contact with editors and media executives. Or that he failed to return the calls of the journalists they employed. There was, confessed one reporter, a strong feeling in the press pack that

> Cameron was a better story if he won. . . . David Davis: we were used to him; we were bored with him; he'd been quite high-handed and arrogant with lots of journalists. Dave: we didn't really know – young, modern; there'd be all sorts of interesting stories about cocaine and drugs, and he was attractive, and his picture looked better on our front pages.

Davis did not disappoint his detractors. His speech ('We need to agree on change. But we don't need a collective nervous breakdown. So let's stop apologizing, and get on with the job') suggested that, unlike Cameron, he underestimated the task in hand. Worse, it was a leaden, stumbling affair that left everyone wondering whether he might turn out to be another Duncan Smith. Indeed, its peroration was so poor that Davis literally had to gesture to his audience that he had finished so they could begin the requisite standing ovation. Naturally, his opponents wasted no time in spinning the whole thing as, in the words of a supporter of Liam Fox (who delivered his own right-wing tub-thumper with considerably more flair than Davis), 'a train wreck'. Even without this, though, it would have been impossible to prevent journalists reporting Davis's effort for the 'triumph of mediocrity' it so obviously represented. The instant verdict of ITN's political editor, Tom Bradby, was devastating: the speech had 'bombed and bombed badly'. As another experienced journalist, looking back on Blackpool, recalled,

> We just piled into Cameron and deserted David Davis, who was left blinking, staring and saying 'What happened?' But also journalists sensed . . . in the hall, that something was happening. They wanted to be on the right side. They wanted to back the winner. They could sense a winner. . . . The herd, they just rushed into him – bought shares in Cameron.

But while the younger man definitely benefited from the media coverage of the speeches, possibly just as important in swinging the votes of MPs was a package on the BBC's *Newsnight* in which Frank Luntz, a controversial US political consultant, treated a large group of floating voters to video clips of each candidate in action. Just as ICM had shown in the *Guardian* the week before, the more people saw of Cameron the more they liked him, and his impact was magnified (some would say blown out of all proportion) by the star-struck hyperbole of the American master of ceremonies.[37] The Cameron team, who had worked hard all week, even padding hotel corridors at dawn to deliver well-designed mailshots, rapidly distributed DVD copies of the BBC package.

The Davis team decided to admit their champion's speech had been sub-par but stressed that there was more to leadership than public speaking. A reorganization also took place: more media-friendly faces like Damian Green, Julie Kirkbride, and David Willetts would take a more hands-on approach with journalists, leaving Davis's long-time lieutenants, Andrew Mitchell and Derek Conway, to try to convince supporters to stay on board. If those MPs took any account of the views of ordinary members, however, it was going to be a difficult task: a YouGov poll for the *Sunday Times* taken at the end of the Conference suggested Cameron, who was supported by 16 per cent of members before Blackpool, had shot into first place on 39 per cent. Clarke was his nearest rival on 26 per cent (down 4 per cent over the week). Fox ended the week where he started it on 13 per cent. But support for Davis had halved from 30 to just 14 per cent. And any Tories who looked at Labour-supporting papers like the *Guardian* and the *Mirror* could see that, for the first time in well over a decade, they were genuinely worried. Hardly surprising, then, that even some of those at the very heart of Davis's campaign team knew, even as they left Blackpool, that 'a knock-out blow' had been delivered and that their man was 'out for the count'.

All over bar the voting

After the 2005 Conference, then, and probably even before it, the leadership was Cameron's to lose. It was always likely he would make it into the membership ballot, though few thought before the Conference that it might be in first rather than second place. Now it seemed likely that he, rather than Davis, would win that ballot. Davis's only advantage (albeit his disadvantage too) was that he was a known quantity. Cameron, on the other hand, had been subjected to nowhere near the same degree of media scrutiny. Was there something, anything, that he could not do? Or, worse, something he had done? The newspapers, intrigued by a well-rehearsed non-reply he had given at a fringe event in Blackpool, did not take long to come up with an answer, or rather a question: had he taken illegal drugs?

For a few days at least, the issue provided a straw at which Cameron's opponents could clutch. Perhaps Cameron and Osborne (who was the subject of even more laughably lurid allegations) would come over not as the personable young family men they liked to present themselves as but as members of a 'metropolitan' elite whose privileged backgrounds and supposedly louche lifestyles meant they had nothing in common with the older, provincial, small-c conservatives who were assumed to make up the ordinary membership. But Cameron's insistence that even politicians were entitled not just to their youthful indiscretions but to keep them private, too, eventually killed the story. Indeed, the whole episode may even have enhanced his reputation by showing that he was 'a normal human being', and more importantly that, despite calls from some of the party in the media (the *Mail* and the *Express*) to 'come clean', he could stick to his guns and keep calm under pressure. By dominating the news coverage of the campaign it also made it more difficult for Davis and co. to mount any kind of fightback. Moreover, the media's obsession with substances meant it failed to focus on substance – the one area where the relatively inexperienced Cameron might have struggled, at least compared to Davis and Clarke.

Cameron went into the first round of parliamentary voting with another key advantage over his opponents, even though all of them did as well as he did in front of their parliamentary colleagues at the hustings held the day before. A BPIX poll for the *Mail on Sunday* which gave Labour a 7 per cent lead over the Tories suggested that with Cameron as leader this would be reduced to 5 per cent whereas under all the other candidates the Party would be even further behind (9 per cent with Clarke and 13 per cent with either Fox or Davis). A *Mail* survey of constituency chairmen suggested that, of those who had made up their minds, 51 per cent supported Cameron, while just 22 and 21 per cent preferred Clarke and Davis, leaving only 5 per cent backing Fox. Even more interestingly, Cameron was said to have a narrow (41–37 per cent) lead in the associations whose MP had publicly declared for Davis, thereby putting pressure on (or giving an excuse to) those MPs to switch in the privacy of the ballot box.

Some of David Davis's declared supporters did indeed defect when it came to the first round of voting. Although his total of 62 was not as bad as some had feared, it was low enough to encourage mischievous speculation that Davis might throw in the towel to facilitate a coronation for Cameron. And though Davis still beat Cameron, whose media-fuelled momentum netted him 56 votes, his younger rival could look forward to the prospect of more to come following Ken Clarke's elimination after he came bottom with 38. More alarming for both the top two was

Liam Fox's score. His 42 votes, and his campaign manager's insistence that he should be seen as 'the champion of the right', meant he was a serious option for Thatcherites who now doubted that Davis could beat Cameron in the membership ballot – doubts shared by the party in the media, all the way from the *Sun* through the *Express* to the *Telegraph*.

As for ordinary party members, a YouGov poll suggested they were not only keener on a Cameron–Fox run-off but that it would be closer than if Cameron were pitched against Davis. The main message, however, was that Cameron would walk it anyway, not least because – following the logic that operated in all the leadership contests since 1990 – he was the candidate who aroused least opposition and was thought most likely to be able to unite the Party. Cameron was way ahead on being the best media performer and the most likely to attract new members and new voters. And he was able to appeal not just to the approximately half of members described as 'One Nation Tories' but also to around a third of the other half – the 'Thatcherite' or 'blue water Tories'. As a result of all this, nearly two-thirds of those who backed Liam Fox or David Davis, either of whom would have polarized opinion rather than achieved reconciliation, said they wouldn't mind if Cameron won.[38]

The fact that it confirmed the common wisdom concerning Cameron meant that the poll was taken seriously by MPs. But it wasn't enough to allow Fox (who, with nine additional votes, finished on 51) to overhaul Davis (who, having shed five votes, ended up with 57). Cameron piled on an extra 34 votes to finish on 90. Even if that total was lower than it might have been because a handful of his supporters had voted for Davis in order to eliminate Fox, it was still a little disappointing, since it suggested that those with doubts about him outnumbered those who did not and that he might face problems if, as leader, he tried to move what was still clearly a right-wing parliamentary party too far into the centre or failed to deliver electoral success.

Given Cameron's message was about style as much as substance, as well as his reluctance (especially now the leadership was almost certainly his) to start writing the Tories' next manifesto four years out from the next election, it was inevitable that Davis would seek to portray the frontrunner as 'policy-lite' and to project himself (via a commitment to tax cuts, grammar schools, abolishing university tuition fees, and renegotiating the UK's relationship with the EU) as an experienced but also a conviction politician. But this was never going to be enough in the face of overwhelming polling evidence that not only Conservative supporters but also voters in general thought much more of Cameron than they thought of Davis.

The same evidence also exposed as hollow Davis's claim that he was the 'Heineken candidate' who could reach into parts of the country that Cameron could not: an ICM survey for the *Guardian* published just as the campaign for the votes of the membership got going showed not only that Cameron was preferred to Davis by 44 to 20 per cent overall but that any regional variation was very small indeed. The same poll also showed Cameron would do much better against the man who, it was assumed, would succeed Tony Blair as PM: whereas voters preferred Brown to Davis by 45 to 32 per cent, Cameron closed the gap to 43–38; among those who said they would consider voting Tory, he actually led Brown 48–33. Given this, it was hard to tell whether some of those who had supported Liam Fox but were now coming out for Cameron – 10 in one day on 31 October – were genuinely taken with what they now claimed was his 'huge talent, intellectual ability and sound judgment' or simply voting, albeit belatedly, for the winner. By 19 November, 116 out of 198 MPs, including William Hague and Liam Fox, had publicly declared for Cameron. Another former leader, Iain Duncan Smith, also supported him – as did (privately) Michael Howard.

Facing an opponent who not only seemed bound to win but had the support of over half the parliamentary party despite his explicit rejection of what he dismissed as the 'core vote, right-wing agenda' which some of them still favoured, Davis did as well as he could have done in the contest in the country. This was not just because he brought in Nick Wood, the man who had spun so hard for Hague and Duncan Smith. Or because he, like Cameron, spent almost all the £100,000 candidates were allowed for the contest. It was because he was actually a very capable performer in the more intimate setting of the TV studio. Indeed, Davis did better than Cameron in an unprecedented head-to-head television debate held just before ballot papers were sent out – one watched by 2.5 million people.

But Davis and his team knew that it was all too late. YouGov repeated its survey of party members and showed that even those with reservations about Cameron saw him as the future and as someone who could deliver victory at the next election – exactly the argument made by the *Mail* when (like the *Sun* and, eventually, the *Telegraph*) it endorsed 'Dave' rather than 'David'.[39] When the result of the ballot of 253,689 members was announced in the first week of December, it was overwhelming. On a turnout of 77 per cent, Cameron beat Davis by two-to-one. Survey evidence suggests that although Cameron cleaned up when it came to party members who believed the Party 'should move towards the political centre with more moderate "One Nation" policies', he also gained about the same proportion as his rival of those who thought it 'should remain firmly on the right of politics and put clear blue water between the Conservatives and the Labour Party'.[40]

After seven months during which the Party had surprised itself by conducting a contest that had for the most part remained civilized, hope had literally triumphed over experience. But the Tories had not simply chosen a new leader, they had also, whether they liked it or not, chosen a new path. Speaking in mid-November, Cameron had made no bones about the 'clear choice' the Party faced in the leadership contest: 'Do we move to the right,' he asked, 'or do we fight for the centre ground? Do we stick to our core vote comfort zone or do we reach out? Do we repeat the mistakes of the past, or do we change to win for the future?'[41] Given this, the Conservatives' new leader could fairly claim a mandate for what he wanted to do. But precisely what that was, and whether he really would be able to do it, remained to be seen.

7

'THE POLITICS OF AND'

DAVID CAMERON, 2005–

Almost the first thing David Cameron had to do after taking over was to go up against Tony Blair at Prime Minister's Questions in the House of Commons. Fortunately it was a task for which the new Leader of the Opposition was supremely well qualified: he had helped Major, Duncan Smith, and Howard prepare for PMQs, and he was already well known for being calm under pressure, quick-witted, and preternaturally articulate. Little surprise, then, that his debut received rave reviews. The real question, though, was not whether he could perform in parliament. After all, William Hague and Michael Howard had usually been able to do that. But neither they, nor Iain Duncan Smith, had come anywhere near convincing the country that the Conservatives should be given a chance to govern. Why should Cameron be any different?

One big reason to think he might be was that, unlike them, he had the wind at his back before he even began. By the very act of taking over, Cameron achieved a step-change in his party's opinion poll rating. Within days of his assuming the leadership, Sunday newspapers were breathlessly reporting ICM and YouGov polls which showed the Conservatives enjoying a slight lead over a Labour Party which, fortuitously for Cameron, was clearly split from top to bottom, not just on policies like education but also on whether Brown should take over from Blair sooner rather than later. Only the most convinced 'Cameroon' (as his supporters had been christened) believed that they were definitely on their way to Downing Street. But this was a better start than most of them had dared hope for. Their man had that most precious of political commodities – momentum. The task now was to keep it up.

Hitting the ground running

Partly due to the time lag between the Tories losing the 2005 general election and electing their new leader, Cameron, unlike his predecessors, was in a position to begin implementing a strategy rather than searching for one. Equally important, it was a strategy to which he (along with those in his inner circle like Steve Hilton, George Osborne, George Bridges, Kate Fall, Ed Llewellyn, and, later on, Andrew Mackay) was not only intellectually but also emotionally committed – again something which could not have been said about his predecessors or many of the people they preferred to have around them. This, plus the fact that the so-called 'Notting Hill Set' (now increasingly referred to as 'Team Cameron') were personal friends with a common project, rather than simply an entourage thrown together by adversity, suggested – even to those who were opposed to them – that they were much less likely to abandon the strategy under pressure. [1]

The strategy had some novel aspects – not least the sheer pace at which it was to be pursued from the outset, the aim being, in the words of one of Cameron's closest advisers, 'not simply to hit the ground running but to hit it sprinting'. But it was essentially a synthesis of several ideas that had been tried before but never with anything approaching the consistency, patience, and message discipline that Cameron could bring to bear. Trailed and tested during his bid for the leadership, the strategy was predicated on the idea (around since IDS became leader) that the Conservative 'brand' needed 'decontamination'. Cameron would begin by doing everything in his power to communicate to the electorate that the Party was changing and, every bit as importantly, was moving back into the centre ground. Media silence would be maintained on the issues that the Party had been 'banging on' about for far too long – not just Europe, which Duncan Smith and Howard had also played down, but also the other parts of the so-called 'Tebbit trinity', immigration and tax. The vacuum created would be filled by Cameron talking about (and creating striking visual images around) issues not normally associated with the Tories, notably the environment, as well as international development, corrosive consumerism, and work–life balance. Meanwhile, Cameron would challenge Labour's automatic ownership of the NHS and state schooling by stressing his own family's reliance on them – and the government's internal divisions on health and education policy – to persuade voters that the Conservatives cared not about the few who could opt out but the many who could not. Public-sector professionals would also be wooed by assurances that they were valued and that their professional discretion, eroded by Labour's 'target culture', would be restored by a Conservative government. At the same time, the leadership would change the system for selecting parliamentary candidates in order to make it more likely that the Party would select more women and people from ethnic minorities. Finally, it would implicitly distance itself from the Thatcher years not by apologizing for them but by stressing that, in effect, that was then but this is now.

The aim of all this was, firstly, to convince the electorate (and particularly the middle classes, who historically have been the Conservatives' real 'core vote') that the Tories were a pragmatic and moderate alternative to Labour, and, secondly, to obtain them 'permission to be heard' from voters who, since the 1990s, had refused even to listen to a party they considered pointless or beyond the pale. It would take time and would require Conservatives to exercise restraint and self-discipline, to avoid the temptation to rush back to 'core' issues if the going got tough or, conversely, if they began to pull ahead of Labour. As Cameron explained to one of the new intake at Westminster – employing an analogy that confirmed his natural ability to communicate in ways that even those outside the Westminster village could understand – 'You know, it's like playing Tomb Raider. If you can't finish off level one, there's no point talking about level two.'[2]

Once voters could be persuaded not to discount Conservative ideas automatically because they emanated from a party that was 'nasty', selfish, old-fashioned, and incompetent, it could carefully begin to play as well to its traditional strengths on, say, crime (and possibly even immigration and Europe). Demands for policy in these and other areas would be countered by the creation of groups and task forces set up by Cameron on becoming leader. These would allow him to signal straight away that the Party was doing some fresh thinking and that it was seeking to reconnect with professional and other pressure groups it had long ignored. They would also allow him to link the Party with popular, even iconic non-party figures, to tie some older Tory states-men into the modernization project, and to help hold off the inevitable demand from Labour for policies, which it could then either steal or rip to shreds. Finally, they would help Cameron placate those on the right of the Party. He anticipated some resistance here but planned if at all possible not to confront them but to take them with him by (a) deliver-ing consistent opinion poll leads and (b) signalling that, although he could not give them the up-front tax cuts and spending restraint craved by the economic liberals, he was personally committed to key aspects of the family-friendly social agenda favoured by the 'High Tories'.

This largely positive strategy also had an important negative edge to it. Whatever the rhetorical commitment to ending what Cameron called 'Punch and Judy politics', the Tories would try to trash the reputation and the character of Gordon Brown, whom they considered eminently beatable, at the same time as doing everything possible to hasten his taking over from Blair – the political magician who had taken out the Tory Party but also taught those now running it many of the techniques that could restore its fortunes. The 'psychologically flawed' Chancellor was, to quote Osborne, not only 'unpleasant and brutal' but 'past his sell-by date'. Blair, to quote Cameron, 'was the future once'; now it belonged, went the narrative, to a revivified Conservative Party.

That such attacks left Cameron's opposite number obviously dis-concerted and Osborne's reportedly livid was in part to do with the fact that Downing Street's famously feud-prone next-door neighbours were having difficulty deciding how to play the new Leader of the Opposition. Should Cameron, as Brown believed, be hit as hard as possible from the outset, portrayed as an effete old-Etonian who had no idea how the other half lived and who, like George Bush in 2000, would talk about compassionate conservatism but act very differently once in office? Or, as Blair seemed to think, should Labour hold its fire, welcome Cameron's apparent move to the centre as testimony to New Labour's ideological hegemony while casting doubt both upon his willingness to make the hard choices involved and his party's readiness to join him on the journey? Here, after all, was a Tory leader who not only cycled to work and shopped at Tesco (and was more than happy to be filmed doing so), but who was happy to declare 'I'm not a deeply ideological person – I'm a practical person', to insist that he hadn't come into politics to be 'the mouthpiece' for the economic interests normally associated with his party, and to claim that, instead of trying to 'turn the clock back', he preferred to ask, 'What has been done which is good and we can build on, and what needs to be changed?'[3]

'Cut-through'

George Osborne was a shoo-in as Shadow Chancellor when Cameron announced his new team. Francis Maude was also reappointed: the malice some bore him in the constituencies and on the right of the Party was not going to make things easy but moving him would immediately have cast doubt on the Party's commitment to modernization, especially on its promise to select more women and ethnic minority candidates. An example in this respect was set by Cameron himself. He included four women and also gave Alan Duncan, the first openly gay Tory MP, Trade and Industry. Another former Thatcherite-turned-modernizer, Andrew Lansley, carried on in his portfolio, Health. David Willetts was forgiven his support for David Davis and given Education. Also absolved was Damian Green, who was brought back onto the front-bench (though not the Shadow Cabinet) and tasked with moderating the Party's previously strident tones on immigration. David Davis kept his post as Shadow Home Secretary to reassure right-wing MPs and his dedicated parliamentary followers, one of whom (Andrew Mitchell) was also kept in post (in his case at International Development). Liam Fox went to Defence, while his campaign manager, Chris Grayling, swapped Shadow Leader of the House for the transport brief. Fox's place as Shadow Foreign Secretary went to William Hague, who agreed to forsake some of his considerable extra-parliamentary earnings to make his first appearance on the Conservative frontbench since stepping down as leader in 2001.

Another former leader, Iain Duncan Smith, was put in charge of one of six new policy groups, his being concerned with social justice. The other five covered national and international security, quality of life, public service reform, overseas aid, and economic competitiveness, under a demoted John Redwood. They would produce reports that would eventually feed into green papers by Shadow Ministers in a process overseen by Oliver Letwin, who spent much of his first few months in the job making it clear (much to the chagrin of some of the party in the media) just how much of the 2005 manifesto might be put out of its misery and how many new kites might be flown.

While Letwin suggested the policy groups were aiming at 'a real intellectual revival of Conservatism', the emphasis, as Stephen Dorrell, one of the group's co-chairs, put it, was not on 'thinking the unthinkable' but on 're-establishing contact with people that the Tory Party hadn't been in serious contact with' for years (academics, policy wonks, pressure groups, and practitioners) and coming up with ideas that could pass what he called 'the Wednesday–Friday test' – electorally attractive before the Thursday on which general elections are always held but also capable of implementation once a Tory Prime Minister moves into Downing Street the day after.[4] The groups were also clearly intended to allow Cameron to appear open-minded and serious about substance as well as style at the same time as continuing to resist attempts to bounce him into policies he might live to regret. Just as importantly, their immediate establishment would suggest even to the vast majority of voters who paid little attention to politics that this was a leadership which had not only hit the ground running but was willing to re-evaluate its positions and come up with fresh ideas based on evidence rather than ideology.

This was exactly what the pollster Nick Sparrow had suggested in his unsolicited advice to the Party after the 2005 election.[5] Cameron was also determined to follow the counsel offered by another pollster closely associated with the Party, Andrew Cooper, who had tried and failed to move things on under William Hague and, in despair during the Duncan Smith years, had set out (along with Michael Gove and under the auspices of Francis Maude's modernizing ginger group C-Change) to show the Party what it needed to do from the outside. In February 2003, Cooper and Gove had called on ordinary party members, local councillors, MPs, indeed anyone who would listen, to:

1. Always try to see ourselves through the voters' eyes.
2. Talk about the issues that matter to voters (not the issues that we're most at home with).

3. Use the language of people, not the language of politicians.

4. Tell people what we stand for – not (just) what is wrong with Labour. Unless we give voters new reasons to support us they won't.

5. Remember Tim Bell's rule: 'if they haven't heard it, you haven't said it' – so repetition is vital.

6. Respect modern Britain. If we seem not to like Britain today, the feeling will surely be reciprocated.

7. Don't be shrill or strident – that's not how normal civilised people behave.

8. Remember that whatever we are talking about, the most important message is what we are saying about ourselves.

9. Face the fact that we lost people's trust because of how we behave (and sound), as well as what we do.

10. Focus on the voters we have to win, don't preach to the converted.

11. Be disciplined and consistent.

Under Cameron, even for those who were unfamiliar with its contents, C-Change's 'roadshow' may as well have been a roadmap.

Cameron's strategy also involved shifting media attention from day one to topics not traditionally associated with the Conservatives. Especially important were those that resonated with 'AB voters' and the opinion-formers in broadcasting, who would, it was hoped, communicate the fact that the Party was changing to voters lower down the socio-economic and educational ladder. The most obvious of these, partly because it was superficially the most counter-intuitive, was the environment – an issue that a number of Conservatives (not least Michael Howard) took very seriously as individuals but which only a few (Tim Yeo and Michael Gove, for instance) thought had electoral potential.[6] The green agenda, which Cameron locked onto in one of his first newspaper contributions as leader, would be looked at by the 'Quality of Life' policy group that would be led by former minister John Gummer and Zac Goldsmith, the dashing (and fabulously wealthy) young editor of the earnest but little-read *Ecologist* magazine.[7] This gave the Tory leader around a year and a half to establish (and parade) his green credentials before he needed to even think about committing to particular policies. The fact that the issue was already claimed (though hardly owned) by the Liberal Democrats was all part of the plan. Playing the environmental card was about repositioning the Conservative Party in the public's imagination, about showing it was changing. But it was also the first skirmish in a wider campaign to 'love-bomb the Lib Dems' signalled by Cameron's call for them to come over to 'the new Conservative Party' and help him 'build a modern progressive, liberal, mainstream opposition to Labour'.

The other group of voters to whom the Party had to pay attention was women. This it could do, Cameron believed, firstly by talking (as he had before the election) about issues like work–life balance, parental leave, and childcare, and, secondly, by pursuing institutional change that would signal an intention to address the grave underrepresentation of women in the parliamentary party. The issue had long preoccupied modernizers like former and current Party Chairmen Theresa May and Francis Maude. And it had recently come to the fore by the launch of a ginger group called Women2Win, which, in the light of the pathetic number of female Tories elected to the Commons in 2005, was not only trying to provide practical help to potential candidates but was willing to say the unsayable, namely that the Party – if it really wanted to do something about its chronic failure to pick women and to pick up women's votes – had to reconcile itself to institutional action that would go beyond exhortation and encouragement.[8]

The precise nature of this action was announced by Cameron less than a week after he took over. Predictably, there were to be no all-women shortlists. However, Cameron did adopt an idea that had been kicking around the Party for a few years but that had been rejected by his predecessors. The Candidates Committee would recruit and select a Priority List (soon nicknamed the A-List) of 100 (rising to 200) people deemed especially eligible for selection, at least half of whom would be women. The list would also seek to include 'a significant proportion' of people from ethnic minority backgrounds and with disabilities. All target seats and seats with sitting MPs planning to retire would have to select from the list, although in 'exceptional circumstances' they would be able to consider a local candidate. Selections would be frozen until the list was compiled and there would be a review of its operation – and the possibility of 'further action' – after three months.

To help this decision achieve 'cut-through' – in other words to get the public to notice what was going on – Cameron appointed Shireen Ritchie (the chairman of a London constituency association who just happened at the time to be the step-mother-in-law of pop-icon Madonna) to assist in drawing up the list. But internally this was not going to be easy. For one thing, the YouGov poll of party members conducted just prior to Cameron's victory in the leadership contest showed that, though nearly two-thirds would like to see more women candidates in winnable seats, they were divided on how to do it, with only 14 per cent agreeing with the idea of requiring them to pick candidates from some sort of A-List.[9] Having chosen that option, the leadership now faced a backlash from those who feared they might not be selected, as well as from those who had to do the selecting and objected to what they saw as the triumph of political correctness over meritocracy. In years gone by this might not have mattered much. But now the website ConservativeHome provided an institutionalized forum for complaints – and one that could be easily accessed by the media, which, after the site's poll of readers had correctly predicted Cameron's winning margin back in December, seemed increasingly happy to use it as a proxy for grassroots opinion.

'Non-stop political pyrotechnics'

Team Cameron knew that after the pre-Christmas blizzard of announcements and blaze of publicity it was going to have to pace itself. Arresting images, catchy soundbites, counter-intuitive interventions, and eye-catching appointments were still the order of the day but they required spacing and sequencing. It made sense, for example, to wait for the post-Christmas lull to announce that the famously foul-mouthed rock-star-turned-anti-poverty-campaigner Bob Geldof would act as an adviser to the policy group on globalization and global poverty chaired by former Deputy Leader Peter Lilley. Geldof was, in marketing-speak, a 'brand signifier': especially to those more interested in Saint Bob and his tabloid-titillating daughters than in anything remotely political. His involvement suggested that Cameron's Conservatives (as the Party's instantly revamped website now billed them) weren't the same old Tories.

Once that story was played out, it was time to show that Cameron (in his Converse sneakers of course) walked the green walk as well as talked the green talk by briefing the media that he had commissioned an 'eco-architect' to remodel his new house, plans for which included solar-panels, water-harvesting, and a roof-mounted wind turbine. This kind of stuff – like Cameron and other Shadow Cabinet members being photographed using their laptops to switch their homes to energy suppliers specializing in 'green tariffs', or Cameron doing a live webchat with mumsnet.com after the birth of his third child, or ordering that only Fairtrade tea and coffee were to be drunk at CCHQ, or hitting the streets with sellers of *The Big Issue*, or complaining about shops exploiting harassed parents by selling sweet stuff at the checkout – was easy to laugh at. But it seemed to be having an impact. Even in early January, a BPIX poll showed 40 per cent of respondents agreeing that Cameron was 'a genuinely different, more sympathetic kind of Conservative'. By March, ICM's online focus groups were comparing an apparently dynamic and virile Cameron to a BMW 5-Series sports car or a thoroughbred racehorse, and, while his social event of choice would apparently be mingling at a Live8 concert, they could see him having fun at a club, 'laughing, talking and most importantly listening'.[10]

In personifying this 'different, more sympathetic' Conservatism, Cameron was doing exactly what he wanted his supporters to do. In his New Year message, he argued that, in order to 'usher in a new type of politics in this country: constructive, thoughtful and open-minded', they should follow Gandhi's edict that 'We must be the change we want to see in the world.' Again, this was easy to parody. Yet, given the widespread public enthusiasm for books, posters, greetings cards, and fridge magnets carrying exactly that kind of inspirational sentiment, who was to say whether it really was as cringe-worthy and counterproductive as some so-called experts rather sniffily assumed? It certainly did not prevent Cameron (aided of course by the fact that Labour and the Lib Dems appeared more interested in doing away with their own leaders than effectively countering the Conservatives) securing his party an opinion poll lead – a lead which would of course make it easier to do the ideological and institutional spadework that still desperately needed doing.

That said, a certain amount of unease from supporters was still expected – even courted. The bullet-pointed statements run in the

Sunday Telegraph on New Year's Day 2006 were a technique borrowed from the Howard years but, in marked contrast to his 'I believe' ad, they were clearly designed not just to reinforce the change message but also to provoke. To those on the centre-left it was motherhood and apple pie stuff: 'Fighting global poverty is our moral obligation: a priority not an afterthought'; 'The right test for our policies is how to help the least well-off in society, not the rich'; 'We should not just stand up for big business but stand up to big business when it's in the interests of Britain and the world', etc. For some on the right, however, it was fighting talk and risked, in the words of one representative of the party in the media, 'leaving millions of natural conservatives effectively disenfranchised – and, even worse, demonised as dinosaurs by the party that is supposed to represent them, but is now telling them to go hang while it tears up everything they believe in'.[11] Clearly, the leadership would not have welcomed such hyperbolic criticism on a daily basis, particularly if it spread from the pages of the *Mail* into parliament (then conveniently in recess). But it served its purpose: it allowed the leader being criticized to 'triangulate'. Blair's claim to occupy the centre ground relied not just on his policies but on his rhetorical position between the hopelessly unrealistic left in his own party and whichever ideologically-driven no-hoper was currently the leader of the Conservative Party. Cameron would attempt to pull off exactly the same trick, in his case using the dogmatic right of his party and a cartoon version of his Labour opponents.[12]

The rebranding of the Party to which such initiatives (and the reaction they provoked) were directed was not, however, merely a matter of words rather than deeds. It had, for instance, become commonplace to cite polling which showed that voters' agreement with certain Tory policies was higher if they were presented to them without being attributed to the Conservative Party, thereby suggesting that the Party's main problem was its image rather than its policies.[13] But there was clearly feedback between policies and image – something Team Cameron obviously understood given the alacrity with which it began not just trying to change the face of the Party but also dumping overboard particularly right-wing policies from the 2005 manifesto. Cameron's first set-piece speech on the NHS at the beginning of January was used, firstly, to junk the patient's passport, which had left voters confused, uninspired, or even hostile at the last election and, secondly, to rule out not only old favourites like tax incentives for taking out private insurance, but also looking at other streams of funding. A few days later it was announced that the Party was ditching its long-term flirtation with a return to the 11-plus and the grammar school system based on it. Also, it would no longer oppose university tuition fees or the government's target to get 50 per cent of pupils into higher education. And it was abandoning the idea of a 'pupil's passport', which would have seen the state subsidize those wishing to send their children to private schools.

This left some on the right, including of course Norman Tebbit, wondering whether Cameron was really 'New Labour Lite', a Tory wolf in Lib Dem sheep's clothing, or for that matter a Lib Dem sheep leading a pack of Tory wolves? 'Or', wondered Tebbit, 'is he the party's Chairman Mao or Pol Pot, intent on purging even the memory and name of Thatcherism before building a New Modern Compassionate Green Globally Aware Party somewhere on the Left side of the middle ground?' [14] But while many of what Tebbit termed these 'non-stop political pyrotechnics' were certain to arouse the suspicion and even the ire of right-wingers, any attempt on their part to coordinate some kind of response was made difficult by the fact that the Commons was still in recess – one of the reasons the leadership acted as quickly as it did. Objections were also stymied by the fact that donations were rolling in. Moreover, polls suggested that Cameron was not only putting his party back in serious contention with Labour but that the brand-based gap between voter responses to Cameron's New Year bullet points when they were (a) unattributed and then (b) attributed to the Tories were narrower than the gaps found when similar exercises were conducted (albeit on much less motherhood and apple-pie statements) in 2005.

Similar considerations seemed to affect grassroots Tories polled by Tim Montgomerie's website, ConservativeHome. The most popular policy asked about was still Cameron's pledge (as yet unrealized) to pull Tory MEPs out of the EPP–ED – supported by 76 per cent. And, as well as serious reservations about the A-List (60 per cent disagreed with it, even if 62 per cent thought it was 'good politics'), there was clearly some disquiet about giving up a return to grammar schools (a stance rejected by 73 per cent and thought to be 'bad politics' by 48 per cent). Yet, although some 20 per cent thought 'modernization' had gone too far, a large majority was pleased with how things were going, with 82 per cent fairly or very satisfied with Cameron's leadership and 76 per cent thinking the Party was on the right course.[15]

Had they been asked about the next instalment in Team Cameron's 'shock and awe' campaign – George Osborne's assertion that economic stability and sorting out the public finances would have to take priority over tax cuts for a future Conservative government – they might have been rather more concerned. And they would have been in good (or at least exalted) company: Rupert Murdoch descended from on high to warn Cameron (who he had now met a couple of times) about making it 'all about image' and to focus on 'facts and real policies', one of which, naturally, had to be 'shrinking taxes'.[16] Even two or three MPs, albeit just the usual Thatcherite suspects like Edward Leigh and Eric Forth (and later on Derek Conway), were now poking their heads publicly above the parapet to ask what the Conservative Party was for if it wasn't for tax cuts.

None of this was unexpected. Nor, once again, was it necessarily unwelcome. It would be nice to have Murdoch on board, but, if his record was anything to go by, this would only happen when and if it became clear that the Tories would win the next election. For the moment, the main aim was to get the Tory leader presented day-in-day-out as a change-maker by the broadcast networks and the centre-left broadsheets; if anything, a couple of Thatcherite 'headbangers' coming out of the woodwork was all grist to the mill. Moreover, Cameron had a ready response which replicated exactly the type of defence that Blair had mounted against his internal critics when he took over the Labour Party in 1994. He had made it clear during his leadership campaign, he pointed out in an article for the *Telegraph*, that on the issues which were provoking concern he would lead the Party 'in a new direction' and that he didn't think there was 'time to hang around'. There was no mystery to what he was doing: just like Disraeli, Churchill, and Thatcher (all of whom were nodded to), he wanted 'to put the Conservative Party back in the mainstream of political debate'. Winning the 120 or so seats that needed to be won meant the Party had 'got to move on from the comfort zone Conservatism of the last two elections'. This wasn't the same as 'turning the party into a pale imitation of New Labour', however. 'I am Conservative', he claimed 'to the core of my being, as those who know me best will testify.' He believed in 'trusting people, and sharing responsibility' and simply wanted 'to apply these core Conservative values to the challenges of our time'.[17]

A few days later, in a speech at Demos, a think-tank often associated with New Labour, Cameron went even further. Blair's great insight, he claimed, was to realize that contemporary politics was about how to meld rather than to trade off social justice and economic efficiency. He shared that view and would not therefore be diverted, as his predecessors had been, both by 'well-intentioned cheerleaders on the right [who] exerted a powerful gravitational pull' and the difficulty of getting media attention without stressing differences between the two parties. The Tories had made 'terrible strategic and tactical mistakes', he lamented. 'As Labour moved to the centre ground, the Conservative Party moved to the Right.' It now had to drag itself back because, as recent years had shown, 'The alternative to fighting for the centre ground is irrelevance, defeat and failure.' [18]

'Plenty more change to be made'

Although Cameron's honeymoon looked likely to last well into the New Year of 2006, he needed to be careful. He managed to persuade his MPs to rescue Blair's Education Bill in the face of a Labour rebellion, thereby contrasting Tory moderation with government division, but some inevitably saw this as too clever by half. Of course, the message from the opinion polls appeared to be encouraging: according to Populus at the beginning of March, the Conservative vote share since Cameron took over was 5.7 points higher on average than over the previous six months, with the biggest improvement among AB voters; there were also signs that the Tories would open up a significant lead once Cameron were pitted against Brown. However, critics could point to the Party's predictably poor performance in the Dunfermline by-election and to evidence beneath the headline figures that suggested the public remained sceptical: a YouGov survey towards the end of February found six out of ten respondents agreeing that the Tories had 'a new freshness and vitality' about them, but the same proportion thought that 'David Cameron talks a good line but it is hard to know whether there is any substance behind the words'.

Labour's high command had finally decided that the best way to attack

Cameron was to play on this concern, to portray him as a 'flip-flopper', an inconsistent phoney who believed he could be Conservative to the core one day, a Liberal Conservative the next, and 'the heir to Blair' the day after. Doubt was also cast on the extent to which he could take his party with him. The Conservatives' response to all this was to announce that they would be balloting members on a statement of values released at the end of February called *Built to Last*. It contained little that was new. Indeed, beyond a claim that 'We believe in the role of government as a force for good', it contained little that most Conservatives, indeed almost anyone, could object to: as Norman Tebbit waspishly noted, 'I agree with all eight principles – but then so do my friends in the Liberal and Labour parties.'[19]

Such comments tapped into concerns within the Party that any repositioning not be taken so far that it erode any differences with the other parties and prevent it from acting as an effective opposition. For instance, the leadership had to take a cautious approach to the growing 'Loans for Peerages' scandal swirling around the Labour government. It ill-behoved a party that had benefited massively from initially unnamed (and foreign) donors and lenders to throw stones in that particular glasshouse, especially when the Tory Treasurer, Jonathan Marland, regarded naming such benefactors as a breach of confidence – a point of principle that within days had to be surrendered as the Party came under intense pressure from both the Electoral Commission and the media.[20] Nevertheless, many Tories believed that it was still only right and proper (constitutionally and politically) to kick Blair when he was down. Cameron, however, was light enough on his feet to conjure up a package of proposals that implied serious criticism of the government at the same time as making the Conservatives look keen to help clean up politics in an apparently cross-party fashion. He was also able to reassure his doubters, at least in part, by going after Brown in a big way: his ferocious attack on him ('an old-fashioned tax and spend Chancellor', 'completely stuck in the past', 'an analogue politician in a digital age') in his response to the Labour government's tenth Budget was seen by many as a particular highlight.

The Conservatives' Spring Forum in Manchester gave Cameron his first chance to address Tory activists publicly since becoming leader. Although he was guaranteed a good reception, some were beginning to ask – as worries began to surface that the Party was failing to build on the bounce it enjoyed when Cameron first came in – whether the change he was trying to promote and personify was having as much impact on voters as it had on journalists. There was also concern that any boost to the leadership's ongoing campaign to persuade AB voters that the Conservatives were sane, middle-of-the-road, and tolerant by Cameron characterizing UKIP as 'a bunch of fruitcakes and loonies and closet racists' might be outweighed by offending those who had voted for it but were now thinking of returning to the Tories. Cameron, however, refused to retreat. Speaking against a backdrop on which the words Optimism, Change, and Hope replaced the word Conservative, and ignoring crime, taxation, Europe, and immigration in favour of family- and environmentally friendly themes and the need for internal institutional reform, he insisted, 'We must fast forward to a new Conservative party' and that 'This change in our party has to get faster; it must go wider and deeper. It's not enough for the leader to change. We all have to change. And we must show that the change is real, that it's lasting.'

The problem of course was going to be demonstrating that. Candidate selection was perhaps the most obvious way of doing it and, as delegates left Manchester, Maude released a new set of rules for the selection process designed both to involve non-members (either as voters or as interviewers of candidates) and to reduce the importance traditionally accorded to the set-piece speeches thought to favour the kind of candidates the Party had always picked in the past. But all this was going to be contentious. Even as the Manchester Forum was winding up, an activist from the city was telling Channel Four News that selecting an ethnic minority candidate in her working-class constituency 'wouldn't work for us', before being told she was 'in the wrong party' by Cameron and issuing a statement declaring she 'completely and utterly' regretted remarks which were 'not what I meant or believe at all'. Moreover, changing the sales force (like coming up with distinctive policy products) would also take time, while marketing Cameron as a breath of fresh air would have to carry on regardless, thus rendering the gap between him and his party – as well as the suspicion that he was 'all spin and no substance' – even more pronounced.

Worse still, there were the first signs of colleagues beginning to allow journalists to voice their concerns – a routine occurrence under

Thatcher, Major, Hague, and Duncan Smith, but something which Cameron, now some four months into his leadership, had, like Howard in his initial honeymoon period, been able to avoid thus far. Speaking to a Sunday TV show just before the local elections, defeated leadership contender and now Shadow Defence Secretary Liam Fox expressed the view that the Party should be aiming to be the kind of broad coalition that Margaret Thatcher managed to put together in opposition: after all, 'If the party is tilted too much in any one direction, that makes us politically less stable and that makes us less attractive.' Speaking off-the-record, however, such criticism could afford to be less oblique. Commenting on the news that Cameron was going to visit – on a dog-sled and with a film crew in tow – an arctic archipelago threatened by global warming, one unnamed Shadow minister declared it was 'barmy to be jetting off to do this in the middle of the local election campaign. There will be Conservatives all over the country knocking on doors, and where is he? He's off looking at glaciers in Norway. I'm afraid he's missing the target – it just has the feel of a gimmick.'[21]

Of course it was a gimmick, argued Cameron's inner circle, but one designed to achieve cut-through to voters largely uninterested in politics. And, in any case, it was all of a piece with the Party's campaign for the local election, summed up by the slogan 'Vote Blue, Go Green'. Insisting – in a clear pitch to Lib Dem voters, who, polls showed, cared most about such matters – that Tory councils had the most environmentally friendly policies did not necessarily attract the ire of grassroots Tories, many of whom, it transpired, were as concerned as anyone else about pollution, preserving the countryside, and cutting household and industrial waste. And Cameron even risked ridicule by having officials hand out silver birch saplings in hemp carrier bags to journalists, telling them to 'think global, act local'. Labour's response was to portray him in an election broadcast as a chameleon willing to say whatever it took.[22] This wheeze was widely considered a flop: the computer-generated 'Dave the Chameleon' was unintentionally cute and in any case could hardly compete with the iconic images of the Tory leader with his huskies in the sharp sunlight and pristine snow of the frozen North. It was another question whether the latter would impress environmentalists (and the 62 per cent of people who told Populus that Cameron was 'only talking about the environment because he thinks it will make people more positive about the Conservative Party, not because he really cares about it').[23] Certainly, the revelation that he was followed on his bike-ride to work by his chauffer-driven Lexus carrying his shoes, briefcase, and a freshly laundered shirt was unlikely to counter such cynicism.

As the local elections approached, however, there appeared to be greater concern about more conventional issues than the environment. For one thing the bad news about hospital deficits seemed to be having an effect on Labour's poll ratings, even if it didn't seem to be doing much for the Conservatives, despite Lansley's energetic campaign against 'Gordon Brown's NHS cuts'. For another, the government (already reeling after news of Deputy Prime Minister John Prescott's love-life leaked out) was having to cope with the fallout from the revelation that it had failed to deport around a thousand foreign prisoners at the end of their jail term – a fiasco that gave Cameron a much-needed opportunity to act like a conventional opposition politician. Whether or not it was this pitch-perfect handling of Labour's troubles, his Arctic photo-op, or a strident stand against the BNP that did it, a YouGov poll for the *Sunday Times* just days out from the local elections gave Cameron a net approval rating of +20, compared to -31 for Blair and -1 for the lacklustre new Lib Dem leader, Menzies Campbell. This was streets ahead of what any of his predecessors since 1997 had managed to achieve.

The question, of course, was whether Cameron could convert his own lead into votes for his party. On the evidence of the local election results, the answer appeared to be yes – though only in some parts of the country. The Tories gained over 300 seats and a projected national share of the vote of around 40 per cent compared to Labour's 26 per cent. Of course, even Hague, IDS, and Howard had been able to claim victory over Labour in local elections. But this time voters appeared to have come across not just from Labour but from the party whose voters Cameron had so assiduously targeted, the Lib Dems. The fears of a few years back that the 'yellow peril' might overtake the Tories were now well and truly put to bed. The Conservatives also did well in London. The only bad news was that their success was limited in the West Midlands, while once again Northern cities proved utterly impervious to the Party's charms. Ironically, however, the fact that it had done well but obviously still had some way to go was helpful: the leadership could claim that its strategy was getting results but that, as Cameron put it, there was 'plenty more change to be made and work to be done'.

Pushing on, pushing through

After the elections, the leadership could now risk releasing the details of the Priority List of supposedly top-drawer candidates that target seats, and seats with retiring Tory MPs, would be called on to choose from. Feelings were likely to run pretty high, especially after the *Telegraph* published details of a leaked memo which showed the leadership was determined to see women in at least 20 of the 30 seats likely to be selected before the Party Conference – so determined, indeed, that it was planning all sorts of apparently underhand means to encourage them to do so, including Cameron just happening to drop in to any meetings that constituency officers may have at CCHQ.[24] As the names on the list began to leak out into the public domain via ConservativeHome, it was obvious, to critics anyway, that some (though by no means all) of the lucky few had been parachuted in without much history of working for the Party and/or that they were 'token' women or minority representatives. The former *Coronation Street* pin-up, underwear model, and reality-TV contestant Adam Rickitt was one example, but others seethed at the inclusion of the chick-lit author Louise Bagshawe and, of course, Zac Goldsmith. Many of those left off, in contrast, had solid records, including, for example, the increasingly ubiquitous Conservative blogger Iain Dale. Comments left on his site, as well as on ConservativeHome, indicated a good deal of discontent, prompting Francis Maude to deny on another activist website that he was trying to 'insert mincing metrosexuals into gritty northern marginal seats' and promising that those currently left off the list had not been 'cast into outer darkness' since the list would be topped up as candidates were selected.[25] His comments were echoed – in an appeal made direct on ConservativeHome – by Cameron himself.[26]

It wasn't just activists who were upset. So too were some MPs. Frontbencher John Hayes, launching a report which stressed the importance of Tory candidates having strong local links, declared, 'The idea that we can parachute insubstantial and untested candidates with little knowledge of the local scene into key seats to win the confidence of people they seek to represent is the bizarre theory of people who spend too much time with the pseuds and posers of London's chichi set and not enough time in normal Britain.'[27] Although not intended as such, his remarks seemed to hint at a lingering resentment within some sections of the parliamentary party towards the so-called Notting Hill Set which surrounded (and included) Cameron.

Certainly one legitimate gripe about the Priority List (although one that was rarely voiced inside the Party) was that, irrespective of the sex and ethnic background of those on it, it was stuffed full of upper-middle-class people, the vast majority of whom worked in the private sector. Of the first 100 on the list, only five seemed to have been employed by the state and even then only in the medical and emergency services rather than in those parts of the public service considered a waste of space (and money) by so many Tories.[28] This may have been due to ideological bias, but it may also have been the tens of thousands of pounds that becoming a candidate costs each individual – something which (along with the advantage of connections) may also help explain why, when it came to the 2005 election, someone who went to Eton was 384 times more likely to become a Tory MP than someone who was state-educated.[29]

The negative reaction towards the A-List among some Tories at Westminster also revealed a genuine anxiety about a trade-off between revamping the Party's image and doing what needed to be done to win on the ground. It also tapped into a wider vein of cynicism, especially among longer-serving MPs, about other leadership wheezes to change public perceptions of the Party. In mid-May, for example, borrowing from an idea first floated under IDS, Tory MPs were sent a request that they spend the second half of the spring recess helping out in 'an appropriate local organization'. Few came forward and one, speaking to a journalist, noted that 'Most of us have booked family holidays and aren't about to cancel them to work in the local Oxfam or whatever left-wing charities Dave wants us to support so he can get a few cheap headlines.'[30]

Such cynicism did not, however, deflect Cameron from his search for those headlines, especially where they might both undermine the impression of the Tories as the political wing of big business and reposition them as advocates of the sort of socially responsible (and family-friendly) capitalism favoured by his chief strategist, Steve Hilton. In early May, he had grabbed headlines by grubbing up an old story about high-street retailer BHS's 'harmful and creepy' line of underwear for pre-pubescent girls and hinting that store-giants like Tesco's needed to act not as profit-driven predators but as 'good neighbours'.[31] A couple of weeks later, and fresh from his appearance at a celebrity-studded party at Posh and Becks' the night before, he declared, 'It's time we admitted that there's more to life than money, and it's time we focused not just on GDP, but on GWB – general well-being.' It was no good saying that government should have nothing to do with helping people develop a work–life balance. Equally, trying to impose such balance by legislation was counterproductive. Surely there had to be a position between indifference and over-regulation?

Whether or not such blatant triangulation really was such a departure from Thatcherism, it was certainly spun as such. This only added to the irritation of those already contemptuous of their leader's frequent forays into the 'touchy-feely' stuff – an attitude that Cameron was more than willing to challenge head on.[32] Their problem – if it was a problem – was that it seemed to be working, at least if opinion polls were anything to go by. An ICM survey published by the *Guardian* in late May not only showed the Tories in the lead (and confirmed it would be even bigger were Brown to take over), it also showed they were picking up support among women voters and, after Labour's recent troubles, were even judged to have the best policies on the NHS and education as well as on law and order and immigration. Apparently, then, the Conservatives still retained their traditional trump cards even though Cameron chose not to play them, and his determination to take on Labour on its traditional territory seemed to be bearing fruit.

Just as importantly, Cameron could also point to a substantial rise in donations being made to the Party – welcome news given it had run up an unprecedented deficit approaching £30 million the previous year. The first three months of the year had seen £9 million flood in, compared to £1.6 million that was raised in the three months after the election of IDS in 2001 and £2.6 million after Michael Howard took over in 2003. Even discounting the amount made up of pre-election loans that were converted to donations after the election (including £2.1

million from car-dealer Robert Edmiston), this was still an impressive figure – and three times that raised by Labour in the same period.[33] In the light of this even the *Telegraph*, which, like the *Mail* and, indeed, many of its readers, had occasionally been pained by what it called Cameron's 'iconoclastic approach to principles and customs that Tories hold dear', felt obliged to admit, however grudgingly, that his overall strategy was working.[34]

Yet Cameron could be cautious where it counted. The death of the outspoken right-wing MP Eric Forth meant a by-election in Bromley and Chislehurst. Cameron, however, made it clear from the outset that the shortlist could include people not on the Priority List. In the event, the nomination went to Bob Neill, the Party's leader in the London Assembly and undeniably a 'blazer and tie Tory' – white, male, middle-class, and a middle-aged barrister. Any disappointment that the association had chosen him ahead of three A-listers was offset, however, by Ipsos MORI giving the Tories, on 41 per cent, their first double-digit poll lead over Labour since the 1980s.

Leads like that made it much easier for Cameron to keep up the pace in other areas. In the 2005 election, the Tories had at times acted as if their main intention was to see how many civil servants they could get rid of in order to pay for tax cuts – not a particularly smart move, perhaps, given that getting on for 6 million voters worked in the public sector, that many of them lived in the North, where the Tories needed to win more votes, and that many were already predisposed not to trust their intentions.[35] Talking to the National Consumer Council, exactly six months into his leadership, Cameron tried to put this right, declaring it was time to stop 'constantly beating up on the public sector and telling it to be more like the private sector', a habit the Conservatives had all-too-easily fallen into over the years:

> In our legitimate desire to drive out government waste and improve public sector efficiency, we have sometimes risked giving the impression that we see those who work in the public sector as burdens on the state rather than dedicated professionals who work hard to improve the quality of people's lives. Anyone working in the public services could easily have heard a pretty negative message from my party, 'There's too many of you, you're lazy and you're inefficient.' This is far from how I

see things. Public service – the concept of working for the good of the community – is a high ideal.[36]

Again, this was hardly music to the ears of the Thatcherite right, be they in Westminster or Fleet Street – 'Cam off it,' cried the *Sun* the next day, while the *Mail* explained, 'Why we hope Dave doesn't believe it.' The message also ran counter (deliberately so) to a speech by Blair on the same day which basically told public servants that they had had about as much extra investment as any government was ever likely to make in them and that it was now time for them to sharpen up their act and learn at last from the private sector. This 'political cross-dressing' both reinforced the overall message that the Party was changing and confirmed that Blair's default tactic – moving rhetorically to the right of centre so the Tories moved even further themselves – was now a busted flush. Cameron's remarks were also a targeted appeal to a group of voters who were the one part of the New Labour coalition that had remained solidly loyal up to and including the general election of 2005. Conservatives who thought they could win a comfortable majority without winning over at least a significant proportion of such voters were deluded. Cameron could not only read the polling evidence, he was the first Tory leader in well over a decade who was realistic enough to act on it.

Likewise, Cameron and those around him were acutely aware they needed to press on with their efforts to woo women voters, and that ultimately it would take more than warm words and soft-focus shots to do it. In a heavily hyped speech to the National Family and Parenting Institute in the third week of June, Cameron did empathy: 'dads' should be present at the birth (a 'magic moment') and spend time with their kids, he thought, and he knew that most women didn't have a choice about going out to work if they wanted to do the best for their children. And he did popular culture, albeit with a Conservative twist: 'Britain's families need Super-Nanny, not the Nanny State.' But he also talked about cold, hard cash, addressing the issue of childcare costs faced by families up and down the land, hinting strongly that the Tories might move towards tax relief on childcare to all working parents rather than targeting it, like the Labour government, at poorer families – in effect offering an expensive subsidy to middle-class voters for both formal and informal types of childcare. A speech in mid-September also called on businesses to support flexible working.

Tougher times

But it could not be full speed ahead on all fronts. As with candidate selection, on touchstone issues like tax and Europe, discretion – or even doubletalk – was deemed to be the better part of valour. But, as with candidate selection, it was not always that easy to get away with. George Osborne, for instance, argued that he was only following Thatcher in 1979 in not promising 'upfront', specific tax cuts, even though a glance at the Tory manifesto of that year would have shown that it contained clear commitments in this respect. He also got into trouble at the beginning of June when he appeared to want to have it both ways on tax, simultaneously dampening expectations and dangling the prospect of cuts.[37] Europe was even more of a minefield. Speaking at the beginning of June, Hague repeated the Howard line – a more flexible Europe and referendums on any further transfer of sovereignty. But he could do little to disguise the fact that Cameron's over-hasty pledge to pull Tory MEPs out of the EPP–ED group in the European Parliament was, in the short term at least, undeliverable, whatever some of them said: apart from the Czech ODS, there were no takers among European centre-right parties for the idea of a new outfit led by the Tories. Sceptics – at Westminster, in Fleet Street, and at the grassroots – were furious: Cameron's guarantee had been one of the main reasons why they had given him the benefit of the doubt in the leadership contest; now the leader and letters pages, and the blog comments, were running hot with warnings that their trust must not be betrayed.[38]

Any hope that Tory sceptics might be placated by Cameron's proposal to replace Labour's supposedly European-driven Human Rights Act with 'a modern British Bill of Rights' proved unfounded. The suggestion earned him derision in the liberal media he had spent so much time stroking. Even if he could pull it off, all those currently 'making a mockery' of British tolerance and common sense by using the 1998 Act would be able to do the very same thing simply by appealing to the court in Strasbourg under the European Convention on Human Rights – an international agreement which a future Conservative government could not renege on, not least because it might be incompatible with EU membership. Europhiles were similarly unimpressed. It emerged that Cameron had failed even to mention the idea to old stager Ken Clarke, who he had appointed to chair the 'Democracy Taskforce' charged with coming up with ideas to improve British governance. When Clarke was asked by journalists, he predictably dismissed the plan as 'xenophobic and legal nonsense'.

But if the debate over the Human Rights Act looked unlikely to distract Eurosceptics, it certainly seemed to take the leadership's eye off the ball when it came to the election in Bromley and Chislehurst. Rather than taking charge of the campaign and ensuring it became an advert for the all-new Conservatism on offer from David Cameron, CCHQ left things to the locals, who clearly wanted it that way. As a Tory seat, it was never going to provide the chance for the Party to show what it could do against a Labour or Lib Dem incumbent. Yet it was inevitably going to be seen as a test and therefore everything should have been done to ensure that it was passed with flying colours. Instead, Forth's majority of 13,342 was slashed to just 633 by the Lib Dems, who fought one of their classic pavement-pounding, no-holds barred campaigns.

Some of those around Cameron may have decided before polling day that a less than impressive performance (as long as it was still a win and not too many votes went to UKIP) would be no bad thing: it would show that fighting a traditionally Tory campaign (as their candidate seemed determined to do) was not the way forward. This was certainly the line pushed by Chairman Francis Maude, whose pager message to Tory MPs ran 'Bromley: disappointing result. This shows change must move faster, wider and deeper.' Whether they were similarly convinced is another matter. Leaked emails from Cameron's PPS, Desmond Swayne, provided confirmation of the uneasiness already felt by backbenchers, some of whom felt ignored by a leadership they clearly considered a clique.[39] But even for those who were more worried than actually discontented, the Bromley result suggested that the Party's opinion poll lead may have had more to do with Labour's unpopularity than its own performance. For some, it was worse than that – a feeling encapsulated by the *Mail*'s pointed leader on 1 July:

Why hasn't Mr Cameron's masterly job of restoring the Tories' fortunes in the opinion polls been reflected in the polls that really matter? Until now, Dave's thinking has been that Tory traditionalists will just have to lump his touchy-feely waffle. He reckoned they had nowhere else to go. Oh no? This week, they showed they did. . . . Mr Cameron needs to realise that there is more to politics than spin and media manipulation. . . . Dave and his crew should start spending more time on creating solid policies. Bromley should teach them that natural Conservative voters are not seduced by . . . pathetic stunts. . . . Put simply, the message from tribal Tories to Mr Cameron is: 'Stop taking us for granted'.

Such a message would almost certainly have stopped Hague, Duncan Smith, and Howard in their tracks. But Cameron was determined to push through, possibly to the point of foolhardiness. Just over a week after the by-election his office began to brief a speech he planned to make about law and order and social breakdown. The resulting head-lines in right-wing newspapers would have left the Tory leader in no doubt about the likely reaction to his plea that youth crime could only be tackled by showing troubled adolescents some understanding as well as by meting out punishment, the real killer being the *News of the World*'s alliterative classic, 'Hug a hoodie says Cameron'. If the leader-ship had been hoping that a more hard-line speech later the same day to the Police Federation was going to balance things out, it was sorely mistaken. 'How much more can we take?', demanded the *Telegraph*'s leader on 10 July, and in the next few days (as any half-way decent media operation would have warned Cameron) the tabloids went to town.

Fortunately for Cameron the government too was still in trouble. Blair's chief fundraiser had been arrested and bailed in connection with the police inquiry into 'cash for honours' – a scandal that had a pur-ported 69 per cent of the public thinking Labour was 'very sleazy and very disreputable', with only 29 per cent now thinking the same of the Tories. This not only allowed Cameron to make a strong showing in front of his troops at PMQs, it also meant that the media eased up on 'hug a hoodie'. By then, however, the damage had been done. Although Shadow Cabinet doubters and other Conservative MPs stayed silent for the most part, few were surprised when YouGov's monthly survey for the *Telegraph*, published at the end of July, showed that only 35 per cent of respondents thought Cameron was doing a good job as Tory leader, down from a peak of 46 per cent just after he took over. The proportion who thought he was doing a bad job had increased from 19 to 33 per cent.

Moreover, 'cash for honours' did not help the Tory leadership bury the bad news on Cameron's EPP–ED pledge. Hague had managed to do a deal with the Czech ODS which would see the two parties set up a 'Movement for European Reform, dedicated to the ideals of a more modern, open, flexible and de-centralised European Union'. But it would not become a European Parliament party group until after the 2009 European elections. The reaction – in the party in the media, among the activists (or at least those visiting ConservativeHome), and at Westminster – was largely, and predictably, negative. Most, though, were realistic enough to accept it as a deeply disappointing *fait accompli*. The elected politicians (as the leadership well knew) were off on their holidays, and anyway there were more pressing matters to consider on the foreign front after Israel invaded Lebanon to try to see off Hezbollah – a move which caused considerable policy divisions within the Party after Hague (to the disappointment of his Atlanticist and pro-Israel colleagues) suggested that 'elements of the Israeli response' were 'disproportionate'.

Cameron's plan to regain momentum – the launch of the final version of *Built to Last*, the statement of aims and values that was to be sent out to the membership with ballot forms at the end of August – did not unfortunately help much. The final draft had doubled in size since February yet was still, argued the *Mail*, 'too long on touchy-feely waffle, too short on detail' for those prepared to 'hope against hope there may be more to Mr Cameron than just a bicycling hoodie-hugger with nice manners'.[40] This was disappointing because efforts had been made to tweak the text, mostly in order to please, amongst others, the party in the media.

The changes were small but significant, at least insofar as the document had any real function beyond demonstrating buy-in by ordinary members for Cameron's leadership. The declaration in the first draft that 'We are a modern, compassionate Conservative party' had been replaced by a commitment to 'a free society and a strong nation state; an opportunity society, not an overpowering state' and the pursuit of a 'responsibility revolution' which would create 'an opportunity society – a society in which everybody is a somebody, a doer not a done-for'. Also gone was explicit criticism of 'opting out' of state-provided health and education, while there was now a commitment to 'fairer, flatter and simpler taxes'. The pledge to support working women was also replaced with a more general (and arguably more traditional) promise to support 'families and marriage' (a word that had not appeared in the first draft). Unfortunately, this recalibration to the right couldn't disguise the fact that the section on the environment had been beefed up rather than watered down. Steve Norris, as Chairman of the Party's policy group on transport, had already set off the tabloids by talking about new taxes on cars and air travel. The document was less alarming but still included 'binding annual targets for carbon reduction' and 'tough targets for carbon reduction in new cars'. Moreover, George Osborne's comments a few weeks later that 'eco-taxes' should be increased to allow reductions elsewhere suggested this was not mere posturing – much to the consternation of the party in the media.[41]

No let-up

For all the changes made, the final draft of *Built to Last* retained the original's commitment to increasing the representation of women and ethnic minorities. Worryingly, though, assiduous work by ConservativeHome suggested that the Priority List was not doing the business in this respect: constituencies were avoiding A-Listers by picking local candidates and only a few were picking women. Cameron, who had just bitten the bullet and decided that the search for the Party's candidate for the London mayoralty would have to be extended after no big names came forward, promptly moved to announce changes to parliamentary candidate selection – changes that went further towards central control than anything contemplated by any of his predecessors. Candidates would henceforth be chosen from a shortlist of four people, two of whom must be women, with the final selection confined in most cases to the association's executive rather than its full membership. Meanwhile the very smallest associations would have to hold open primaries.

The reaction from the grassroots, at least as relayed by ConservativeHome, was lukewarm at best. Cameron was just about to jet off to a meeting with Nelson Mandela, a 'brand signifier' *par excellence* – a trip nicely synchronized with the production of a Sunday newspaper article calculated to reinforce once again how different he was by his expressing regret over previous Conservative governments' stances towards the anti-apartheid movement.[42] But he once again took the trouble to reply direct to activists' concerns on 'their' website. Speaking with the renewed confidence that came with a *Guardian*/ICM poll putting the Tories on 40 per cent and the Electoral Commission reporting second-quarter donations to the Party running at nearly £5 million, Cameron stressed in other media that no-one should doubt how serious he was about tackling the problem of underrepresentation; indeed, he would review progress at the end of the year and if necessary take further action.[43]

As the long run-up to the party conference season began, the Tory leadership inevitably began to feel the heat from those who believed that it was, in the words of the *Mail*'s eve-of-Conference leader, 'time for Cameron to put flesh on the bones'. These calls came not just from the party in the media and from think-tanks and pressure groups, but also from right-wingers at Westminster. The No Turning Back group, for instance, trailed a Selsdon Group pamphlet calling on the Party to commit itself to reductions in taxation – something it regarded at best as 'compulsory charity' and at worst 'theft by kleptocrat politicians'. There then followed a leak of the likely recommendations of the Tax Reform Commission set up before Cameron became leader and chaired by the Thatcherite peer Michael Forsyth. This was a move clearly aimed at preventing Osborne watering the recommendations down before publication – something the leadership was later to prove better able to do when it came to the policy groups established by Cameron himself.[44]

The leadership, however, could point to polling which supported its insistence that the Party had to move forwards not backwards. In Populus's pre-Conference survey for the *Times*, voters continued to place both Cameron and his party further to the right of them than they placed Labour and Blair to the left. Although Labour had lost its edge on many issues and people wanted hard-line policies from the Tories on crime, immigration, and even tax, the government still had the advantage on the economy and on statements like 'cares about the problems ordinary people have to deal with' and, especially, 'is for the many, not just the few'. Some 57 per cent of respondents agreed that 'Behind all the spin and PR, David Cameron probably still believes in the same old right wing policies that the Conservatives have proposed in the past' and 72 per cent agreed that 'David Cameron is the best leader the Conservatives have had in a long time, but he has to prove that the whole party has changed before most people will be ready to vote for them again.'

These findings were echoed by YouGov, the *Telegraph*'s pollster, which compared respondents' answers with those given to the same questions just a couple of months into Cameron's leadership. The proportion of those agreeing with the statement 'David Cameron talks a good line but it is hard to know whether there is any substance behind the words' had, at 60 per cent, barely changed, although the proportion agreeing he was 'proving a good leader of the Conservative Party' had dropped from 47 to 35 per cent, as had the proportion agreeing that 'Under David Cameron the Conservatives reflect the values and aspirations of the British people better than they used to' (down to 31 from 35 per cent). Just over half of respondents agreed that it was 'hard to know what the Conservative Party stands for at the moment', although 42 per cent thought that one of the reasons it wasn't doing better was that the Tories still couldn't be 'trusted to run public services such as schools and hospitals'. Voters' preferences for a Conservative Party that, rather than going for big tax cuts and a smaller state, decided to 'commit itself to running public services pretty much along the same lines as now and to spending as much money as necessary on them' while cutting waste and overregulation were clear and remained unchanged since February: the second option was favoured by 51 to 18 per cent.

All this bolstered Cameron and Osborne's determination to hold the line on taxes and their insistence that the Party had to be seen not simply to modernize institutionally and individually but also to moderate ideologically. Only this would counter what was still obviously a widespread belief that the Tories were well to the right of the political spectrum: with zero as the mid-point on a scale running from -100 on the left to +100 on the right, the Labour Party was on average placed at -19, Blair on +5, and Brown on -20; Cameron was placed at +35 and his party at +50, both barely changed from where voters had placed them in February.[45] This was still better than under Howard, but given almost two-thirds of those voters placed themselves at or close to zero – smack bang in the centre – there was still a long, long way to go.

Whether or not the process could be helped along by a change of logo was a moot point, but the leadership had decided that it was worth spending tens of thousands trying. Out went the so-called 'Torch of Liberty' that had first been adopted in the eighties and in came a breezy blue-trunked, green-leaved oak tree designed to emphasize values like 'strength, endurance, renewal and growth', as well as 'solidity, tradition, friendliness towards the environment and Britishness'.[46] Whatever members' views of the finished product, no-one could argue, as they gathered in Bournemouth for the 2006 Conference, that the leadership had failed to apply the makeover across the board: on the cover of the conference agenda, 'A New Direction', sunshine flooded optimistically through blue skies and the branches of (what else?) an oak tree. Those not lucky enough to make it to Bournemouth in person could catch most of the imagery on the Party's redesigned website or, like those who were much less interested in politics, simply make do with the characteristically iconic image of Cameron out relaxing with his family which was plastered all over the papers as the Conference began.[47]

Given voters' doubts that the Party had changed as much as its leader, Cameron's first autumn conference in the post had to be all about showing he was bringing the membership with him. Unfortunately, *Built to Last* proved to be a bit of a damp squib in this respect. True, the 93 per cent majority in favour of the document was impressive but rather less so when it became obvious that only 27 per cent of those balloted had bothered to vote. Moreover, the number of ballot papers issued (at 247,000 some 6,000 less than had been issued for the leadership contest) gave the lie to the tales told earlier in the year of the thousands of new members brought into the Party by Cameron.

The impression of a changing (if not a changed) party would therefore rest in part on the way the Conference looked and was run. The Tories' commitment to 'society' would be demonstrated by activists and MPs getting together to turn a disused church into a community centre. Their commitment to new ideas and a more open debate would be symbolized by the participation of non-party 'brand signifiers' in the debates – George Monbiot on the environment, Will Hutton on the economy, and, on law and order, Liberty's Shami Chakrabarti, who would have been about as welcome at past Tory conferences, one sketch-writer suggested, 'as a dead mouse in a bowl of egg nog'.[48] Delegates would be able to text in ideas, which would be projected on the backdrop of the main stage during debates. The US presidential hopeful John McCain (who even compared Cameron with JFK in media interviews) would address delegates and do a piece to camera for a site called webCameron that would be launched at the Conference. The site would host video clips from Cameron and others, and, it was hoped, give the impression that the Party was trying to reach out to a new audience put off by conventional politics but who might respond to a less orthodox approach – one symbolized by Cameron's first contribution, which featured him apparently extemporizing as (ever the new man) he washed up in the kitchen surrounded by his kids.[49] Back at the Conference there would even be a GWB (General Well-Being) café, though the wholesome snacks and fruit smoothies it offered delegates clearly weren't enough to calm those constituency activists who booed and hissed Francis Maude, Shireen Ritchie, and Bernard Jenkin as they tried to stick up for the A-List.

Candidates did not get a mention in Cameron's opening speech on 'social responsibility', designed to set the tone for the Conference. The speech did not, however, shy away from stressing how much the Party still needed to do. It had to avoid getting hung up on ideology or particular policies. It didn't need to apologize for the glory years but it did need to get over them. And it had not only to change but also to be patient, to 'stick to the plan'. As Cameron reminded his audience,

> Getting ready for the responsibility of government is like building a house together. Think of it in three stages. First you prepare the ground. Then you lay the foundations. And then . . . , brick by brick, you build your house.
>
> These last ten months, we have been preparing the ground. Our Party's history tells us the ground on which political success is built. It is the centre ground. Not the bog of political compromise. Not the ideological wilderness, out on the fringes of debate. But the solid ground where people are . . . where you find the concerns, the hopes and the dreams of most people and families in this country.
>
> In 1979, they wanted a government to tame the unions, rescue our economy and restore Britain's pride. Margaret Thatcher offered precisely that alternative. And this Party can forever take pride in her magnificent achievements. Today, people want different things. . . . But for too long, instead of talking about the things that most people

care about, we talked about what we cared about most. While parents worried about childcare, getting the kids to school, balancing work and family life – we were banging on about Europe. As they worried about standards in thousands of secondary schools, we obsessed about a handful more grammar schools. As rising expectations demanded a better NHS for everyone, we put our faith in opt-outs for a few. While people wanted . . . stability and low mortgage rates, the first thing we talked about was tax cuts.

For years, this country wanted – desperately needed – a sensible centre-right party to sort things out in a sensible way. Well, that's what we are today. In these past ten months we have moved back to the ground on which this Party's success has always been built. The centre ground of British politics. And that is where we will stay.

If the speech was some way from delivering the red meat they wanted, the *Mail* and the *Telegraph* (which was split down the middle on how to handle Cameron) seemed prepared still to give the benefit of the doubt to a Tory leader who, in contrast to his predecessors, was clearly determined not to be dictated to.[50] In fact, for all their talk of rumbling opposition to this repositioning, there was little on public display in Bournemouth. Indeed, the parliamentary party in particular contin-ued to demonstrate the tight-lipped discipline which had for the most part characterized it ever since Cameron had assumed the leadership. This was thanks in no small part to his poll lead but also to the work of his hugely experienced and widely respected Chief Whip, Patrick McLoughlin. True, a handful of keepers of the Thatcherite flame like Edward Leigh and Norman Tebbit fulminated on the fringe, while No Turning Back's plea for tax cuts was finally published. But all this was containable, not to say functional, allowing George Osborne in particu-lar to reassure the Party that, unlike Brown, he wanted tax cuts in the long term but to reassure the country that he would put public services and low interest rates first, even if it meant having to say to those who were supposedly foaming at the mouth for 'upfront promises of tax cuts now' that 'We will not back down' – tough talk and triangulation all at the same time.

Cameron's closing speech said little about crime and nothing about Europe or immigration. Instead it risked discomfiting delegates by celebrating marriage 'whether you are a man and a woman, a woman and a woman or a man and another man'. The latter was important because the Tories not only had to change; they also had to be about an optimistic future rather than an attachment to the past and the policies of the past: 'We must not', Cameron declared, 'be the party that says the world and our country is going to the dogs. We must be the party that lifts people's sights and raises their hopes.'[51] As for those who clamoured for more substance, 'What they really mean is that they want the old policies back. Well, they're not coming back. And we're not going back.'

Just as importantly, Cameron also used his second speech to move even further onto Labour territory by re-committing the Party to the NHS – the section of the speech that was briefed in advance to the media. Unlike his explicit commitment to the centre ground – something Hague, Duncan Smith, and Howard had eschewed – this move was not unprecedented: all Cameron's predecessors since 1990 had done the same. It was just that he was much better at it. As the father of a disabled child, he could, unlike them, garner both sympathy and credibility from his personal experience. He knew that the Health Service ('a symbol of collective will, of social solidarity' and 'one of the greatest achievements of the Twentieth Century') was vitally important to everyone in Britain because it was so important to him: 'When your family relies on the NHS all the time – day after day, night after night – you really know just how precious it is.' So,

> For me, it's not a question of saying the NHS is 'safe in my hands.' My family is so often in the hands of the NHS. And I want them to be safe there. Tony Blair once explained his priority in three words: education, education, education. I can do it in three letters. NHS.

Characteristically, this was not merely a dead-cert soundbite for broadcasters needing a few snatches of the speech for the evening news, it also dovetailed into the re-launch the following week of the Conservative's long-term campaign to overturn Labour's traditional (and electorally crucial) lead on the NHS. Helped by the hostile reception handed out to Health Secretary Patricia Hewitt by nurses and the continuing concern about hospital deficits, the Party once again called on the public to help it 'Stop Gordon Brown's Cuts'. And now it floated the idea of an 'NHS Independence Bill' that would 'take the politics' out of the Health Service by creating a board to run it free from direct government control – an echo of Labour's successful attempt to buy credibility on the economy by handing over control of monetary policy to the Bank of England.

Airborne

If the first PMQs of the new political season was anything to go by, the Tory leader looked set to wipe the floor with Blair in the Commons, boosting morale among his MPs, who, in return, elected only one recognized right-winger to the three places newly reserved for them on the Party Board. With this kind of wind in the leadership's sails, it proved relatively easy to handle the report of Michael Forsyth's Tax Reform Commission. Predictably, it recommended not just simplification of the tax system but also £21 billion's worth of reductions in business and personal taxation. Equally predictably, Labour treated it as an authentic statement of Conservative Party policy – a trick it was determined to play as each of the reports of Cameron's policy groups was released. Osborne, however, deftly welcomed the document as 'a menu of options that merit serious consideration' some of which would be accepted, some of which would be modified and some of which may be rejected. And, while repeating that the Tories would 'not be promising upfront, unfunded tax reductions at the next election', he moved the debate on by saying that the Party planned to 'rebalance' the tax system by ensuring that 'taxes on pollution will rise to pay for reductions in family taxes' – an approach swiftly confirmed by Cameron.[52]

Inasmuch as voters had even noticed all this, it had clearly done the Party no harm at all. Both ICM and YouGov reported soon afterwards that the gap between the Tories and Labour had, if anything, widened and, indeed, looked set to grow bigger still (from 7 to 13 points according to YouGov) if Brown replaced Blair. Unless and until this happened, however, the Tories were still in hung parliament territory and so could not afford to rest on their laurels. But the improving poll position did raise the hopes of Team Cameron that it could improve its relationship with the party in the media. The *Mail* was going to be difficult:

its editor, Paul Dacre, remained frustrated by Cameron's refusal to be dragged back to tax, crime, immigration, and Europe. But there were high hopes with regard to the *Telegraph*, which (apart from the unremitting hostility of Simon Heffer, the star columnist it had poached from the *Mail*) was slightly friendlier and might become more so under its new editor, 37-year-old Will Lewis. The loyalty of the *Express* could be pretty much guaranteed, even though it would have preferred a rather more right-wing platform than Cameron and co. were prepared to offer, at least for the moment. The *Times*, which prior to Cameron had been something of a bolt-hole for modernizing Tories, was also reasonably supportive. The real prize, electorally speaking, however, was the *Times'* tabloid stablemate, the *Sun*.

Cameron and Osborne had met a few times with Murdoch and his lieutenant Irwin Stelzer, both of whom had indicated publicly that they would at least consider supporting the Tories at the next election. While in the end such a switch would depend on which way readers were swinging, it was something the Conservative leadership was keen to achieve sooner rather than later, believing (almost certainly correctly) that a steady drip-drip of even implicitly pro-Tory copy was worth more than an explicit last-minute campaign endorsement. But there was a problem: Cameron's more liberal line on youth crime – reiterated in a speech made at the start of November that the *Sun* instantly branded 'love a lout' – did him few favours. Even so, it might be forgiven once the Tory leader felt confident that he had earned 'permission to be heard' and began before the election to introduce harder-line policies. Any attempt to align the Party with prevailing public opinion on Iraq was a no-no, however, as Cameron found when he had Tory MPs join Scottish and Welsh Nationalists and left-wing Labour rebels in voting for an immediate inquiry into the war – a decision which earned scathing next-day notices in both the *Times* ('Absent without leave') and the *Sun* ('Dave the dope').

Cameron, however, was determined, unlike some of his predecessors, not to confuse media and public opinion. While the Tory vote for an inquiry made for slower progress with Murdoch, and caused some disquiet among MPs (just as Howard's attempts to reposition the Party on the issue had done), it put it onside with most voters. Also, given the significant gender differences in support for the Iraq war, it may even have contributed to a development recorded by an increasing number of polls, namely that the Conservatives were now doing significantly better among women than Labour – a lead that was even more pronounced when female respondents were given a choice between the Tories under Cameron and Labour under Brown, who, given this image problem, should have been rather less pleased than he looked when Blair compared him to 'a big clunking fist'.

Repositioning on Iraq, however, was only ever going to be a tiny piece of the jigsaw when it came to Cameron persuading the public not only that he was modern and moderate but that his party was joining him on his journey to the centre ground and beginning to look at least a little more like the country it hoped to govern. Unfortunately, progress on the latter was still uneven at best. True the media helpfully paid far more attention to the women and ethnic minority candidates who were selected than the steady stream of middle-class white men who were still selected in greater numbers. Journalists were particularly keen, for example, to report on the selection of a right-wing Asian woman in an Essex seat, especially in view of the fact that Bernard Jenkin, one of those in charge of candidates, had just been obliged to step down after allegedly telling another Asian A-Lister that (although he clearly regretted the fact himself) he would 'be shocked if they didn't pick a white, middle-class male'.[53] But even the most sympathetic journalists did the maths now and then – or simply borrowed figures from ConservativeHome that showed that female and Black and Minority Ethnic (BME) candidates were still finding things difficult.

Meanwhile, if they so chose, journalists had little difficulty digging up individual party members with ideologically unreconstructed ideas about women, homosexuals, and ethnic minorities.[54] It was brave in such a context for Cameron to allow David Davis and Damian Green to go ahead with the release of a policy pamphlet on *Controlling Economic Migration*. But even its measured emphasis on the need for better control of non-EU economic immigration and decoupling the debate from the issue of asylum (upon which the Tories no longer proposed imposing quotas) attracted a pretty sniffy reaction from left-leaning papers, suggesting that the Tories, in liberal circles at least, still hadn't earned the proverbial permission to be heard.[55]

Cameron, however, was clearly determined to keep trying. The

Queen's Speech in November made it obvious that Labour, via its latest 'hard-man' Home Secretary, John Reid, was out to outflank the Tories (apparently all hug-a-hoodie and no-to-ID-cards) on crime and security issues. But the Conservative leadership seemed happy to respond by sanctioning the release of a pamphlet on social exclusion co-authored by Greg Clark, the Party's former Head of Policy but now a frontbencher.[56] It argued that the Tories had made 'a terrible mistake' by ignoring the gap between rich and poor that opened up in the 1980s and 1990s and that they should now take the concept of relative poverty fully on board. Moreover, in one particularly provocative section that made the headlines, it suggested they should forget about the sort of safety-net welfare envisaged by their hero Winston Churchill and look to more contemporary analysts, such as the left-liberal columnist Polly Toynbee – a woman many Conservatives loved to hate as a champagne socialist whose cure for inequality was to insist government throw more of the middle classes' hard-earned cash at the problem. This was simply too much for some Tory MPs, who had until now proved remarkably reticent about being quoted (even anonymously) criticizing their leader. One MP, who spoke for many, declared, 'I can change my tone, but I draw the line at a political sex change.'[57]

In truth, not all MPs, even on the right, were so unsupportive. Clark's pamphlet was welcomed by those who, like John Hayes and other Cornerstoners, saw themselves less as 'grumpy old men' than High Tory true-believers in 'compassionate conservatism' and backed Iain Duncan Smith's ongoing efforts to persuade the Party to take social justice seriously.[58] Yet even some of those who were sympathetic were concerned about their colleagues' reaction to the idea of 'dumping Churchill': one anonymous frontbencher warned, 'David has done well in countering the negative image we had. We're now airborne. But if he does not throttle back, we could crash-land.'[59] Once again, however, Cameron ostentatiously refused to ease up. In a speech which the leak of Clark's pamphlet had been designed to trail, he confirmed his party's commitment to tackling relative poverty and, while he insisted that 'the large, clunking mechanisms' of the (presumably Brownite) state were not the answer, also criticized the right's naïve faith in 'trickle-down economics' and its belief that a rising tide lifts all boats.

Cameron's last-minute decision a few days later to skip the 2006 conference of the Confederation of British Industry (CBI) in order to visit troops in Iraq was forced on him by military rules. Yet some still chose to see his missing the conference as all-of-a-piece with the Tory leader's efforts to distance his party from the business interests which many voters still thought that it ultimately represented – especially after his stand-in, George Osborne, declared that 'for too long' the Conservatives had 'abandoned issues like the environment, flexible working and social responsibility to our opponents on the left' and were not going to apologize for taking them up now.[60] Fortunately for Osborne, even if the CBI didn't warm to him, many of his colleagues still thought of him as an asset, especially when, on the same day, he revealed that a graphologist he had commissioned to analyse Brown's handwriting suggested 'the writer shows unreliable and poor judgment, was not in control of their emotions at the time of writing and there are signs the writer can be evasive'. While stunts like this hardly represented an end to Punch and Judy politics, they were not merely banter but the latest stage in the Tory leadership's long-term effort to undermine Blair's successor and, it was hoped, minimize any bounce he might enjoy after taking over.

Calibration

Early December 2006 inevitably brought forth a rash of media assessments of Cameron's first year as leader. They were by no means wholly negative, especially when based on opinion polls, which contained encouraging news. Some 52 per cent of respondents to YouGov's monthly poll believed Cameron was 'improving the Conservative's image' against only 27 per cent who did not. Meanwhile, 45 per cent believed he was 'moving the party in the right direction' compared to just 19 per cent who disagreed. Just as importantly, two-thirds of Tory voters thought Cameron was 'right to be cautious – to heed what voters are saying and to be reluctant to set out party policies in detail until nearer the next election'. Findings like these undermined the ability of those opposed to the leadership's line to claim that it was turning away Tory voters and that, in true populist fashion, they were speaking up for some kind of silent majority both inside and outside the Party.

In fact, the most common line of argument against Cameron one year on was that he should be doing even better against a government clearly in freefall, and that he would only begin to do so when he began to deliver policies that – surprise, surprise – would 'make our streets and neighbourhoods safe from violence and intimidation, control Britain's borders and transform public services so that they actually serve the taxpaying public rather than the interests of the bureaucrats who staff them'.[61] Cameron's first anniversary also saw what had hitherto been largely private criticism of his closest adviser, Steve Hilton, begin to leak out into the press, which managed to obtain anonymous quotes from frontbenchers and backbenchers worried about both his supposed Svengali-like influence over Cameron and (later on) his allegedly astronomical salary.[62] The tendency to blame those around the leader instead of blaming the leader himself is of course age-old and by no means limited to the Conservative Party. Nor, of course, was Hilton the only lightning rod: he might be public enemy number one by those opposed to the ideological direction in which Cameron appeared to be heading, but Francis Maude was just as, if not more, unpopular among grassroots activists as the face of the institutional changes to candidate selection that Cameron was pursuing.

Cameron marked his first anniversary by stressing his determination to carry on regardless. 'I've had plenty of criticisms this past year,' he told the BBC in a set-piece interview on 5 December, 'I've ignored them. I've stuck to the path I want to take to get my party to the centre ground, to address the issues people care about, to modernize the Party.' In fact, this overstated the seriousness of the internal criticism the leadership had faced during his first year and simultaneously underplayed the extent to which it was willing to respond to pressure by giving the Party at least a little of what it fancied – often at the same time as it courted liberal opinion-formers. For example, in outlining the Tories' thinking on education in early December, Cameron might not have mentioned grammar schools, but he did make it crystal clear that he wanted to see more traditional methods and subjects; he also wanted an expansion of setting by ability within schools. Similarly, he may have used a trip to Brussels around the same time to persuade left-liberal titles like the *Guardian* that he was more prepared to take a constructive stance than his predecessors, but grassroots Tories reading the right-wing press's treatment of the same trip would have been more than happy to learn that, in the words of the *Mail*, he apparently 'blasted' the EU's 'culture of hopelessness'. Likewise, an intervention on the integration of ethnic and religious minorities that drew praise from left-liberal commentators could be written up in the *Sun* as Cameron declaring that 'Britain's multiculturalism experiment has failed and that while religious groups can carry on their traditions and cultures, all must show allegiance to traditional British values.'[63]

By the same token, Cameron's reaction to the first report of the Social Justice Policy Group, chaired by former leader Iain Duncan Smith, suggested he wanted it (and was sometimes able to have it) both ways on poverty. On the one hand, Cameron could once again point to the fact that the Party was taking it seriously: as IDS himself admitted, part of his mission was political, to get voters who thought the Tories promoted selfishness 'to say, rather like they say about Labour, actually these people are OK, they are decent people, their heart is in the right place'.[64] On the other hand, Cameron (encouraged by his special adviser Danny Kruger) could endorse the conclusion of a Report that personal responsibility and stable family structures, rather than just state help, should be at the heart of any strategy to tackle 'Breakdown Britain'. His was therefore the kind of country, he insisted, that *Mail* readers wanted to see.[65] Such reassurance earned him good notices from the party in the media, as well as a donation of half a million pounds from a Christian city trader, Mike Farmer – very helpful considering that, although plenty of money was coming in and the Party had finally managed to sell its old HQ in Smith Square, it was still in considerable debt and spending more than it raised.[66]

The familiar gap between outgoings and expenditure might have encouraged parallels with his recent predecessors, but what distinguished Cameron from them was not only his explicit references to the centre ground but his ability to switch back and forth between the traditional and the innovative. Rather than 'lurching to the right', Cameron was continually calibrating. So, while he went into Christmas 2006 talking all about marriage and the family, he came out in the New Year of 2007 with what was basically a left-wing populist attack on supermarkets and energy providers, declaring that the Conservatives, 'unlike Labour, . . . will be a party that is for working people, not rich and powerful vested interests'.[67] A week later, however, he was back in reassurance mode, responding to concerns about possible defections and donations to UKIP (which, claimed ConservativeHome, was the second favourite party of nearly half of all Tory members). He stressed his continued attachment to 'freedom under the law, personal responsibility, sound money, strong defence and national sovereignty' – 'the ideas that encouraged me as a young man to join the Conservative Party and work for Margaret Thatcher'.[68]

This kind of ideological calibration was institutionally vital: the activists on the ground had to be kept motivated. Organizationally, the Party was still weak (and even non-existent) in parts of Northern England where it would need to take seats to form a government. The situation in Scotland was even worse – so bad in fact that some Tories (without, it should be said, any encouragement from the leadership) were publicly discussing the benefits not just of 'English votes for English laws' but even of independence, which could prevent Labour from winning a general election ever again.[69] Improvements south of the border would, it was hoped, be facilitated by the setting up of a dedicated 'Northern Board' under William Hague with regional campaign offices in Bradford, Salford, and Newcastle. Survey research suggested, however, that the Party's uneven performance across the country was as much an ideological problem as an institutional one. Populus, polling in early February, asked people whether they agreed that the Conservative Party 'understands and speaks for people in my part of the country as much as any other part of Britain'. In the South East and the Midlands, some 54 and 53 per cent agreed. At the opposite end of the spectrum was Scotland, where only 29 per cent agreed. In Wales and the South West 44 per cent agreed, but in Northern England the figure dropped to just 37 per cent. When people were asked whether they saw the Conservatives as 'mainly the voice of people who are already quite well-off, rather than ordinary working people', some 56 per cent of those in the South East agreed – worrying enough in itself. But in the North the figure rose to 67 per cent (and was of course even higher in Scotland, at 72 per cent).[70]

Increasing the Party's support in Northern England was the second of 'seven aims for 2007' which featured on a laminated wallet-sized card not released to the media but given to MPs and officials at a meeting called by Cameron and Ashcroft (who also used the occasion to try to dispel the idea that UKIP presented a serious threat). In fact, all the aims made it clear how important it was to reach beyond the Party's core vote (which, the leadership calculated, had nowhere else to go) and into Labour and Lib Dem territory, ideologically, geographically, and demographically (with regard to the youth vote).[71] The Party's lack of presence in Northern England was also given as one of the reasons why at the end of January, the leadership decided to make it easier for seats to choose from a wider range of candidates. Henceforth, associations would be allowed to choose from the much bigger approved list and, just as importantly, all candidates (not just 'A-Listers') would be kept fully posted of vacancies. The only sting in the tail was the closing of a loophole which had allowed associations going beyond the Priority List and holding open primaries to get around the obligation to have two women in the final shortlist of four.

Judging from the fairly muted reaction of activists on ConservativeHome, this was a quid pro quo that many of them considered reasonable. In effect, the Priority List no longer meant that much and both the media and, if truth were told, the leadership paid much less attention than it had done to the issue. Although constituency chairmen were informally encouraged to pick women, the pressure was off, with predictable results. By July 2007, it looked as if a healthy overall majority for the Conservatives would bring in 50–60 women MPs, a big advance on the 17 already in the Commons. But looking beneath the headlines and the media puffery about a new kind of candidate, it was obvious that women had made less progress than met the eye.[72] Whether one looked at the top 10, 20, or 30 women, it was clear that the majorities they had to overcome were around twice those facing their male counterparts.[73] By the end of 2007, by which time most winnable seats had been selected, the proportion of women chosen had dropped to just 28 per cent.[74]

Steel core

Those Tories who had already made it into the Commons were less exercised than activists about candidate selection. But, as opinion polls emerged which could be spun as suggesting the Party might be losing a few voters to UKIP, and as Cameron had to put up with the media discovering he was punished for smoking pot at school, some of them scented an opportunity. Once again, the bugle was sounded by Edward Leigh of the Cornerstone group, some of whose members were not best pleased by Cameron's announcement that, while he would allow his party a free vote, he personally supported the government's decision not to allow Catholic adoption agencies to opt out of legislation preventing them from turning away gay couples.[75] Published on 12 February 2007, the day Cameron went to visit the modernizing leader of Sweden's conservative party, Leigh's article in Westminster's *House* magazine claimed the leadership was 'in danger of taking our core vote for granted'. It was time, he declared, 'to revisit our roots'.

Yet, once again, there was no sign of anyone falling in behind Leigh. For one thing, only the truly blinkered (and the *Mail*) could look at the opinion polls and think it was worth worrying more about the fraction of Tory voters that might defect to UKIP than about how best to bring over the huge numbers of those now fed up with Labour and the Lib Dems. In any case, the idea that the man *Time* magazine had just called 'Britain's Boy Wonder' wasn't standing up for 'faith, flag and family' could hardly be reconciled with his heavily trailed criticism in January and February of Muslim extremism or the Party's renewed determination, announced in March, to stymie the passage of a revived Constitutional Treaty.[76] Nor could it easily be squared with his argument in speeches in February and March that the proper response to a critical Unicef Report on the UK's children and a spate of teenage murders was an emphasis on 'personal responsibility', 'common sense', and a declaration that 'the foundation of society is – or should be – the care of children by the man and the woman who brought them into the world'.

That Cameron accompanied this message with an assertion that 'businesses have an overriding corporate responsibility to help . . . make it easier for parents to find the proper balance for their lives' may have chafed a little. But, as he calculated, the right would find it difficult to criticize one part of his intervention without seeming to criticize the other: was this not what ConservativeHome's founder Tim Montgomerie had, even back in the days where he worked for IDS, called 'the politics of and'?[77] In fact, even MPs who preferred the politics of either/or were buying into the decontamination strategy being pursued by a leader who, whatever his roots, came over as an affable, pragmatic guy, in tune with contemporary Britain. After all, weren't the polls suggesting not only that the Tories were on course for an over-all majority but that over 90 per cent of those who saw themselves as basically Conservative would vote for the Party?[78]

The Tory leader was not, however, bullet-proof. In spite of the fact that he had begun to talk tougher on law and order for a few months, Labour still believed it could turn Cameron's famously more under-standing approach to the causes of crime (and his rejection of ID cards) to its advantage. In this context, the front-page photo carried by Britain's bestselling daily on 23 February was a gift to the government. It showed a 17-year-old hoodie pointing an imaginary gun at Cameron as he walked through a Manchester housing estate on a visit set up to talk about teenage gun crime. One didn't need a degree in semiotics to decode the message sent by the image, and the *Sun*'s screaming headline – 'I suppose a hug is out of the question?' – made it even easier. Here was a posh politician whose pleas for love and understanding showed how out of touch he was with the dangerous reality on what many in the media were bent on portraying as Britain's chav-infested mean streets.

Neither was Cameron (or Osborne) immune to grumbling (albeit in private) from within the Shadow Cabinet. The policy groups already meant that anything spokesmen said was strictly provisional. Now, apparently, the release of the groups' reports would be staggered, firstly, to ensure that they were not buried by media speculation about a pos-sible 'Brown bounce' in the polls when, as expected, the Chancellor became Prime Minister, and, secondly, to limit the extent to which Labour could expose the inevitable contradictions between the various reports. Frontbenchers were also miffed when, after Labour criticism that the cost of the Party's pledges so far was already running into the billions, leaked emails between Osborne and his advisers revealed their admiration for the way Brown, when in opposition, had 'relied on the force of his personality as well as leaks, threats, counter-briefings and pre-emptive policy announcements to maintain spending discipline amongst colleagues'.

So far, neither Cameron nor Osborne had really had to resort to such black arts to keep colleagues in line, relying instead on the fact that most of them were ambitious for office, had in some cases seen men more senior than they were miss out on it, and were determined not to let the same happen to them. In the second week of March 2007, however, Cameron, faced with a situation all too familiar to his predecessors, was called upon to display his underlying ruthlessness – what one MP interviewed called the 'steel core' beneath the 'charming man'. Patrick Mercer, the Party's frontbench spokesman on homeland security and a former army officer, remarked in the course of a media interview that he had come across 'a lot of ethnic minority soldiers who were idle and useless, but who used racism as cover for their misdemeanours', and that racial taunts such as 'you black bastard' were regarded in the same way as taunts relating to a soldier's being fat or red-haired. There was no suggestion that Mercer himself was racist or had ever used such language – indeed, he apparently had a very good rapport with ethnic minority recruits. However, this was a detail that was bound to get lost in the media furore, ensuring that the story risked offending the socially liberal voters Cameron had been so keen to woo.

Within just a couple of hours the Tory leader instructed Mercer to stand down and extracted a statement from him deeply regretting the offence he had caused. Moreover, the tone of the Tory leader's condemnation ('They are shocking remarks, completely unacceptable. . . . Racism is disgusting and it has no part in any part of our society, and you can't make excuses for it') was unequivocal. The media verdict was largely positive, although the *Mail* couldn't help wondering 'whether Mr Cameron had to act with such puffed up, politically correct zeal'.[79] It was also clear that some activists (and fellow MPs) thought he had acted precipitously and taken Mercer's comments out of context. Such protestations, and the incident itself, would inevitably reinforce the view that, as one *Sun* columnist put it, 'the Tory leader has an uphill battle to get the many lumbering dinosaurs still in his party to embrace his touchy-feely style and jump on board his shiny smiley battle bus'.[80] Taken as a whole, however, Cameron almost certainly made the best of a bad job.

The same could probably be said of the Tory leader's calm handling, just a few days later, of rumours that the Tories were about to land the travelling public with big tax rises on airline travel once they exceeded an annual individual quota of miles flown – proposals that got a big thumbs down from polls, the media, and aviation interests. In any case, the media (apart from the *Sunday Mirror*, which, in mid-March, stooped so low as to go through the Cameron family's bins to show he was less eco-friendly than he appeared) had moved on to the government's difficulties in persuading its backbenchers to vote for the renewal of Trident, the UK's independent nuclear deterrent. This allowed Cameron to use the Tories' continued support for the system to save the government's bacon – all in the national interest, of course. By also cleverly connecting the vote to the radical poses being struck by the candidates in Labour's deputy leadership contest and its refusal to agree to a cap on donations in order to maintain its union funding, he argued that Labour was 'abandoning the centre ground of politics' and that, with Blair going and Brown unable to keep control, it would revert to its 'gut instincts' – 'left-wing, pro-union, anti-defence'.[81]

Cameron had the message discipline, however, to ensure that, as planned, the Party's 2007 Spring Forum was basically a showcase for its apparent determination to save the NHS from Gordon Brown's cuts. Yet when the Chancellor tried to wrongfoot him by introducing a budget which both raised child benefit and education spending and delivered a headline-grabbing cut in the basic rate of income tax targeted at middle-income families, Cameron impressed with a swift response that called the whole thing a con at the same time as congratulating the Chancellor on seeing the light. He was well aware, however, that some in his own party might use Brown's move to put pressure on him to come up with tax cuts of his own in short order. Even more seriously, the Budget suggested that the Prime Minister in waiting was thinking of calling Cameron's bluff and holding a snap election once he had secured office.

On the face of it, the Tories stood a chance of winning such a contest. They were, after all, ahead by up to 10 points in the polls, and even those voters who weren't particularly enthusiastic about the prospect of a Conservative government were no longer so worried about it. Compared to 2005, the proportion of people telling YouGov in March 2007 that they would be dismayed by the election of a Tory administration had dropped from 46 to 31 per cent, while the proportion saying they wouldn't mind either way had risen from 25 to 36 per cent. However, the ideological 'decontamination' of the Party's image was still incomplete, while institutional innovations like the Northern Board would take time to bear fruit.

An internal report based on focus group research, 'The State of the Conservative Party Brand', noted Cameron himself was a plus. 'But,' it concluded, 'his fresh attitude has not filtered down to the party ranks. One respondent compared the Tories to 'a British telephone box, which looks appealing on the outside, but if you open the door, it smells really bad'.[82] It went on to add that 'The party is losing younger voters. There are continuous improvements in the South-East, but momentum gained in the West Midlands has stalled and the party's not doing very well at all in the North' – something it probably had to do if it were to turn an otherwise impressive share of the national vote into an overall majority. Meanwhile, Tory plans to employ pro-hunting activists from the Countryside Alliance's offshoot, Vote-OK, in marginal constituencies were not as well advanced as they would later become.

In short, a well-timed rush to the polls by Labour at the height of some sort of 'Brown bounce' had to be prevented. The best way to do that was to continue to undermine the Chancellor by attacks on his supposed psychological flaws and by linking him with the failings of what was now a highly unpopular government: as Cameron let slip during a conversation which rather belied his nice-guy image, 'We're quite happy Blair's going. He's trying to get out of the shit and can't. Brown thinks he still can, so we have to push his face back in it.' [83] The local elections, meanwhile, provided an opportunity to scare Brown off by showing the Conservatives were back in contention – something which depended on squeezing the Lib Dems.

This squeeze would be achieved, it was hoped, partly by focusing the Party's campaign on 'Fighting Crime and Grime' – appealing to both traditional and (like the ubiquitous 'Vote Blue, Go Green' slogan) more novel Conservative concerns. But it also involved Cameron sending 'personal' letters to around 140,000 people in key constituencies who were thought to have voted Liberal Democrat at the general election. These missives highlighted common ground with the Tories on civil liberties, the environment, 'localism', and public services – all part of what Cameron called in a campaign speech 'a new liberal Conservative consensus in our country'. News of attempts by the Tory leadership to lure over Lib Dem frontbenchers was also allowed to pass into the public domain. It was less pleased, however, about the leak of its plan to persuade Ming Campbell to join Cameron in endorsing as an 'independent' candidate for the London mayoralty Greg Dyke – previously a Labour donor and the Director General of the BBC until he was forced out over its reporting of the 'dodgy dossier' on Iraq's WMD. While this showed Cameron's willingness to look for creative, cross-party solutions, it shocked some activists and signalled a degree of desperation about the Party's inability to come up with a sufficiently weighty candidate of its own.

Anyone thinking, however, that these shenanigans might harm the Tories' chances in the May 2007 local elections appeared to have been proved wrong when the results came flooding in. The Conservatives gained over 900 seats. 'Love bombing the Lib Dems works', wrote CCHQ's George Bridges, as, with the odd exception, the Party cemented its pre-eminence throughout the South East of England on a notional share of the vote of around 40 per cent.[84] The Tory gains meant that there would be hundreds and possibly thousands of grass-roots members more inclined than ever to pound the pavements for the Party at the next general election. Looked at a little more closely, however, the results suggested that the Conservatives, although they did well in some places in the Midlands (notably Birmingham), had failed to make the kind of breakthrough in the North that they needed if they were to win an overall majority. Meanwhile, the Lib Dems' failure to take seats from Labour in the North, though encouraging, also meant that Labour's losses, though dreadful, were not quite as spectacular as some had hoped for. Still, they were bad enough to suggest that the gap Brown would have to make up really was, at 27–40, as large as, if not larger than, the national opinion polls were indicating.

The risk presented by this apparently impressive result was complacency. The leadership was therefore keen to demonstrate that it had no intention of resting on its laurels. Within days of the local election, Oliver Letwin was outlining – to a media bemused by some of his jargon and anyway too interested in Blair's impending departure to take much notice – what he understood to be the intellectual and ideological thrust of 'Cameron Conservatism'. This apparently included the recognition that twenty-first-century politics would revolve less around the economy (the battle for free markets having apparently been won) than around society and the extent to which governments would have to step in directly to deal with market failure and supply public goods or instead create a climate in which people helped not just themselves but others too.[85] Meanwhile, the Tory leader, it transpired, had spent a couple of days living with a supposedly ordinary Muslim family in Birmingham, providing some fine photo-ops and some good copy in the liberal media that was supposedly the favourite reading of broadcasters and Lib Dem voters.[86]

'Skid-mark'

In mid-May 2007, as Cameron was about to move on to his next fact-finding trip (as a teaching assistant in Hull), his Education spokesman, David Willetts, gave a speech to the CBI on Tory plans to build on Blair's 'city academy' scheme. These plans would force Brown either to declare for the legacy of his outgoing leader or to retreat from it. They would also do more for the educational and life chances of poorer children than the Party's old call for a return to grammar schools – an idea already ruled out by Cameron and which, noted Willetts, flew in the face of 'overwhelming evidence that such academic selection entrenches advantage, it does not spread it'. The reaction of a pressure group like the Grammar Schools Association was predictably negative. But Willetts had neither expected nor sought the backlash that greeted his remarks at the grassroots and among Conservative MPs.[87] In a first for the Cameron regime, MPs other than the usual suspects began to break cover to criticize what was, strictly speaking, only a reiteration of party policy. Among their number was Shadow Europe Minister Graham Brady, who was almost immediately forced to issue a statement accepting the current position. Unfortunately, Cameron could not be there in person to close things down quickly. Even more unfortunately, he issued a statement that reflected his irritation at what was a distraction from his photo-friendly work experience in a Humberside comprehensive: 'A pointless debate about creating a handful of extra grammar schools', he warned, 'is not going to get us anywhere and I won't have it.'

Suddenly, however, people were piling in on all sides to attack a policy change that they had supposedly, if grudgingly, swallowed months previously. That the criticism went beyond the usual suspects reflected, at least in part, a feeling in the media that Cameron and the Conservatives had probably had it too easy for too long. But the issue itself also aroused strong passions even among Tories not fundamentally opposed to the wider Cameron project. Even Michael Howard, one of the 25 per cent of Tory MPs who had been to grammar schools and one of those whose constituents still used them, did little to hide his displeasure with his protégé. Although grammar schools now represented only 5 per cent of state secondary schools, they were seen by many Conservatives as symbolic of a commitment to social mobility and old-fashioned excellence. They were a touchstone that went beyond ideology and fed into class tensions that were reflected even at Westminster, where many MPs felt excluded from the inner circle of advisers and gatekeepers around Cameron – labelled by one 'a group of very privileged and arrogant public schoolboys'.[88] Many were prepared to concede that support for grammar schools may not be politically expedient, but were nonetheless unwilling to be told by one of their own that such schools simply did not do the job that, within the Party, they were widely assumed to do. This turned a decision not to build more grammar schools into a criticism – albeit implicit – of those that currently existed, as well as threatening their right to expand in response to demand or demographics.

The defence of grammar schools, then, took on a symbolic value out of all proportion to its substantive importance. Between December 2005 and May 2007, the Conservative Party had put up with an awful lot from a leadership that it didn't always agree with but which, it had to admit, appeared to be delivering the goods electorally. Now that Blair was definitely going, to be replaced by a man whom all the polls suggested would only make things worse for Labour, many members believed the next election was all but won. To them, this meant that Cameron could afford to ease up on his efforts to distance the Party from its past and drag it towards the politically correct centre. And if he did not, it was about time he was told when he'd gone too far.

Cameron did not set out to engineer a 'Clause IV moment', though some of his advisers now thought he may as well make it one. Whatever, he was worried about being seen simply to buckle under internal pressure. He therefore issued 'a clear and uncompromising message to those who think they can perpetuate a pointless debate about grammar schools: we will never be taken seriously by parents and convince them we are on their side and share their aspirations if we splash around in the shallow end of the education debate'. A couple of days later, he declared it was 'completely delusional' to talk about building more grammars, claiming it was 'a key test for our party. Does it want to be a serious force for government and change, or does it want to be a right-wing debating society muttering about what might have been?' This proved too much for Graham Brady, who, after launching a one-man media offensive on behalf of grammar schools, resigned from the frontbench.

Worried the situation was spinning out of control, Cameron decided on this occasion (as on some others) that discretion would have to be the better part of valour, calling a halt to hostilities by agreeing that more grammar schools could be built in areas which still used the 11-plus exam if population increases required. Reports that Willetts might lose his job in the next reshuffle were allowed to circulate and there was lots of talking of setting and streaming within secondary schools as a whole. All this was inevitably interpreted as a climb-down and a cave-in to his critics, and anyone watching Cameron in the Commons in the days and weeks that followed could see he'd had some of the stuffing knocked out of him.

It would certainly have been a brave man who declared the episode – graphically described by the former frontbencher Bernard Jenkin as the 'first skid-mark' of Cameron's leadership – as anything other than a setback. The monthly poll on ConservativeHome showed Cameron's net satisfaction rating had plunged from +49 per cent before the row to +22 per cent after it, leading its editor to warn Cameron that 'it is not his party to do with as he wishes. The grassroots members are stakeholders in the party. . . . They are not deluded. Their concerns are not pointless. They deserve a little more respect.'[89] And Cameron's problems weren't merely internal: with the Chancellor set to take over as Prime Minister, opinion polls were beginning to register a 'Brown bounce' and to suggest that the Conservatives were now seen, for the first time in a very long time, as more divided than Labour. They also showed that voters stubbornly continued to think that the Conservative Party was far further to the right of themselves than Labour was to the left. In mid-June, the average voter placed him- or herself at +1 on YouGov's left–right scale, on which zero was the mid-point. Brown was placed on average at -26 and Labour at -22. Cameron was further away from the average voter on +33 but nowhere near as far away as his party, on +52. And asked whether the Conservative Party would 'prevent David Cameron's policies from being as moderate as he would like them to be', only 17 per cent disagreed, while 44 per cent agreed.[90]

The only upside of 'grammarsgate' was that the mauling Cameron received in the press lent weight to the argument that the Party had to do something to strengthen its media operation. Accordingly, at the beginning of June it duly announced that Andy Coulson, former editor of the bestselling Sunday, the *News of the World*, would take up the new post of Head of Communications and Planning on a salary that supposedly topped £275,000 a year. While, according to a *Telegraph* profile, Coulson was 'a classic Thatcherite Tory with hard-line views on Europe, immigration and lower taxes' as well as law and order, he had little experience of political reporting. What he did have was Murdoch's ear and a feel for popular culture and for what played well with readers: it was, after all, on Coulson's watch that the *News of the World* had come up with 'hug-a-hoodie'. The relationship between the Tory leader and the Labour-supporting *Mirror* was beyond repair.[91] But if anyone could get Cameron and the Conservatives better coverage in the rest of the red-tops, it was Coulson.

Some Tories, of course, worried about entrusting things to someone associated with (though not involved in) a *News of the World* operation to bug the phones of members of the royal family that had resulted in criminal convictions. Others were understandably concerned that he might turn out to be another Amanda Platell. On the other hand, as long as Cameron ensured, unlike Hague, that his head of media did not drive (or, more accurately, drive out) strategy but merely made it more effective by providing what one of his colleagues called a bit of 'working-class grit in the oyster', he might be no bad thing. Certainly, they reasoned, a sharper media operation might have prevented Hugo Swire, Cameron's Shadow Culture Secretary (and, as luck would have it, a fellow old-Etonian), announcing – much to the disgust of the *Sun*, for instance – that the Tories were considering scrapping the obligation on national museums and galleries not to charge the public for entry. This was hardly earth-shattering stuff, and could be reconciled with the Party's commitment to decentralization. Swire, though, was forced to recant within hours – but not before his announcement was, like the policy on grammar schools, judged typical of a party stuffed with politicians so privileged that they were unable to understand that a change that meant nothing to them could make quite a difference to ordinary people.

Sticky patch

Given this suddenly hostile environment, Cameron clearly needed all the friends – and the friendly coverage – he could get. In what was immediately dubbed by opponents as a 'Save Dave' move, William Hague and David Davis went into bat for the leader on the airwaves and in newsprint, with Davis comparing the two of them to guarantors: 'If we think things are OK, most Tories will probably think they're OK.'[92] Then Cameron, in the course of a widely trailed speech in late June designed both to un-ruffle feathers and to provide a context for the forthcoming reports of the Party's policy groups, announced that Davis would be heading up an additional taskforce on social mobility. Few could have failed to notice either that the speech also made much of the differences between, on the one hand, a 'progressive' Conservative Party that emphasized the family and individual initiative as well as social responsibility and, on the other, a Labour Prime Minister designate who apparently believed the state should and could do everything. Cameron's assurance that every comprehensive school would have 'a grammar stream' was taken as the concession it was intended to be. Privately, he was again insisting to MPs that he believed in 'the politics of and' – that the Party could protect the environment but also promote private enterprise, could defend UK sovereignty but fight global poverty, could prioritize public services but also talk about crime, immigration, and the family.

Cameron was also anxious to minimize any controversy surrounding the imminent reports of the Party's policy groups. The leadership would have sight of drafts before they were published but Cameron nonetheless thought it best to involve not just Oliver Letwin but also the less gaffe-prone George Bridges, his political director and a trusted figure in his inner circle – a move which subsequently ran into trouble when Bridges, wanting a break from politics, resigned a few weeks later. In fact, nobody was paying much attention anyway. All eyes were on Brown, especially when, just days before the handover from Blair, the

Observer published an Ipsos MORI survey that put Labour ahead of the Tories (by 39–34 per cent) – a result echoed a few days later by YouGov and ICM and the first time any major polling organization had recorded a Labour lead in eight months. Cameron had expected a bounce – and, however much he put Brown down in public, had warned colleagues in private not to underestimate him.[93] Quite a few, though, had failed to heed the warning and were now distinctly uneasy. Some even wondered whether the relentless attacks on him by Cameron and Osborne, combined with his lack of charisma and lack of loyalty to Blair, had backfired by so lowering expectations of the new Prime Minister that he was almost bound to look better than most voters expected.

This unease turned quickly to shock when, as Brown prepared to move into Number Ten and put together a 'government of all the talents', Labour announced that Tory MP Quentin Davies – a Europhile but by no means a liberal Conservative – had decided to join its ranks. Not only that but he had written publicly to Cameron in a manner surely calculated to confirm people's worst suspicions about the Tory leader. Under his leadership the Conservative Party had apparently 'ceased collectively to believe in anything, or to stand for anything', its 'sense of mission . . . replaced by a PR agenda'. Davies accused Cameron of having 'displayed to the full both the vacuity and the cynicism of your favourite slogan "change to win"' and of coming out with policy statements that appeared calculated 'merely to strike a pose, to contribute to an image'. Finally, he told Cameron, 'Although you have many positive qualities you have three – superficiality, unreliability and an apparent lack of any clear convictions – which in my view ought to exclude you from the position of national leadership to which you aspire.'[94]

This blow, combined with the fact that Brown was clearly bent on demonstrating he was sticking to the centre rather than 'lurching to the left' as the Tories had predicted, was bad enough. But things were made even worse by the fact that, after attempts to set off bombs in central London and Glasgow airports ended in failure, the new man in Number Ten appeared to have successfully handled a terrorist crisis – the sort of event that put a premium on the strength and experience that Brown was supposed to have in spades and Cameron conspicuously lacked. Speculation about a snap election started within days – and was not squashed by Labour, not just because Brown hadn't ruled out the possibility but also because he believed it might scare the Tories into showing their hand too early.

This was unlikely, not least because, with the policy groups only just getting ready to report, the Tories had no hand to show. Cameron in any case believed that Brown would not go early. Just in case, however, he tasked Letwin with overseeing an emergency manifesto, effectively accelerating a process already underway to weave together those proposals emerging from the policy groups that stood some chance of escaping what some insiders referred to as an inevitable 'bonfire of the lunacies' that some of them were bound to come up with. Cameron also allowed Michael Ashcroft to beef up his target and marginal seats campaign team with the Central Office veteran Stephen Gilbert and Gavin Barwell (soon to become a candidate himself).

This last move was not, however, greeted with universal acclamation. Within the Party there were those who worried (and, notwithstanding a confidentiality agreement introduced in January 2006, were prepared to tell journalists) that Ashcroft was gaining too much influence – although quite what this amounted to and why it should be seen as malign was never really explained.[95] Labour, meanwhile, was panicking about the way the Target Seats and Marginal Seats Fighting Fund overseen by Ashcroft was channelling money to Conservative candidates when it could not be limited or regulated by electoral law that only applied to spending in the immediate run-up to elections. This charge conveniently forgot about the donations to Labour candidates by businessmen and the trade unions, not to mention the Commons allowances that effectively subsidized sitting MPs' campaigning efforts.[96] But concern that the impact of Ashcroft's efforts would increase as time wore on encouraged some in Brown's immediate circle to urge him to capitalize on any bounce by calling an election sooner rather than later.

Despite Brown's 'dream start', however, Cameron still believed he had the measure of an opponent whom he was sure the public would sooner or later rumble as a man with nothing new to offer. He was also confident that he could take him apart at PMQs – a confidence that seemed more than justified after their first joust in early July. This improved morale, but a meeting with the Executive of the 1922 Committee during which Cameron tried to persuade them that groups like Cornerstone (whose leading-light, Edward Leigh, was yet again calling for a return to core issues) needed reining in did not go well. It did suggest, however, that Cameron was determined not to get dragged too far rightwards during a Brown bounce that he (and most if not all of those closest to him) believed would be temporary. As one of them, Michael Gove, put it, '[W]hat really drives the political tide is not the appearance of change at the top, but the shift in the deep currents underneath.' Brown's attempt to pinch some of Cameron's clothes by claiming to want to move away from top-down targets and more legislation as the answer to everything was 'just froth on the crest of one breaking wave. Underneath, a real sea-change [was] taking place' and there was nothing that the new Prime Minister could do to stop it.[97]

As rumours of a Tory reshuffle gathered pace, two men who knew they were staying put, George Osborne and William Hague, hit the TV studios with the message that the Party was foursquare behind Cameron and that there would be 'absolutely no change in strategy'. The faces, as widely predicted, however, did change. Francis Maude, who had acted as a lightning rod for Cameron over the A-List and whose tell-it-like-it-is modernizing style had never been popular with activists, was moved to a policy coordination role and replaced as Chairman by the more emollient Caroline Spelman. Her presence would, it was hoped, help counter the charge that the Tories lacked women at the top – one Labour was bound to push now it had elected Harriet Harman as Deputy Leader. Hugo Swire paid the price not so much for putting his foot in it over museum charges as for being an old-Etonian on a frontbench supposedly too full of 'toffs'. Given that he had been one of Cameron's earliest and most faithful backers in the leadership campaign, his removal suggested his friend did indeed possess the kind of steel required of a political leader. The fact that Michael Gove and not David Willetts was given the new Children, Schools, and Families portfolio was surely a peace offering after grammarsgate.

The other new boys promoted, Jeremy Hunt and Nick Herbert, preserved the ideological equilibrium. Cameron also brought in, from outside the Commons, Sayeeda Warsi, a 36-year-old female (and Muslim) lawyer, as the Shadow Minister for Community Cohesion, and Pauline Neville-Jones, the former head of the Joint Intelligence Committee, as National Security Adviser. Like all such exercises, then, it was a balancing act, an opportunity to bring in some new blood and attract attention, as well as a chance to deal with some of the criticisms. And, as always, who was left out was as interesting as who was brought in: by not promoting Boris Johnson, Cameron ensured the high-profile MP for Henley would be much more likely to have a crack at the London mayoralty – a risk, perhaps, but better than seeing a non-entity crushed by Livingstone.

Equally interesting was Cameron's response to the release of the second of the reports from the Social Justice policy group, chaired by former leader Iain Duncan Smith. Weighing in at nearly 700 pages and containing almost 200 recommendations for the leadership, *Breakthrough Britain* was heavily trailed for days before its publication, with Cameron making it clear that, while he could not commit to specifics, he endorsed the general thrust of the report – in particular its emphasis on tackling welfare dependency and addiction and its support for marriage as the foundation of a more healthy (and wealthy) society. All this, thought the leadership, would enthuse its core supporters – so much so that a 20-page summary of the report, a 'citizens repair manual' in the style of the iconic Haynes DIY car guides, was prepared and distributed free with the *Sunday Telegraph* on 22 July.

Cameron's decision to stand shoulder-to-shoulder with IDS, to approve his analysis, and to pick up on some of his suggestions went down a storm with the party in the media: the *Mail*, for example, headlined its admiring editorial on 11 July with 'At last Mr Cameron sounds like a Tory.' Modernizers, however, were worried – and prepared to say so (albeit for the most part anonymously) to the media. As ever, John Bercow was brave enough to go on the record, but one of his unnamed colleagues spoke for many when he told the *Times* that 'This is straight back to the "nasty party". God knows why David has done it.' Even those who thought this was over the top were concerned about the practicalities of defending any policy that (to use an example ministers were already citing) left an abandoned wife worse off than a man on his fourth marriage.[98]

After much dithering, Boris Johnson announced on 16 July that he would indeed throw his hat into the ring to become the Conservative candidate for Mayor of London – a decision that would eventually see him (with the help of Lynton Crosby) win the mayoralty in May 2008.[99] But in the summer of 2007 it was an election in just one small part of the capital that was beginning to attract attention. Labour, obviously hoping to capitalize on the Brown bounce, had announced it would hold the by-election occasioned by the death of the MP for Ealing Southall on 19 July. Rather than playing safe, and in a move that caused ructions in the constituency association, the Conservatives had picked a personable young Sikh millionaire and media entrepreneur, Tony Lit, who had only joined the Party at the end of June. The leadership was determined to show that, even if the Tories couldn't win, they could at least mount a credible by-election campaign, especially after their woeful, albeit winning performance in Bromley in June 2006.

The campaign started well: a number of Labour councillors even defected to the Tories. But a few days out from polling day things began to go badly wrong. For one thing, an ICM poll put Labour nationally on 40 per cent and the Tories on 33. For another, newspapers revealed that Tony Lit had attended a Labour Party fundraising event just eight days before being selected, only three weeks previously, as the Tory candidate. Even worse, he had had his photo taken with his arm round Tony Blair – a photo that was now plastered all over the press. Unfortunately, Cameron could do nothing by that stage to avoid being personally associated with what was turning into a fiasco: somehow the decision had been taken to label the candidate on the ballot paper as 'Tony Lit – David Cameron's Conservatives'. The Tory leader therefore decided to tough it out, making yet another personal appearance in the constituency just before polling day. But it was all in vain. Labour held Ealing Southall and its loss of vote share (at just over 7 per cent) was the smallest it had suffered in 18 by-elections that had been held in Labour-held seats since 1997. It could also heave a sigh of relief as it was announced that there would be no prosecutions over 'cash for honours' and that it had also managed to hold on to the Sedgefield seat vacated by Tony Blair. There the Tories slipped to third place, while in Ealing Southall they were again beaten to second place by the Lib Dems, winning just under 23 per cent of the vote, only 1 per cent up on 2005.

Gravitational pull

Inevitably, there was alarm throughout the Party and the inquest began almost immediately. London MP Mark Field joined the angry activists on ConservativeHome to launch a stinging attack on the conduct of the by-election, criticizing in particular the way Tony Lit had been foisted on the association. The party in the media argued the defeats suggested the Tories were being outflanked by a Prime Minister selling himself as both a social conservative and as anti-spin; to get back in the game the Party needed to 'reset its co-ordinates' and Cameron could not allow pride to prevent him from changing a strategy that had left his party looking 'soft and complacent'.[100] What Cameron, back in January 2006, had called 'the powerful gravitational pull' of 'cheerleaders on the right' was getting stronger.

Discontent was widespread on the right of the party at Westminster. And even those who were more sympathetic to Cameron were concerned that his long-planned trip to visit a group of 43 Tories (including 8 MPs) working for a couple of weeks in Rwanda to demonstrate the Party's commitment to international development sent out the wrong message. On the other hand, even if it was unwise of Andrew Mitchell, the Shadow International Development Secretary, who organized the trip to Rwanda, to condemn 'the gutless wittering of unnamed colleagues', only two or three MPs – as well as former donors (and well-known right-wingers) like Stanley Kalms and Stuart Wheeler – joined Field in going on the record with their doubts. Some MPs, although they thought he was mistaken, were impressed that Cameron had held his nerve and gone, and even those who were not recognized there was no point in panicking. As one right-winger acknowledged, 'David Cameron is the only game in town. We win or lose with him' – a sentiment shared, reassuringly, by the party in the media, which may have wanted a change of tack but wanted it carried out by Cameron.[101]

Cameron, hoping the trip to Rwanda would provide an arresting backdrop to the release of the Party's policy group on globalization and poverty, went ahead with the trip. His predecessors had lost their nerve at this point, but it got them nowhere and he was determined not to follow them down that cul-de-sac. As he put it before flying off, 'What we are not going to do is retreat to the comfort zone.' This was admirable but underestimated the extent to which his decision to go just as unseasonable rain was causing floods in central England could be spun by Labour as a dereliction of duty, proof that he was out of touch and more concerned with Africans than he was with the plight of his own people. Readers of the *Daily Star* are not generally known for their interest in politics, but its headline on 24 July, 'Cam deserts Brit victims', may well have achieved what Team Cameron itself liked to call 'cut-through'.

The pressure on Cameron to rush headlong into the populism pursued by his recent predecessors was mounting. Polls were suggesting that a key component of his strategy – persuading voters that Brown did not represent anything like the change they wanted or needed – was not working; they were also picking up a good deal of unease among the apparently shrinking ranks of Tory voters about Cameron himself. And on his return from Rwanda he was bested at PMQs by Brown, who, while he would not concede an EU referendum, was clearly bent on attacking from the right by pinching the Conservatives' idea of some kind of border police force and also by seeking to extend the length of time terrorist suspects could be held without charge. The Tory leader's response was not to panic, but nor was it to do nothing. Rather it was to think about bringing forward – partly in anticipation of an early election, partly to reassure his troops – what was always going to be the next phase of his overall strategy, namely the reincorporation of some more populist themes, having, it was hoped, done enough to signal the Party's move back into the moderate mainstream to ensure they didn't drown out everything else. As one frontbencher who had supported Cameron from the very start put it, what Cameron was doing was always going to be

a bit like one of those Rolf Harris paintings, when he paints a whole picture and puts on a canvas one colour, and you look at it and think 'What the bloody hell is that?' You don't recognize it at all. And until he gets his other three paintbrushes out and fills in the gaps and puts on the other colours . . . then you stand back and say 'Ah, I get it now!' For the first few months people just saw . . . an unfinished product. . . . People were thinking that we would never get on to being tough on crime, never get onto talking about the economy, about the burden of taxation. We were, but it was a staged process.[102]

As a result, Cameron's end-of-term appearance in front of the 1922 Committee did not turn into the showdown some had hoped for.

Indeed, Cameron's calm conviction that things would turn around when the media tired of Brown, his call for 'discipline, passion, and hunger', his reminder that elections were won in the centre ground, and his promise of a 'summer offensive' went down well with MPs. Under Major, Hague, and IDS, the crack that Conservative MPs were willing to be led but only in the way that Henry VIII was willing to be married had the ring of truth.[103] But under Cameron, as under Howard, the majority had little time for colleagues who rushed into the media to whisper against a leader whom most of them thought was the only conceivable man for the job. They were also buoyed by the news that for the first time in six years the Party was raising more money than it was spending. Nor, apart from a few grumbles from (mostly former) donors about the Cameron regime, was there any indication that its current income stream was about to dry up – a pleasing contrast with the parlous state of Labour's finances.

This peer pressure was not enough to silence all of the usual suspects on the right, of course, with Messrs Leigh, Brady, and Conway characteristically happy to tell anyone who would listen where Cameron was going wrong. Once again, though, both David Davis and William Hague, neither known as liberal-lefties, went into the media to defend Cameron: 'The whole point about politics', claimed Davis, 'is you don't persuade anybody if you lurch . . . on the back of a few opinion polls. The party absolutely has to hold its nerve.' People should remember 'We have lurched to the right before and it doesn't work.'[104] Hague, given his experience in the top job, spoke with even more authority: the Party had 'to persist' not 'change tack'. Anyone thinking differently needed to remember 'We've fought two elections on tax, Europe and immigration and we know what the results of those elections were.' Moreover, he assured his interviewer, 'David Cameron's not doing a Hague because he has Hague standing over his shoulder ensuring he's not doing a Hague.'[105]

Rebalancing

Given that by the end of July, YouGov was showing Labour with a 41–32 lead over the Tories, Cameron could not hope to stop speculation about an early election. But he still believed he could stop one actually being called. For those not yet on their summer holidays, indeed, he soon provided a clue as to how he intended to respond after he came back from his. An inordinate amount of press attention was paid to his using a radio interview on the last day of the month to slap down an Asian A-Lister, Ali Miraj, who had just contributed a damning piece to ConservativeHome, by noting Miraj had been to see him about a peerage just before publishing it. More notice should have been paid, though, to a GMTV interview the day before. Asked, 'Is there a bit of you that thinks there is too much focus on climate change and on things abroad when what people care about is water in their taps, crime and the issues at home?' Cameron replied, 'Of course and you have to get the balance right.'

During the first half of Cameron's break, the Tories, led by the Shadow Secretary of State for Work and Pensions, Chris Grayling, concentrated on trying to undermine Brown's claim to be a breath of fresh air. They weren't helped, however, by sniping over the paid outside interests of many frontbenchers – 'second jobs' which arguably made them less hungry for power than their New Labour equivalents had been in the early 1990s. They were also hampered by the fact that the media, having shifted its attention from floods to the outbreak of foot and mouth, had its mind elsewhere. Nevertheless, the issuing of *Gordon Brown's First Month: The Small Print* at least provided Tory spokesmen with a 'line to take' that was rather more convincing than the claim that the new Prime Minister was 'lurching to the left'.

The second half of Cameron's break, however, saw the Conservatives concentrate on the tax and deregulation proposals put forward by the policy group co-chaired by John Redwood. George Osborne was heavily involved, not just to ensure that Redwood remained on message with the commitment that tax cuts had to be funded, but also to signal to the Party and the voters that the Conservatives, for all their claim to have moved into the centre ground, were still interested in lowering the burden on business and individuals. Much of the report consisted of what the *Guardian* called 'vintage Vulcanomics', concerned with reducing taxes and 'red tape' on firms – a category that on Redwood's reading involved some health and safety and labour market legislation, as well as regulations on, for example, mortgage lending and financial services. As such, the report was predictably cheered to the rafters in the right-wing press, with the *Sun*, for example, suggesting on 18 August that Cameron, if he was wondering how to win a snap election, 'should be throwing caution to the wind and giving these proposals a clear thumbs-up'. On its release, however, Osborne's main focus was on Redwood's proposal to cut or even abolish inheritance tax. Although any reduction would have to be funded from other sources, most obviously (if rather vaguely) 'green levies', this was something the Tories were apparently working on doing – an initiative that predictably went down a storm with the party in the media, which had been agitating against death duties for years. So, too, did Cameron's use, on his return, of a *Sun* headline to try to bury his 'hug-a-hoodie' reputation: tough discipline and punishments (what the *Sun* billed as 'a blitz on yobs') were needed, he claimed, if society were to tackle 'anarchy in the UK'. Andy Coulson, it appeared, was starting to earn his supposedly stratospheric salary.

In order to counter Labour's inevitable accusation that the Party was 'lurching' back to right, the Tories then moved to switch to the NHS (as they had originally planned to do before the outbreak of moral panic over knife crime). Cameron, fresh from his condemnation of teen violence, went so far as to promise Brown 'a bare-knuckle fight' over hospital cuts and closures. This may have worked out fine had he and his Shadow Health Secretary, Andrew Lansley, not been let down by poor research, which resulted in some of the trusts named by the Tories as under threat denying they were contemplating closures. It was hardly surprising, then, that Cameron switched back from health to law and order, calling for the scrapping of the Human Rights Act – currently the subject of a media frenzy because it was widely (though wrongly) blamed for preventing the deportation of a high-profile murderer who was about to be released after completing his time in jail. Cameron then went on to call for young people convicted of violent offences to be punished by losing not just their liberty but their right to a driving licence or benefits on the grounds that 'you need to hit them where it hurts'. As the *Sun* itself commented on 23 August, 'Not so much "hug a hoodie" as "mug a hoodie". Quite a U-turn there. But at least it's in the right direction.'

Meanwhile, just as it had in February 1993, the massive publicity surrounding the death of a young boy in Liverpool lent credence to the opposition's message that something was going badly wrong in Britain.

Cameron, keen to show he was in tune with the mood of the country after the shooting of Rhys Jones, moved in with impressive speed, assisted by Davis and roared on by the grassroots. As well as claiming that the government was 'in denial' over gun crime, he used an interview and a heavily trailed speech to claim that the Tories would fight the next election primarily on trying to fix the UK's 'broken society'. After pausing for breath only to lay into Brown's refusal to grant a referendum on the revised EU Constitutional Treaty, Cameron was back on the beat with his third speech on crime in a week. And this time the tone ('time to draw a line in the sand', 'enough is enough', 'fight back against the drugs, the danger and the disorder') was even more uncompromising, suggesting that Cameron was learning from his recent appearances on talkback radio, as well as benefiting from the sharper edge lent to the Tories' media operation by Coulson.

'At last,' declared the *Mail* (forgetting that it had used almost exactly the same headline when Cameron had stood up for traditional families in July), 'Mr Cameron is talking like a Tory.' And that was before it got wind of the Tory leader's interview on BBC TV's agenda-setting *Newsnight* show the next day. A week previously, Shadow Home Secretary David Davis had garnered a few headlines after re-entering the debate on immigration.[106] Notoriously reluctant even to mention the 'i-word', Cameron's failure to press home the attack surprised nobody. So his admission during the interview that he considered the level of immigration into Britain had been 'very high' and required 'some fairly tough and rigorous action' did raise some eyebrows, as did his acknowledgement that

> people have a very real concern about levels of immigration and not because of different cultures or the colour of their skin. I think that people's concern is about services. It's the pressure on schools, pressure on hospitals, pressure on housing. It is important to understand that if your child is going into a reception class and suddenly 20 new kids turn up because lots more families have arrived then that is a big pressure.[107]

To liberals, of course, this – much more so than Michael Howard's telegraphed messages in the run-up to the 2005 election – really was dog-whistle stuff. You talked empathetically about an issue that resonated with your opponents' core vote and was inevitably suffused with racial prejudice, cultural antipathy, and urban myth, all the while insisting that your concerns – and the concerns of those worried about it – were wholly practical. Cameron might have demurred from using the word 'swamped' but, to his opponents in the other parties, he may as well have done. Such criticism resonated sufficiently with one of the Conservatives' Deputy Treasurers (and key lenders), Johan Eliasch, to prompt his resignation and his decision to work with the government on one of his keen interests, climate change. To those who were more supportive, however, it was about finally having the guts to speak up about a topic that was simply too important to too many people to become a taboo in democratic politics. If they were Conservatives, they also hoped it might warn a notoriously cautious Prime Minister that, even facing Cameron, he wouldn't be able to fight any snap election entirely on issues that were supposedly Labour territory.

To label Cameron's artful interventions on crime and immigration as nothing less than 'a lurch to the right' *à la* Hague, IDS, and Howard, however, was to overstate the extent to which Cameron had moved to the left in the past 18 months and to misunderstand more generally the nature of his project. Throughout Cameron's time as leader he had tempered his modernizing and moderate rhetoric by, for example, making it obvious that he shared Duncan Smith's concern with family breakdown as the root of many social problems and that he retained his long-term aspirations to make Britain a lower-tax, more lightly regulated country that continued to preserve its national sovereignty. He had also been careful not to push the Party too far when it came to candidates and had compromised over grammar schools, while the promotions and demotions within his Shadow Cabinet had given the right little to complain about.

In any case, Team Cameron's strategy had never been simply about moving the Party to the centre, important though that was. It had also been about making counter-intuitive gestures in order to emphasize to both opinion-formers and certain sections of the electorate (notably Lib Dem voters and public-sector employees) that the Conservatives were changing. In so doing, the aim was to earn 'permission to be heard'. Once that permission had been granted, the plan had always been to begin a return to more traditional Tory territory, albeit one that, in contrast to past efforts, was carefully phrased and which complemented rather than crowded out the Party's reassuring messages on public services. In short, when Cameron said he was a believer in 'the politics of and', he meant it. As he told an audience of candidates and activists in the first week of September: 'Forget about those on the Left who say I shouldn't talk about Europe, crime or lower taxes or those on the Right who say I shouldn't talk about the NHS, the environment or wellbeing. That is a false choice and one I will not make.' [108]

As if to confirm this analysis, George Osborne launched a surprise of his own. Osborne's assurance that there would be 'no election promises of up-front, un-funded tax cuts' and that '[a]ny reduction we offer in one tax will have to be matched by a tax rise elsewhere' confirmed what most Tories, however grudgingly, already acknowledged. What was unexpected (though hardly novel since various Shadow Chancellors since 1997 had made similar promises) was his announcement that a Conservative government would match Labour's public spending totals for the years 2008–9 to 2010–11 – the mirror image of Brown and Blair's promise to stick for two years to what most of their supporters considered the unreasonable totals outlined by the Conservative government before the 1997 election. This predictably upset some in the Party – especially those who had some sympathy with what (in view of the rebalancing already underway) was an oddly mis-timed attack on Team Cameron by Michael Ancram. In a pamphlet, the former Deputy Leader counselled against 'trashing our past or appearing ashamed of our history' and urged the Party to return to the eternal verities of tax cuts, marriage and family, and national sovereignty.[109]

Ancram's intervention was both irritating and helpful. It distracted media attention not only from Osborne's announcement but also from the release of *Restoring Pride in our Public Services*, the final report of the policy group co-chaired by the impeccably moderate Stephen Dorrell – a document whose mix of innovative and practical suggestions contained something for everybody, not least the public-sector professionals Cameron had been courting from the outset of his leadership.[110] Also, Ancram's concerns were wide of the mark. One of the things that Cameron had been careful to do, even when getting some distance on it, was, as Michael Howard stressed, to avoid 'rubbishing the Conservative past, the Conservative record' so as not to alienate those who were proud of it: he came not to apologize for his Party's history, simply to treat it as such.[111] However, the fact that Ancram's attack attracted little public support from right-wingers showed most were genuinely happy that Cameron had chosen to lead his 'fight-back' by talking more about an agenda they could relate to. On the other hand, a rant from someone dismissed by Cameron in a combative interview with the *Sun* as 'a blast from the past' helped reassure those modernizers who had been a little uncomfortable with the renewed focus on tax, Europe, crime, and immigration that the leadership remained committed to change and to the centre ground.

The publication of *Restoring Pride* meant that only one of the Party's policy groups had still to report. Unfortunately, the Quality of Life group co-chaired by 'millionaire eco-warrior' Zac Goldsmith and veteran MP John Gummer was the one that looked set to produce some of the politically riskiest proposals. As with the other reports, the leadership, the Policy Unit, and the CRD were given the chance to see an early draft and thus the opportunity to try to talk the chairmen out of radical recommendations. In the event, although the leadership managed to prevent *Blueprint for a Green Economy* rejecting nuclear power and saying anything too silly or alarming, some of its recommendations were singled out for particularly rough treatment by the media. The idea that plasma-screen televisions may have to go and that local councils be allowed to force out-of-town retail parks and supermarkets to charge for parking provoked howls of derision and warnings even from friendly newspapers that they were tantamount to electoral suicide.[112]

Consequently Cameron, though keen to maintain his hard-won green credentials, made it clear that he would not be adopting the report wholesale and even went so far as to claim any additional green taxes would be earmarked and paid into a 'family fund' that would be used to pay for more conventional tax cuts. Underworked proposals like this suggested that the Party's recently recruited Head of Policy and Research, Policy Exchange's James O'Shaughnessy, was going to have his work cut out. They also lent weight to the argument inside the Party that the green stuff was all very well but that it risked getting out of hand.

In spite of this the media still found it difficult to dredge up Tory MPs willing publicly to criticize the report. This was the case even in the wake of the decision of Margaret Thatcher to pay a call on the new occupant of Number Ten in the full glare of the television cameras – an event that provoked renewed comment on Gordon Brown's chutzpah and some speculation that the former Tory leader was feeling underappreciated by the man who now held the post. Party discipline had clearly recovered after 'grammarsgate', helped by the possibility of an imminent election and the leadership's evident willingness to press home the Party's attack on Europe, whether it be on the need for a referendum or EU migrants claiming UK child benefit for dependants living abroad. That said, the Party soon went quiet, if not completely silent, on the environment, suggesting to some that Steve Hilton's influence had begun to wane (and the Conservatives' head of media's had begun to rise).[113] As a result: as one journalist asked rhetorically, albeit off-the-record, 'Where's Zac Goldsmith? He was the great white hope of the party. Andy Coulson has buried him in a cemetery in Richmond and he won't be allowed to see the light of day until after the general election.'

Nerve

Zac Goldsmith or no Zac Goldsmith, the environment was in any case about to drop a long way down everyone's agenda. Northern Rock, one of the building societies that had taken advantage of financial deregulation to turn itself into a bank, suddenly ran into serious trouble, forcing the government, after a few days of damaging delay, to step in to prevent a further run on deposits. Ignoring accusations of opportunism, and the fact that he was obliged to back the bailout of the bank, Cameron went straight for the jugular, claiming the government had 'presided over a huge expansion of public and private debt without showing awareness of the risks involved' and that, as a result, 'Though the current crisis may have had its trigger in the United States, over the past decade the gun has been loaded at home.'[114] Labour's electorally vital reputation for economic competence was on the line and neither Cameron nor Osborne was going to waste what might be an opportunity to help destroy it and to make it even less likely that Brown would call an early election – a contest which the Tory leadership, notwithstanding its calls for Brown to bring it on, did not believe privately it was likely to win at that point.

The first polls taken after the banking story broke, however, showed Labour well in the lead, Cameron's approval rating sliding into negative territory, and a general public appearing to place more faith in the experience of Brown and Darling than in the untried Tory team. Indeed, the aggressive response of the latter now looked counterproductive: instead of receding, the prospect of an early election, fought on what still appeared to be Labour's trump card, the economy, loomed larger than ever. Panic would have been too strong a word, but many Tories were getting very, very nervous, especially after Brown made a speech to the Labour Conference which saw him pitch to 'Middle England' by ranging all over traditional Tory territory without mentioning the Party or its leader even once.

As delegates arrived in Blackpool, the pre-Conference polls were as dire as they had been under previous Tory leaders. Anthony King, the *Telegraph*'s resident reader of the runes, may have been too harsh when he claimed that to more and more voters Cameron (whose approval rating had fallen from +8 to -27 according to YouGov) was looking like 'a rich man's Iain Duncan Smith: well-meaning but ineffectual and politically inept'.[115] However, his party, which trailed Labour by 43–32 per cent, wasn't seen to have changed that much, nor did it inspire much confidence. Some 40 per cent believed one of the reasons it wasn't doing better was because 'The Conservatives can still not be trusted to run public services such as schools and hospitals', down only 2 per cent from the year before.

On YouGov's left–right scale, where zero was the mid-point, the average voter placed him- or herself at -3 while Brown and Labour were well to the left on -20 and -22, respectively. Cameron came in at +28 and his party was placed way over to the right at +46. This still represented a move to the centre compared with previous polls but, given the results of ConservativeHome's monthly survey of activists, this perception of the Party as right-wing could hardly be called an exaggeration: as Tim Montgomerie noted in his summing up, 'Grassroots members would like to see a manifesto that reduces taxation, increases prison places, increases funding for the armed forces, scraps ID cards and delivers English votes for English laws.' Moreover, 55 per cent wanted to see the Party campaign more on immigration, while they disagreed (24–64) with Osborne's pledge to match Labour's spending plans for the next three years.[116]

By toying with the idea of a snap election, Brown hoped at the very least to exacerbate these tensions between Tories. But it quickly became apparent at the Conservative Party Conference in Blackpool that his teasing was having the opposite effect. Without the threat of a dash to the polls, the Conference could have turned into a bad-tempered squabble over why the Party wasn't doing as well as it should have been against an opponent many had assumed would be far easier to tackle than Tony Blair. But instead of falling apart, the leadership and the delegates – both buoyed up by Boris Johnson's easy win in the race to represent the Party in London – managed to pull together. Without a show of unity they stood no chance of stopping Labour calling an election or winning one if it did. Blackpool had to be about showing the Tories were up for a fight and had one or two policies that just might burst Brown's bubble.

Given the task had to be to rally the faithful, the leadership knew that it would have to bring traditional Tory themes up in the mix but sought to stress that they could complement rather than conflict with the concerns it had been emphasizing since December 2005. This (and not an attempt to distance himself from Cameron and Hilton) was the message George Osborne wanted to send in an interview with the *Spectator* published just before Blackpool:

> I don't take the kind of über-modernising view that some have had, that you can't talk about crime or immigration or lower taxes. It is just that you can't do so to the exclusion of the NHS, the environment and economic stability. I have always argued for a more balanced message, and that is what I hope you would see at this party conference.[117]

That said, he used other interviews to make it clear that he wasn't about to start charging people to park outside supermarkets or limiting the number of foreign holidays they could take. And he made clear that he and Cameron, not Blair and Brown, were 'successors of the Thatcher inheritance'. They had no intention of 'dumping Margaret Thatcher'. Their solutions might not be the same as those put forward in the 1980s but – to the evident approval of both the *Mail* and the *Telegraph* – they were 'based on the same kind of Conservative principles – trusting people, giving people more choice over their own lives, releasing people's aspirations, stronger families and stronger communities and a secure nation'.[118] A four-page newspaper, two million copies of which were sent into 70 marginal constituencies in the week before the Conference, however, focused not only on law and order but also on health. And the Conference themes, too, supposedly struck a balance: the Winter Gardens were plastered with the mantras 'empowering people', 'making families stronger and society more responsible', and 'making Britain safer and greener'.

The set, however, was one thing; the selling points the leadership had decided on were another. Before the Conference even opened it drip-fed details of eye-catching tax cuts including scrapping stamp duty for first-time buyers on all properties under £250,000 (a move that would benefit the average purchaser by around £2,000) and raising the threshold for inheritance tax to take all but the very wealthy out of its reach. As well as all this, delegates (and voters) were reminded of the Party's plan to build more prisons and scrap early release, of its intention to create a dedicated border police force to tackle 'out of control' immigration, and of its promise of a referendum on every transfer of powers to the EU. They were also offered 'pioneer schools' to be financed but not run by the state, a 'pensions lifeboat' to help those who had supposedly lost out due to Labour's 'raid' on pension funds back in 1997, and an end to 'the compensation culture' that was apparently ruining children's lives.

With the possible exception of education policy, none of this was particularly modernizing or even indicative of a party seriously prepared yet for government. And to describe it, as did one enthusiastic member of the party in the media, as 'a coded *mea culpa* from the Cameroons' was going too far. That said, the same observer was right to read it as a signal to the Party that 'the hoodie-hugging, Polly-praising, huskie-drawn days [were] over'.[119] As such, it was undeniably effective. The Conference's deafening roar of approval as Osborne announced that under a Tory government only millionaires would pay inheritance tax – a sentiment echoed in the party in the media the next day – suggested that the leadership had hit the spot. Without being too expensive, it was a clear commitment to cutting taxation, and it focused on what many people, Conservative or not, had come to see as an attack on aspiration, on family, and on the property-owning democracy. Moreover, it would only apply to millionaires and would be paid for, in true populist fashion, by fleecing fantastically wealthy 'non-doms', apparently proving that the Conservatives were standing up for the middle class but not in hock to the super-rich. Best of all, polling in marginal constituencies after the Conference would soon show that it had cut-through not just to the London journalists who stood to gain personally from the policy but to voters all over the country, even those unlikely ever to be affected by it. This was just what the focus groups had predicted.

Meanwhile, Gordon Brown kindly confirmed pretty much everything Conservative politicians were saying about him by just happening to pay a visit to British forces in Basra in order to announce a reduction of troop numbers that turned out to be distinctly less impressive than he was suggesting. Shadow Defence spokesman Liam Fox's decision to rush into the media to condemn the Prime Minister for 'shameless and cynical electioneering' was a brave one that paid off, especially after former PM John Major made one of his rare interventions in contemporary affairs and, clearly furious, condemned Brown just as strongly. Cameron's 'unscripted' effort the next day – 'I can tell you we are not going to be lurching to the left, we are not going to be lurching to the right, we are just going to provide the good solid leadership that this country needs' – was as fine a speech as he had ever given, serving both to rally his own forces and to remind Labour just how formidable a foe he would prove during an election campaign. He had proved himself cool under fire and able to inspire. Moreover, the opinion polls published straight after Blackpool – some of their research completed even before Cameron left the stage to the strains of Jimmy Cliff's reggae standard, 'You can get it if you really want' – suggested a significant turnaround in political fortunes. Populus and YouGov both had Labour's double-digit lead narrowing to just 3 or 4 per cent and according to ICM the parties were now neck-and-neck. Brown moved almost immediately to rule out an election. As the headline over the *Sun*'s post-Conference leader column put it, 'Job done.'

Breakthrough?

Just as the Conservative leadership had hoped, the Prime Minister's failure to go to the country provoked screaming headlines that labelled him everything from 'Bottler Brown' to 'Gordon Clown'. He then compounded what was already looking like a classic career-limiting move by insisting that his decision to postpone a contest had had nothing to do with whether he thought he could win it or not but was taken because he wanted more time to set out his 'vision for change in Britain'. It was not only a pathetic lie but the fact he even tried to get away with it suggested he thought voters were idiots – an attitude, opinion polls later revealed, those voters did not take kindly to. Even worse, his decision to announce there would be no election in an exclusive interview with the BBC infuriated other political journalists already irritated at having wasted time and energy preparing for something that now wasn't going to happen. They duly turned on him at a press conference he held the next day and gave a lot of coverage to Cameron laying into him in the Commons for double-counting troop withdrawals from Iraq, thereby playing with 'people's lives and the families of our brave servicemen'. Then, just to top things off, Brown had Alistair Darling, his Chancellor, announce a big rise in the threshold at which people would pay inheritance tax – a move which, instead of looking clever, not only came across as overly complicated in comparison to the Tories' scheme but made it look as if Labour was prepared to copy anything they proposed in a desperate attempt to keep up. The government's protests that it had always intended to make such a move fooled nobody. And the Tories could, for the first time in years, claim to be making the weather on tax and spending.

The carefully crafted Brown 'brand' – that of a strong, straight-talking, patriotic, agenda-setting, decisive, conviction politician – was blown apart. Cameron, in contrast, had been tested and not found wanting and this appeared to have a knock-on impact on his party's fortunes. Polling on 25–6 September, before the Tory Conference, YouGov had found only 21 per cent of respondents thinking Cameron was doing a good job, as against 48 per cent who disagreed; the same fieldwork showed 32 per cent intending to vote Conservative. Polling on 5–6 October, after the Conference, the same company found 54 per cent of respondents thinking Cameron was doing well, as against 34 per cent who thought he was doing badly, with 41 per cent saying they planned to vote Tory. 'Not since the Falklands war', observed YouGov's Peter Kellner, 'has public opinion moved so far, so fast.'[120]

The same could be said about Party opinion. Before the Conference, Cameron could have expected to face major problems: indeed, the normally feisty ConservativeHome editor, Tim Montgomerie, had been so worried about how poorly the Tory leader was regarded by activists that he actually withheld the results of his site's September survey showing net satisfaction with Cameron running negative for the first time ever, fearing that the media would use it to sink any hope he had of rallying the troops at Blackpool. By the end of October, Cameron's rating had gone from -1 then to +78. Indeed, in the days and weeks after the Conference, having snatched back the lead from the hapless Brown ('the first Prime Minister in history to flunk an election because he thought he was going to win it', as Cameron put it during a devastating performance at PMQs), the Tory leader could for the moment do no wrong. He flew off to California to meet Governor Schwarzenegger, knowing that on his return he would be able to clock up more credit with Party and public alike as the government prepared not only to sign the UK up to the EU's Lisbon Treaty but to insist that it would be ratified without a referendum.

Conservative opposition to Lisbon was not, however, without its own risks. Although Cameron had played some traditional Tory tunes in Blackpool, he was determined to resist the gravitational pull that saw his predecessors retreat to the laager never to re-emerge again. Taking the fight to the government over its refusal to grant a referendum allowed the Conservatives to present the Prime Minister as running away from the voters yet again. But declaring open season might also tempt the Party's hard-line Eurosceptics to 'bang on' about the EU, thereby refuelling suspicions that the Party was, if not so much divided on the issue, then as obsessed with it as ever. Without explicitly rejecting calls for a retrospective referendum, Cameron and Hague stressed that their aim was to try to defeat the Lisbon Treaty in parliament, knowing full well that this was never a serious prospect. Fortunately, however, the Party's widening opinion poll lead meant that even the most ardent sceptics were prepared, for the moment at least, not to push the point either on this or on a new system for selecting candidates for the European elections in 2009 that clearly favoured even Europhile incumbents.

If Cameron was the obvious victor of the election-that-never-was, its first casualty was Menzies Campbell, the leader of the Liberal Democrats. In trouble from the moment he took over, Campbell had been able to do nothing to prevent his party being squeezed. Sensing he was going nowhere, they had forced him out, eventually picking the supposedly more dynamic and presentable Nick Clegg in the hope that he might be able to recover some of their support. In an attempt to head off, or at least minimize, this, Cameron used the first of what was to become a regular monthly press conference to promise voters who cared about the environment, civil liberties, education, and localism that his 'liberal Conservative Party' would welcome them with open arms.

But Cameron continued to calibrate. A speech made a few days later in which he called for 'a grown-up conversation' about reducing immigration garnered some predictably good headlines from the right-wing media ('Cameron throws down the gauntlet on immigration', 'Cam: You can't come in'). Encouragingly, though, the relatively muted reaction of the centre-left of British politics to what was his first speech dedicated to the subject since he had taken over as Party leader also suggested that, unlike his predecessors, he might be able to talk about it without provoking howls of outrage.

How much this had to do with Cameron's eminently reasonable tone and his refusal to return to talk of abandoning the Geneva Conventions, stranding asylum-seekers on offshore islands, and clamping down on gypsy camps, and how much it had to do with Brown moving the debate rightward by making absurdly nationalistic promises of 'British jobs for British workers' is a moot point. Still, Trevor Phillips, Head of the new Equality and Human Rights Commission, went so far as to suggest that Cameron's handling of the issue marked an historic 'turning point'. Given how Phillips had laid into Michael Howard's approach at the 2005 election, this really did represent 'permission to be heard'. Even then, the subject was still a minefield. Only a few days after Cameron's speech, the Party felt obliged to deselect a Conservative candidate in the West Midlands who refused to apologize for what some saw as an inflammatory newspaper article referring to 'the way we roll out the red carpet for foreigners while leaving the locals to fend for themselves' and noting Enoch Powell was right in arguing that immigration would dramatically change the country.[121] Judging from the outrage expressed at his treatment on ConservativeHome, many (though by no means all) activists sympathized with him.

The Tories' energies at this point, however, were focused on destroying what little credibility and coherence the 'hapless and hopeless'

Brown government had left after the election débâcle and following its chaotic handling of the revelation that the number of migrants in the country was much bigger than previously thought. One wheeze – a tongue-in-cheek poster listing the policies the country was missing out on because of Brown's failure to call a contest – was testimony to the rebalancing that had occurred since September. Only two ('stopping NHS cuts' and 'taxing pollution, not families') could be said to point towards a more centrist strategy; the others ('abolition of stamp duty for nine out of ten first time buyers', 'abolition of inheritance tax for everyone except millionaires', 'teaching by ability and more discipline in schools', 'National Citizen Service for every school leaver', 'proper immigration controls and a new Border Police Force', 'a vote on the European Constitution', and 'ending the early release of prisoners') did not. On the other hand, the release a few days later of detailed plans for an arm's-length board to run the NHS, at the same time as providing patients with a clear statement of their entitlements and a newly created watchdog to help enforce them, looked 'progressive'. And Cameron's use of an address to the Conservative Women's Organization to give a hard-hitting speech on 'the need to end sexual violence against women' could hardly fail to go down well right across the political spectrum.

Brown's first Queen's Speech inevitably turned out to be something of a damp squib since virtually all the policies in it had already been trailed as tasters for the election that never was. Once again, however, Cameron's attack was in large part *ad hominem*: 'Say what you like about Tony Blair,' Cameron told parliament in his reply, 'at least he was decisive. Isn't the only change we have had to swap a strong Prime Minister for a weak one?' The near-total command of the Commons displayed in such a performance, combined with the Conservatives' improving poll ratings, meant their leader faced virtually no opposition – serious or otherwise – from his parliamentary party, or indeed the party in the country. They might not love him, but they were beginning to trust him, and they were increasingly convinced he could deliver them power.

To make it back into Downing Street, however, the Party would need to boost its share of the vote to over 40 per cent and, ideally, to widen the gap with Labour to give it a double-digit lead. There were encouraging signs: an ICM poll in the second week of November gave the Conservatives 43 per cent – their highest rating since 1992. Labour, however, was still at 36 per cent. Eroding that figure still further was going to need the criticism of Brown that was working so well at Westminster, and going down so well with the Tory grassroots, to cut through to people who paid a lot less attention than they did to politics. This in turn required the discipline to repeat it to the point where those who did pay it attention were driven almost mad with boredom. Partly because they had learned it from New Labour, partly because neither felt much personal warmth towards the Prime Minister, and partly because they were the individuals they were, this kind of 'message discipline' was fortunately one of Cameron's and Osborne's strongest suits.

In the event, they were helped too by an unprecedented chapter of accidents that befell the government in November 2007 and provided proof, if proof were needed, of Macmillan's old adage about 'events, my dear boy, events' providing the greatest challenge for any Prime Minister. The Chancellor's clever-clever plans to bring in more revenue via a complex increase in capital gains tax came to pieces in his hands just as the public woke up to the fact that taxpayers might never recover the money he'd used to rescue Northern Rock. The Home Secretary, Jacqui Smith, was blamed for the failure of a quango, the Security Industry Authority, to vet applicants for their immigration status, allowing the tabloids to suggest she had allowed 'illegals' to endanger the public. A defence minister cast doubt on his government's own anti-terrorist measures in the morning but insisted he supported them by lunchtime. Worst of all, the Prime Minister – just as he came under attack for his treatment of the armed forces by former defence chiefs – had to apologize to parliament and the nation for the loss by HM Revenue and Customs of two computer disks containing the personal and financial details of over 7 million families receiving child benefit. And, finally, Labour's General Secretary resigned after a businessman revealed he had given the party hundreds of thousands of pounds using friends and colleagues as intermediaries so it could keep his generosity a secret.

By the end of November, even before the last revelation, Labour's opinion poll rating had dropped below 30 per cent and its reputation for competence – economic and otherwise – was in tatters. Brown, as Vince Cable, the acting leader of the Lib Dems, memorably put it at PMQs, had undergone a 'remarkable transformation in the past few weeks – from Stalin to Mr Bean'. Cameron, about to fly off to Washington for the first meeting between a Tory leader and the US President since 2002, was less amusing but every bit as wounding. Everyone was asking, he said, 'Is this man simply not cut out for the job?' By the middle of December, a YouGov poll showed that Brown's net approval rating, which had touched +48 in August, had plummeted to -26. Cameron's had moved up to +20, while his party led Labour by 45–32 per cent – its strongest position in over 15 years. ICM research published just before Christmas suggested that the Tories were at last beginning to attract support in the North of England – a finding seemingly borne out a few months later when, on 22 May 2008 at Crewe and Nantwich, a swing of nearly 17 per cent from Labour gave the Conservatives their first by-election gain since June 1982.

Between 1997 and 2005, the Conservative Party had lost three elections on the trot – all of them badly. Now, after David Cameron had been in charge for just two years, it was in with a serious chance of forming the UK's next government. But how much this turnaround was due to the Tories' own efforts to 'change to win' and how much it was due to the collapse of confidence in Gordon Brown remained debatable. In January and February 2008, two YouGov polls came up with some interesting findings. Some 41 per cent of respondents agreed that 'the Conservatives under David Cameron are more moderate than they used to be under Michael Howard and Iain Duncan Smith'. This suggested Cameron had gone some way to repositioning his party but was far from convincing everyone: after all, 21 per cent disagreed that it was more moderate and 38 per cent were unsure. In large measure the Party continued to be most strongly identified with those issues it traditionally owned (especially immigration, law and order) rather than with those to which Cameron had spent time trying to stake a claim. It had improved its position (and helped erode the government's lead) on some traditional Labour issues. But this improvement (and this erosion) seemed to owe more to an overall loss of confidence in Labour than to a widespread re-evaluation of the Conservative Party.

In only one area – the environment and global warming – was the rise in the number of people picking the Tories as best able to handle the issue bigger than the fall in the number picking Labour. Ironically, as the economic outlook grew more and more worrying, that was one issue about which Cameron and co. seemed less and less keen to talk.

Whether their emphasis for the New Year – a distinctly traditional promise to get tough on people not in work and claiming welfare – would resonate with a public increasingly likely to find themselves (and their friends and family) in such a position was debatable. The fact that the Conservatives were willing and able to launch such a policy, however, was testimony to their leader's confidence that, by sticking to his strategy but recalibrating when necessary, he had managed to convey a commitment to the pragmatic centre ground without ever moving too far away from the Party's ideological instincts. As Cameron himself put it in an interview in October 2007, 'I'm a mixture of sometimes being quite radical and wanting changes, and on the other hand being quite cautious and thoughtful about how to bring it about.' [122]

8

GETTING THE MESSAGE

A CONCLUSION

'When you look at things in perspective,' John Major told an interviewer in March 2007, 'you see reality rather than current dramas. It takes a long time. You need to wait for the academics.'[1] That the leader of the Conservative Party between 1990 and 1997 should choose to put more faith in academic than journalistic observers of politics is understandable but misguided. Understandable because there is no doubt that Major was badly treated by newspaper proprietors and editors who, even discounting his thin-skinned paranoia, really were out to get him. Misguided because many political reporters and columnists do an amazing job, often penning pieces that are as prescient, accurate, and analytical as any of those produced by academics who have more time to reflect on events. Moreover, when those academics do get round to making a judgement, they are not necessarily as kind to Mr Major as he might hope – or possibly even deserve. On the other hand, unlike some of his fiercest critics in the press, they do at least try to remember that when he took over from Margaret Thatcher the Conservative Party was already in serious trouble.

The puzzle restated

By 1989, voters were tired of the Tories in general and Mrs Thatcher in particular. Many of those she had helped by lowering direct taxes, freeing up the economy, and 'making Britain great again' had banked what they'd been given and were now looking around for a kinder, gentler alternative that would spend more on public services like health and education. The Conservative Party in parliament responded – rationally some would say – by getting rid of Thatcher in November 1990. By playing on voters' nagging doubts about the Labour Party, and by promising to govern not only more competently than his opponent but also more consensually than his predecessor, Major then snatched victory at the 1992 election. Once it became clear, however, that he was only a little less right-wing and a lot less lucky than his predecessor, the game was up. By the time Tony Blair took over the leadership of the Labour Party in the summer of 1994, the Tories' troubles had turned terminal. 'Black Wednesday', bad behaviour by Conservative MPs, tax rises, arguments with and over the EU, as well as weak leadership and widespread worries about the neglect of public services, meant that Blair inherited a poll lead of around 25 percentage points. Although the Conservatives narrowed this to 12.5 per cent on polling day in 1997, they were still left with fewer than two hundred seats in parliament for the first time since 1945.

The Tories' performance in 2001 was just as dismal, and in 2005 it was only slightly improved, largely, it has to be said, because the shine had finally come off Tony Blair. Clearly, the Conservative Party was unlucky until then to have faced an unusually gifted opposition politician who went on, while he was Prime Minister anyway, to run a government that presided over an unprecedentedly benign economy. This allowed it to devote equally unprecedented sums to health and education spending even as it intervened militarily all around the world – interventions that became unpopular but from which the Tories derived little or no electoral benefit. However, many of the wounds the Conservative Party suffered in its battle against Blair (and Brown) were essentially self-inflicted. They also represented a marked contrast with the Party's historical experience. The twentieth century had seen the Tories trounced before but they had usually recovered in fairly short order. Indeed, the common wisdom even in the mid-nineties was that 'The Party is driven by what might be called lethal pragmatism' and that 'Nothing concentrates the Conservative mind so wonderfully as election defeat.' [2] Few, then, would have predicted that it would have taken the Tories so long to sort themselves out, especially after 1997.

What the Tories needed to do was not that hard to fathom, especially since the UK appears to have moved into an era of what the academics call 'valence' rather than 'position' politics – an era in which voters value leadership competence and credibility over commitment to a cause or class.[3] The Conservative Party needed to present itself as a proficient alternative administration rather than an ideologically inspiring but potentially fissiparous crusade. And it had consistently and convincingly to project some kind of progress back to the centre ground on which, in Britain at least, elections are generally won. Labour had faced the same test after 1979 and similarly flunked it until 1983. After its defeat under Michael Foot, however, it had elected a series of leaders who, despite operating under rules, doctrines, and procedures which constrained them far more than their Tory counterparts, made it their mission from 1983 onwards to manoeuvre their party back into the mainstream.[4] Successive Conservative leaders, despite having more power to determine their party's policy direction and appoint its key personnel, made only the most half-hearted attempts, or no attempt at all, to do the same.

One can argue, of course, that Labour should have changed further and faster than it did, and observe that it failed to win office until 1997. But this misses the point. Whatever the pace and extent of the changes made by Kinnock, Smith, and Blair, and however long it took them to bear fruit electorally, the fact is that they got the message after just one landslide defeat. This, then, was our puzzle: how and why did it take two such defeats, as well as a further defeat in which its pathetic performance was only disguised by the government's own loss of support, for the Conservative Party – an organization renowned for its 'appetite for power' – to get the message? And how and why was it then able, relatively swiftly, to 'change to win'?

Laying out the pieces

In a world where the commentator who apparently 'knows one big thing' is bound to attract more attention, even if he or she is wrong, than the one who 'knows many things', it is sorely tempting to come up with an explanation of the Tories' lack of movement that identifies an overriding cause that can be summed up in a single sentence.[5] But, sadly, it would not be credible. Put bluntly, this is the real world: stuff happens for a reason, but not because of one big thing.

Any explanation worth its salt has to begin by acknowledging that there are plenty of reasons why leaders see change as unnecessary and/or risky, and that many of these apply to the Conservative Party after 1989. A satisfying explanation has to capture the interplay between ideas, institutions, and interests, as well as individuals. It also has to recognize the importance of 'path dependency' – the tendency of earlier decisions to determine or at least limit what happens later on. And it has to focus, like all studies of 'high politics', on the sometimes shockingly small world that politicians inhabit without presuming (a) that those politicians will simply say anything to advance themselves or (b) that they are irrevocably ideologically blinkered or (c) that they are unwitting captives of the organization in which they have invested so much of their lives and aspirations or (d) that a Conservative Party elite which is 'thoroughly, and indeed one might say extravagantly, capitalist in character' is populated by mere ciphers of the economic interests the Party was set up (and continues) to promote and protect.[6] Moreover, a credible explanation has fully to appreciate the fact that the partisan press plays a very big role in that very small world. Indeed, we cannot hope to understand the Conservatives without including 'the party in the media' – those ideologically driven leader-writers, columnists, and reporters with disproportionate influence on the politically obsessed they write for and write about.

To do all this means digging into the detail to produce an analytical narrative – one woven together in the preceding chapters and summarized below. It is a narrative, and an explanation, populated by people making rushed decisions not just according to their own individual quirks and prejudices but based on short-term concerns that, in hindsight, can seem ridiculously ephemeral but which require teasing out if we are to render what they did intelligible rather than inexplicable – or even inexplicably stupid. Likewise, we have to remember that political jobs (including the top political jobs) go to real people rather than factors of production that can be refashioned or replaced at will when they prove less than productive. Parties, unlike most firms, have to make the best of what they've got rather than do the best they can – at least in the short to medium term. The product, in other words, often has to be adjusted (or, indeed, left relatively unchanged) in order to meet the needs and the capacities of the CEO and the salesforce, not the other way around.

As the preceding chapters show, many of the generic explanations for the failure of parties to change, for the failure of their leaders to change them, did indeed apply to the Conservative Party after 1989. To those in charge before David Cameron, change was not merely difficult, it was by no means clear to them it was even rational. Tory leaders could not guarantee that moderating their offer to the electorate would work. It risked confusing voters and upsetting an increasingly Thatcherite parliamentary party, as well as their activists, their donors, and the party in the media, which (unlike, say, the *Guardian* or the *Mirror* in the 1980s) urged not moderation but more of the same. Time horizons being what they are in politics, any initiative that failed to pay off pretty quickly was liable to attract ferocious criticism. But, truth to tell, those leaders were just as ideologically convinced as the followers they had to keep on board. They believed that politics was about giving people what they supposedly need rather than what they say they want. Moreover, they were able to insulate themselves from those in their party who wanted to change things or who simply wanted them to consider additional evidence. Tory leaders also believed – not always without reason – that calls for innovation had more to do with a desire to replace them as individuals than with a genuine commitment to a different way of doing things ideologically or institutionally. In addition, decisions taken, and events which occurred, early on in their leadership (or even prior to them taking over) rendered any new departure either incredible or practically impossible given the time available before the next election – an event they simply could not afford to see beyond.

But while research suggests that inertia is the default setting for political parties, they do of course change – primarily, it would appear, in response to precisely the combination of electoral setbacks and changes of leadership that the Conservatives faced once Labour began to get its act together.[7] Indeed, many Tories grudgingly admired some of the techniques that allowed Labour to beat them so badly in 1997. After an initial (and deeply damaging) period of complacency during which they were convinced the electorate would get wise to Tony Blair, many Conservatives were all but transfixed by him. The upside of this fascination was that some of them believed they could learn from him. The downside was that even they forgot how much groundwork had been done by his predecessors. They failed fully to appreciate the extent to which New Labour was more than just a political conjuring trick by a master magician but also a profound, genuine, and sometimes agonizing move away from long-held positions and prejudices towards the preferences of the electorate and even the policies of its opponent. If the Tories wanted to emulate (and perhaps even short-circuit) the process, they too would have to sacrifice some sacred cows, not simply take a couple of quick bites of humble pie before carrying on as before. Their failure to adapt was in no small part a refusal, at times unconscious, at times wilful, to do that – or, as Labour had done, to find leaders who would make them do it.

It is easy to criticize, of course, especially for those of us with no sunk costs in, or ideological commitment to, what the Conservative Party became after Thatcher was elected its leader in 1975. The Party was run by real people in real time and, as Tolstoy famously observed,

> most men – not only those considered clever, but even those who are very clever – can seldom discern even the simplest and most obvious truth if it be such as obliges them to admit the falsity of conclusions they have formed, perhaps with much difficulty – conclusions of which they are proud, which they have taught to others, and on which they have built their lives.[8]

We are dealing, in other words, with decision-makers who are as prone as any other human being to the 'cognitive biases' that psychologists and economists – and, if the bestseller lists are anything to go by, the rest of us – find so fascinating.[9] Neither journalistic nor academic accounts of party politics tend to take these seriously yet, but the account presented in the previous chapters suggests they ought to think about doing so.

Some of these biases are individual and some are collective. When it comes to the former, there are a few of obvious relevance to our explanation. One is 'the endowment effect', namely the tendency of people to value what they already have over what they might (but only might) gain by risking its loss. An example? Conservatives who valued the issues they 'owned' more than those they didn't and believed it was better for the Party to hang on to the support it already had rather than lose some of it (perhaps to UKIP) by diluting its offer to attract new voters. Another is 'hyperbolic discounting' – the tendency to overvalue a lower payoff due in the near future than a higher payoff due sometime down the line. An example? Conservative leaders who were preoccupied with tactics rather than strategy, thinking more about tomorrow's headlines than where the Party needed to position itself in the months and years to come. Then there is the so-called 'base rate fallacy' – the tendency to ignore readily available and objectively persuasive statistical data in favour of specific or anecdotal evidence which seems to prove it wrong. An example? Conservatives who dismissed polls and focus groups in favour of what they were hearing 'on the doorstep' or in the *Dog and Duck*. Similarly, politicians are no less prone than anyone else to 'anchoring' (relying too heavily on one stand-out event, characteristic, or piece of information) and to the 'contrast effect' (placing too much stress on recent occurrences). An example? Conservatives who believed that a reasonable result in a European or local election, or a tabloid campaign on travellers or immigrants, meant that had to be the path to follow.

Collective biases also affected Tory politicians. We know that small groups of decision-makers, especially where there is no mechanism to ensure the input of new information and that someone plays devil's advocate, tend not just towards what passes for conventional wisdom in their circle but towards more extreme versions of it. Even those who start out with doubts will, if they stay the course, overcome them, partly in order to fit in and partly because people tend to take their lead not only from each other but from the top. Thus, if a bunch of politicians start out convinced that a particular approach will, eventually, do the trick, even if it has to be tempered or leavened a little, they can, over time, end up believing even more strongly in their original approach – which is fine if it's a good one, but not if it's not. Likewise, professional politicians are no more immune than professional investors to the flaws that affect all of us: they herd together, they overrate their own impact and skill, and blame poor results on bad luck and forces beyond their control. These collective biases are exhibited irrespective of the intelligence of the individuals in the group because, in most cases, they are more alike (and indeed more like their supposedly tiresome activists) than their superficial differences suggest.[10] Bearing all this in mind we are now able to summarize what stopped, and what eventually facilitated, the Tory Party's recovery after 1989.

Putting all the pieces together

Margaret Thatcher did not so much fail to respond to the message coming from the opinion polls and her own MPs as fail to get the message in the first place. Previous experience had taught her that the middle of any parliament was bound to be difficult but that any loss of support to the Labour Party – especially one led by the publicly distrusted Neil Kinnock – would be temporary. Making it up would of course involve engineering a pre-election boom but would not necessitate a fundamental change of direction. Such a change was, in her opinion, self-evidently against the long-term interests of the country, as well as against the ideas she had increasingly come to see as eternal verities rather than useful tools. The shifts being called for would anyway have been beyond her by that stage. She was prepared to countenance the massaging of the Poll Tax with which she was so personally associated, but not to see it axed. Meanwhile, pumping more money into health and education would be throwing good money after bad, especially when her introduction of quasi-markets would sort them out anyway.

To Thatcher, then, there was little point in listening since nothing could or should come of it. And much of the disquiet, she believed, came from those without the firmness of purpose required for government or from those who didn't just disagree with her approach but had long been hoping to see the back of her. Since they had, in the opinion of most of those closest to her, neither the right nor the numbers to depose her, their complaints were merely a distraction, especially when they didn't appear to be shared by the interests that would fund the Party's next election campaign. Those individuals who could have challenged this complacency were no longer around, while those who were still around only reinforced it and added to her isolation. Given the neutrality of the Whips' Office and the dysfunctionality of her Cabinet (many of whose members had simply given up trying to reason with her), there was no institutional mechanism that might have made a difference. Moreover, the rules of the game were against her. It was the right time of year for a leadership contest and it was one she needed not just to win but to win convincingly. Those rules also meant she could be replaced very quickly by MPs alone, especially if those who were sympathetic to her agenda, but who thought she personally had become a liability, could rapidly fix on someone broadly acceptable both to them and to the country at large.

John Major appeared to be that someone. Thatcher (in marked contrast to what happened after he was elected) seemed satisfied with him; he was clubbable, competent, and safely (though not aggressively) right-wing; and the polls suggested he would do as well as Heseltine, whose elevation to the leadership would have created a rump of Thatcherite irreconcilables. There was also no doubt that, before the election at least, he got the message. The Poll Tax went, spending on state-provided health and education – to which Major stressed his personal debt – went up, while the EU was kept at bay (yet not rejected) at Maastricht. The Tory leader was also able to rely on talented individuals committed to combining his own emollient appeal with a highly negative campaign carried out hand-in-glove with the party in the media. Unfortunately for Major, however, it was precisely that section of the Party which, along with Thatcherites at Westminster, felt most betrayed when the government's policy and popularity collapsed after the exit from the ERM. His critics were strengthened because the Tories' big lead over Labour in vote share had given them only a small majority in parliament. Attempts to conciliate those critics by pointing out that the government remained committed to further privatization and to bearing down on public spending proved fruitless, although it further alienated voters who already felt taken for a ride and resented tax and interest rate hikes which slowed recovery from recession. Reneging on Maastricht or ruling out the euro would have helped, but were regarded by Major both as bad ideas and as impossible to achieve given the opposition of his highest-ranking Cabinet colleagues. This did not mean, however, that those colleagues abandoned their leadership ambitions, especially at a time when the party in the media and many MPs at Westminster were attempting to engineer a contest – attempts which gained momentum after Blair took over as leader of his party and the Tories were comprehensively beaten (and, just as worryingly, outspent) by Labour at the European elections of 1994.

The fact that Major called and won a leadership contest in 1995 made no difference because it could do nothing to boost the Conservative Party's popularity – the rock on which its leader's authority ultimately depends. After all, the only credible contenders were offering a prospectus even more right-wing than the one voters were already clearly on the verge of rejecting, thereby reducing what little impetus there was towards a more centrist approach. Major's tendency to try to conciliate all sides of an increasingly factionalized parliamentary party bought him time, during which he hoped – in vain – that economic recovery would bring voters back to the Tory fold. But it also earned him widespread contempt inside the Party and a reputation for fudging and weakness outside it. The inability of the Tories to come up with a consistent strategy to take on Blair was testimony not just to the latter's skill but to their having forgotten what it was like to fight a credible, mainstream contender – something which, along with a widespread belief that the opinion polls would get it wrong again, led them to think they would do much better than expected at the election. That they eventually lost it so badly also reflected the fact that the voluntary party in the country had withered on the vine, while many Tory MPs (when they weren't worrying about the post-election leadership contest or preserving their extra-parliamentary earnings) were more preoccupied with fighting off the challenge from minor parties to their (Eurosceptic) right than the unspoken tactical alliance between Labour and the Liberal Democrats that was about to sweep so many of them away.

The complacency and self-obsession that characterized the Conservatives before the 1997 election carried on after it. Strapped for cash, straight into a leadership contest, and complacently convinced that voters would soon wise up to a Labour government which had supposedly lost the ideological argument and would soon implode, the Tories failed to realize how much they would have to shift back to the centre ground. Instead, having rejected as leader on ideological grounds the one man (Ken Clarke) who might have helped them make such a shift, they prioritized sorting out what they regarded as their key problems – Europe, sleaze, and a party machine that had shown itself manifestly inferior. Contrary to common wisdom, there was no initial attempt by Hague, beyond a few disastrous photo-ops and a speech or two, to make a serious move back into the mainstream or to reach out to a new electoral constituency. Inasmuch as there was a strategy, it was to renew the Party institutionally so it would be ready in government to take to the next level the Thatcherism of which Hague and most of his colleagues were unquestioning devotees. By the time some began to question the viability of such an approach and to recommend a rather more conciliatory one, it was too late. For one thing, anyone who suggested some sort of move to the centre was torn apart by the party in parliament and the media, with many of those who would later go on to embrace modernization being among the fiercest critics: Lilley's Butler lecture was a critical juncture in this respect. For another, huge opinion poll deficits combined with Hague's poor PR and judgement had called his leadership into question, the response to which was to refashion the Tory leader as a populist, commonsense defender of Middle England against asylum-seekers, criminals, political correctness, and, of course, Brussels. The urging of newspapers, plus the seeming success of the Party's 1999 highly sceptical European election campaign, cemented in the increasingly hard-line approach and froze out advisers who had more faith in opinion research than in gut instincts and media 'hits'.

Things were only made worse in late 1999 by the re-entry of Michael Portillo, who was beginning to grasp the magnitude of the changes the Party might have to undergo. He, and the Shadow Cabinet Members who agreed with him, came to realize that, in the Conservative Party at least, the leader's colleagues have little or no hold over him even when it comes to matters within their own portfolio. To voters, the Party was clearly in two minds about not just 'social issues' but also tax and spending. Meanwhile, the threat posed by a more charismatic colleague turned Hague's inner circle into a praetorian guard. This limited the access of those who disagreed with the direction in which the Party was going, and ensured (media) tactics would continue to crowd out (political) strategy. To Hague and his inner circle, the Tories' occasional forays onto Labour territory had proved fruitless and therefore the Party was best off avoiding the bread-and-butter issues, like health, education, and the economy, which conventionally decide elections. Instead, it would attempt to appeal to voters (and mobilize activists) on issues on which the Tories were stronger and stood some chance of breaking up New Labour's coalition – crime, immigration, Europe, and (to a lesser extent) tax. This pitch would have the added advantage of authenticity since it accorded with Hague's instincts. But with voters mainly happy to give Labour another chance, it flopped just as badly as the Tories' own opinion pollster had predicted. After four wasted years, they were back at square one.

Anyone thinking that things could only get better, however, was in for a disappointment. Tory MPs' doubts about Portillo, as well as his own concerns that they simply weren't ready to do what needed to be done to put the Party back into contention, combined with an electoral system giving the final say to the wider membership to see Iain Duncan Smith elected as leader. As an individual, IDS was no more capable than his predecessor of capturing the affection or the imagination of the public and the media. As a result, he was quickly written off as an embarrassing liability by the bulk of his own MPs. Some simply wouldn't or couldn't work with him, and either retreated into private pursuits or joined modernizing ginger groups. Others still despised him for the trouble he caused Major over Maastricht. Most just wanted him out but didn't know how they could do it without precipitating a contest that might land them with another leader no-one wanted. This, as well as the fact that IDS, like Hague, spent so much time worrying about his own position and was prone to venting his populist pet peeves in the media, meant he gained little credit for his halting efforts to reposition the Party as one that cared about social justice. In any case, there was little point in talking about 'helping the vulnerable' and public services if the proposed solutions were still so ideological, involving shrinking the state to free up room for tax cuts and subsidizing the tiny minority who had the wherewithal to opt out of state healthcare or education. Likewise, acknowledging the Party had to reach out to women and ethnic minorities was pointless if, because of both ideological objections and the difficulty of overriding the institutional autonomy of the constituencies, the Party shied away from taking the necessary measures to make it happen. It also sat ill with a response to government equality legislation that suggested the Tories' newfound tolerance toward minorities was far from infinite.

Those advisers who tried to keep IDS on a more moderate,

modernizing message were soon cast aside in favour of people who were more in tune with the leaders' traditionalist instincts and whose answer to terrible opinion polls was to go out and buy some better ones. Yet Duncan Smith, whose neo-conservative support for the US ruled out any possibility of the Party capitalizing on public disquiet over the Iraq war, hung on – mainly because Tories at Westminster still feared the consequences of another leadership election decided by the grassroots. By the end of 2003, however, concerns that the Party would become a laughing stock overtaken by the Lib Dems, threats by high-profile donors to withdraw their funding, and the probability that MPs would be able to avoid a contest by electing a replacement unopposed saw IDS ousted (with the help of his own Whips' Office) in favour of Michael Howard.

If, like Labour's Michael Foot, IDS did his party some good by being so bad, he also resembled him in handing over a policy legacy that any successor wanting to change things would need to dismantle. But any hopes that Howard would use his unusually powerful position to do this and so broaden the Party's appeal died within days of the heavily spun, supposedly 'modernizing', speech he made as he took over – a critical juncture, an opportunity missed. The elevation of a 'grown-up' to the leadership boosted discipline and morale, but it came at a price. The Party's new leader had no interest in renewing the (admittedly faltering) steps taken by Duncan Smith towards changing public perceptions by talking about social exclusion and broadening its base of candidates. However, he continued to believe the Tories could find sufficient waste in government to finance a few eye-catching tax cuts. IDS's neo-liberal wheezes on health and education were retained, even if they were de-emphasized in favour of a focus on delivery and a crack-down on crime, immigration, and gypsies – populist issues Howard had long thought of as electorally powerful and which guaranteed plenty of coverage from the party in the media, which, as ever, called for red meat and plenty of it.

Howard could understand, and to some extent even sympathize with, modernizers' arguments for a more moderate approach. And he, like Hague, was prepared to concede that Labour could not be beaten unless its spending plans for schools and hospitals were matched. But, he believed, it had to be worth giving an authentically Conservative platform just one more try: in any case, given who he was and how much time he had, it was the only one he could credibly sell – a point made not just by those colleagues who were ideologically inclined towards it but even by those who, like David Cameron, were not. It didn't help, however, because, while voters had tired of Labour, they didn't trust the Tories on public services. Howard was easily portrayed as a blast from the past and, because of his agonizing attempts to distance the Tories from the government on Iraq, as an untrustworthy opportunist. His party was still seen as too right-wing, too out-of-touch, too nasty, and too unrepresentative of ordinary people – possibly good enough for the protest vote his campaign tried to whip up, but not for a government-in-waiting. The result was woeful. True, the Tories picked up extra seats in 2005 whereas in 2001 they had virtually stood still. But they still won less than Labour had done at its own low point in 1983.

Within less than a year, however, the Conservative Party had elected a leader who made no secret of the fact that it would have to moderate and modernize. In this respect, at least, Michael Howard can justly claim to have done David Cameron, and therefore his party, a favour or two. Firstly, by at least holding the Party together and preventing the meltdown that many feared would occur if it went into an election still led by IDS, he ensured that, in the light of Labour's declining popularity, Westminster would see an influx of over fifty new Tory MPs, many of whom were right-wing but prepared to think and act more creatively. Second, he effectively tested to destruction the claim that, if only the Conservatives shouted louder rather than really listened to the electorate, they would persuade it to listen. If the options open to political parties eventually come down to a choice between 'preference shaping' (the heroic assumption that you can get voters to see things your way) and 'preference accommodation' (the assumption that you need to meet them halfway), then the Tories' result in 2005 encouraged more of them finally to consider giving the second option a go – especially after Howard organized a series of forums for his post-election parliamentary party where they were treated to presentations on how poorly the Party was perceived by the public. Finally, Howard, despite putting up with considerable flak for doing so, managed to delay a leadership contest for half a year. This made victory all the more likely for his favoured candidate – a pragmatic modernizer prepared to make some gestures to the right and a man with much better media skills and much less baggage than his only serious rival.

We noted in the introduction the argument that those who are most heavily invested in an organization are therefore most likely to deceive themselves that things are OK. But we also noted that, once they realize things can't carry on in the same way, they can sometimes do even more to achieve a change in its direction than those who were always unhappy with it. Howard is a good example, but so too are many of those who have played a big role under Cameron. This is an important point. The Conservative Party – like many other parties – is not full of talent, or so meritocratic and open, that it can easily rid itself of people who, in an earlier guise, have been deeply associated with embarrassment and/or failure. As a consequence, while a change of leader normally implies a change of regime, the next change of leader often sees not a full-fledged restoration but a degree of circularity. However, that circularity, or at least circulation, need not lead to atrophy or entropy. This is because those who pop up and bounce back are not the same people they were at the beginning of the story: they become, for instance, rather less strident or ideological, either because they have a genuine change of heart or because their earlier stances had more to do with staying in the game than stating the truth. This recalls the warnings of those who follow the 'high politics' approach that principles are about positioning rather than conviction. But it also recalls the argument that individuals' responses to their organization's decline vary – and can oscillate – between exit, voice, and loyalty. David Cameron, like many of those who work closely alongside him, is a case in point.

The complete package

The Conservatives now look like a party capable of winning the next general election. When accounting for this, we are dealing with more than just another case of 'The economy, stupid.' After all, it is possible to argue that the global credit crunch stood at least a chance of reviving the fortunes of a Labour Prime Minister who had, at the end of 2007, looked out for the count. Moreover, a Tory victory began to look possible within days of David Cameron assuming the leadership – long before things turned truly pear-shaped on the financial front. Given his party had been 'flatlining' for around a decade, such a rapid turnaround requires some explanation too.

Clearly not all the reasons behind the shift have to do with Cameron himself. The challenges presented to him both by the external environment and by the state of his own party provide a sharp contrast to those faced by his predecessors. They faced, especially after 1994, one of the most popular party leaders this country has ever seen and one whose government was able to deliver economic growth and massive investment in public services, along with policies on crime, Europe, and immigration that, while by no means as hard-line as most voters would have liked, were tight enough to prevent them defecting to the Tories. Cameron, by contrast, started his time as leader of the opposition facing a Prime Minister well past his sell-by date and a party consumed with personal and policy differences. He was also aided by the widely predicted failure of Blair's successor to connect with the British public, at least after his initial bounce was cancelled out by the incredible run of ill-fortune which followed his 'bottling' of an early election. Moreover, voters were beginning to chafe against the more or less stealthy rises in taxation used to pay for improvements in public services that people either banked without much gratitude or regarded with some scepticism. More recently, of course, Labour's luck on the economy has run out, too – something the Tories had predicted for so long that they had begun to believe it would never happen.

But it is not just the external environment that is more benign. David Cameron also leads a party which, irrespective of his own efforts, is both more malleable and more manageable than the one with which his predecessors were confronted (sometimes in the literal sense of the word). There are many reasons for this. One is simply that the people and the issues that made it so hard for them – even if they didn't exactly help themselves – have moved on. To take one obvious example, one does not need to sink into the armchair Freudianism that puts the Party's troubles down to the matricide of Margaret Thatcher to realize that her transformation from a constantly carping critic into a frail old lady has provided its own form of 'closure'. The heat, too, appears, at least for the moment, to have gone out of the issue that became her *casus belli*: the realization that this country is unlikely to adopt the euro and the obstacles faced by the Lisbon Treaty has put Europe where it has long been for most of the electorate, if not most of the Conservative Party – namely, way down the list of priorities.

In any case, the parliamentary party Cameron leads is not the same one that witnessed Thatcher's glory days, or her going, at first hand. Indeed, over half of Tory MPs elected in 2005 won their seats after 1997. The gradual exit from the Commons, either by death or by retirement, of the old and the bold who remembered who said what to whom on the night their heroine was 'stabbed in the back' has also drained some of the poison. Anyone who talks to more than a handful of Conservative MPs quickly realizes that, while the new intakes of 2001 and 2005, and to a lesser extent 1997, are not necessarily less right-wing than the people they replaced, they are different. They regard Euroscepticism as a given rather than a touchstone, and they admire Thatcher without worshipping her. They – and some of the younger members of the still shrinking party in the country – are also more comfortable with the UK as it is rather than how it used to be. Political correctness may still be frowned upon, especially of course when 'gone mad', but it no longer encompasses the defence of words or deeds that are explicitly or even implicitly discriminatory towards women and ethnic minorities.

By the same token, while they would of course deprecate the idea that a party should form its policies solely on the basis of survey research or focus groups, fewer and fewer believe that the saloon bar of the *Dog and Duck*, or for that matter the pages of the *Mail*, are a far better way of finding out what voters really think. That in itself is a marked contrast with the attitudes of many of those with whom the Party's pollsters and Central Office strategists had to cope for years after Labour's landslide. Also in marked contrast to the Party bequeathed by John Major to his successors is the comparative lack of hard-and-fast factions. Meanwhile, as the Party ticked off the years between 1997 and 2005, exhaustion gave way first to frustration and finally to hunger. Many of those most recently elected have seen the men and women they worked for as researchers and volunteers spend the best years of their political lives in opposition and they have no intention of doing the same themselves.

These attitudes have even spread to some of those who are widely regarded as keepers of the Thatcherite flame. After all, as one of them put it, 'You can't keep chopping and changing leaders. It's not as if we're at a wine tasting where you just swill it around your mouth and spit it out. This is grown-up business.' [11] This applies as well to the party in the media, which has likewise changed in a way that has made things easier for the leadership since 2005. It would be an exaggeration to say that the Tory press is wholly convinced by the Cameron project: the *Mail* is still edited by Paul Dacre, hardly a mincing metrosexual, while the *Telegraph* titles continue to have their doubts. But both recognize that Cameron is the only game in town, now and in the foreseeable future. They may have criticized him, particularly in the first year and a half of his tenure, but he never had to cope with the kind of leadership speculation that Hague, and in particular Duncan Smith, had to put up with within months or even days of taking over. The *Express* is fully on board, while Rupert Murdoch's News International titles are likely, as always, to follow their readers, which on current form suggests relatively favourable coverage: it is hard to imagine, for example, the *Sun* these days going with a front page comprising David Cameron's head superimposed, like Hague's was, on the body of a dead parrot.

This is partly, it must be said, because Cameron is who he is – a presidential politician happy to provide journalists with arresting and intimate visuals and to talk about (and invite them into) his family life. In sharp contrast to his predecessors, who were either unwilling or unable to come up with the goods in this respect, here is a politician who is recognizably a human being despite his highly privileged background. But it is also because the party in the media, like the party in parliament and in the country, can read the opinion polls. When Hague, Duncan Smith, and Howard took over, the polls barely registered it and, if they did improve, it was not for very long. Simply by becoming leader, Cameron achieved a step-change in his party's rating and, the Brown bounce aside, he delivered it the most sustained lead it had enjoyed since before Black Wednesday in 1992. This ensured that donations began arriving in much greater amounts and much earlier on in the political cycle than at any time since the 1980s: by 2008 they were running at an annual rate of £15.8 million, including not only big donations from corporate backers but more individual gifts as well. [12] Moreover, as real election results began to confirm the opinion polls, critics both at Westminster and in the media found it harder to complain that whatever Cameron was doing was not only wrong but not working. Opinion polls create either a vicious or a virtuous cycle: it may seem trite to say Cameron clearly benefited from the latter, just as his predecessors often suffered from the former, yet it is true nonetheless.

But explaining why the Conservative Party has moved under Cameron in a way it did not move under his predecessors requires us to do more than note that he has had it easier than they did. We also have to acknowledge that, unlike them, he has done all the things that Tory oppositions have traditionally (and very successfully) done to put themselves back in contention.[13] The most obvious difference between Cameron and his predecessors, then, relates to strategy: he had time to think about one; he was elected on the basis that he would implement it by a party that, for once, had been forced to pause for thought; and he had people around him who agreed with him wholeheartedly that things had to change. Moreover, it was the right strategy, focused first and foremost on conveying change, modernization, and, most vitally of all, a move onto the centre ground. True it picked up on a few of the ideas that some of Cameron's predecessors had toyed with, in their unconvinced and unconvincing way, before tossing them aside. Under Cameron, however, those ideas were pursued with a consistency and a coherence, with a will and a wider message discipline, that none of them came even close to matching.

Just as importantly, Cameron acted quickly. His election was immediately followed by a series of counter-intuitive initiatives and announcements, by the dumping of particularly toxic policies and the delaying of all the rest, by unapologetic raids on Labour and Lib Dem territory, and by action to make the Party look at least a little more like the country whose votes it was seeking. Ideology was out and pragmatism was in. Thatcherism wasn't so much apologized for as turned into history.[14] Nothing, or nothing very much, was to be said about Europe, crime, tax, and immigration – until, that is, the Tory brand had been decontaminated and the Party had earned 'permission to be heard' and passed 'the dinner-party test'. It could then begin to hum some of the old tunes as well as the new ones.

Crucially, however, one element in Cameron's 'politics of and' was stressed even during the so-called 'decontamination' phase. The refusal to promise the upfront tax cuts and spending restraint craved by economic liberals was bound to create some discontent on the right. But Cameron effectively split the latter by emphasizing his personal commitment to key aspects of the social agenda favoured by the 'High Tories' – marriage, the family, mending 'Broken Britain' by civil society rather than state solutions. The goodwill thus created overrode not only his failure to deliver immediately on his promise to pull Conservative MEPs out of the EPP–ED but also his insistence on respecting the rights of, and according due respect to, women, homosexuals, and ethnic minorities. And as long as right-wingers could support that stance in public, as well as the ruthless removal of anybody who made remarks that appeared to contradict it, Cameron was happy to bring them onto the frontbench – a 'big tent' approach that also helped keep them on board.

The patience and discipline displayed by those on the right after December 2005 was remarkable, but it was far from infinite. Cameron, however, was willing to adjust rather than be bounced into a confrontation, and he made no attempt to engineer a so-called 'Clause IV' moment. The A-List was only pushed so far, for instance: once the appearance (and at least a modicum) of change had been achieved, it was watered down and then quietly done away with – and detailed research suggests that the cultural and institutional obstacles to women candidates within the Party remain.[15] Likewise all talk of green taxes died after they were given a pretty rough reception. Once it became obvious that Brown was seriously considering a general election in the autumn of 2007, the Tory leader brought forward the rebalancing that the leadership had always planned, calculating (correctly it turned out) that the public was now ready to hear some tougher talk on crime and a signature (but supposedly fully funded) cut in inheritance tax. Once the emergency had passed, however, the leadership did not take its success as a signal that it could abandon its attempt to claim the centre ground. Cameron carried on talking tender as well as tough, or tried to combine the two.

Unlike his predecessors, then, Cameron did not so much lurch as calibrate. And, while he had a reverse gear (as he showed when he ran into an unplanned spot of bother over the totemic issue of grammar schools), he used it not to effect a three-point turn, but simply to back up a little in order to drive around whatever was in his way – something he was better able to do than his predecessors because, unlike them, he not only knew where he wanted to go but had a good idea of how he intended to get there. This also meant that he had no need to consult, as they did, the maps foisted on him by the Party's supposed friends in the print media. While he evidently tried very hard to keep them on board – spending time *en famille* with editors was not uncommon – it was clear that, if necessary, he would stop, let them out, and continue on his way without them if he had to. And, although Cameron tried by all accounts to run a relatively collegial Shadow Cabinet and (perhaps less successfully) to avoid the charge of inaccessibility levelled at his predecessors, MPs with any ambition to serve in government soon became aware that what applied to the party in the media also applied to them. Indeed, this subordination of individual interests to the collective good was if anything reinforced by Cameron's immediate insistence, in the wake of the expenses scandals that hit parliament in May 2009, that those Shadow ministers deemed to have made inappropriate claims repay the money instantly.

Cameron's apparent firmness (presaged by his earlier removal of the Conservative whip from Derek Conway over his alleged abuse of parliamentary allowances), his willingness to demote colleagues who got him into trouble with the party in the country or the media, and his decision to pass responsibility for the Party's media operation from an old chum to a former tabloid editor suggested to many Tories that their leader's judgement and ruthlessness more than made up for his lack of experience. Likewise, the Conservative leader's impressive performances in the Commons removed from the outset any doubts that he would be able to hold his own against Blair and Brown – the latter a man whose character and reputation the Tory leadership did their best to rip to shreds even before Cameron took over. No party leader, of course, can ever afford to be as nice as he looks, and Cameron couldn't convince some voters: a majority of respondents told YouGov in February 2009 that they saw him as 'caring' and as an asset to his party, but most people also saw him as 'a lightweight' and more thought he couldn't be trusted than thought he could be. Polls like these also suggested that Cameron may not have changed his party, at least in the eyes of voters, as much as some suggest. Nor, incidentally, has he done anything to halt its decline in membership – human capital which, experts believe, still counts at election time, notwithstanding the more efficient distribution of other campaign resources by Michael Ashcroft and his team.[16] Even so, Cameron has come far, far closer than any of his predecessors to being (as Tony Blair once was) 'the complete package'.

Harsh realities

How Cameron will handle the switch from opposition to government – one that Blair apparently found difficult – remains to be seen. So, too, does the extent to which that government, if it does come about, really will mark a departure from the kind of Conservatism practised by the Tory governments of the 1980s and 1990s, especially given the straitened economic circumstances it is bound to face.[17] Just before Cameron won the leadership, he claimed, 'I'm certainly a big Thatcher fan, but I don't know whether that makes me a Thatcherite.'[18] Some see this as more than clever positioning. To them, Cameron is genuinely striving not so much for a new consensus as for a new synthesis – a Tory equivalent to New Labour's claim to combine social justice with economic efficiency and environmental sustainability.[19] Others are convinced, as one put it (approvingly, mind) even before they took over, that 'Cameron, Osborne and co.' are 'useful idiots, putting a caring and optimistic face on the old Tory dog' – a timeless beast that 'distrusts whiz-bang politics' and is 'eternally sceptical of government schemes for the improvement of humanity', a beast which 'thinks the apparatus of state will absorb as much gold as you throw at it, and still cry for more', that 'people do not like to pay taxes', that 'politics is not only about renaissance and reform, but also about the clash of interests, and that you can't please everybody'.[20]

If such an analysis sounds unduly cynical, however, the politics of recession suggest it might not be so wide of the mark. But they also posed something of a dilemma.[21] The decision made by Cameron and Osborne in late November 2008 not only to abandon their year-old pledge to match Labour's spending plans until 2010–11 but to go even further than the government in trying to find efficiency savings in order to reduce borrowing suggested that the global downturn exposed the limits of the Party's rhetorical commitment to the centre ground. The decision was generally welcomed within the Party: the commitment to Labour's spending plans was always seen, especially after the collapse of the Brown bounce, as a regrettable insurance policy taken out against an early election that never came; moreover, there was widespread scepticism among Tories as to whether Labour's much vaunted 'fiscal stimulus' would do any good, always assuming it wouldn't make things even worse. That said, there were some Tories who worried about the impact of the economic downturn on Cameron's strategy, not least because it was constructed around a narrative in which the country's economic problems had supposedly been solved in the 1980s and 1990s by a Conservative Party now dedicated instead to sorting out its social malaise and putting it on the path to environmental sustainability.

Much of that story, and the often optimistic tone in which it was told, no longer seemed relevant once it became obvious that the economy had fallen off a cliff. At least initially, Cameron struggled to come up with a new narrative – a struggle that threatened in the autumn of 2008 to undermine his characteristic message discipline. His eventual decision to contrast savings and sound finance with 'Labour's debt crisis' helped in this respect. But it was nevertheless a brave one, especially for a party which, according to polls and despite Cameron's best efforts, had yet to convince voters that it really understood and represented ordinary people. After all, the Party needed the support of millions of people with anything but fond memories of the Conservatives' largely laissez-faire response to the recessions of the early 1980s and 1990s. As a result, the Tories could ill afford to give the impression that they were, as Labour dubbed them, the 'do-nothing party', promising all pain and no gain. Nor, on the other hand, were they necessarily going to find it easy to persuade people that they could reduce government borrowing and avoid post-recession tax hikes simply by cutting down on 'quangocracy'. Surely a Conservative government would also have to squeeze spending on frontline public services or seriously slim the defence budget or cut state subsidies to the middle classes as well as the poor.

David Cameron was clearly alive to the risks of his decision to take a tough line on the economy, to stop talking about 'sharing the proceeds of growth' and start softening up people for what he feared his government, indeed any government, would have to do in order to restore the national finances. Hence his framing the new line in proverbial clichés: he wanted, he claimed in a speech on 5 January 2009, 'an economy where government and its citizens live within their means, save for a rainy day, waste not and want not'; this, he told the Party's Spring Forum at the end of April, is 'the age of austerity' in which 'we risk becoming the sick man of Europe again', our children 'weighed down with a millstone of debt' unless we wake up to the fact that this is 'no time for business as usual' but a moment for 'a government of thrift' determined to deliver 'more for less'. And hence his concern to prevent his team using rhetoric that might remind voters of the 'if it's not hurting, it's not working' mantras of the Major years.[22] The same concern drove the decision in March 2009 to upset some on the right, and the party in the media, by making it clear George Osborne was unlikely to reverse Labour's plan to raise the top rate of taxation. It was also evident in a heavily hyped speech on the economy made a few days later by Cameron himself – one in which he was careful to try to reassure voters by promising that 'Paying down our debt must not mean pushing down the poor' and that he was all about 'fiscal responsibility with a social conscience'. Whether this particular example of 'the politics of and' could carry the Conservatives unscathed through the heat of an election – one in which they required a massive swing and a double-digit lead in order to win with a workable majority – was a moot point. The electorate might be persuaded that the country needed a little honesty and possibly even some 'tough love'. But would they trust the Conservatives not to take the latter too far?

At least, though, Cameron's clear stance looked like leadership. This is something that research suggests is increasingly important to voters and which, according to opinion polls, they felt was in increasingly short supply from Gordon Brown, especially as the row over MPs' expenses which began in May 2009 knocked the deepest economic crisis in decades off the front pages and threatened to blow British politics apart. Clearly, Labour had most to worry about: any backlash against incumbent members at Westminster for 'flipping'[23] and outrageous claims was by definition bound to hit the party with the most seats hardest. Likewise, whichever party had provided the Commons with a Speaker so manifestly incapable of carrying out reform would have attracted more than its fair share of opprobrium. But the *Telegraph*'s revelations about the moats, mowers, and manure (and chandeliers, tennis courts, swimming pools, forests, and duck houses) claimed for by Tory MPs posed a particular problem for the Conservatives in that they fed into pre-existing, and highly stubborn, stereotypes of the Party as an institution still stuffed full of rich people with no idea of how the other half lives.

Cameron's response, however, was a brilliant example of what any organization has to do when it runs into trouble – one that could have been torn from the pages of a PR textbook. Surveys consistently point to the premium consumers put on companies that listen to complaints, own up to their mistakes, and rapidly try to put things right.[24] And this was exactly what Cameron did. As the first revelations about Conservative MPs were about to break on the morning of 10 May, Cameron was ready with a statement on the evening of the 9th: 'We have to acknowledge just how bad this is. The public are really angry and we have to start by saying, look, this system that we had, that we used, that we operated, that we took part in, it was wrong and we're sorry about that.'

Within a day or so, Cameron was calling his MPs together, apparently to read them the riot act and to confirm he was setting up a 'Scrutiny Panel' to look into individual cases, as well as expecting Shadow Cabinet members, at least, to repay any claim that he did not consider passed a 'reasonableness test' – measures which ensured admiring headlines in the media and left Brown playing catch-up yet again. By 14 May the Tory leader had obliged Andrew MacKay MP to resign from his advisory team and on 15 May he scrapped the Party's planned election broadcast in favour of a straight-to-camera apology to the nation and outlining of the action he was going to take. Behind the scenes, pressure was brought to bear on backbenchers thought to have shown particularly poor judgement, a handful of whom agreed to step down in advance of possible moves to deselect them by their associations. Quite how Cameron was going to handle the characteristic determination of some association chairmen to stick with their MP, or whether he was going to have the courage to try to subject more high-profile members to the same penalty, was admittedly unclear. But this probably mattered less than the fact that Cameron was seen by the public to have acted like a leader – in marked contrast, rightly or wrongly, to the Prime Minister, who, unlike the Tory leader, just didn't seem to 'get it'. At the height of the revelations, a BPIX poll for the *Mail on Sunday* suggested some 53 per cent of voters thought Cameron had handled things well, with only 17 per cent saying the same of Brown – a judgement borne out by other surveys over the next few days.

Cutting the complacency

Hopes that Cameron had been better able than Brown to limit the damage done to his party by the expenses scandals seemed to be borne out by the results of the local government and European Parliament elections at the beginning of June. With the government in virtual meltdown as Labour frontbenchers began to resign and speak out in the hope that their colleagues could be bounced into ditching the Prime Minister, the Conservatives could claim a national vote share of 38 per cent, compared to the Lib Dems' 28 and Labour's 23. They also gained control of the four remaining county councils held by Labour in England and, just as encouragingly, won seats from the Lib Dems in the South West. The Conservative vote share, however, was down from the 44 per cent it managed in 2008, suggesting that the Party had taken something of a hit on expenses and was not benefiting as much as it should have been from the government's unprecedented unpopularity. The latter became even more obvious when the European Parliament votes were counted: Labour took only 15.7 per cent of the vote and was beaten into third place by UKIP, whose 16.5 per cent of the vote was enough to reduce the Tory share to just under 28 per cent, in effect repeating the results of the 2004 contest.

Cameron understandably chose to talk up the fact that the Tories had beaten Labour in Wales and other former strongholds. He also made it clear that he would not be backtracking from his intention to form a new group in the European Parliament based on an alliance with the Czech Civic Democrats and Poland's Law and Justice. Cameron's call for an early election, repeated after it became clear that Brown's internal opponents lacked (at least for the moment) both the courage and the numbers to oust him, was equally predictable.

Nevertheless, the Tory leader's post-election warning to his party that it must avoid complacency was sensible. And, interestingly, it contained a specific as well as a general message. 'We have to say to people', Cameron pointed out, 'that we are the party of public services . . . especially a good National Health Service for everybody.' With the party in the media increasingly open about its belief that, to quote the *Spectator*'s political editor, 'the only tool worth using when he makes it through the door of Number 10 is a hatchet' – one he would need to use to make brutal reductions in public spending – Cameron was understandably nervous that the Party remained vulnerable to Labour attacks on 'Tory cuts'.[25] It was therefore unsurprising that the Conservative leadership was furious when, in an attempt to use a media interview to provide reassurance on the NHS a few days later, Shadow Health Secretary Andrew Lansley appeared to suggest that its ring-fencing (along with the ring-fencing of spending on international aid and schools) meant that other departments would be facing cuts of 10 percentage points under an incoming Conservative government – not perhaps coincidentally the very same figure suggested by the *Spectator* a couple of weeks previously.

Brown, of course, seized on Lansley's words to suggest that the Tories had finally let the cat out of the bag, attempting in so doing to reassert the 'dividing lines' that Labour had used to such devastating effect in 2001 and 2005. To many this was sheer hypocrisy from a Prime Minister who knew that whoever made it into Downing Street after the next election would need to clamp down hard on public spending. Indeed, the party in the media went further: the episode, they hoped, would encourage Cameron really to level with the electorate about the extent to which cuts would need to be made – something for which he would, they felt sure, be given considerable credit. Some even urged Cameron to drop 'the sacred cow status' accorded to the NHS; healthcare could no longer be free at the point of use but would have to be financed by a mixture of private insurance and 'co-payment'.[26] Whether the public, especially in the wake of swine flu being officially declared a global pandemic, would see it the same way was another matter – as Cameron, still more cautious than the zealots, was well aware.

The politics of power

David Cameron quickly proved himself one of the most skilful leaders of the opposition Britain has ever seen. In this respect at least, he was better even than Thatcher and truly 'the heir to Blair'. But government, as the latter found, is a little more difficult. The politics of support is one thing, the politics of power another. The essence of statecraft is to reconcile and, ideally, to integrate them so that one election victory leads inexorably to the next. This is no easy task even with a wealth of experience – something Cameron's Conservative Party, especially in the House of Commons, inevitably lacks, just as it also lacks the in-built majority in the House of Lords that previous Tory administrations could take pretty much for granted.[27] The task is rendered all the more difficult when economic constraints make it even harder than usual to turn slogans into policies. It is difficult to imagine, for example, how one can scrap top-down targets at the same time as calling on departments to deliver 'more for less', or to see how the latter can mean anything other than a reduction in the number of those employed by government – a classic Conservative remedy that, back in the days when it seemed the good times would never end, Cameron claimed was no longer the Party's instinctive reflex. By the same token, how does one shift the burden of taxation from families to 'eco-taxes' when that burden will have to rise and when industrial growth is slow or non-existent?

Yet perhaps the most serious, but also the most predictable, mismatch between the politics of power and the politics of support involves Europe – and its implications go way beyond whom the Tories team up with in the European Parliament.[28] Despite the agreement not to 'bang on' about it, there exists a widespread assumption at all levels in the Conservative Party on the need to renegotiate Britain's relationship with the EU, beginning with the repatriation of selected powers and limitations on the reach and competence of the European Court of Justice. Arguably, this illustrates how little Cameron really has managed, or even sought, to challenge his party's core beliefs.[29] But it is also tantamount to fantasy politics. There is no likelihood that agreement will be forthcoming from the other member states. Anyone thinking a British threat to leave the EU would concentrate their minds is not living in the real world. No Prime Minister should ever threaten to do something he or she cannot deliver. There is no evidence that a majority of voters, bureaucrats, businesses, or even newspapers believe quitting the EU is in the country's long-term national interest. Anyone willing to bet, then, that a Conservative government can live up to the inflated expectations of some of its supporters on matters concerning the EU is as deluded as they are.

By the same token, 'faith, flag, and family' Tories who hope, on a free vote held in a parliament filled with socially conservative new members, to roll back the so-called 'permissive consensus' on matters moral – most obviously on abortion or gay adoption – had better think very carefully.[30] Like it or not, there is a permissive majority in Britain, on matters like these, if not on law and order and immigration. Because that majority is latent and largely passive, it would indeed be relatively easy for a Conservative-controlled Commons to ride roughshod over it. However, *ex post facto*, when people wake up to what has happened, the backlash could be serious – even if Cameron, Osborne, and their colleagues try to disclaim responsibility for the actions of their less liberal backbenchers. Those most bothered about any winding back of the clock will be the articulate, educated, and liberal middle classes who (thanks to Labour's not altogether selfless obsession with expanding access to higher education) are a growing force in society. Their votes are crucial and they simply do not see things in black and white terms. This is not America. It would be electoral suicide for any Tory administration worth the name to think differently.

In Britain at least, changes of government are precipitated not by a burning sense of right and wrong but by a vague feeling that things have gone too far in one direction and that some kind of correction is needed to bring them back into balance. After a while, voters bank the good things that a government has given them and look to the other party to deliver them from the bad things. They got the welfare state from the Attlee government, for instance, but after five years of sacrifice they were longing to do some shopping. They got something like full employment from a series of Labour and Conservative governments but they also got higher taxes and over-mighty trade unions and so turned to Mrs Thatcher. She and John Major sorted out those problems but kept health and education on such short rations that voters elected New Labour, at least in part, to build them back up again. It did so, but did little or nothing to tackle the underlying vulnerabilities of a growing welfare state reliant on an economy built increasingly on debt and unwarranted confidence that the good times could never end.[31]

If successful statecraft is about reconciling the politics of power with the politics of support, it is also about understanding this politics of correction. Stripping everything back, David Cameron has to think about what it is that ordinary people – not just Conservatives – think needs fixing. It need not be his only concern by any means. All of us should make wish-lists once in a while. But we should never forget that it is our to-do lists that really matter. And, just as was the case for Margaret Thatcher, Cameron will ultimately be judged and defined by what he does, not simply on what he says. 'Yes,' he told the Conservative Spring Forum in 2009, 'We're the party of strong borders, law and order and low taxes – and we always will be. But today we're also the party of the NHS, the environment and of social justice too.' We shall see.

Afterword

THE ELECTION, THE COALITION, AND BEYOND

Even the most talented politician sometimes allows his fondness for a fine phrase to trump his better judgement. For David Cameron, the alliterative 'age of austerity' was one such occasion. Together with George Osborne's announcement at the Party's 2009 Conference in Manchester that he intended to scrap programmes, squeeze benefits, and freeze public-sector salaries, what was surely a soundbite too far reawakened fears among voters that the Conservatives, whatever they might say, would simply revert to Thatcherite type once safely ensconced in government.[1] As a result, the chances of the Tories returning to office suddenly started to shrink. Until the end of 2009 they held on to a double-digit lead, but by the New Year the margin began to slip down into single figures, with surveys revealing a lack of confidence in the Party's capacity and willingness to manage the faltering economy and maintain jobs and services. Cameron responded in late January by ruling out 'swingeing cuts'. The media talk of backtracking, muddle, and confusion that inevitably followed – exacerbated by the Party's ongoing difficulty in spelling out exactly how it was going to support marriage through the tax system – was considered a price worth paying in order to avoid accusations that the Tories were about to kill off a recovery that had barely started. But it was not exactly the ideal way to begin the battle for Downing Street.

Missed opportunity or historic achievement? Election 2010

Not all was doom and gloom, of course. The party in the media was pretty much onside and now included the *Sun*, which had at last come out for the Conservatives in September 2009 following over a decade of support (at least at election time) for Labour. Moreover, to great relief all round, Cameron's risky decision not to promise a referendum on the EU Lisbon Treaty once it had been ratified by all member states was greeted with resignation rather than widespread indignation. Finally, with huge financial resources (the Party raised £20 million between October 2009 and March 2010 alone) and plenty of staff able to marry up opinion research, canvassing, and demographic information provided by commercial credit referencing agencies, the Conservative campaign looked like being one of the best-prepared, best-funded, and most technically advanced campaigns ever launched by a British party.[2] At its heart were Osborne, and the directors of strategy and media Steve Hilton and Andy Coulson. They were joined by old hand George Bridges. Also important were veteran campaign director Stephen Gilbert (who worked closely with Deputy Chairman Michael Ashcroft), Ed Llewellyn, Cameron's chief-of-staff, and pollsters Andrew Cooper and Johnny Heald.

The team was not as tight as it might have been, however. The Party's narrowing opinion poll lead generated internal friction, some personal, some strategic: should the emphasis be on attacking Labour and a focus on the economy, for instance, or a more positive, 'change' message? This dilemma was never fully resolved, although the Party's decision to move its advertising from Euro RSCG (which had produced an upbeat, and impressive, campaign featuring ordinary people explaining why they'd decided to vote Tory for the first time) to old-stagers M&C Saatchi (whose efforts were characteristically far more negative) arguably spoke volumes. Media leaks concerning these tensions, and the fact that no one individual seemed to have the final say on anything, did little to calm growing nervousness. Nor did the return, in March, of the longstanding saga of Ashcroft's tax status, which risked reviving the Tories' image as a wealthy, self-serving tribe and, worse, calling into question Cameron's judgement. Surely this should have been sorted long before the election?

Despite these doubts, and despite the first opinion polls of the campaign pointing to a hung parliament, most Conservatives still felt that an overall majority was just within their reach – a feeling strengthened by what was widely regarded as a strong start. Their all-out attack, supported by prominent business people, on Labour's National Insurance rises (dubbed its 'tax on jobs') seemed to cut through to the electorate. The party's manifesto, launched against the dramatic backdrop provided by London's Battersea Power Station, and supposedly lent substance by being a hundred pages longer than the 2005 effort, was also well received. Even some of those who were well disposed to the Tories, however, had their doubts about the manifesto's key theme – 'The Big Society'. The idea that ordinary people could be encouraged by a caring Conservative government to take the initiative on social problems rather than simply leave them to the state to sort out was one that Cameron shared with Steve Hilton. But it had only been given its first proper outing by the Tory leader in a public lecture in November 2009. While the idea was welcome in theory, some (including the American freelancer brought in to assist with the campaign, Bill Knapp) argued that the Party should have prepared the public for it rather than launch it – without even testing it on focus groups – at the start of the election campaign proper. This concern was reinforced by polling that showed that even those voters prepared to believe that the Big Society was more than simply code for shrinking the welfare state didn't know what it meant. It would have been better to have gone instead with a gimmick used later on in the campaign – one that did seem to resonate with voters – Cameron's so-called 'contract with voters', three million copies of which were produced in the week before polling day.

By then, however, the Tory campaign had been effectively thrown off-course by the televised leaders' debates. Lib Dem leader Nick Clegg's impressive performance during the first of the three had allowed him (temporarily at least) to wrest the mantle of 'the change candidate' from Cameron, provided an apparently game-changing boost to his party's ratings, and got the Conservative leader criticized for agreeing to take part in the debates at all – criticism that only increased after the election when it became apparent that the team prepping him had realized in rehearsals they were going to have a 'Clegg problem' but had been unable to decide how to deal with it. Still, by the third debate Cameron more than had the measure of his opponent and the Clegg 'surge' turned out to be more of a soufflé that collapsed just before polling day. Rather than adding substantially to their 2005 seat tally, the Lib Dems suffered a small net loss and ended up winning in just 57 constituencies. Labour lost just short of a hundred seats, finishing on 258. The Conservatives, needing a minimum of 323 for an overall majority, could only manage 306 (if one excludes John Bercow as the Speaker of the House of Commons).

But if the election of 2010 was dominated by the televised leaders' debates, it was not decided by them. The Conservative Party did not fail to win an overall majority simply because Clegg's charisma queered its pitch. Rather, his emergence as a plausible alternative reflected the fact that the Tories had been unable, in the years and months leading up to the election, to 'seal the deal' with voters. Polls and focus groups, private and public, pre- and post-election, make it clear that the electorate was indeed fed up with Gordon Brown and his government. But despite being reasonably well disposed to David Cameron, a significant number of voters were still not sure about the party he led. There were, in the end, just too many people who continued to doubt whether the Tories could be trusted, especially in a downturn, to improve the economy, protect public services, and prioritize the needs of ordinary people over those of the rich. And even if this had not been the case, the Conservatives would have been hard pressed to win outright given how much ground they had to make up under an electoral system which – partly because of the overrepresentation of areas of the country where Labour is strong (Scotland and the inner cities) but mostly because its vote is simply more efficiently distributed – does the Tories few favours. Moreover, an increasing share of the UK vote is going to parties other than the top two. In 1951 Labour and the Conservatives secured 97 per cent of the vote between them. By 2005, this had fallen to just 68 per cent. The backlash against the biggest parties occasioned by the parliamentary expenses scandal was unlikely to do anything to help reverse the trend in 2010.[3] At the same time, the number of 'marginal seats' (those liable to change hands rather than being safe bets) was shrinking: in contrast to the 'golden age' of two-party politics in Britain, when around 150 constituencies flipped fairly easily between Labour and the Tories, the same could be said of only around 100 constituencies in 2005.[4]

All this presented the Conservatives with (to borrow from the title of one relatively optimistic internal briefing) an uphill challenge. Indeed, to put things into historical perspective, for David Cameron to have won an overall majority in 2010, just over four years after assuming the leadership of a party with around two hundred Commons seats, would have been the equivalent of Labour leader Neil Kinnock winning a similar victory in 1987. Clearly Cameron was luckier than Kinnock in his opponent. Yet in order to secure a majority in the Commons of just one, he still needed to win an additional 117 seats. The last time the Tories had achieved anywhere near this was in 1950 under Winston Churchill, when they gained 85. But that was achieved on a swing of under four per cent. Ted Heath in 1970 and Margaret Thatcher in 1979 could boast higher swings (just under and just over five per cent, respectively) but gained fewer seats (69 and 62). On the other hand, unlike Churchill in 1950, they had managed to eject Labour from Downing Street and form a majority government. To do the same, Cameron needed a swing of almost seven per cent. In the end the swing in 2010 was 5.1 per cent and the Conservatives gained 96 seats, beating Labour by 7.3 percentage points – a slightly bigger margin of victory than Thatcher had achieved in 1979 and far bigger than those achieved by any of her predecessors in the post-war period. This was an historic achievement by any measure. But because it wasn't enough to secure an overall majority, and because the Party's share of the vote, at 37 per cent, represented an increase of only 3.8 points on the previous general election, it nonetheless came as a grave disappointment to Conservatives convinced that an election in the face of one of the worst recessions the country had ever seen, and presided over by one of its least popular Prime Ministers, should surely have produced an outright win. And for some this dovetailed with a long-held belief – one apparently unaffected by a string of general election defeats and a raft of research which suggested the opposite – that moving into the centre ground was bound to make things worse rather than better.

In fact, the Party did not fail to win outright because it modernized and moved into the centre. It failed because, for some voters at least, that process had not not gone far enough – not so much on social/moral questions (indeed, the Conservatives have to be careful not to be outflanked on the right by Labour on such matters) but on the economy and public services. Arguments that the Party could have short-circuited such concerns by talking more about immigration or spending even more time than it did in bashing Brown may have appealed to the right, but they fly in the face of both the evidence and elementary logic. The Prime Minister was already dead in the water: to have spent even more time and money on attacking him – time and money that could have been spent on reassuring voters with a more positive message about Conservative plans – would have been akin to drowning a corpse. Likewise, immigration was an important issue for the country, but most voters did not see it as that significant for themselves or their family, especially when compared to the economy. As in previous elections, most of those particularly concerned about the issue would either be voting Conservative already or were likely to stick with Labour because they retained a residual faith in the latter's capacity to protect their jobs or to protect them from poverty should they lose them. And, as in previous elections, a more strident stance on the issue would have risked alienating the middle-class 'small-l liberals' whom the Conservative Party needed to win back. In any case, the Party made a considerable effort to have its cake and eat it on the issue. For one thing, although the Tories themselves made relatively little noise about immigration in the campaign, except to join Labour in laying into the Liberal Democrats' amnesty for illegal immigrants, they could rely on the party in the media not to forget about the issue, especially after Gordon Brown was overheard calling a voter who had raised it with him 'a bigoted woman'. For another, immigration was featured in some of the 17 million pieces of direct mail that the Party sent out to swing voters in target constituencies as part of its 'ground war' – an effort which failed to stop Labour exploiting anxiety about welfare benefits and public-sector jobs and preventing a catastrophic loss of votes translating into an equally catastrophic loss of seats, but helped to ensure that the Conservatives emerged as the biggest single party after polling day.[5]

Of lemons and lemonade: forming the coalition

The fact that the election gave no party an overall majority accurately reflected the mood of the country: tired of Labour, not yet sure about the Tories, intrigued but far from convinced by the Lib Dems. It also suggested that attempts to frighten voters about the consequences of a hung parliament had fallen, for the most part, on deaf ears. Not unnaturally, the Conservatives had been at the forefront of those attempts. One of their pre-election ads, for instance, contrasted what people might think would happen in the aftermath of an inconclusive result ('a fresh new dawn'; 'more open and democratic government with everyone cooperating for the national good'; 'a new consensus of the best policies for Britain to get us through the recession') with what would really happen ('parties will get behind closed doors and horse-trade between each other over posts and power'; 'haggling between politicians'; 'delay and indecision'). Could those two scenarios now be reconciled? 'When fate hands us a lemon,' the original self-help guru Dale Carnegie exhorted his readers, 'let's try to make a lemonade.'[6] On 7 May David Cameron – a man whose can-do confidence Carnegie could only have admired – woke up determined to do just that. After making his intentions clear to colleagues, he called a press conference and announced, 'I want to make a big, open, and comprehensive offer to the Liberal Democrats.'

There have been articles, books, and documentaries about the 'Five Days in May' that followed that announcement. Doubtless a film will appear in due course: after all, if Michael Sheen can do Tony Blair, David Frost, and Brian Clough, then why not David Cameron? There is little point, therefore, in going over the ground they cover, in empha-sizing the personal chemistry between Clegg and Cameron and their negotiating teams, in dwelling on the divisions between Labour's main players, in swallowing or seeing through the claims that they were never seriously interested, or that, Brown or no Brown, the Lib Dems, lacking faith in Labour's ability to deliver and privately preferring the Tories' 'tough but fair' deficit reduction plan, had made their minds up before the whole thing even began.[7] Better instead to keep it simple, to forget, for the most part, about who said what to whom and when, and focus on the hard underlying realities, remembering that, in the end, every-thing in such situations flows from the maths and how much people are prepared to trade off their party's principles – some of which they have never really shared anyway – in return for the opportunity actually to do things rather than simply talk about them.

The Conservative leadership might not have wanted to think too hard about a hung parliament. But, as illustrated by their ability (courtesy of Oliver Letwin) to conjure as if from nowhere a paper which set out both the overlaps between the two parties' policies and the obstacles they would need to overcome, the Tories were by no means totally unprepared. If the Party beat Brown – something even the most pessimistic Conservatives were fairly confident of doing – but fell short of a majority, then, providing Labour and the Lib Dems were unable to form a majority coalition (which, in the event, was indeed the case), Cameron knew he stood a reasonable chance of becoming Prime Minister. There seemed, then, to be two alternatives. He could try to form a minority government, perhaps in the hope that a second election could be called later on in the year that might (but only might) secure him an overall majority. Or he could attempt to persuade the Liberal Democrats not simply to tolerate or support such a government from the outside but instead to join the Conservatives in a full-blown, majority coalition. The media and many fellow Tories may have thought the first alternative was the best and most likely option, but they were profoundly mistaken. A minority government, political science suggests, can only form and survive if it can pretty much guarantee it will not be defeated on motions of no-confidence and on its budget. Given that most of the other parties in the House of Commons were located somewhere to the left of the Conservatives, this was highly unlikely. Indeed, the most feasible minority government may well have been a Labour–Lib Dem combination, relying on the votes or the abstentions or even the partnership of the assorted nationalist parties. This, however, would not have provided the stability which the Lib Dem leadership thought was necessary at a time of economic uncertainty. And it, too, might have led to a second election which they had next to no money to fight. An arrangement with the Conservatives (represented at the negotiating table by Hague, Osborne, Letwin, and Llewellyn) would, it seemed, stand a much better chance of reassuring the financial markets and avoiding what some claimed (and perhaps really believed) was the imminent risk of a 'Greek-style' crisis.

The real question for Clegg and co., then, was whether Cameron would offer some kind of 'confidence and supply arrangement' – a deal which would have seen them responsible for supporting a minority Conservative administration but denied them seats in Cabinet – or whether he would instead invite them to join him in government. It was Cameron's genius to realize much earlier than many of his colleagues that, as long as he did that, and offered the Lib Dem leadership a coalition agreement that it could sell to fellow MPs and to the grassroots, then its decision was ultimately a no-brainer, not least because Clegg and some of his colleagues were actually much closer to the Conservatives ideologically than many observers had realized – something that, research suggests, makes what political scientists call 'a minimum winning coalition' (i.e. one that delivers the least number of parties an overall majority) all the more likely. Cameron's other masterstroke, after the Lib Dems admitted mid-way through that they had also begun talking to Labour, was to persuade his parliamentary party (on the only occasion they were consulted) to endorse his offer to Clegg of a referendum on the alternative vote (AV) as the price of a coalition agreement, which, considering how little they were asked to give up and to give away, represented a great deal for the Conservatives.[8]

This may have needed some sleight of hand. It required Cameron to play down his belief that the coalition would not only stymie a long-dreamt-of Lib–Lab reconciliation and provide political cover for some serious spending cuts, but would, by showing that the Conservatives could work with a supposedly centre-left party, complete the brand decontamination that had ultimately eluded him in opposition. Nor could he afford to celebrate the fact that going with Lib Dems allowed the dumping or postponement of policies that were always going to be awkward to implement, most obviously repealing the Human Rights Act and changes to inheritance tax. Most controversial, however, at least among Tory MPs after the event, was whether Cameron had been telling them the truth when he told them Brown was prepared to deliver Clegg electoral reform on a plate. Their response – sanctioning the counter-offer of a referendum on AV – was the key which turned the lock that opened the door to Downing Street.

Early days

An hour or so after he had walked through the door of Number Ten as the youngest Prime Minister since 1812, David Cameron was given a rapturous welcome by his MPs at a hastily convened meeting of the

Parliamentary Conservative Party. If any of them were critical of the leadership's failure to secure an overall majority, or still smarting at the lack of consultation during the coalition negotiations, or wondering whether they would be the ones to lose out to Liberal Democrats when the jobs were eventually handed out, they hid it well. Most were simply glad to be back in government. For many, especially those who went on to receive preferment, however lowly, that feeling would continue to trump everything for the foreseeable future. That said, even they found one of their leader's earliest decisions just a little worrying.

Before they'd even got a chance to get their breath back after the election and the dramatic days that followed, Tory MPs were told by David Cameron that he wanted a fundamental change to the way their only collective body, the 1922 Committee, worked. Traditionally, a move into office saw membership restricted to backbenchers, with ministers (including the PM) joining them only at the invitation of the Committee's Executive in order to explain government policy. Apparently on the advice of John Major, whose experience of such meetings as Premier had proved less than positive, Cameron proposed that the Parliamentary Party as a whole should vote to open membership to all MPs, irrespective of whether they were part of the so-called 'payroll vote' with government jobs. Assuming Cameron's recommendation were accepted, said payroll vote would be able to participate in the upcoming elections for the Chair and the Executive – a move, it was widely assumed, which would make it less likely that the '22 would be led by anyone likely to make trouble for the leadership.

The hastily called ballot was won by 168 to 118. But the margin of victory (only achieved by virtue of the payroll vote), as well as the willingness of many backbenchers to make clear their unhappiness to journalists, suggested that the move had backfired badly. Even some of the Prime Minister's biggest fans wondered whether it didn't make him look like a control-freak who had forgotten that one of the '22's primary functions was to serve as a safety valve and an early-warning light – a venue where those who were unhappy with the government could blow off steam, watched by the Whips, without necessarily voting against it on the floor of the House. Meanwhile, those who were less ideologically inclined towards Cameron saw in his action confirmation of their suspicion that he was determined to use the coalition with the Lib Dems as a way of isolating and ignoring his own right-wing – a suspicion that even led them to wonder out loud (but without a shred of evidence) whether the Prime Minister was actually relieved not to have won an overall majority, since that might have left him more reliant on their votes than he would have liked; indeed, some went so far as to suggest that Cameron believed a change to AV would lead to a permanent coalition of the centre that would allow him to marginalize the right forever.

Faced with all this, Cameron characteristically elected to compromise: declaring (to widespread amusement) that he had only ever wanted to open up meetings to ministers, he made it clear that backbenchers alone would be allowed to vote and stand for the Chairmanship and the Executive. And when a few days later, Graham Brady – the right-winger who had resigned from the front bench during 'grammarsgate' back in 2007 – beat the rather more emollient Richard Ottaway to become Chairman, Cameron was quick to congratulate and to meet with him. Brady, it must be said, was keen to come over as equally constructive, stressing, for example, that the Committee's intended review of the election campaign would be complementary to, rather than cutting across, CCHQ's own efforts.

Of course, Brady's election, and the fact that the majority of those elected onto the Committee with him were also on the right, may well have reflected not just a desire to stick it to the leadership but also the balance of ideological opinion among ordinary Tory MPs. Just under half (147 out of 306) of those elected in 2010 were first-time MPs and therefore a largely unknown (or at least unmeasured) quantity. There seems every reason to believe, especially if one were to compile the answers given by those who replied to the 'Twenty Questions for the Class of 2010' set for them by the increasingly influential ConservativeHome, that today's Parliamentary Conservative Party is every bit as right-wing as its predecessors – indeed possibly more so.[9] Certainly, anyone looking not just at the '22 Executive but also at those MPs elected to chair the Party's newly configured backbench subject committees (covering Economic, Home, and Foreign Affairs, Public Services, and the Environment), as well at as those chosen to represent MPs on the Party Board (Brian Binley, Priti Patel, and Charles Walker), would have come away with the distinct impression that the right was predominant.[10] The willingness and capacity of various right-wing clubs

– the '92 group, Cornerstone, and No Turning Back – to run 'slates' of candidates for such contests was surely testimony to their (arguably renewed) vigour. The latter, plus the fact the groups were now coordinating their efforts via a weekly steering group, may, for instance, have helped in the successful campaign to limit the rise in capital gains tax announced in Osborne's first budget to just 28 per cent rather than the 50 per cent that the Lib Dems hoped to get.

On the other hand, feelings on that issue ran high across the parliamentary party, going beyond the nucleus of around a dozen right-wing irreconcilables and even the ten to fifteen MPs prepared on occasion to join them in defying the Whips.[11] The opposition to AV coming from this quarter proved insufficient to derail the government's plans to hold a referendum. Moreover, despite the history of bad blood between the parties at local level, relations with Lib Dem MPs were generally (and genuinely) cordial. However, party managers were far from complacent: many of the new intake were doughty local campaigners who might easily be persuaded that their best hope of holding on to their marginal seats was to be seen to be acting independently and according to their principles – an approach that might also appeal to those Tories concerned about losing out personally as a result of the reduction of parliamentary constituencies. The Whips could only hope that the mini-rebellion by 37 Tory MPs on the UK's financial contribution to the EU which occurred in mid-October 2010 was not a sign of things to come. In opposition it had proved relatively easy to deal with Europe simply by adopting a more sceptical line. In government, when the leadership is obliged to consider the national interest too, things are bound to get more complicated, as Cameron found when, at the end of October, he permitted a treaty change in order to help Eurozone countries and could only limit (rather than prevent) a rise in the EU's budget. The passing of legislation at Westminster to ensure a 'referendum lock' on further transfers of sovereignty to Brussels may help calm frayed nerves, but, as one MP interviewed put it, 'Once you start talking about Europe up go the barricades and out come the guns.'

Sociologically, as opposed to ideologically, the MPs elected in 2010, both old and new, aren't so very different from those elected in 2005 and before, with one or two obvious differences.[12] After the 2005 election there were 17 Tory women; after 2010 there were 49. Although an increase of only 7 points (from 9 to 16 per cent of the total), it was enough to make a visible difference, which was always the main rationale for Cameron's halting attempts to persuade his Party to pick more women. True, while there is evidence that, on average, 'A-Listers'(whether male or female) did better in 2010 than their non-A-List counterparts in seats the Tories failed to win in 2005, female Tory candidates in general did no better than the men. On the other hand, they fared no worse. The same cannot be said for candidates of Black and Ethnic Minority (BME) origin, who, at least in constituencies where BME voters were thin on the ground, performed significantly less well than their white counterparts.[13] Still, after the election there were 11 rather than just two Tories of BME origin sitting in the Commons, many of whom were likely to be around for quite some time given the size of their majorities.

Whether these MPs, be they BME or women or both, could be said to be typical of the groups or the gender they 'represent', however, is a moot point: the vast majority came from highly paid occupations in the private sector, such as business, banking, and the law. This makes them much more like other Conservative MPs than like the population as a whole: almost 50 per cent of the parliamentary party elected in 2010 had backgrounds in business, accountancy, and PR; 20 per cent of them were lawyers; with the third biggest group (at 10 per cent) being gainfully employed in politics before becoming an MP; only two Tory MPs (one the highly respected and highly able Chief Whip, Patrick McLoughlin, a former miner) could claim to have worked in a manual occupation. More worryingly for a party with big plans for the reform of education and the NHS, there were no teachers or lecturers on the Conservative benches after 2010 and fewer than ten people with backgrounds in the health professions.

All this will come as no surprise. What may strike some as significant, however, is that the election of 2010 continued the trend towards a more state- than privately-educated party: in 1979 just under 75 per cent of Conservative MPs had been to independent schools; by 2010 it was only 54 per cent (with a 50–50 split when it came to the new intake), though we should of course note that in the population as a whole considerably less than 10 per cent of pupils are educated outside the state sector. Whatever their background, though, those aspiring one day to become a Tory MP and worrying that they may not make it (or may not have made it) to Oxford or Cambridge could take heart from the fact that fewer than half of university graduates sitting on the Tory benches after the 2010 election were products of those universities – a proportion that drops to around a quarter if one takes only the new intake into account.

Few people interested in politics will know or care that the average age of those Tories fortunate enough to be elected or re-elected in 2010 was 47. But many will recall that back in the 1990s the average age of the ordinary member of the party in the country was 62. Recent research suggests that things have improved on this count – at least marginally. A survey conducted in July 2009 found that the average age of the Conservative grassroots had dropped to 55. Then again, those who were 55 and older still made up 60 per cent of the total membership, some three quarters of which was in occupational groups ABC1.[14] The research also confirmed the finding that grassroots members of the Party, although generally right-wing (on a scale of 1–7 they rated themselves on average at 5.62), were by no means all the 'swivel-eyed' extremists of legend, on either the state–market or the authoritarian–libertarian dimension. Indeed, 'Thatcherites' (characterized as those who 'support cuts in tax and spending, but are hostile to environmentalism, European integration, immigration and gender-related reforms') accounted for about the same proportion (36–38 per cent) of the membership as 'Traditionalist Tories', 'the largest, most working class and most female of the intra-party tendencies', who 'are surprisingly progressive on a number of specific proposals and issues, including taxation and public spending, gender issues and the institutional reform of politics' – some of which they have in common with 'Liberal Conservatives', who made up the remaining 25 per cent and who are 'the youngest, most male, . . . most active of these tendencies, and are distinguished by being the least hostile to Europe and immigration, to environmentalism or to feminist values'. It is this, along with the deal Cameron managed to get and the fact grassroots members are simply glad to be back in government, that helps explain why he had relatively little trouble convincing them that the decision to enter coalition was the right one.

That said, Cameron made a concerted effort from the off to reassure both Tory members and voters (and probably MPs as well) that, as he stressed in articles and interviews in the *Mail*, the *Telegraph*, and the *News of the World* over the weekend of 21–3 May, he was still a Conservative PM delivering an agenda on immigration, on Europe, on spending cuts, and on education and health reform, of which they could be proud.[15] His arguments almost certainly failed to convince those Tories still unpersuaded that Cameron was really 'one of us'. But most were prepared to at least suck it and see, even if they had reservations here and there. ConservativeHome's reader surveys showed a growing but not necessarily universal belief that the coalition was a good thing, not only for the country but also for the Party itself.[16] They also pointed, though, to those areas of most concern (constitutional reform, law and order, and delays to tax cuts) and to a (possibly unrepresentative) desire to see the NHS (as well as the overseas aid budget) included in the deficit reduction exercise that would culminate in the Comprehensive Spending Review (CSR) announced at the end of October 2010. Perhaps significantly for the future, they pointed in addition to a fair amount of scepticism about the idea, floated within months of the coalition's formation, that the Lib Dems and the Conservatives should conclude some sort of non-aggression pact or even field joint candidates at the next general election.[17]

Were the leadership of the Party to decide that this was indeed the way they wanted to go, then this reluctance on the part of the membership could prove a huge obstacle. The exclusive right to select parliamentary candidates is one of the few attractions of joining a party, and is already under threat from the possible extension (using state funds) of selection via open and even postal primaries. Taking away that right, especially if it occurs after a few years of defeats in local elections and involves a call to support a Lib Dem or 'coalition' candidate instead of an out-and-out Conservative, could make it even harder for the Tories to put 'boots on the ground' at the next general election – something which can make the difference between winning and losing in a marginal seat. The incentives to join the Party (indeed any party) are already fairly paltry. As one jaded contributor to a thread on ConservativeHome observed in August 2010: 'Being a member, at the moment, merely means paying, going to meetings where no one wants to hear you, attending expensive social dos where you don't know anybody, getting all sorts of requests to do unpleasant things at elections and receiving endless appeals for more money.'[18] Reducing those incentives still further may not be a good idea, unless of course one believes, as some academics and activists allege, that those at the top of political parties would actually prefer to dispense with members altogether.

The evidence suggests, however, that parties are keen, for the moment anyway, to find some way of slowing, if not actually reversing, what seems like an inevitable and widespread trend away from 'high-intensity' political participation. Senior Tories, at least those in the voluntary party, are clearly worried and have already begun to think about how they might use paid professionals – 'Voluntary Party Managers' – not so much to replace as to generate more activity in the party in the country. On the other hand, the introduction to the discussion paper on the topic, released late in the summer of 2010, suggests a worrying degree of wishful thinking when it claims the Party is able to call on 100,000 active supporters.[19] The Party lost approximately 80,000 members between 2005 and 2010, by which time the total had dropped to around 177,000.[20] The 2009 membership survey suggests that no more than a third of party members consider themselves active – and even that proportion would come as a surprise to many of those who do actually deliver leaflets and knock on doors. Whatever the real figure, however, one would be hard-pressed to argue that David Cameron has inspired large numbers of people to join or stick with his party. Certainly, there is no sign at all of a new generation of young Conservatives falling over each other to sign up or, having signed up, to do much. In September, Conservative Future, the Party's youth branch, which supposedly boasts a membership of 18,000, held elections for its national Chair and Committee: the winner was elected by a paltry 113 votes to 60 – a figure so low that it can't be explained by admittedly chaotic administration. The likelihood of the Party being able to reverse this trend, especially in government, when few parties ever do much about reforming or rebuilding their grassroots organization, is virtually nil.

Whether this matters, given that that the Tories' rivals are facing the same long-term trends, and given that the Party's members (for all the brave talk of an expanded role for some sort of policy forum) will have virtually zero influence on policy-making, is a moot point.[21] However, unless the Party can enlist the help of the cash-strapped Lib Dems to push through legislation which radically boosts state funding, its inability to hold on to or replace its members will make it ever more dependent on the type of donations and loans which have the potential to bring it into disrepute. Within months of the election, for instance, the Tories were facing awkward questions about fund-raising activities that seemed to offer privileged access to minsters and about the business dealings and tax affairs some of their wealthiest donors. As a result, the man announced as the Party's new Treasurer, David Rowland, never actually took up the post.

The task of ensuring that, despite such stories, the party in the country and the party in Central Office maintained its capacity and its morale would be down to its co-chairmen, Andrew Feldman and Sayeeda Warsi. The former (a long-term personal friend of Cameron's) wasted little time in authorizing managerial reform.[22] But motivation was down to the latter – one of the few women, and the only person from an ethnic minority, sitting around a Cabinet table mainly occupied on the Conservative side by colleagues who were largely white (95 per cent), male (80 per cent), independently educated (60 per cent), and (if press reports that all but four of them were worth over a million were true) extremely wealthy. Inevitably this gave rise to whispers about tokenism – whispers that only grew louder after Warsi failed to impress early on in the other essential task of the Party Chairman – handling the media. Cameron's decision to appoint Michael Fallon (a shrewd and smooth media performer) as Deputy Chairman in September suggested he sensed there was indeed a gap that badly needed filling. That said, the Tories had little to complain about – at least initially – when it came to their treatment by the press and broadcasters. The objectivity of the latter, and particularly the BBC, is a perennial concern among Conservatives, many of whom are convinced that the corporation is chock-full of left-wingers intent of turning the country against them. Any journalist thus tempted, however, could not have failed to read the warning signals coming from above: no sooner had Jeremy Hunt taken up his post at the Department of Media, Culture, and Sport than he was warning the Beeb that it, like everyone else, would have to do more with less. Meanwhile, the BBC's Director General appeared particularly keen to reassure Cameron personally of his organization's good intentions.

The print media, like the blogosphere with which it is increasingly enmeshed, was a different proposition, however. Most Tory papers and bloggers were prepared to welcome the formation of the coalition or to give it the benefit of the doubt. And many were more than happy to help the government begin softening up the public for its measures to reduce the size and the supposed perks of public-sector workers and those on benefits: Chris Grayling, Minister of State at Work and Pensions, for example, must have been particularly pleased in the late summer/early autumn to see press releases turned straight into splashes with headlines like '76% of those who say they're sick "can work"' (*Mail*, 28 July) and '£28bn Bill for workshy scroungers' (*Express*, 16 August). However, this did not necessarily guarantee Cameron and his colleagues a uniformly easy ride from what we have called 'the party in the media' – the commentators, columnists, and leader writers whose voices count in Conservative circles. Even leaving aside criticism of the election campaign and early accusations of sell-out and betrayal occasioned by the Party going into government with the Lib Dems,[23] there was an obvious determination to try to prevent Cameron moving too far off their interpretation of what constituted a Tory agenda. Of particular concern, for instance, was immigration.[24] So too was the apparent willingness not only to forgo the opportunity of 'repatriating powers' from Brussels but actively to sign up to initiatives that appeared (to Eurosceptics at least) to dilute UK sovereignty, notably the European Investigation Order, which granted foreign police forces rights to act within Britain. In addition, at least outside the pages of the *Sun* and the *Times* (keen perhaps to curry favour with a government deciding on whether Rupert Murdoch could take a controlling stake in the satellite broadcaster Sky), there was also a willingness to warn Cameron over certain policy choices. The decision to stop paying child benefit to households containing a higher-rate taxpayer, which derailed the Party's 2010 Conference, it was said risked alienating traditional Tory voters and trampling on values (in that case, family-friendliness and aspiration) that they held dear, thereby opening up an opportunity for Labour to claim concern for the so-called 'squeezed middle'.[25]

Certainly, there were plenty of policy choices being made in the first few months of the new government's life, suggesting that Francis Maude's pre-election Implementation Unit had realized its ambition to help Cameron (looking and sounding every inch the Prime Minister from the get-go) to hit the ground running.[26] Some were predictable. As expected, it was full-steam ahead with plans laid out by Michael Gove (who managed to survive early criticism over his handling of the ending of a large school-building programme) to increase the supply of good state schools by encouraging those which wanted more independence from their local authorities to apply for academy status and enabling the setting up of new, so-called 'free schools'. Equally predictable was the drip-feed of announcements (with Eric Pickles, the former Party Chairman and now Minister for Communities and Local Government in the vanguard) concerning the scrapping of what, at least to Tories, were self-evidently stupid targets, regulations, and quangos.

Other Tory ministers provided more in the way of surprises. Whilst most thought William Hague would, like Cameron, take a sensibly pragmatic line in his early dealings with the EU, not everyone expected the government to set a date (2015) for the withdrawal of British combat forces in Afghanistan.[27] On the domestic front, the new Home Secretary, Theresa May, looked more prepared than her Tory predecessors to take on the police, whose leaders were quick to cast doubt on the idea that they should be placed under the control of directly elected commissioners and that they would be able to cope with fewer resources. Many wondered, however, whether she would keep her nerve when and if crime began to rise. Similarly, Justice Secretary Ken Clarke worried many traditional Tories when he made clear his scepticism about the value of short but costly jail sentences for relatively minor offenders, although most of their criticisms were directed at his junior minister, Crispin Blunt, who suffered at the hands of the party in the media after appearing to go soft on prisoners. By way of contrast, Iain Duncan Smith, the man who beat Clarke to the party leadership in 2001, and then made such a hash of it, received rave reviews bordering on beatification for his apparently successful campaign as Secretary of State for Work and Pensions to persuade the Treasury to allow him to undertake long-term radical reform of welfare in return for delivering short-term savings – one of the few instances (the others are Hague and Home) of a modern politician who, having utterly failed to convince in the top job, is apparently able to shine lower down the batting order. Whether, though, Duncan Smith's reforms really would deliver a less complex and more cost-effective system remained to be seen. The same applied to Health Secretary Andrew Lansley's announcement of fundamental changes to the NHS, which, given the impression previously created that the last thing the Tories wanted to do was to foist yet another reorganization on one of Britain's best-loved institutions, was possibly the most surprising (and politically risky) of all the government's early decisions.

Health, of course, was one of just two departments (the other being International Development) whose budgets were supposedly protected in the CSR, debates about the shape and scope of which inevitably dominated the Party's first few months in government and would define its position – and possibly determine its electoral fate – in the years to come. Prior to its announcement, voters were invited to share their ideas for savings on a government website.[28] They were also treated to ringside seats at what became a no-holds-barred fight over military spending between Defence Secretary (and former leadership contender) Liam Fox and Chancellor George Osborne – a fight which (following US pressure and Prime Ministerial intervention) resulted in a compromise that left a fair few Tory MPs unhappy and left the Treasury looking for last-minute savings elsewhere. Crucially, however, Osborne did not allow all this to distract him from successfully pursuing his main task: persuading the public of three things prior to the CSR being announced. Polls at that point showed that the British believed, first, that the deficit had less to do with the global financial meltdown and consequent economic downturn than it did with Labour's profligate policies; secondly, that immediate and drastic action to reduce it was unavoidable; and, thirdly, that the emphasis should be not on tax rises but (by an extraordinary ratio of 3:1) on spending cuts. These, the Chancellor and the Prime Minister insisted, would be 'tough but fair' and taken 'together in the national interest' and in anticipation of the 'Big Society'.

Where to now?

In their unguarded moments, many Tories may have shared the view of former leadership contender David Davis, overheard treating friends to his views on what he dubbed 'the brokeback coalition' in the Boot and Flogger (!) wine bar, that the Big Society amounted to little more than 'Blairite dressing' for the cuts to come. The plain fact was that in order to spend less the state would henceforth do less and give less – something made crystal clear by the CSR, announced on 20 October 2010, which made significant (and some argued deeply regressive) reductions in the government payroll and in money spent on welfare and given to local government, albeit claiming to have protected politically more popular services and groups, such as health, schools, and the elderly.

The CSR may have been an economic gamble – testament to the fact that Conservatives remain as convinced now as they ever were that shrinking the state will energize the economy. But the biggest gamble was political. This was not simply because the measures involved might make the Party unpopular in the short term: Tory MPs were prepared for this. It was because they entailed a Conservative Prime Minister – one who had failed to win a general election outright because he had been unable to persuade enough people to trust his party-choosing, like Margaret Thatcher in 1979, to risk confirming their suspicions rather than, as Winston Churchill had been determined to do after 1951, to allay their fears. Churchill, of course, had it easier: the post-war boom brought with it buoyant revenues that he could use to square the circle between voters' demands for more of everything and Tory resistance to tax and spend. But he was also more cautious: his reluctance to return to the Treasury orthodoxy of the thirties was born of the belief that people wouldn't put up with it – not when they could turn to a Labour Party whose support essentially matched and might easily exceed his own. Margaret Thatcher, at the height of her powers, showed that such caution was unnecessary as long as one was prepared not to worry too much about poverty and unemployment outside the more prosperous (and more heavily populated) South and was fortunate enough to be facing a discredited and divided opposition.

But Thatcher had a couple of crucial things going for her which, crucially, Cameron does not. First, she made sure – prior to the Poll Tax at least – that she never hit natural Tory supporters where it hurts: the middle-class welfare state was always safe in her hands. Cameron, possibly in a bold move to sever the connection between such people and government help in order to undermine the cross-class solidarity so crucial to Labour's social democratic political economy, has decided instead to let middle England fend for itself. Second, Thatcher could rely on enough residual support in the leafier suburbs and rural constituencies above the line that runs from the Severn to the Wash to provide her party with the majorities to which it all-too-easily became accustomed.

Those days, it seems, are long gone. Even presuming he is able to reduce the number of seats in parliament, and with it the system's tendency to favour Labour, Cameron (who, thanks to Mrs T, operates in a country where entire cities remain, like Scotland, virtually Tory-free zones) will still need a far bigger share of the vote than she did to win outright. And, because the coalition (knowing how long it would take to reduce the deficit and get the economy growing) agreed on a five-year fixed parliamentary term, he will not be able, as Thatcher was, to guarantee going to the country at precisely the right time.

Cameron seems to have given up on the Scottish Conservative Party and, given the impact of the CSR on the UK's lopsided economy, is unlikely to win many new friends in the North.[29] However, he has engineered one big advantage that Thatcher never enjoyed. By persuading Britain's third party to join him in government, he has, even if the Lib Dems do survive intact, almost certainly reduced the chances that they will siphon off voters who might otherwise vote Conservative – a phenomenon that historically (1929, 1950, 1964, 1974, 2010) cost the Tories dear. On the other hand, Clegg's decision to enter the coalition and associate his party with policies diametrically opposed to those it had advocated in opposition virtually guarantees (unless everything comes spectacularly right by the next general election) that many of those who voted Lib Dem in 2010 will think seriously about doing so again. The same may well apply to some of those who voted Tory, especially if economic growth remains anaemic, unemployment stays stubbornly high, public services deteriorate or disappear, immigrants stick around, and (especially if prison places and police numbers are reduced) crime begins to rise. David Cameron is running a Conservative-led government that, partly (but not wholly) owing to the Liberal Democrats within it, is both socially liberal and economically on the right. Only a minority of voters are loyal to either party, while the bulk of the electorate remains socially authoritarian and economically on the centre-left. All of this presents Labour with an opportunity. Whether it is able to take advantage of it may depend, at least in part, on whether it can learn some of the lessons contained within this book.

NOTES

Chapter 1 Solving the Puzzle: An Introduction

1 John Ramsden, *An Appetite for Power* (London: HarperCollins, 1998), p. 495.

2 Stuart Ball, 'Factors in opposition performance: the Conservative experience since 1867', in Stuart Ball and Anthony Seldon (eds), *Recovering Power: the Conservatives in Opposition* (Basingstoke: Palgrave Macmillan, 2005), pp. 4–5.

3 Andrew Hindmoor, *New Labour at the Centre: Constructing Political Space* (Oxford: Oxford University Press, 2004).

4 Kieron O'Hara, *After Blair: David Cameron and the Conservative Tradition* (Thriplow: Icon, 2007).

5 For an example of an academic article that uses manifesto data to try to question this assumption, see Thomas Quinn, 'The Conservative Party and the "centre ground" of British politics', *Journal of Elections, Public Opinion and Parties*, 18 (2), 2008, pp. 179–99. For the record, on a scale of 1–10 where 5 is dead centre, respondents to the BPES and BES election surveys on average placed the Tories at 6.18 in 2000, 6.76 in 2001, and 6.81 in 2005, with the figures for Labour being 4.14, 4.53, and 5.17: see Jane Green, 'A Test of Party Competition Theories: the British Conservative Party since 1997' (unpublished D.Phil.

dissertation, University of Oxford, 2006), p. 142. At the very least, then, the Party failed to progress toward the centre even if it didn't become particularly extreme. Any 'convergence' since the 1980s, and especially since 1997, has largely been down to Labour.

6 Oleg Smirnov and James H. Fowler, 'Policy-motivated parties in dynamic political competition', *Journal of Theoretical Politics*, 19 (1), 2007, pp. 9–31. See also James F. Adams, Michael Clark, Lawrence Ezrow, and Garrett Glasgow, 'Understanding change and stability in party ideologies: do parties respond to public opinion or to past election results?', *British Journal of Political Science*, 34 (4), 2004, pp. 589–610.

7 Robert Harmel, 'Party organizational change: competing explanations?' in K. Richard Luther and Ferdinand Müller-Rommel (eds), *Political Parties in the New Europe: Political and Analytical Challenges* (Oxford: Oxford University Press, 2002). See also James Adams and Zeynep Somer-Topcu, 'Policy adjustments by parties in response to rival parties' policy shifts: spatial theory and the dynamics of party competition in twenty-five postwar democracies', *British Journal of Political Science*, in press.

8 Torben Iversen, 'The logics of electoral-politics: spatial, directional, and mobilizational effects', *Comparative Political Studies*, 27 (2), 1994, pp. 155–89.

9 See James F. Adams, Samuel Merrill, and Bernard Grofman, *A Unified Theory of Party Competition* (Cambridge: Cambridge University Press, 2005), see especially pp. 7–11, 168, 182–7, 227–34.

10 Ian Budge, 'A new spatial theory of party competition: uncertainty, ideology and policy equilibria viewed comparatively and temporally', *British Journal of Political Science* 24, 1994, p. 446.

11 Herbert Kitschelt and Philipp Rehm, 'Work, family, and politics: foundations of electoral partisan alignments in postindustrial democracies', paper presented at the annual meeting of the American Political Science Association, Washington, DC, September 2005. See also James M. Snyder and Michael M. Ting, 'An informational rationale for political parties', *American Journal of Political Science*, 46, 2002, pp. 90–110.

12 James Adams and Zeynep Somer-Topcu, 'Moderate now, win votes later: the electoral consequences of parties' policy shifts in 25 postwar democracies', *Journal of Politics*, 71 (2), 2009, pp. 678–92.

13 Albert O. Hirschman, *Exit, Voice, and Loyalty: Responses to Decline in Firms, Organizations, and States* (Cambridge, MA: Harvard University Press, 1970).

14 Justine Greening, interview, 25 April 2007.

15 An exception to this rule, albeit a specialized one, is provided by Jennifer Lees-Marshment, who has written about the Party from a comparative 'political marketing' perspective. See her *Political Marketing and British Political Parties* (Manchester: Manchester University Press, 2008).

16 Obvious examples include (from a political studies perspective) Andrew Gamble and Philip Norton, as well as Andrew Denham, Peter Dorey, Mark Garnett, Kieran O'Hara, Timothy Heppell, Richard Kelly, Philip Lynch, Andrew Taylor, and Philip Tether, and (from a historical perspective) Stuart Ball, John Charmley, John Ramsden, Andrew Thorpe, John Turner, and, of course, the indefatigable Anthony Seldon and his collaborators Peter Snowdon and Daniel Collings.

17 Geoffrey Wheatcroft, *The Strange Death of Tory England* (Harmondsworth: Penguin, 2005).

18 Pippa Norris and Joni Lovenduski, 'Why parties fail to learn: electoral defeat, selective perception and British party politics', *Party Politics*, 10 (1) 2004, p. 90.

19 Jane Green, 'Conservative Party rationality: learning the lessons from the last election for the next', *Journal of Elections, Public Opinion and Parties*, 15 (1), 2005, pp. 111–27. See also Green, 'A Test'.

20 Hugh Heclo, 'Ideas, interests and institutions', in Lawrence C. Dodd and Calvin Jillson (eds), *The Dynamics of American Politics: Approaches and Interpretations* (Boulder, CO: Westview), pp. 372, 375.

21 On 'path-dependence' – the 'historical institutionalist' notion that certain events are 'critical junctures' which 'lock-in' certain courses of action and preclude other possibilities, see Paul Pierson,

Politics in Time: History, Institutions, and Social Analysis (Princeton: Princeton University Press, 2004).

22 Edmund Burke, 'Speech on American taxation, 19 April 1774'. See Edward John Payne (ed.), *Select Works* (London: Lawbook Exchange, 2005), p. 97.

23 Maurice Cowling, *The Impact of Labour 1920–1924: the Beginning of Modern British Politics* (Cambridge: Cambridge University Press, 1971), pp. 1–12.

24 See Robert Crowcroft, 'Maurice Cowling and the writing of British political history', *Contemporary British History*, 22 (2), 2008, pp. 279–86.

25 See, for example, Andrew Rawnsley, *Servants of the People* (Harmondsworth: Penguin, 2001).

26 George Canning, who became Prime Minister in 1827 but died after only 119 days in office, made the remark in a speech to the Commons on 9 December 1802.

27 Jo-Anne Nadler, *Too Nice to be a Tory* (London: Simon and Schuster, 2004), p. 161.

28 Andrew Marr, *Express*, 16 February 2000.

29 Cowling, *Impact*, p. 11.

30 For the Tories, see Paul Whiteley, Patrick Seyd, and Jeremy Richardson, *True Blues: the Politics of Conservative Party Membership* (Oxford: Oxford University Press, 1994) and Rupert Morris, *Tories* (Edinburgh: Mainstream Publishers, 1991). On the UK more generally, see Pippa Norris, 'May's law of curvilinear disparity revisited: leaders, officers, members and voters in British political parties', *Party Politics*, 1 (1), 1995, pp. 29–47. For the international evidence, see, for example, Iversen, 'Logics'.

31 Nadler, *Too Nice*, p. 77.

32 See Martin Smith, 'The core executive and the resignation of Margaret Thatcher', *Public Administration*, 72 (3), 1994, pp. 341–63. See also Richard Heffernan, 'Prime ministerial predominance? Core executive politics in the UK', *British Journal of Politics and International Relations*, 5 (3), 2003, pp. 347–72.

33 Robert McKenzie, *British Political Parties* (London: Mercury Books, 1963), p. 145.

34 Liam Fox, interview, 18 February 2008.

35 The phrase is credited to John Ramsden. See Peter Hennessy, 'Churchill and the premiership', *Transactions of the Royal Historical Society*, 11, 2002, pp. 295–306.

36 Kenneth Newton, 'May the weak force be with you: the power of the mass media in modern politics', *European Journal of Political Research*, 45 (2), 2006, pp. 209–34.

37 Hans Mathias Kepplinger, 'Reciprocal effects: toward a theory of mass media effects on decision makers', *The Harvard International Journal of Press/Politics*, 12 (2), 2007, pp. 3–23.

38 Emma Nicholson, *Secret Society: Inside – and Outside – the Conservative Party* (London: Indigo, 1996), pp. 113–15. See also Philip Norton, 'The parliamentary party and party committees', in Anthony Seldon and Stuart Ball (eds), *Conservative Century* (Oxford: Oxford University Press, 1994).

39 John Rentoul, 'Young, sunny David versus old, snarling Gordon: oh, that life were so simple', *Independent on Sunday*, 23 October 2005.

40 Richard Cockett, *Twilight of Truth, Chamberlain, Appeasement and the Manipulation of the Press* (London: Weidenfeld and Nicolson, 1989), p. 187.

41 Cowling, *Impact*, p. 11.

42 Enoch Powell (interviewed by Robert McKenzie) 'I am a loner by nature', *Listener*, 28 May 1981.

Chapter 2 Losing the Plot: Thatcher to Major, 1989–1997

1 Andrew Gamble, 'An ideological party', in Steve Ludlam and Martin Smith (eds), *Contemporary British Conservatism* (London: Macmillan, 1996), p. 23. See also Simon Jenkins, *Thatcher and Sons* (Harmondsworth: Penguin, 2006), Chapter 10. For a more heroic (though by no means wholly blinkered) take, see Claire Berlinski, *There is No Alternative: Why Margaret Thatcher Matters* (New York: Basic Books, 2008). Another historically inclined but above all measured reassessment is provided by Richard Vinen, *Thatcher's Britain* (London: Simon and Schuster, 2009).

2 Ivor Crewe, '1979–96', in Anthony Seldon (ed.), *How Tory Governments Fall: the Tory Party in Power since 1783* (London: Fontana, 1996), pp. 401–8 and David Denver, 'Electoral support',

in Philip Norton (ed.), *The Conservative Party* (London: Prentice Hall/Harvester Wheatsheaf, 1996), pp. 180–3.

3 Philip Norton, '"The lady's not for turning" but what about the rest? Margaret Thatcher and the Conservative Party 1979–89', *Parliamentary Affairs*, 43 (1), 1990, pp. 41–58.

4 Alistair McAlpine, *Once a Jolly Bagman: Memoirs* (London: Phoenix, 1998), p. 257.

5 Tristan Garel-Jones, interview, 25 April 2007. See also John Major, *The Autobiography* (London: HarperCollins, 2000), pp. 168–9.

6 Michael Heseltine, *Life in the Jungle* (London: Hodder and Stoughton, 2000), p. 351 and Margaret Thatcher, *The Downing Street Years* (London: HarperCollins, 1993), p. 830.

7 Douglas Hurd, *Memoirs* (London: Little, Brown, 2003), pp. 365–6.

8 Major, *Autobiography*, p. 173.

9 Tim Renton, *Chief Whip: People, Power and Patronage in Westminster* (London: Politico's, 2005), pp. 44–7.

10 Crewe, '1979–96', pp. 401–8.

11 George Walden, *Lucky George: Memoirs of an Anti-Politician* (London: Allen Lane, 1999), p. 302. See also Gillian Shephard, *Shephard's Watch: Illusions of Power in British Politics* (London: Politico's, 2000), pp. 183–4.

12 Michael Crick, *Michael Heseltine: a Biography* (Harmondsworth: Penguin, 1997), p. 343.

13 See Alan Watkins, *A Conservative Coup: the Fall of Margaret Thatcher* (London: Duckworth, 1991), p. 182.

14 Michael Foley, *John Major, Tony Blair and a Conflict of Leadership* (Manchester: Manchester University Press, 2002), p. 17.

15 Thatcher, *Downing Street*, pp. 836–7 and Kenneth Baker, *The Turbulent Years: My Life in Politics* (London: Faber and Faber, 1993), p. 419.

16 Steven Norris, *Changing Trains: an Autobiography* (London: Hutchinson, 1996), pp. 153–4. See also Alan Clark, *Diaries: In Power 1983–1992* (London: Phoenix, 1994), 17 and 19 November 1990.

17 Tristan Garel-Jones, interview, 25 April 2007. See also Norman Lamont, *In Office* (London: Warner, 1999), p. 10.

18 Probably the best blow-by-blow (but still reasonably concise) account of Thatcher's replacement by Major is provided by Robert Shepherd, *The Power Brokers: the Tory Party and Its Leaders* (London: Hutchinson, 1991), pp. 1–79.

19 Matthew Parris, *Chance Witness: an Outsider's Life in Politics* (Harmondsworth: Penguin, 2003).

20 Walden, *Lucky George*, pp. 300–1. See also Douglas Hurd, *Memoirs* (London: Little, Brown, 2003), pp. 363, 399–400.

21 Renton, *Chief Whip*, pp. 68, 20, 116 and Baker, *Turbulent*, p. 388.

22 Watkins, *Coup*, p. 149.

23 Norris, *Autobiography*, p. 149.

24 Clark, *Diaries: 1983–1992*, 4 November 1990

25 McAlpine, *Bagman* p. 258.

26 Baker, *Turbulent*, p. 320.

27 Woodrow Wyatt, *Journals*, Volume II (London: Macmillan, 1999), 23 April 1989.

28 Geoffrey Howe, *Conflict of Loyalty* (London: Pan, 1995), pp. 636 and 670. See also Alan Clark, *The Tories: Conservatives and the Nation State, 1922–97* (London: Phoenix, 1999), pp. 492–3, Baker, *Turbulent*, p. 368, McAlpine, *Bagman*, p. 266 and Norris, *Autobiography*, p. 148.

29 Parris, *Witness*, pp. 199, 188.

30 Hurd, *Memoirs*, p. 399.

31 Major, *Autobiography*, p. 169.

32 See Timothy Heppell, *Choosing the Tory Leader: Conservative Party Leadership Elections from Heath to Cameron* (London: I.B. Tauris, 2008), p. 9.

33 Shepherd, *Power Brokers*, p. 63.

34 Peter Lilley, interview, 26 March 2007.

35 The best academic account remains Philip Cowley and John Garry, 'The British Conservative Party and Europe: the choosing of John Major', *British Journal of Political Science*, 28 (3), pp. 473–99. One of the best insider accounts is provided in Ian Lang, *Blue Remembered Years* (London: Politico's, 2002), pp. 94–113. See also Crick, *Heseltine*, p. 355–6 and Lamont, *Office* pp. 19–29.

36 Heppell, *Tory Leader*, p. 92.

37 Jenkins, *Thatcher and Sons*, p. 159.

38 See, for example, Wyatt, *Journals*, 3 and 28 March 1991.

39 Parris, *Witness*, p. 385.

40 Lamont, *Office*, pp. 21, 15.

41 Major, *Autobiography*, pp. 200, 209.

42 Sarah Hogg and Jonathan Hill, *Too Close to Call: Power and Politics – John Major in No. 10* (London: Little, Brown, 1995), p. 23.

43 Ivor Crewe, 'Electoral behaviour', in Dennis Kavanagh and Anthony Seldon (eds), *The Major Effect* (Basingstoke: Macmillan, 1994), p. 100.

44 Christopher Gill, *Whips' Nightmare: Diary of a Maastricht Rebel* (Spennymoor: Memoir Club, 2003), p. 33. See also Norman Fowler, *A Political Suicide: the Conservatives' Voyage into the Wilderness* (London: Politico's, 2008), pp. 78–82.

45 John Sergeant, *Maggie: Her Fatal Legacy* (London, Pan Books, 2005), pp. 209, 357.

46 Tristan Garel-Jones, interview, 25 April 2007.

47 Norris, *Autobiography*, p. 219.

48 Major, *Autobiography*, p. 246.

49 Hogg and Hill, *Close*, p. 205.

50 McAlpine, *Bagman*, pp. 264–5.

51 Anthony Seldon, *Major: a Political Life* (London: Phoenix, 1998), p. 219.

52 Michael Ashcroft, *Dirty Politics, Dirty Times* (London: MAA Publishing, 2005), pp. 56–7.

53 Seldon, *Major*, pp. 220–1 and Hogg and Hill, *Close*, pp. 86, 108.

54 Hogg and Hill, *Close*, p. 125.

55 Lamont, *Office*, pp. 157, 190.

56 See Wyatt, *Journals*, 1 April to 7 April 1992.

57 On the presidentialization of the Tory campaign in 1992, see Foley, *Major, Blair*, pp. 43–8. On campaign tensions, see Hogg and Hill, *Close*, pp. 206, 215 and Seldon, *Major*, pp. 257, 269, 280.

58 See John Curtice and Michael Steed, 'The results analysed', in David Butler and Denis Kavanagh, *The British General Election of 1992* (Basingstoke: Macmillan, 1992).

59 Tristan Garel-Jones, interview, 25 April 2007.

60 Major, *Autobiography* p. 307. See also Shephard, *Watch*, pp. 56, 59.

61 One Thatcherite who acknowledges the insidious power of this assumption is Peter Lilley: see Lilley, interview, 26 March 2007.

62 Shephard, *Watch*, p. 59.

63 Sergeant, *Maggie*, pp. 237 and Seldon, *Major*, p. 285.

64 Major, *Autobiography*, p. 347.

65 Alan Duncan, quoted in Shephard, *Watch*, p. 57.

66 See David Baker, Andrew Gamble, and Steve Ludlam, 'More "classless" and less "Thatcherite"? Conservative ministers and new Conservative MPs after the 1992 election', *Parliamentary Affairs*, 45 (4), 1992, pp. 656–68.

67 David Baker, Andrew Gamble, and Steve Ludlam, 'Backbenchers with attitude: a seismic study of the Conservative Party and dissent on Europe', in Shaun Bowler, David M. Farrell, and Richard S. Katz (eds), *Party Discipline and Parliamentary Government* (Columbus: Ohio State University Press, 1998).

68 Major, *Autobiography*, p. 352.

69 Gill, *Whips' Nightmare*, p. 27.

70 Emma Nicholson, *Secret Society: Inside – and Outside – the Conservative Party* (London: Indigo, 1996), p. 97 and Gyles Brandreth, *Breaking the Code: Westminster Diaries* (London: Phoenix, 2001), p. 55.

71 Peter Lilley, interview, 26 March 2007.

72 Walden, *Lucky George*, pp. 345–6.

73 Major, *Autobiography*, p. 359.

74 Gill, *Whips' Nightmare*, p. 123.

75 Donald MacIntyre, 'The dinner: sour hangover from a convivial farewell', *Independent*, 17 January 1994. See also Tim Bale and Karen Sanders, '"Playing by the book": success and failure in John Major's approach to Prime Ministerial media management', *Contemporary British History*, 15 (4), 2001, pp. 93–110.

76 Colin Seymour-Ure, 'Mass media', in Kavanagh and Seldon (eds), *Major Effect*, p. 417.

77 Fowler, *Suicide*, pp. 105–6ff. See also Justin Fisher, 'Party finance', in Norton (ed.), *Conservative Party*.

78 Philip Tether, 'The party in the country I: development and influence', in Norton (ed.), *The Conservative Party*, pp. 123–5.

79 Parris, *Witness*, p. 207. See also Tether, 'Development', p. 108 and Michael Pinto-Duschinsky, 'Tory chiefs in danger of losing their troops', *Times*, 10 October 1994.

80 Tether, 'Development' and 'The party in the country II: members and organisation', in Norton (ed.), *Conservative Party*, pp. 110 and 125.

81 Paul Whiteley, Patrick Seyd, and Jeremy Richardson, *True Blues: the Politics of Conservative Party Membership* (Oxford: Oxford University Press, 1994).

82 Seldon, *Major*, p. 543.

83 Robin Harris, 'The ring of no confidence', *Spectator*, 20 May 1995.

84 Lamont, *Office*, pp. 341, 362, 366, 377. See also Brandreth, *Westminster Diaries*, p. 191.

85 Malcolm Balen, *Kenneth Clarke* (London: Fourth Estate, 1994), pp. 252–9 and Brandreth, *Westminster Diaries*, pp. 184–5.

86 Fowler, *Suicide*, pp. 168–9.

87 Crewe, 'Electoral behaviour', p. 114.

88 Hugo Young, 'The Prime Minister', in Kavanagh and Seldon (eds), *Major Effect*, p. 27.

89 'The day the high ground crumbled', *Guardian*, 22 November 1994.

90 Shephard, *Watch*, pp. 62–3.

91 Nicholson, *Secret Society*, pp. 9–13.

92 Major, *Autobiography*, p. 352.

93 Gill, *Whips' Nightmare*, p. 107.

94 Walden, *Lucky George*, p. 362. See also Paul Webb, *The Modern British Party System* (London: Sage, 2000), p. 187 and Timothy Heppell, 'The ideological composition of the Parliamentary Conservative Party 1992–97', *British Journal of Politics and International Relations*, 4 (2), 2002, pp. 299–324.

95 Teresa Gorman, *The Bastards* (London: Pan, 1993), pp. 126–30. See also David Baker, Andrew Gamble, and Steve Ludlam, 'Whips or scorpions? The Maastricht vote and the Conservative Party', *Parliamentary Affairs*, 46 (2), 1993, pp. 151–66.

96 Those who were punished were joined by an MP who resigned the Whip in protest at Major's action.

97 John Redwood, *Singing the Blues: the Once and Future Conservatives* (London: Politico's, 2004), p. 128.

98 Gill, *Whips' Nightmare*, p. 74. This anecdotal evidence is supported by more rigorous study: see Tether, 'Members and organisation', pp. 115, 120.

99 Philip Cowley and Philip Norton, 'Rebels and rebellions: Conservative MPs in the 1992 Parliament', *British Journal of Political Science*, 1 (1), 1999, pp. 84–105.

100 Renton, *Chief Whip*, p. 319.

101 Hywel Williams, *Guilty Men: Conservative Decline and Fall, 1992–1997* (London: Aurum Press, 1998), p. 35 and Seldon, *Major*, p. 547.

102 Williams, *Guilty Men*, p. 42.

103 Brandreth, *Westminster Diaries*, p. 367. See also Philip Norton, 'Parliamentary party' and 'Party committees', in Anthony Seldon and Stuart Ball (eds), *Conservative Century* (Oxford: Oxford University Press, 1994).

104 Brandreth, *Westminster Diaries*, p. 247 and Seldon, *Major*, p. 438.

105 As with the 1990 campaign, one of the best insider accounts is provided in Lang, *Blue*, pp. 213–46. The best accounts from the Redwood camp are Williams, *Guilty Men* and Gill, *Whips' Nightmare*, pp. 157–67.

106 Michael Portillo, interview, 25 January 2007. Redwood, *Singing*, pp. 134–5.

107 Williams, *Guilty Men*, p. 43.

108 See Keith Alderman, 'The Conservative Party leadership election of 1995', *Parliamentary Affairs*, 49 (2), 1996, p. 318.

109 Williams, *Guilty Men*, p. 115.

110 Williams, *Guilty Men*, p. 91.

111 Heseltine did, however, have the edge over Major in some later polls: see Foley, *Major, Blair*, pp. 137–40.

112 Heppell, *Tory Leader*, p. 112.

113 Heppell, *Tory Leader*, p. 111.

114 For details of 'Operation Overrule', as this strategy was known, see Lang, *Blue*, pp. 231ff.

115 Michael Howard, interview, 5 March 2008.

116 Brandreth, *Westminster Diaries*, pp. 388, 433.

117 Nicholson, *Secret Society*, p. 203.

118 See the interview Major gave to Bruce Anderson, 'We have an absolute right to say no to a single currency', *Times*, 25 July 1996. See also Lamont, *Office*, pp. 499, 501.

119 Fowler, *Suicide*, pp. 170–2.

120 See Jenkins, *Thatcher and Sons*, p. 163 and chapters 11–13; and Wyatt, *Journals*, 1 March 1991. See also Gamble, 'Ideological party', p. 33 and Webb, *Party System*, p. 129.

121 Young, 'Prime Minister', p. 22.

122 Ian Gilmour and Mark Garnett, *Whatever Happened to the Tories? The Conservatives since 1945* (London: Fourth Estate, 1998), p. 366.

123 'Get off your knees', *Telegraph*, 18 April 1996.

124 Brandreth, *Westminster Diaries*, p. 492.

125 Heseltine, *Life*, p. 528.

126 Michael Pinto-Duschinksy, 'Decline in party membership shows rising disillusionment', *Times*, 23 April 1997.

127 Pinto-Duschinsky 'Tory chiefs', *Times*, 10 October 1994 and Whiteley et al., *True Blues*. p. 43.

128 Major, *Autobiography*, p. 691.

Chapter 3 Tactics over Strategy: William Hague, 1997–2001

1 Byron Criddle, 'MPs and candidates', in David Butler and Dennis Kavanagh, *The British General Election of 1997* (Basingstoke: Macmillan, 1997), pp. 186, 202.

2 Anthony Seldon, 'When Tory governments fail', in Seldon (ed.), *How Tory Governments Fall: the Tory Party in Power since 1783* (London: Fontana, 1996), pp. 453–62.

3 They were not alone in this, of course: Labour's apparent embrace of Thatcherism is taken as a given by many. See Richard Heffernan, *New Labour and Thatcherism: Political Change in Britain* (Basingstoke: Palgrave Macmillan, 2001).

4 Paul Webb, *The Modern British Party System* (London: Sage, 2000), p. 181, For a detailed breakdown, see Timothy Heppell, 'The ideological composition of the Parliamentary Conservative Party 1992–97', *British Journal of Politics and International Relations*, 4 (2), 2002, pp. 299–324.

5 Hywel Williams, *Guilty Men: Conservative Decline and Fall, 1992–1997* (London: Aurum Press, 1998), p. 189.

6 Michael Crick, *In Search of Michael Howard* (London: Pocket Books, 2005), pp. 373–90. See also Nicholas Kochan, *Ann Widdecombe: Right from the Beginning* (London: Politico's, 2004), pp. 215–32.

7 Williams, *Guilty Men*, p. 192.

8 Philip Cowley, 'Just William? A supplementary analysis of the 1997 Conservative leadership contest', *Talking Politics*, 10 (2), 1997/8, pp. 91–5.

9 Alan Clark, *Diaries: the Last Diaries 1993–1999* (London: Phoenix, 2003), 6 June 1997.

10 Ken Clarke, interview, 23 November 2006.

11 Michael Hill, 'The Parliamentary Conservative Party: the Leadership Elections of William Hague and Iain Duncan Smith' (unpublished Ph.D. thesis, University of Huddersfield, 2007), pp. 168–77.

12 Tim Hames and Nick Sparrow, *Left Home: the Myth of Tory Abstentions in the Election of 1997* (London: Centre for Policy Studies, 1997).

13 For a critique, see David Willetts, 'Conservative renewal', *Political Quarterly*, 69 (2), 1998, pp. 110–17.

14 Rick Nye, interview, 18 December 2006.

15 Michael Portillo, interview, 25 January 2007.

16 John Bercow, interview, 17 January 2007.

17 John Redwood, *Singing the Blues: the Once and Future Conservatives* (London: Politico's, 2004), pp. 141–2 and Gillian Shephard, *Shephard's Watch: Illusions of Power in British Politics* (London: Politico's, 2000), pp. 173–6.

18 Stuart Ball, 'Factors in opposition performance: the Conservative experience since 1867', in Stuart Ball and Anthony Seldon (eds), *Recovering Power: the Conservatives in Opposition* (Basingstoke: Palgrave Macmillan, 2005), pp. 12–14, 24–6.

19 For a detailed account of how Tory MPs reached this compromise, and a superb analysis of its pros and cons, see Keith Alderman, 'Revision of leadership election procedures in the Conservative Party', *Parliamentary Affairs*, 52 (2), 1999, pp. 260–74. For a formal comparison with the Labour Party, see Thomas Quinn, 'Leasehold

or freehold? Leader-eviction rules in the British Conservative and Labour Parties', *Political Studies*, 53, 2005, pp. 793–815.

20 Shephard, *Watch*, pp. 199–200 and Peta Buscombe, 'Sometimes it's hard to be a Tory woman', *Spectator*, 1 September 2001.

21 Michael Ashcroft, *Dirty Politics, Dirty Times* (London: MAA Publications, 2005), Chapter 8.

22 Archie Norman, interview, 23 February 2007.

23 James Landale, 'Local Tories spurn Hague cash appeal', *Times*, 31 January 2000.

24 Jo-Anne Nadler, *William Hague: In His Own Right* (London: Politico's, 2000), p. 211.

25 Archie Norman, interview, 23 February 2007.

26 Paul Routledge, 'William's clumsy friend', *Independent*, 21 September 1997.

27 Rick Nye, interview, 18 December 2006. Also Peter Stanford, 'Is there anybody out there?', *Independent on Sunday*, 7 June 1998.

28 Hill, 'Parliamentary Conservative Party', p. 142. Also David Baker, Andrew Gamble, and David Seawright, 'Sovereign nations and global markets: modern British Conservatism and hyperglobalism', *British Journal of Politics and International Relations*, 4 (3), 2002, pp. 399–428.

29 The Referendum Party and UKIP may have cost the Tories up to 16 seats and 2 seats, respectively. See Ian McAllister and Donley T. Studlar, 'Conservative Euroscepticism and the Referendum Party in the 1997 British General Election', *Party Politics*, 6(3), 2000, pp. 359–72.

30 Geoffrey Evans, 'Euroscepticism and Conservative electoral support: how an asset became a liability', *British Journal of Political Science*, 28, 1998, pp. 573–90.

31 See Simon Heffer, 'The Tories stand for . . . er, what?', *New Statesman*, 3 July 1998.

32 Ken Clarke, interview, 23 November 2006.

33 Jo-Anne Nadler, *Too Nice to be a Tory* (London: Simon and Schuster, 2004), p. 205.

34 Nadler, *Hague*, pp. 234, 251–2 and pp. 120, 138, 169. See also Colin Hughes, 'The Guardian Profile: William Hague: Just William', *Guardian*, 4 July 1998.

35 Webb, *Party System*, p. 129.

36 Michael Ancram, interview, 9 June 2008.

37 Michael Portillo, 'Essay', *Independent*, 3 October 1998.

38 Andrew Cooper and Danny Finkelstein, 'Kitchen Table Conservatives: a Strategy Proposal', Conservative Party internal document, October 1998.

39 Cooper and Finkelstein, 'Kitchen Table'.

40 Peter Stanford, 'Is there anybody out there?', *Independent on Sunday*, 7 June 1998.

41 Andrew Cooper, interview, 23 November 2006.

42 'Cranborne sacked; Blair upstages Hague', *Guardian*, 3 December 1998.

43 'Without peers; Hague can't afford another split', *Guardian*, 4 December 1998.

44 Archie Norman, interview, 23 February 2007.

45 See 'Blue Peter's recipe for victory', BBC interview, 28 March 1999, available at *http://news.bbc.co.uk/1/hi/uk_politics/302679.stm*.

46 For a transcript, see *http://www.guardian.co.uk/politics/1999/apr/20/conservatives*. For an example of one of the trailing articles, see David Hughes, 'Tories turn a somersault to support the welfare state', *Mail*, 19 April 2008.

47 Michael Howard, interview, 5 March 2008.

48 David Lidington, interview, 1 November 2006.

49 Peter Lilley, interview, 26 March 2007.

50 Stephen Glover, 'The madness of disowning Maggie', *Mail*, 27 April 1999.

51 Michael Gove, 'A striptease that costs too much', *Times*, 27 April 1999.

52 Andrew Grice, 'Conservative Party: Portillo attacks Hague's relaunch', *Independent*, 27 April 1999.

53 Andrew Pierce, 'Tory mutiny over end of Thatcherism', *Times*, 28 April 1999.

54 'William Hague and Thatcher's heritage', *Mail*, 29 April 1999.

55 Andrew Pierce and Tim Hames, 'Hague retires, bloody and confused', *Times*, 1 May 1999.

56 William Hague, 'The NHS is safer in our hands', *Times*, 23 April 1999.

57 David Hughes, 'Portillo tells Hague: You're dumping the wrong policies', *Mail*, 27 April 1999.

58 Grice, 'Portillo'.

59 Michael Prescott, 'Hague banishes Thatcher to conference sidelines', *Sunday Times*, 2 May 1999.

60 Numerous interviewees made this point. See, for example, Andrew Lansley, interview, 11 September 2008.

61 Simon Walters, *Tory Wars: Conservatives in Crisis* (London: Politico's, 2001), p. 118.

62 Andrew Grice, 'Hague told: win or you're out', *Independent*, 30 April 1999.

63 See Mark Garnett, 'A question of definition? Ideology and the Conservative Party, 1997–2001', in Mark Garnett and Philip Lynch (eds), *The Conservatives in Crisis* (Manchester: Manchester University Press, 2003), pp. 120–1.

64 David Lidington, interview, 1 November 2006.

65 Colin Rallings and Michael Thrasher, 'Fickle electorate exposes Tory and Labour frailties', *Sunday Times*, 10 May 1999.

66 Steve Richards, 'One of Hague's closest allies admits it: the Tories are incoherent and have to get back to the drawing-board', *New Statesman*, 10 May 1999.

67 Robert Shrimsley, 'Ffion dreams up strategy to revamp her action man' and 'Project Hague and the women determined to make us love him', *Telegraph*, 12 August 1999.

68 Rick Nye, interview, 18 December 2006.

69 Malcolm Gooderham, interview, 2 September 2008 and Andrew Pierce, interview, 1 December 2008.

70 Andrew Cooper, interview, 23 November 2006.

71 Nick Wood, interview, 7 March 2007.

72 Andrew Grice, 'Hague plots secret strategy to save his job amid election fears', *Independent*, 6 May 1999.

73 Ken Clarke, interview, 23 November 2006.

74 David Butler and Martin Westlake, *British Politics and European Elections 1999* (Basingstoke: Macmillan, 2000), p. 184.

75 See Philip Lynch, 'The Conservatives and Europe, 1997–2001', in Garnett and Lynch (eds), *Conservatives*, pp. 154–8.

76 See John Curtice and Michael Steed, 'Appendix: an analysis of the result', in Butler and Westlake, *European Elections 1999*, p. 246.

77 Anne McElvoy, 'We shall overcome', *Spectator*, 10 February 2001.

78 Andrew Lansley, interview, 11 September 2008.

79 Walters, *Tory Wars*, pp. 118–19.

80 Andrew Lansley, 'Accentuate the negative to win again', *Observer*, 3 September 1995.

81 Daniele Albertazzi and Duncan McDonnell (eds), *Twenty-First Century Populism* (Basingstoke: Palgrave Macmillan, 2008), p. 3. See also Cas Mudde, 'The populist zeitgeist', *Government & Opposition*, 39 (4), 2004, pp. 541–63.

82 Jill Sherman, 'Taxpayer funds Tory army of spin-doctors', *Times*, 23 September 1999.

83 Andrew Lansley, interview, 11 September 2008.

84 Nicholas Rufford, 'Hague takes the accent off Yorkshire', *Sunday Times*, 10 October 1999.

85 William Rees-Mogg, 'Hague sets the seal on a Thatcherite triumph', *Sunday Times*, 10 October 1999.

86 Michael Gove, 'Hague has the guts for the job', *Times*, 5 October 1999.

87 The on-the-hoof decision to pull the stunt is best captured by Walters, *Tory Wars*, pp. 53–5.

88 On the Eurosceptic wooing of the *Sun* by Hague, see Stephen Glover, 'The fascinating affinities between William Hague and the editor of the *Sun*', *Spectator*, 23 October 1999.

89 Simon Walters, 'I stopped the Tory Party going out of existence', *Mail on Sunday*, 2 April 2000. For the full story, see Ashcroft, *Dirty Politics*.

90 Ewen MacAskill and Lucy Ward, 'Hague's generalship consolidated', *Guardian*, 15 June 1999.

91 See Walters, *Tory Wars*, Chapter 4.

92 John Maples, 'Dear William: what you're doing wrong', *Times*, 15 February 2000.

93 Michael Portillo, interview, 25 January 2007.

94 Walters, *Tory Wars*, p. 27.

95 Michael Portillo, interview, 25 January 2007.

96 Melissa Kite, 'Portillo backs NHS and state schools', *Times*, 1 April 2000.

97 David Butler and Dennis Kavanagh, *The British General Election of 2001* (Basingstoke: Palgrave Macmillan, 2001), p. 54.

98 Nick Wood, interview, 7 March 2007.

99 Archie Norman, interview, 23 February 2007.

100 Francis Maude, interview, 8 June 2007.

101 David Hughes, 'Hague is pandering to the NF on asylum seekers, says Straw', *Mail*, 1 May 2000.

102 Jane Green, 'A Test of Party Competition Theories: the British Conservative Party since 1997' (unpublished D.Phil. dissertation, University of Oxford, 2006).

103 Webb, *Party System*, p. 126.

104 Nick Wood, interview, 7 March 2007.

105 Andrew Grice, 'Massow defection highlights Hague's right-wing populism', *Independent*, 3 August 2000.

106 Paul Waugh and Sarah Schaefer, 'Hague under fire as Tories' poll revival falls flat', *Independent*, 26 August 2000.

107 David Thompson, 'Labour welcome for Hague deserter', *Daily Record*, 11 January 2000.

108 Ivan Massow, 'The Tory Party has become nasty and intolerant', *Independent*, 2 August 2000. The Tory grassroots' equally predictable traditionalist views on the family and sexuality were revealed in a leaked Conservative Policy Forum document: see Andrew Grice, 'Tories are out of touch on family, warns leaked report', *Independent*, 8 August 2000.

109 Andrew Grice, 'Cook accuses Hague of using asylum to "legitimise" racism', *Independent*, 11 September 2000.

110 Walters, *Tory Wars*, pp. 65–71.

111 Archie Norman, interview, 23 February 2007.

112 Tom Baldwin, Philip Webster, and Roland Watson, '"Mods and Rockers" fight for power', *Times*, 5 October 2000.

113 Michael Gove, 'What kind of tonic would lift Tory spirits?', *Times*, 3 October 2000.

114 Kochan, *Widdecombe*, pp. 293–304.

115 Damian Green, interview, 4 December 2006 and Ian Taylor, interview, 13 July 2006. See also Damian Green and Ian Taylor,

Restoring the Balance (London: Tory Reform Group, 2000) and Ian Taylor, 'The Conservatives, 1997–2001: a party in crisis?', in Garnett and Lynch (eds), *Conservatives*.

116 Based on BBC reports, 302,987 ballots were sent out, 50,508 were returned, with 49,932 voting yes.

117 For a dramatic reconstruction of the bust-up see Walters, *Tory Wars*, pp. 86–100.

118 Michael Ancram, interview, 9 June 2008.

119 Tim Collins, 'Tory way forward', letter to the *Times*, 15 February 2002.

120 Butler and Kavanagh, *Election of 2001*, p. 61.

121 Nick Sparrow, 'A Review of ICM Research on Behalf of the Conservative Party' (unpublished: London, 2001).

122 Nadler, *Too Nice*, pp. 209–10.

123 Julia Hartley-Brewer, 'Hague to trigger new race storm', *Daily Express*, 4 March 2001.

124 'Hague's error', *Sun*, 7 March 2001.

125 Anne McElvoy, 'We shall overcome', *Spectator*, 10 February 2001.

126 Michael Portillo, interview, 25 January 2007; Archie Norman, interview, 23 February 2007.

127 For the most notorious example, see Paul Gilfeather, 'There is very funny footage of Hague being chased by men in masks . . .', *Daily Mirror*, 4 May 2001.

128 Walters, *Tory Wars*, pp. 160–3.

129 Thomas Quinn, 'The Conservative Party and the centre ground of British politics', *Journal of Elections, Public Opinion and Parties*, 18 (2), 2008, pp. 183–4.

130 Quinn, 'Conservative Party', pp. 183–4.

131 Anthony King, 'Campaign is making no impact on voters', *Daily Telegraph*, 19 May 2001.

132 Kamal Ahmed, 'Glum Tories want Hague to quit', *Observer*, 4 March 2001.

133 Will Self, 'Brave Billie watches as the magus weaves her strange spell', *Independent*, 23 May 2001.

134 'A true leader', *Mail*, 23 May 2001.

135 Steve Richards, 'It's not just Portillo who has an identity crisis', *Independent on Sunday*, 3 December 2000.

136 Lynch, 'Conservatives', pp. 159–60.

137 Andrew Pierce, 'How Euro-plot was born among the heather', *Times*, 2 March 2001 and Patrick Wintour and Michael White, '£2 million deal to shield Tory marginals', *Guardian*, 3 March 2001.

138 Daniel Collings and Anthony Seldon, 'Conservatives in Opposition', *Parliamentary Affairs*, 54, 2001, pp. 631–5.

139 For a clear discussion of media influence, and the obstacles to it, see Kenneth Newton, 'May the weak force be with you: the power of the mass media in modern politics', *European Journal of Political Research*, 45 (2), 2006, pp. 209–34.

140 Eleanor Laing, interview, 31 July 2007, Michael Ancram, interview, 9 June 2008, and Nick Sparrow, interview, 23 November 2006.

141 Nick Sparrow, interview, 23 November 2006.

142 Andrew Lansley, interview, 11 September 2008.

143 Andrew Grice, 'How Hague's "shift to the centre" ran out of time', *Independent*, 28 May 2001.

144 Anthony King, 'Hague looks doomed as Blair powers ahead', *Telegraph*, 9 February 2001.

145 Micheal Jones, Michael Prescott, Eben Black, Adam Nathan, and Christopher Morgan, 'You're a loser, baby', *Sunday Times*, 3 June 2001.

Chapter 4 'Simply Not Up to It': Iain Duncan Smith, 2001–2003

1 See Anthony Seldon, *Blair* (London: Free Press, 2004), p. 461.

2 Andrew Lansley and Tim Collins, 'We now have a foundation for the future', *Telegraph*, 15 June 2001.

3 Simon Walters, *Tory Wars: Conservatives in Crisis* (London: Politico's, 2001), p. 6.

4 Richard Kelly, 'The party didn't work: Conservative reorganisation and electoral failure', *Political Quarterly*, 73 (1), 2002, p. 39. See also Bill Deedes, 'How Tories lost their precious volunteer army', *Telegraph*, 8 June 2001.

5 Philip Cowley and Mark Stuart, 'Parliament: mostly continuity, but more change than you'd think', *Parliamentary Affairs*, 55, 2002, pp. 274–5.

6 Timothy Heppell, 'The ideological composition of the

Parliamentary Conservative Party 1992–97', *British Journal of Politics and International Relations*, 4 (2), 2002, pp. 299–324. Pippa Norris and Joni Lovenduski, using a different dataset, found that new Tory MPs were more right-wing and Eurosceptic than their more experienced counterparts: see their 'Why parties fail to learn: electoral defeat, selective perception and British party politics', *Party Politics*, 10 (1), 2004, p. 94.

7 On the supposed skulduggery used by the Conservative Way Forward group to get potential Portillo supporters into parliament to secure him the leadership after the election, see Walters, *Tory Wars*, Chapter 11.

8 Malcolm Gooderham, interview, 2 September 2008. Gooderham was Portillo's press secretary.

9 Michael Portillo, interview, 25 January 2007.

10 Many Conservatives interviewed for this book were, without prompting, adamant that, while IDS was a 'thoroughly decent' man, he was, in the words of one, 'just not bright enough to hold a senior job in politics'. On the voting, see Michael Hill, 'The Parliamentary Conservative Party: the Leadership Elections of William Hague and Iain Duncan Smith', unpublished Ph.D. thesis, University of Huddersfield, 2007, p. 190.

11 Simon Hoggart, 'Tension mounts, the votes are in and, er – everyone's a winner', *Guardian*, 11 July 2001.

12 'Not so fast', *Telegraph*, 13 June 2001 and Paul Eastham and Michael Seamark, 'We don't want you as leader', *Mail*, 12 July 2001.

13 Malcolm Gooderham, interview, 2 September 2008.

14 Heppell, 'Ideological Composition', pp. 299–324.

15 Keith Alderman and Neil Carter, 'The Conservative Party leadership election of 2001', *Parliamentary Affairs*, 55 (3), 2002, pp. 578–80. See also Nicholas Kochan, *Ann Widdecombe: Right from the Beginning* (London: Politico's, 2004), pp. 306–7.

16 Francis Maude, interview, 8 June 2007. A thorough ideological and social breakdown of the support given to each of the final-round candidates is provided by Hill, 'Parliamentary Conservative Party', pp. 177–85.

17 Michael Portillo, interview, 25 January 2007.

18 Hill, 'Parliamentary Conservative Party', p. 155.

19 Alderman and Carter, 'Conservative', p. 585.

20 *http://www.icmresearch.co.uk/pdfs/2001_august_telegraph_conserva-tive_party_membership_poll.pdf.*

21 Paul Whiteley, Patrick Seyd, and Jeremy Richardson, *True Blues: the Politics of Conservative Party Membership* (Oxford: Oxford University Press, 1994).

22 Ian Taylor, interview, 13 July 2006.

23 See Rachel Sylvester and Philip Johnston, 'Racism "endemic in Tory Party"', *Telegraph*, 1 September 2001.

24 Nick Kent, 'The party I joined was full of nice old people; today it is full of nasty old people', *Guardian*, 5 December 2001.

25 Alderman and Carter, 'Conservative', pp. 575ff.

26 Tom Baldwin and Melissa Kite, 'Dismay as leader appoints allies and mavericks', *Times*, 15 September 2001.

27 Andrew Grice, 'Howard returns from the dead to shadow Brown', *Independent*, 15 September 2001.

28 Gaby Hinsliff, 'New Tory leader "on probation"', *Observer*, 16 September 2001. Norris, who had backed Portillo and then Clarke, was relieved of his post as Vice-Chairman of the Party.

29 Colin Brown, 'Two year deadline for Duncan Smith', *Independent on Sunday*, 16 September 2001.

30 Rachel Sylvester and George Jones, 'The navel-gazing is over', *Telegraph*, 6 October 2001.

31 See Janet Daley, 'Tories have rediscovered the joys of revolution', *Telegraph*, 5 December 2001.

32 Andrew Cooper, 'Trust in health', in Edward Vaizey (ed.), *The Blue Book on Health: Conservative Visions for Health Policy* (London, Politico's, 2002).

33 Iain Duncan Smith, 'Putting money in this NHS is like putting water in a colander', *Telegraph*, 5 December 2001.

34 Robert Skidelsky, 'They're anti-intellectual Europhobes', *Guardian*, 16 October 2001.

35 Rachel Sylvester, 'We must change to survive, say Tory webmasters', *Telegraph*, 8 December 2001.

36 Michael Ashcroft, 'A modern political party needs to be mean, lean and hungry', *Independent*, 10 October 2001.

37 See Greg Clark and Scott Kelly, 'Echoes of Butler? The Conservative Research Department and the making of Conservative policy', *Political Quarterly*, 75 (4), 2004, pp. 378–82.

38 Quentin Letts, 'Sorry, but Dunkers is no cop in the Commons', *Mail*, 13 December 2001.

39 Oliver Letwin, 'Beyond the Causes of Crime', Keith Joseph Memorial Lecture, Centre for Policy Studies, 2002. Melanie Phillips, 'At last, a truly moral solution to rising crime', *Mail*, 7 January 2002.

40 Robert Shrimsley, 'Freedom and choice in a modern world', *Financial Times*, 17 January 2003.

41 Michael Gove, 'It is time for the Tories to turn away from Thatcher', *Times*, 19 March 2002.

42 Sam Lister, Melissa Kite, and Tom Baldwin, 'Thatcher wrong on Europe say Tories', *Times*, 22 March 2002.

43 Rachel Sylvester, 'We want to be sure all our policies help the vulnerable', *Telegraph*, 23 March 2002.

44 Joe Murphy, 'Surprised and delighted', *Sunday Telegraph*, 7 April 2002.

45 Alastair Campbell, *The Blair Years* (London: Arrow, 2008), p. 617.

46 Amanda Platell, 'The next Tory Prime Minister', *Sunday Telegraph*, 28 April 2002.

47 Iain Duncan Smith, 'Why the French are laughing at us this morning', *Mail*, 24 May 2002.

48 John Hayes, interview, 1 November 2006.

49 Andrew Grice, '"Unpopular" Tories will not lead anti-euro vote campaign', *Independent*, 5 June 2002.

50 Stephen Glover, 'Self-loathing and cowardice', *Mail*, 11 June 2002.

51 Francis Maude, 'Male, white, straight – and doomed', *Times*, 24 June 2002.

52 Andrew Rawnsley, 'It's all about image for the Tories, too', *Observer*, 14 July 2002.

53 Nick Wood, interview, 7 March 2007.

54 Nick Sparrow, 'One right note doesn't make a symphony', *Times*, 27 December 2002.

55 Dominik Diamond, 'IDS is in a spin', *Daily Star*, 31 July 2002.

56 Matthew D'Ancona, 'Diana Rigg meets Sybil Fawlty', *Sunday Telegraph*, 28 July 2002.

57 Alice Thomson, 'I didn't want to be called barmy', *Telegraph*, 27 September 2002.

58 Norman Tebbit, 'Who cares what Alan Duncan does under his duvet? What the Tories need is political clout', *Spectator*, 3 August 2002. For an extended critique along similar lines published around the same time, see Rupert Darwall, *Paralysis or power? The Centre Right in the 21st Century* (London: CPS, 2002).

59 Tom Baldwin, 'Tories want flag-waving old guard out of sight', *Times*, 23 August 2002.

60 Jo-Anne Nadler, *Too Nice to be a Tory* (London: Simon and Schuster, 2004), p. 273.

61 Peter Oborne, 'It's crunch time for the Tories', *Spectator*, 5 October 2002.

62 Graeme Wilson, Tahira Yaqoob, and Claire Saunders, 'Clarke's broadside as IDS revolt grows', *Mail*, 5 October 2002.

63 Rachel Cooke, 'Will the last person to leave the Tory Party please turn out the light', *Observer*, 6 October 2002 and Melissa Kite, 'Tory panels spurn plea to choose more women', *Times*, 22 November 2002.

64 Jonathan Oliver, 'We don't want white men in our safe seats', *Mail on Sunday*, 6 October 2002.

65 Nick Wood, 'True blue murder!', *Mail*, 22 January 2004.

66 Trevor Kavanagh, 'May Day warning', *Sun*, 8 October 2002.

67 'Duncan Smith vows to finish Thatcher reforms', *Telegraph*, 7 October 2002.

68 Rachel Sylvester, 'The Chingford polecat has not lost his bite', *Telegraph*, 12 October 2002.

69 Ben Macintyre, 'Quiet man weighs the benefit of becoming mute', *Times*, 17 October 2002 and Quentin Letts, 'Painful, pitiful . . . it was like drowning kittens', *Mail*, 24 October 2002.

70 See Sarah Richardson, 'Changing the face of Conservatism', in Chris Philp (ed.), *Conservative Revival* (London: Politico's, 2006), pp. 78–80.

71 Andrew Sparrow, David Millward, and Nicola Woolcock, 'Tory activists rally behind their leader', *Telegraph*, 2 November 2002.

72 Paul Waugh and Nigel Morris, 'Party reaction – angry response reflects a seething discontent', *Independent*, 6 November 2002.

73 Simon Hoggart, 'The bastards' bastard shows his suicidal side', *Guardian*, 6 November 2002.

74 Michael Crick, *In Search of Michael Howard* (London: Pocket Books, 2005), pp. 410–17.

75 Iain Duncan Smith, 'Tories will offer better public services – and lower tax', *Telegraph*, 3 December 2003.

76 Kirsty Walker, 'Even the faithful say that their characterless leader must go', *Express*, 23 December 2002.

77 Stephan Shakespeare, 'When spin and reality seem to be polls apart', *Telegraph*, 8 January 2003.

78 Paul Webb, 'Parties and party system: prospects for realignment', *Parliamentary Affairs*, 56 (2), pp. 283–96.

79 Francis Elliott and James Hanning, *Cameron: the Rise of the New Conservative* (London: Fourth Estate, 2007), p. 209.

80 Tom Baldwin, 'Duncan Smith's "comfort blanket" polls alarm aides', *Times*, 4 October 2003.

81 David Maclean, 'What a crazy time to raise a challenge to the leadership', *Telegraph*, 24 February 2003.

82 Andrew Pierce, 'Don't mention the Tory leadership to Kenneth Clarke', *Telegraph*, 26 February 2003.

83 The slides for 'Why Conservatives Lose and How We Can Win Again' were made available on C-Change's website and detailed in Michael Gove, 'It's still the nasty party', *Spectator*, 26 April 2003.

84 Elliott and Hanning, *Cameron*, pp. 197–9, 234–5.

85 For example, Iain Duncan Smith, 'Stop illegals and save £1.3 billion', *News of the World*, 9 March 2003.

86 IDS in Graham Turner, 'Can the Conservative Party recover?', *Telegraph*, 8 October 2002.

87 David Hughes, 'Now will you listen Mr Blair?', *Mail*, 17 June 2003.

88 'Tory eurovision', *Telegraph*, 11 July 2003.

89 Nic Cecil, 'IDS vows Tories will stem tide of asylum', *Sun*, 29 August 2003.

90 Rosemary Bennett and Melissa Kite, '. . . but Tory tempers are at boiling point', *Times*, 8 August 2003.

91 Tim Hames, 'Conservative leader: Arnie is just made for the part', *Times*, 18 August 2003.

92 Tim Shipman, 'Exclusive poll forecasts oblivion for top Tories', *Sunday Express*, 21 September 2003.

93 'Tories get the blues', *Telegraph*, 20 September 2003.

94 Peter Riddell, 'Voters think the Conservatives are out on a limb', *Times*, 22 September 2003.

95 Tim Hames, 'It's as simple as AB, Tories still aren't nice enough', *Times*, 6 October 2003.

96 Nick Gibb, 'It's not just the leader – we Tories need a new direction', *Guardian*, 7 October 2003.

97 Matthew Parris, 'Sorry, Iain, but the truth is you are simply not up to it', *Times*, 4 October 2003.

98 Rachel Sylvester and George Jones, 'Tax cuts and an all-out war on waste: the Quiet Man has started to roar', *Telegraph*, 4 October 2003.

99 Michael Gove, 'IDS lost his head, he now deserves to lose his crown', *Times*, 14 October 2003.

100 Colin Challen, *Price of Power: the Secret Funding of the Tory Party* (London: Vision Paperbacks, 1998).

101 Michael Howard, interview, 5 March 2008.

102 Michael Ashcroft, *Dirty Politics, Dirty times* (London: MAA Publications, 2005), p. 281.

103 Tim Renton, *Chief Whip: People, Power and Patronage in Westminster* (London, Politico's, 2005), pp. 330-1.

104 Iain Duncan Smith, 'Back me: I'm ready to address my leadership's shortcomings', *Times*, 29 October 2003.

105 Wood, 'True Blue'.

Chapter 5 Like Moths to a Flame: Michael Howard, 2003–2005

1 Richard Littlejohn, 'We've had nice and look where that got us . . .', *Sun*, 31 October 2003.

2 Rosemary Bennett and Tom Baldwin, 'Howard's manoeuvring makes him firm favourite', *Times*, 29 October 2003.

3 Archie Norman, interview, 23 February 2007.

4 Matthew Parris, 'He is not a rotter and I wish him well (warily)', *Times*, 31 October 2003.

5 Michael Howard, interview, 5 March 2008.

6 Michael Howard, interview, 5 March 2008.

7 Andrew Pierce, interview, 1 December 2008.

8 Greg Clark and Scott Kelly, 'Echoes of Butler? The Conservative Research Department and the making of Conservative policy', *Political Quarterly*, 75 (4), 2004, p. 381.

9 Michael Howard, interview, 5 March 2008.

10 Benedict Brogan, 'Howard calls in tycoons to set up Tory trust fund', *Telegraph*, 12 December 2003.

11 Justin Fisher, 'Money matters: the financing of the Conservative Party', *Political Quarterly*, 75 (4), 2004, p. 406.

12 See Ron Johnston and Charles Pattie, 'Conservative constituency parties' funding and spending in England and Wales, 2004–2005', *Political Quarterly*, 78 (3), 2007, pp. 392–411.

13 Benedict Brogan and Toby Helm, 'Letwin changes tack on refusal to offer tax cuts', *Telegraph*, 10 December 2003.

14 Michael Howard, 'I declare war on red tape', *News of the World*, 4 January 2004.

15 Michael Portillo, 'Howard reinvented himself, now he has to reinvent a party', *Sunday Times*, 4 January 2004.

16 Patrick O'Flynn, 'Daily Express victory as Blair does a u-turn on immigrants: gypsies: you can't come in', *Express*, 5 February 2004.

17 'Mr Howard has put the Tories back in contention', *Independent*, and 'Euro crusader', *Sun*, both 13 February 2004.

18 Alice Thomson, 'We're gearing up for October, says Fox', *Telegraph*, 5 April 2004.

19 Nick Sparrow, interview, 23 November 2006.

20 Michael Portillo, 'Another slow Tory crash into the buffers of Europe', *Sunday Times*, 6 June 2004.

21 Francis Elliott and James Hanning, *Cameron: the Rise of the New Conservative* (London: Fourth Estate, 2007), p. 243.

22 Alastair Campbell, 'My strategy for a Tory triumph', *Times*, 20 November 2004.

23 Michael Howard, 'Tony Blair must be more honest over Iraq', 20 May 2004.

24 'Blair has held the line: Howard, please note', *Telegraph*, 21 May 2004. An article by the paper's former editor, Charles Moore, published the same day and entitled 'Iraq deserves more than cheap shots' was even blunter.

25 Patrick O'Flynn, 'No votes in being posh say critics: Howard's Tory toffs take over', *Express*, 27 June 2004.

26 Those with strong stomachs should read Paul Callan, 'Sandra, the wife with an eye on No. 10: Howard unveils his secret weapon', *Express*, 7 July 2004.

27 Nick Robinson, 'After ten years, the champ still has the technique to floor the challenger', *Times*, 23 July 2004.

28 Norman Tebbit, 'Howard needs to put a rocket up the Tories', *Mail on Sunday*, 25 July 2004.

29 George Pascoe-Watson, 'Howard should gamble it all on law and order', *Sun*, 6 August 2004.

30 Anthony King, 'Verdict on the Tories', *Telegraph*, 30 July 2004.

31 Peter Oborne, 'Howard profits from the rise of the Notting Hill Tories', *Spectator*, 19 July 2004. On the *Telegraph*'s role, which is a fine illustration of the osmosis between the party in the media and parliament, see the interview with its editor in Maggie Brown, 'Newland unleashed', *Guardian*, 15 November 2004. The original *Telegraph* article (which appeared on 26 July) is now strangely unavailable in the electronic archives.

32 Elliott and Hanning, *Cameron*, pp. 70–7.

33 Alice Thomson, 'Young Tories will inherit the earth', *Telegraph*, 23 July 2004.

34 George Osborne, 'Bush is giving the Tories a masterclass in how to win', *Times*, 31 August 2004.

35 Mary Ann Sieghart, 'The female of the species is angrier than the male', *Times*, 7 May 2004 and 'More women Tory MPs? It's still jobs for the boys', *Times*, 20 December 2004.

36 Simon Walters, 'There IS something of the night about you Michael', *Mail on Sunday*, 12 September 2004.

37 Toby Helm, 'Howard accused of "wilfully" dividing Tories', *Telegraph*, 13 September 2004.

38 Rosa Prince, 'Haven't we heard that Tory before?', *Mirror*, 23 September 2004.

39 Tanya Gold, 'My trip to Ukipland', *Guardian*, 5 October 2004.

40 Data from an ICM survey of 300 party members reported in Alan Travis, 'Old story is bad news for Howard', *Guardian*, 18 November 2004.

41 Quantitative research by Martin Harrison shows just how much the Tories became 'a one-man band' during the election. See Dennis Kavanagh and David Butler, *The British General Election of 2005* (Basingstoke: Palgrave Macmillan, 2005), pp. 105–6, 183.

42 Jackie Ashley, 'A liberal who knows only way back is to recapture the centre', *Guardian*, 4 October 2004.

43 Alice Thomson, 'Speakers rush to press the Right buttons', *Telegraph*, 4 October 2004.

44 Michael Portillo, 'Tories pick the wrong enemy . . . and a right-wing suicide', *Sunday Times*, 10 October 2004.

45 Toby Helm and Brendan Carlin, 'Howard gives protégé major election role: young MP groomed as next party leader', *Telegraph*, 27 November 2004.

46 Bruce Anderson, 'There is a simple explanation for the Tories' failure to put up a decent fight: David Davis', *Spectator*, 8 January 2005.

47 'Tories must grasp the nettle or they'll be stung', *Telegraph*, 5 January 2005.

48 Melissa Kite, '"I asked myself do I want Michael Howard or Tony Blair to be Prime Minister?"' *Sunday Telegraph*, 16 January 2005.

49 'Asylum: Facing up to the truth', *Mail*, 24 January 2005 and George Pascoe-Watson, '97% back curb on migrants', *Sun*, 26 January 2005.

50 Matthew Parris, 'The problem with the Tories is that they crave to be like New Labour', *Times*, 12 February 2005.

51 Oliver Duff, 'Conservatives moving in on BNP turf', *Independent*, 21 February 2005.

52 Tim Hames, 'All that phoney baloney', *Times*, 28 March 2005.

53 Kavanagh and Butler, *Election of 2005*, pp. 185–6.

54 Michael Portillo, 'The Tories undone by their Victor Meldrew manifesto', *Sunday Times*, 24 April 2005.

55 Kavanagh and Butler, *Election of 2005*, pp. 87–9.

56 Geoffrey Evans and Robert Anderson, 'The impact of party lead-

ers: how Blair lost Labour votes', *Parliamentary Affairs*, 58 (4), 2005, pp. 818–36.

57 David Denver, 'The results', in Andrew Geddes and Jonathan Tonge (eds), *Britain Decides: the UK General Election of 2005* (Basingstoke: Palgrave Macmillan, 2005).

Chapter 6 *'Cometh the Hour, Cometh the Dave': The Long Leadership Contest, May–December 2005*

1 Matthew Parris, 'The force is with David the unruffled', *Times*, 10 December 2005.

2 ebay.co.uk: item 7321890885, sold 20 May 2005.

3 Peter Oborne, 'The man who (finally!) brought the Tories back to life', *Mail*, 7 May 2005.

4 Andrew Cooper, *The Case for Change* (London: C-Change, 2005) and Nick Sparrow, 'Can the Conservative Party Win?' (unpublished: London, 2005).

5 Michael Howard, interview, 5 March 2008.

6 John Bercow, 'We must change', *Independent*, 10 May 2005.

7 David Davis, 'Our timeless principles will prevail', *Telegraph*, 11 May 2005.

8 Francis Maude and Stephen Dorrell, 'We have let the Lib Dems steal the middle ground', *Sunday Telegraph*, 8 May 2005.

9 Colin Brown, 'The Conservative Party's problem is us, not Labour', *Independent*, 16 May 2005.

10 Justine Greening, interview, 25 April 2007.

11 Conservative Party, *A 21st Century Party*, available at *http://www. conservatives.com/pdf/21stCenturyParty.pdf*.

12 Michael Howard, interview, 5 March 2008.

13 Francis Elliott and James Hanning, *Cameron: the Rise of the New Conservative* (London: Fourth Estate, 2007), pp. 560–7.

14 Martin Kettle, 'With the Tories off the map, the centre is up for grabs', *Guardian*, 5 October 2004. See also Marie Woolf, 'Me as Tory leader?', *Independent*, 28 February 2005.

15 Available online at *http://www.timesonline.co.uk/tol/comment/article529075.ece*.

16 David Davis, 'What is it we Tories can do for Britain?', *Sunday Telegraph*, 5 June 2005.

17 David Charter and Peter Riddell, 'Rifkind joins the runners', *Times*, 8 June 2005.

18 David Davis, 'The Tories will champion the poor', *Observer*, 12 June 2005.

19 David Cameron, 'What my son has taught me about caring', *Mail on Sunday*, 12 June 2005. IDS had been busy with his Centre for Social Justice and at the end of May had published *Good for Me, Good for My Neighbour: the Conservative Way to Social Justice* (London: Centre for Social Justice, 2005). See *http://www.centreforsocialjustice.com/*.

20 Peter Preston, 'Tick here for the top job', *Guardian*, 13 June 2005.

21 Matthew Parris, 'There's no doubt about it – the next Tory leader has to be David', *Times*, 16 July 2005.

22 See *http://cornerstonegroup.wordpress.com/about/*. Note, though, that the existence of a website, a list of supporters, and a hyperactive front-man (in this case the irrepressible Edward Leigh) does not mean the group is a cohesive bloc or a major player in the parliamentary Conservative Party. Nor, given the fact that some of its younger members would go on to serve on the frontbench, was it merely a home for has-beens or a gathering of grumpy old men with a grudge.

23 Iain Duncan Smith, 'The Tory grassroots are more in touch with the real world', *Telegraph*, 24 May 2005.

24 John Major, 'Tories have to win hearts and minds and recapture the centre', *Telegraph*, 28 June 2005.

25 Ian Taylor, interview, 13 July 2006.

26 John Hayes, interview, 1 November 2006.

27 David Cameron, 'Where is the most civilised place on Earth?', *Times*, 1 September 2005.

28 Liam Fox, 'Britain must control its own destiny', *Telegraph*, 8 September 2005.

29 Alice Thomson and Rachel Sylvester, 'Dr Fox prescribes a tonic for the Tories', *Telegraph*, 14 September 2005.

30 Andrew Gimson, 'Bash Street Kid comes a cropper as he attacks Little Lord Fauntleroy', *Telegraph*, 30 September 2005. One of Davis's team, in a confidential interview, calculated that they spent around £4,000 on his launch compared to Cameron's £20,000.

31 Damian Green, interview, 4 December 2006. On generational resentments, see Mary Ann Sieghart, 'Tory old guard outsmarted by rise of young Etonian', *Times*, 21 May, 2005.

32 Keith Simpson, interview, 12 July 2006.

33 Andrew Robathan, interview, 29 April 2008. For extended coverage of the bookmakers' odds, and another view of this and other leadership contests, see Andrew Denham and Kieron O'Hara, *Democratising Conservative Leadership Selection: from Grey Suits to Grass Roots* (Manchester: Manchester University Press, 2008). See also Timothy Heppell, *Choosing the Tory Leader: Conservative Party Leadership Elections from Heath to Cameron* (London: Tauris, 2007).

34 For the crucial difference between the two, see Stephen Bayley and Roger Mavity, *Life's a Pitch* (London: Corgi, 2008).

35 Greg Barker interview 22 February 2008.

36 For the record, the tee-shirts were designed and worn by the women on their own initiative and on the grounds that '[i]f blokes are going to look at your boobs, they might as well learn something in the process'. See Jonathan Isaby, 'Spy', *Telegraph*, 4 October 2005.

37 Nick Cohen, 'How a celebrity pollster created Cameron', *Observer*, 10 December 2006.

38 Anthony King, 'A Cameron–Fox contest is what most grassroots Conservatives want', *Telegraph*, 20 October 2005.

39 Anthony King, 'Cameron holding a course to victory', *Telegraph*, 12 November 2005. Also 'Why we believe (with some misgivings) that it should be Cameron', *Mail*, 12 November 2005.

40 John Garry, 'The Political Attitudes of Conservative Party Members', unpublished MS, Queen's University Belfast, 2006.

41 Andy McSmith, 'Cameron tells party: choose me or lose another general election', *Independent*, 11 November 2005.

Chapter 7 'The Politics of And': David Cameron, 2005–

1 See, for example, an interview Cameron gave in *Cameron on Cameron: Conversations with Dylan Jones* (London: Fourth Estate, 2008), p. 60. For more detail on 'Team Cameron', see Andy Beckett, 'Club Cameron', *Guardian*, 21 March 2007.

2 Grant Shapps, interview, 19 July 2007.

3 Andrew Rawnsley, 'The Cameron interview', *Observer*, 18 December 2005. See also David Cameron, 'I don't believe in isms', *Mail on Sunday*, 1 January 2006.

4 Stephen Dorrell, interview, 4 June 2008.

5 Nick Sparrow, 'Can the Conservative Party Win?' (unpublished: London, 2005).

6 See Michael Howard, 'And what if the sceptics are wrong?', *Guardian*, 7 June 2005 and his speech to the Environment Forum on 13 September 2004, available at *https://www.iema.net/news/ envnews?startnum=41&archive=2004-09&aid=4806*. See also Michael Gove, 'Yes, you can be deep blue and green at the same time', *Times*, 14 September 2004 and David Cameron, 'Change our political system and our lifestyles', *Independent*, 1 November 2005.

7 David Cameron, 'Quantity and quality', *Guardian*, 9 December 2005.

8 Anne Jenkin and Andrew Griffiths, interview, 1 November 2006.

9 *http://www.yougov.co.uk/extranets/ygarchives/content/pdf/ TEL050101052_1.pdf.*

10 Patrick Wintour, 'Cameron = sports car. Brown = tank', *Guardian*, 15 March 2006.

11 Melanie Phillips, 'Bold, refreshing – but what about Conservatism?', *Mail*, 2 January 2006.

12 David Cameron, 'An end to polarisation', *Guardian*, 10 January 2006.

13 Chris Philp (ed.), *Conservative Revival* (London: Politico's, 2006), see especially Chapters 1 and 2.

14 Norman Tebbit, 'Change is needed: but be careful, Mr Cameron', *Sunday Telegraph*, 8 January 2006. See also Richard Littlejohn, 'Forget about the "middle" ground, Dave. Fight for the middle classes', *Mail*, 10 January 2006.

15 ConservativeHome, 'Most members disagree with Cameron on grammar schools and candidates' A-List', 22 January 2006, *http://conservativehome.blogs.com/torydiary/2006/01/most_members_ di.html.*

16 Colin Brown, 'Murdoch hints at switch if Cameron pledges tax cuts', *Independent*, 23 January 2006.

17 David Cameron, 'Tories have a massive mountain to climb', *Telegraph*, 23 January 2006.

18 David Cameron, 'Modern Conservatism', Demos, 30 January 2006 *http://www.demos.co.uk/files/davidcameronmodernconservatism. pdf.*

19 Celia Walden, 'Spy', *Telegraph*, 10 March.

20 Andrew Pierce, 'Tories pay back £5m to hide names of lenders', *Times*, 1 April 2006.

21 Graeme Wilson, 'Cameron under fire as he heads for glacier during election campaign', *Telegraph*, 10 April, 2006.

22 See *http://www.youtube.com/watch?v=bRKbTQHrtdk* and *http:// www.youtube.com/watch?v=-dRwOq4yWio.*

23 For a sceptical perspective, see Robert Macfarlane, 'Deep blue sea', *Guardian*, 22 April 2006.

24 A photograph of the leaked memo is available at *http://con-servativehome.blogs.com/.shared/image.html?/photos/uncategorized/ candidatesemail_1.gif.*

25 This other site, Tory Radio, run by Jonathan Sheppard, can be found at *http://www.toryradio.com/.*

26 *http://conservativehome.blogs.com/goldlist/2006/06/david_cameron_g. html.*

27 *http://conservativehome.blogs.com/torydiary/files/were_you_up_for_ twigg.pdf* and *http://conservativehome.blogs.com/torydiary/2006/05/ the_keys_to_bei.html.*

28 See Rosemary Bennett and David Maxwell, 'Tories change the face of their candidates, but not their jobs', *Times*, 12 June 2006.

29 See *http://conservativehome.blogs.com/goldlist/2006/08/the_costs_of_ be.html.* See also Chris Philp, 'Introduction', in Philp (ed.), *Conservative Revival*, p. xvi.

30 Guy Adams, 'Now Cameron orders his troops to volunteer', *Independent*, 19 May 2006.

31 Nigel Morris, 'Cameron: I'm not afraid to stand up to business', *Independent*, 10 May 2006.

32 David Cameron, 'Money ISN'T all . . . family life IS', *Mail*, 24 May 2006.

33 Andrew Pierce, 'Cameron factor triggers big surge in donations for Tories', *Times*, 26 May 2006.

34 'Tories must get in shape for the final assault', *Telegraph*, 26 May 2006.

35 See Nick Randall, 'No friends in the north? The Conservative Party in Northern England', *Political Quarterly*, 80 (2), pp. 184–92.

36 Tim Shipman, 'Blair and Cameron battle for the public sector vote', *Mail*, 6 June 2006.

37 Benedict Brogan, 'After the muddle Tories promise: We will cut taxes', *Mail*, 2 June 2006.

38 See for example, *http://conservativehome.blogs.com/torydiary/2006/06/hague_prepares_.html* or the *Telegraph*'s leader and letters pages on 8 June 2006.

39 Patrick Wintour, 'Cameron aide warns of Tory backbench misgivings', *Guardian*, 12 July 2006.

40 'There may yet be hope for Cameron', *Mail*, 17 August 2006.

41 For a typical reaction to Norris's comments, see James Chapman, 'Tories to milk the motorist in "green" tax blitz', *Mail*, 19 August 2006. For a reaction to Osborne's, see 'Think again, Osborne', *Telegraph*, 1 September 2006.

42 David Cameron, 'How my party got it so very wrong on apartheid', *Observer*, 27 June 2006.

43 Cameron's response is at *http://conservativehome.blogs.com/goldlist/2006/08/david_cameron_r.html*.

44 Philip Webster, Alice Miles, and Helen Rumbelow, 'No tax cuts promise by Tory leaders', *Times*, 30 September 2006.

45 *http://www.yougov.co.uk/extranets/ygarchives/content/pdf/TEL060101018_1.pdf*.

46 Anthony Browne, 'Tories go for oak in an attempt to soften their image', *Times*, 15 September 2006.

47 For an unflinching deconstruction of the shot, see Lucy Mangan, 'It's a family affair', *Guardian*, 3 October, 2006.

48 Simon Hoggart, 'Leader's bus gets stuck in a ditch', *Guardian*, 3 October 2006.

49 *http://www.conservatives.com/Video/Webcameron.aspx?id=cf3f8baf-40e2-4472-9506-847ebc78e0c8*.

50 For an analysis of the relationship between Team Cameron and the two titles, see Stephen Glover, 'With friends like the *Telegraph*,

does Cameron need enemies?', *Independent*, 9 October 2006. See also Martin Newland, 'Is Cameron really equipped to deal with social division?', *Guardian*, 5 October 2006.

51 This 'painting the sky blue rather than black' had long been a part of Cameron's repositioning strategy. See Daniel Finkelstein, 'Top Tory tips: climb the ladder, check out the ceiling and smell the cheese', *Times*, 30 November 2005.

52 David Cameron, 'I won't promise tax cuts until I'm sure we can afford them', *Telegraph*, 20 October 2006.

53 Anthony Browne, 'Top Tory quits as race row threatens "A-list" candidates', *Times*, 8 November.

54 On immigration, an obvious case in point was that of Ellenor Bland, a local government politician and a Tory candidate at the 2005 general election. See Sam Coates, 'Tories suspend councillor over e-mail poem about immigrants', *Times*, 7 November 2007. The offending email should still be available at *http://image. guardian.co.uk/sys-files/Politics/documents/2006/11/06/1106poem. pdf*.

55 'Closed borders, closed minds', *Independent*, 10 November 2006.

56 Greg Clark and Peter Franklin, *First Principles: Poverty is Relative and Social Exclusion Matters* (London: Conservative Party Social Justice Policy Group, 2006).

57 Fraser Nelson, 'Political sex change too far', *News of the World*, 26 November 2006.

58 David Burrowes, interview, 26 March 2007.

59 Brendan Carlin, 'Churchill v Toynbee: and the anatomy of a stunt that backfired' and 'Backlash against Cameron's caring image', *Telegraph*, 24 November 2006.

60 James Harding, 'Opposition leader slights suits at his peril', *Times*, 28 November 2006.

61 'Cameron's key to Number 10', *Sunday Telegraph*, 3 December 2006.

62 Andrew Pierce, 'Unease among senior Tories over Cameron adviser', *Telegraph*, 4 December 2006. Anthony Barnett, 'What price a Tory kingmaker?', *Observer*, 19 March 2006. Oliver Duff, 'Tories' makeover man takes pay cut', *Independent*, 6 December 2006.

63 Yasmin Alibhai-Brown, 'I feel British, but I don't want enforced patriotism', *Independent*, 29 January 2007 and George Pascoe-Watson, 'Rest of Britain', *Sun*, 29 January 2007.

64 See the interview with IDS in Jackie Ashley, 'Quiet man finds his voice in campaign for social justice', *Guardian*, 21 May 2005.

65 Sarah Sands, 'I'm ready to get serious', *Mail*, 11 December 2006.

66 Andrew Pierce, 'Tories £8m in debt despite sale of HQ', *Telegraph*, 19 February 2007.

67 See *http://conservativehome.blogs.com/torydiary/2007/01/pocket_the_diff.html*.

68 David Cameron, 'Tories will replace Labour, not ape it', *Telegraph*, 15 January 2007.

69 See Tom Brown, 'Mission Impossible', *Sunday Express*, 14 January 2007. The leadership was, however, prepared to consider 'English votes for English issues' and in April 2007 was obliged to deny a report by the *Spectator*'s Fraser Nelson that it was thinking of allowing the Party north of the border complete autonomy.

70 Peter Riddell, 'Tories must woo Newcastle as well as Notting Hill', *Times*, 7 February 2007.

71 *http://conservativehome.blogs.com/torydiary/2007/02/tory_mps_told_t.html*.

72 For examples of the kind of profile piece guaranteed to warm the cockles of the leadership's heart, see Melissa Kite, 'Meet the New Tories (They're not the usual suspects)', *Sunday Telegraph*, 19 April 2007 and Sarah Oliver, 'Shaun's a gymnast . . .', *Mail on Sunday*, 18 November 2007.

73 See *http://conservativehome.blogs.com/goldlist/2007/07/fifty-or-sixty-.html*

74 *http://conservativehome.blogs.com/goldlist/2007/11/who-has-been-se.html*.

75 A total of 85 Conservative MPs voted against the Equality Act (Sexual Orientation) Regulations 2007 on 19 March, with 29 voting for them and 82 abstaining. Some 12 Shadow Cabinet Ministers joined Cameron in voting for them, and the rest (even David Davis) abstained, suggesting some informal whipping of the Shadow Cabinet went on. For a taste of the concern the issue provoked among traditional Tories (including some on the front-

bench), see Benedict Brogan, 'Cameron support for gay adoption sparks Tory anger', *Mail*, 30 January 2007.

76 *http://www.time.com/time/world/article/0,8599,1582025,00.html*. See also William Hague, 'Europe can't keep ignoring the will of its peoples', *Sunday Express*, 4 March 2007.

77 *http://conservativehome.blogs.com/tenthings/2006/04/the_politics_of.html*.

78 Only 76 per cent of Labour identifiers said they would do the same for their party. See Andrew Grice, 'Conservatives take 11-point lead over Labour', *Independent*, 27 February 2007.

79 'A blow to harmony', *Mail*, 9 March 2007.

80 Lorraine Kelly, 'New Tory', *Sun*, 10 March 2007.

81 David Cameron, 'Why I saved Blair and Brown's bacon', *Sun*, 16 March 2007.

82 Vincent Moss, 'Tories are like old red phone boxes', *Sunday Mirror*, 29 April 2007.

83 Lesley White, 'Dave New World', *Sunday Times Magazine*, 22 April 2007.

84 See Melissa Kite, 'Tories still the problem, Cameron warns', *Sunday Telegraph*, 27 May 2007.

85 Oliver Letwin, 'Cameron raises his standard in the battle of ideas', *Times*, 8 May 2007.

86 David Cameron, 'What I learnt from my stay with a Muslim family', *Observer*, 13 May 2007.

87 For grassroots reaction, see *http://conservativehome.blogs.com/torydiary/2007/05/cameron_and_wil.html* and *http://conservativehome.blogs.com/torydiary/2007/05/david_willetts_.html*.

88 See Allison Pearson, 'My harsh lessons for Dave', *Mail*, 23 May 2007.

89 *http://conservativehome.blogs.com/torydiary/2007/06/grassroots_memb.html*.

90 *http://www.yougov.co.uk/extranets/ygarchives/content/pdf/ANA070101002_1.pdf*.

91 For the grisly details, see James Robinson, 'Gloves come off as Mirror and Cameron declare war', *Observer*, 10 June 2007.

92 David Davis, 'I understand the grumpiness but I guarantee this marriage is solid', *Telegraph*, 23 June 2007.

93 David Willetts, interview, 25 July 2007.

94 For the full text, see *http://www.guardian.co.uk/commentisfree/2007/jun/26/whyiamdefectingtolabour.*

95 See Peter Oborne, 'Cameron, Lord A and a very Conservative coup', *Mail*, 25 August 2007.

96 Michael Ashcroft, 'Labour wants to hamstring Tories who threaten its MPs', *Telegraph*, 18 October 2007 and Sam Coates, 'Union cash for marginals exposes flaw in challenge on party funding', *Times*, 5 November 2007.

97 Michael Gove, 'Make no mistake – the Cameroons are coming', *Observer*, 1 July 2007.

98 See Francis Elliot, 'Cameron cash reward for marriage plan "is a mistake"', *Times*, 13 July 2007.

99 For the full story, see Giles Edwards and Jonathan Isaby, *Boris v. Ken. How Boris Johnson Won London* (London: Politico's, 2008).

100 'The Conservatives need to stop digging', *Telegraph*, 21 July 2007.

101 Nicholas Watt and Jo Revill, 'Cameron wobbles as road turns rocky', *Observer*, 22 July 2007 and 'The Tories need Dave – and he needs them', *Mail*, 23 July 2007.

102 Greg Barker, interview 22 February 2008.

103 Bruce Anderson, 'David Cameron is not a man plagued by self-doubt', *Independent*, 30 July 2007.

104 Nigel Morris, 'Cameron under pressure to widen his party's appeal', *Independent*, 30 July 2007.

105 Alice Thomson and Rachel Sylvester, 'David Cameron has not had a baseball cap moment', *Telegraph*, 4 August 2007.

106 David Davis, 'Let in best immigrants, but keep out the rest', *Telegraph*, 22 August 2007.

107 David Cameron, interview on BBC's *Newsnight*, 29 August 2007.

108 Philip Webster, 'Cameron takes a swipe at critics on both wings of the Tory party', *Times*, 8 September 2007.

109 *http://www.ancram.com/images/IASAC.pdf.*

110 The report is hard to find online: the page where all the reviews were hosted and comment invited on the Tories own website soon disappeared. Try *http://blog.isc.co.uk/wp-content/uploads/2007/10/perry-dorrell.pdf.* For an example of Cameron's courting of the

public sector, see Patrick Wintour. 'Cameron vows to bring in gradual changes to Blair's "hysterical" reform', *Guardian*, 26 January 2007.

111 Michael Howard, interview, 5 March 2008.

112 See, for example, 'Calamity Cam', *Sun*, 11 September 2007. For the full report, see *http://www.qualityoflifechallenge.com/*.

113 See Neil Carter, 'Vote Blue, Go Green? Cameron's Conservatives and the environment', *Political Quarterly*, 80 (2), 2009, pp. 233–47 and James Connelly, 'Voting Blue and going green: David Cameron and the environment', in Simon Lee and Matt Beech (eds), *The Conservatives under David Cameron: Built to Last?* (Basingstoke: Palgrave Macmillan, 2009).

114 David Cameron, 'These are the fruits of a reckless "prudence"', *Sunday Telegraph*, 16 September 2007.

115 Anthony King, 'Not one single ray of sunshine amid the Tories' gloom', *Telegraph*, 29 September 2007.

116 *http://conservativehome.blogs.com/torydiary/2007/09/grassroots-memb.html*.

117 See Fraser Nelson, 'Inside George Osborne's War Room', *Spectator*, 26 September 2007.

118 Rachel Sylvester and Alice Thomson, 'We are in a win situation, says Osborne', *Telegraph*, 28 September 2007.

119 Fraser Nelson, 'The hoodie-hugging, Polly-praising, huskie-drawn days are over', *Spectator*, 3 October 2007.

120 Peter Kellner, 'Violent swings in the opinion polls prove a week is a long time in politics', *Telegraph*, 8 October 2007.

121 See *http://www.expressandstar.com/2007/11/05/britain-seen-as-a-soft-touch/*.

122 Interview in Jones, *Cameron on Cameron*, p. 108.

Chapter 8 Getting the Message: A Conclusion

1 John Major interviewed in Julia Langdon, 'I shouldn't have read the papers so much when I was PM', *Observer*, 4 March 2007.

2 A.J. Davies, *We the Nation: the Conservative Party and the Pursuit of Power* (London: Little, Brown and Company, 1995), pp. 449, 204.

3 Harold D. Clarke, David Sanders, Marianne C. Stewart, and Paul

Whiteley, *Political Choice in Britain* (Oxford: Oxford University Press, 2004).

4 Eric Shaw, *The Labour Party since 1979: Crisis and Transformation* (London: Routledge, 1994) and Steven Fielding, *The Labour Party: Continuity and Change in the Making of New Labour* (Basingstoke: Palgrave, 2002).

5 The distinction between thinkers who, like the hedgehog, know 'one big thing' and those who, like the fox, know 'many things' was made famous by Isaiah Berlin. There is room for both, but research suggests that the latter may get it right more often: see Philip E. Tetlock, *Expert Political Judgment: How Good Is It? How Can We Know?* (Princeton: Princeton University Press, 2006).

6 For a take-no-prisoners Marxist account, see John Ross, *Thatcher and Friends: the Anatomy of the Tory Party* (London: Pluto Press, 1983), p. 23.

7 Robert Harmel, 'Party organizational change: competing explanations?' in K. Richard Luther and Ferdinand Müller-Rommel (eds), *Political Parties in the New Europe: Political and Analytical Challenges* (Oxford: Oxford University Press, 2002).

8 Leo Tolstoy, *What Is Art?* (trans. Aylmer Maude, New York: Liberal Arts Press, 1960), p. 131.

9 See Tim Harford, *The Undercover Economist* (London: Abacus, 2007), Steven Levitt and Stephen Dubner, *Freakonomics* (Harmondsworth: Penguin, 2007), and Barry Schwartz, *The Paradox of Choice: Why More is Less* (London: HarperCollins, 2005), especially Chapter 3.

10 There is a massive academic literature on all this, but it is approachably summarized by James Surowiecki, *The Wisdom of Crowds: Why the Many are Smarter than the Few* (London: Abacus, 2004), especially pp. 182–91, 231.

11 Gerald Howarth, interview, 17 January 2007.

12 Francis Elliot and Sam Coates, 'New breed of donor bankrolls Cameron', *Times*, 1 May 2009.

13 Philip Norton, 'The future of Conservatism', *Political Quarterly*, 79 (3), 2008, pp. 324–32.

14 See Stephen Evans, 'Consigning its past to history? David Cameron and the Conservative Party', *Parliamentary Affairs*, 61 (2), 2008, pp. 291–314.

15 See Sarah Childs, Paul Webb, and Sally Marthaler, 'The feminisation of the Conservative parliamentary party: party members' attitudes', *Political Quarterly*, 80 (2), 2009, pp. 204–13.

16 For details, see Ian Kirby, 'Gone-servative Party!', *News of the World*, 20 December 2008. See also Charles Pattie and Ron Johnston, 'The Conservatives' grassroots "revival"', *Political Quarterly*, 80 (2), 2009, pp. 193–203.

17 See Tim Bale, Steven Fielding, and Andrew Denham (eds), Special issue on Cameron's Conservatives, *Political Quarterly*, 80 (2), 2009 and also Simon Lee and Matt Beech (eds), *The Conservatives under David Cameron: Built to Last?* (Basingstoke: Palgrave Macmillan, 2009).

18 Interview on BBC's *Newsnight*, 17 November 2005.

19 See, for example, Alan Finlayson, 'Making sense of David Cameron', *Public Policy Research*, May–March 2007, pp. 3–10 and Kieron O'Hara, 'The iron man: is Cameron true blue?', *Public Policy Research*, September–November 2007, pp. 181–5. See also Peter Kerr, 'Cameron Chameleon and the current state of Britain's "consensus"', *Parliamentary Affairs*, 60 (1), 2007, pp. 46–65.

20 Matthew Parris, 'You don't have to be barking to believe in the old Tory dog's growls', *Times*, 19 March 2005.

21 See Peter Dorey, '"Sharing the proceeds of growth": Conservative economic policy under David Cameron', *Political Quarterly*, 80 (2), 2009, pp. 259–69.

22 Andrew Grice, 'Watch your words, Tories told', *Independent*, 19 December 2008.

23 MPs representing constituencies outside central London can claim an allowance for a second home. Investigations revealed that some of them were switching which of their properties was classed as their main residence and which was classed as their second home. This 'flipping' allowed them not only to claim the allowance on the property with the largest mortgage or rent but also to take advantage of the fact that anyone selling a property is not liable for capital gains tax if said property is defined as their main residence.

24 Corporate Culture, *Customer Trust Index (CTI) Report*, January 2007.

25 Fraser Nelson, 'David Cameron will need a scowl and a hatchet to stop us going bust', *Telegraph*, 28 May 2009.

26 'Labour must be honest about public spending', *Telegraph*, 11 June 2009.

27 Philip Cowley, 'The parliamentary party', *Political Quarterly*, 80 (2), 2009, pp. 214–21.

28 See Philip Lynch, 'The Conservatives and the European Union: the lull before the storm?' in Lee and Beech (eds), *Conservatives*.

29 Andrew Gamble, 'Shifting sands', *Soundings*, 34, Autumn 2006, pp. 94–102. See also Tim Bale '"A bit less bunny-hugging and a bit more bunny-boiling"? Qualifying Conservative Party change under David Cameron', *British Politics*, 3 (3), 2008, pp. 270–99. On these attitudes, at least as reflected by candidates, see the survey reported by ConservativeHome.com on 3 July 2009.

30 Francis Elliot, 'Greenhorns with no green credentials', *Times*, 30 April 2009.

31 For more on Labour's record, see Terrence Casey (ed.), *The Blair Legacy: Politics, Policy, Governance, and Foreign Affairs* (Basingstoke: Palgrave Macmillan, 2009).

Afterword: The Election, the Coalition, and Beyond

1 The state of pre-election public opinion, gathered by both quantitative and qualitative methods, appears in detail in Michael A. Ashcroft, *Minority Verdict* (London: Biteback, 2010).

2 For details, see Ashcroft, *Minority Verdict*, especially Chapter 5, and Justin Fisher, 'Party finance: normal service resumed?', *Parliamentary Affairs*, 63 (4), 2010, pp. 778–901. Whether the money was always well spent – up to half a million was apparently used for some edgy cinema advertising that never saw the light of day – is another matter. See also Dennis Kavanagh and Philip Cowley (eds), *The British General Election of 2010* (Basingstoke: Palgrave Macmillan, 2010), which remains the standard work on the election and helps inform this account of the Conservative campaign and coalition negotiations.

3 In the event, the two-party share of the vote dropped even further in 2010 to exactly two-thirds of the total.

4 See John Curtice, Stephen Fisher, and Robert Ford, 'Appendix 2:

An analysis of the results', in Kavanagh and Cowley (eds), *British General Election of 2010*, p. 414. After 2010, the figure is down to just 85.

5 This is argued forcefully, and in fairly persuasive detail, in Ashcroft, *Minority Verdict*, Chapters 5 and 6.

6 Dale Carnegie, *How to Stop Worrying and Start Living* (New York: Simon and Schuster, 1984 [1944]), p. 157.

7 For a balanced and informative account, see Kavanagh and Cowley (eds), *British General Election of 2010*, Chapter 10, and/or Ruth Fox 'Five days in May: a new political order emerges', *Parliamentary Affairs*, 63 (4), 2010, pp. 607–22.

8 See *http://programmeforgovernment.hmg.gov.uk/*. See also Fox, 'Five days'. Note that the two parties agreed to no fewer than six commissions and 28 reviews on problematic policy areas.

9 See *http://conservativehome.blogs.com/parliament/*. The blog is a must-read for Tory MPs and staffers, and, as one MP put it in an interview, 'nobody wants to get on the wrong side of ConHome'.

10 On the 'Tory left', such as it is, see *http://conservativehome.blogs.com/thetorydiary/2010/07/toryleft.html*.

11 For a running record of rebellion, see *http://conservativehome.blogs.com/parliament/2010/10/conhome-identifies-the-most-and-least-rebellious-conservative-backbenchers-.html*.

12 The following two paragraphs rely on data provided in Byron Criddle, 'More Diverse yet more uniform: MPs and candidates', in Kavanagh and Cowley (eds), *The British General Election of 2010*.

13 For details, see Curtice et al., 'Appendix 2: An analysis of the results'.

14 This, and the following statistics on, and characterisations of, the membership are taken from Paul Webb and Sarah Childs, 'Wets and dries resurgent? Intra-party alignments among contemporary Conservative Party members', *Parliamentary Affairs*, 2011, and Childs and Webb, *From Iron Ladies to Kitten Heels: Women and the Conservative Party* (Basingstoke: Palgrave Macmillan, 2011).

15 See also Cameron's 'end of term report' to his party: *http://blog.conservatives.com/index.php/2010/07/30/weve-hit-the-ground-running/*.

16 See *http://conservativehome.blogs.com/thetorydiary/2010/08/60-of-tory-members-say-cameron-is-giving-away-too-much-to-libdems.html*.

17 See, for example, Nick Boles, *Which Way's Up?* (London: Biteback, 2010).

18 David Sergeant, 20 August 2010, thread in response to *http:// conservativehome.blogs.com/thetorydiary/2010/08/jeremy-middletons-. html.*

19 *http://conservativehome.blogs.com/centreright/2010/08/jeremy-middle ton-conhome-readers-should-lobby-national-conservative-convention- members-with-their-vi.html.*

20 See *http://conservativehome.blogs.com/thetorydiary/2010/10/tory-mem bership-down-by-a-third-to-177000-since-cameron-became-leader. html* .

21 See *http://conservativehome.blogs.com/thetorydiary/2010/10/a-rein vigorated-conservative-policy-forum-is-set-to-give-party-members- new-opportunities-to-contribu.html.*

22 See, for example, *http://conservativehome.blogs.com/thetorydiary/ 2010/07/appointments-confirmed-after-the-restructuring-of-cchqs- campaigning-department.html.*

23 See Simon Heffer, 'David Cameron will rue the day he betrayed the Conservatives', *Telegraph*, 22 May 2010.

24 'Tories must never forget their promise to cut immigration', *Mail*, 11 September 2010.

25 Janet Daley, 'The Conservatives' child benefit plans sent precisely the wrong signal', *Sunday Telegraph*, 10 October 2010. So, some argued, did the lifting of the cap on University tuition fees.

26 Kavanagh and Cowley (eds), *British General Election of 2010*, pp. 89–90.

27 For Hague's exposition of his EU policy on 3 June 2010, see *http:// www.publications.parliament.uk/pa/cm201011/cmhansrd/chan9.pdf*, pp. 25ff.

28 *http://spendingchallenge.hm-treasury.gov.uk/* and see George Osborne, 'You decide', *Sun*, 9 July 2010.

29 See Hamish Macdonnell , 'Scots Tories "cast adrift" by David Cameron', *Scotsman*, 5 September 2010.

INDEX